RUSSIA'S STILLBORN DEMOCRACY?
FROM GORBACHEV TO YELTSIN

# Russia's Stillborn Democracy?
# From Gorbachev to Yeltsin

GRAEME GILL

and

ROGER D. MARKWICK

OXFORD
UNIVERSITY PRESS

# OXFORD

UNIVERSITY PRESS

Great Clarendon Street, Oxford OX2 6DP

Oxford University Press is a department of the University of Oxford.
It furthers the University's objective of excellence in research, scholarship,
and education by publishing worldwide in

Oxford New York

Athens Auckland Bangkok Bogotá Buenos Aires Calcutta
Cape Town Chennai Dar es Salaam Delhi Florence Hong Kong Istanbul
Karachi Kuala Lumpur Madrid Melbourne Mexico City Mumbai
Nairobi Paris São Paulo Singapore Taipei Tokyo Toronto Warsaw

and associated companies in Berlin Ibadan

Oxford is a registered trade mark of Oxford University Press
in the UK and in certain other countries

Published in the United States
by Oxford University Press Inc., New York

© Graeme Gill and Roger D. Markwick 2000

The moral rights of the author have been asserted

Database right Oxford University Press (maker)

First published 2000

British Library Cataloguing in Publication Data

Data available

Library of Congress Cataloging in Publication Data

Gill, Graeme J.
Russia's stillborn democracy?: from Gorbachev to Yeltsin /
Graeme Gill and Robert D. Markwick.
Includes bibliographical references.
1. Russia (Federation—Politics and government—1991– .
2. Soviet Union—Politics and government—1985–1991.
3. Democracy—Russia (Federation).
4. Political culture—Russia (Federation).
I. Markwick, Roger D.   II. Title.
JN6695.G55   2000   947.086—dc21   99–059003

ISBN 0–19–829782–3
ISBN 0–19–924041–8 (Pbk.)

1 3 5 7 9 10 8 6 4 2

Typeset by Hope Services (Abingdon) Ltd.
Printed in Great Britain
on acid-free paper by
Biddles Ltd
Guildford and King's Lynn

# PREFACE

Democracy has become the watchword of contemporary politics. Almost everywhere, from Eastern Europe to Latin America, casting off the shackles of authoritarian rule has been done in the name of democracy. But the reality of post-authoritarian transitions has often fallen short of the democratic ideal. The appointment of Mikhail Gorbachev as General Secretary of the CPSU in March 1985 and his subsequent proclamation of perestroika, glasnost, and democratization raised hopes that at long last the Soviet Union was erasing the shadow of Stalinism. But having reached its peak in 1987–8, the perestroika process began to falter amidst economic decline and nationalist upheaval. Popular hopes, and with them the first shoots of what looked like an active civil society, began to wither. New elite actors began to appear on the scene, notably the disgraced former Politburo member Boris Yeltsin. In the name of democracy and Russian sovereignty, he actively worked to seize the initiative from Gorbachev. As Russia's first elected president, he affirmed a commitment to the democratic principles that Gorbachev's reforms had failed to realise, not by restructuring the Soviet system but by transforming it through the market in an independent Russia. Once again, however, hopes have been dashed. Russia today barely complies with the procedural requirements of a representative democracy.

The desire to understand why the reform process in the Soviet Union and the subsequent transformation of Russia both fell short of their democratic aspirations is the principal motivation for this book. In this study we seek to identify the driving forces for political and social change in Soviet and post-Soviet Russia and the domestic impediments to successful change. A particular concern is to note the course of the emergence of civil society and its subsequent demise. For us, the languishing of civil society goes a long way towards explaining the ultimately undemocratic outcome of the process born in the Gorbachev years. 'Stillborn' Russian democracy has proven to be, but as the question-mark in the title of the book indicates, it did not have to be that way. The social forces were emerging that could have breathed democratic substance into the Russian polity. They still are, and given the chance, democracy in Russia may yet have its day.

This book would not have been possible without substantial financial, institutional and personal support. A grant from the Australian Research Council in

1994–6 provided the resources for the project. Visiting fellowships at Moscow State University, the St Petersburg University of the Means of Communications, and the Moscow School of Social and Economic Sciences, provided research opportunities and the contact with Russian reality that is so vital to such work. In this respect, particular thanks to Renfrey Clarke in Moscow who has been a generous host and provided assistance on more than one occasion. The Department of Government and Public Administration at the University of Sydney has provided a stimulating and congenial environment within which to work. Finally, the research and writing could not have been pursued without the forbearance and support of our respective families, especially our partners, Heather and Therese. To them, our thanks.

Graeme Gill and Roger Markwick

*Department of Government and Public Administration,*
*University of Sydney*
*July 1999*

# CONTENTS

*List of Tables*                                                    viii
*Abbreviations*                                                       ix

1. The Reformers' Inheritance                                         1

2. The Attempt at Liberalization                                     24

3. From Reform to Transformation                                     61

4. The Struggle for a Hegemonic Presidency                          121

5. A Debilitated President                                          167

6. A Stunted Civil Society                                          205

7. Conclusion                                                      251

*Bibliography*                                                      259
*Index*                                                            273

# LIST OF TABLES

1.1.  Soviet growth rates                              17
2.1.  Age of leadership                                 29
2.2.  Leadership change, 1985–1986                      30
4.1.  Results of Yeltsin's referendum                  159
5.1.  Parliamentary election results, 1993             169
5.2.  Parliamentary election results, 1995             188

# ABBREVIATIONS

| | |
|---|---|
| AFL-CIO | American Federation of Labor-Congress of Industrial Organisations |
| AKKOR | Association of Peasant Farms and Agricultural Cooperatives of Russia |
| CC | Central Committee |
| CIS | Commonwealth of Independent States |
| CPD | Congress of People's Deputies |
| CPSU | Communist Party of the Soviet Union |
| DPR | Democratic Party of Russia |
| DVR | Democratic Choice of Russia |
| FAPSI | Federal Agency for Government Communications and Information |
| FIG | financial industrial group |
| FNPR | Federation of Independent Trade Unions of Russia |
| FPS | Federal Border Service |
| FSB | Federal Security Service |
| FSK | Federal Counter-intelligence Service |
| GDP | gross domestic product |
| GDR | German Democratic Republic |
| GKI | State Committee on Property |
| GOPU | Main Socio-Productive Administration |
| GPU | State-Legal Administration |
| GUO | Main Security Directorate |
| IMF | International Monetary Fund |
| INF | intermediate range nuclear forces |
| KGB | Committee for State Security |
| KPRF | Communist Party of the Russian Federation |
| KRO | Congress of Russian Communities |
| LCP | Lithuanian Communist Party |
| LDPR | Liberal Democratic Party of Russia |
| MMNK | Moscow International Oil Club |
| MVD | Ministry of Internal Affairs |
| NBN | On Big Nikitskoi Street |
| NDR | Our Home is Russia |

| NSF | National Salvation Front |
|---|---|
| NTTM | Centre for the Scientific and Technical Creativity of Youth |
| NTV | Independent Television |
| ORT | Russian Public Television |
| PPSR | People's Party of Free Russia |
| PRES | Party of Russian Unity and Accord |
| RF | Russian Federation |
| RSFSR | Russian Soviet-Federative Socialist Republic |
| RSPP | Russian Union of Industrialists and Entrepreneurs |
| SVR | Foreign Intelligence Service |
| TEK | fuel and energy complex |
| UES | United Energy Systems |
| US | United States of America |
| USSR | Union of Soviet Socialist Republics |
| VPK | military–industrial complex |
| WTO | Warsaw Treaty Organisation |

# 1

# The Reformers' Inheritance

It would be difficult to exaggerate the dimensions of the changes that have occurred since 1985 in what was the Soviet Union. The single-party rule of the Communist Party has been overthrown and replaced by a variety of regime types in the former republics of the union. The centrally directed command economy has broken down, and in its place have emerged economies based to varying degrees upon the operation of market forces. Nationalism has become more intrusive as a force within the political process, in some places generating serious conflict. New social forces have emerged, based in part upon the economic changes, and have contributed to the growth in social polarization. All of these changes have had a massive effect upon the societies of the Soviet successor states, and continue to mould the way in which they develop. The key to the transformation of the former Soviet space is the political and economic changes, usually labelled democratization and marketization. But how these changes are to be explained and whether these labels are appropriate is a matter for debate.

One line of explanation of these changes focuses upon the international dimension. Although there are a variety of lines of explanation which have been offered here,[1] the basic proposition is that the failure of the Soviet system needs to be seen in terms of its international location. As the forces of globalisation gathered pace during the last three decades of this century, the Soviet experiment of autarchic development became unsustainable. As the logic of

---

[1] For an early survey of some of these, see Daniel Deudney and G. John Ikenberry, 'Soviet Reform and the End of the Cold War: Explaining Large-scale Historical Change', *Review of International Studies*, 17 (1991), 225–50. Also see Daniel Deudney and G. John Ikenberry, 'The International Sources of Soviet Change', *International Security*, 16: 3 (Winter 1991/2), 74–118. For the argument that the domestic Soviet structure was in part a response to international competition, see Graeme Gill, 'Russian State-Building and The Problems of Geopolitics', *Archives europeennes de sociologie*, 37: 1 (1996), 77–103. For an argument that Russia's peripheral location in the international political economy is an important determinant in the prospects for democracy, see Roger D. Markwick, 'A Discipline in Transition?: From Sovietology to "Transitology" ', *The Journal of Communist Studies and Transition Politics*, 12: 3 (Sept. 1996), 255–76.

international interdependence, powered by the driving force of capitalist development, ground remorselessly on, the Soviet economy was dragged ever more into this net, and with this its inadequacies became apparent. Increasingly it was unable to compete with the more productive capitalist economies of the West, a development which eroded the bases of the system. The attempt to respond to this challenge was ultimately unsuccessful, resulting in the collapse of the system in 1991.

There is much to recommend this sort of explanation. But a focus upon international forces alone is inadequate, because what is important for the explanation is the internal reaction to those forces. The Soviet Union was not a case just of international pressure causing its collapse; not only was the domestic reaction of political elites to this pressure important, but also significant were longer-term developments within Soviet society itself. The external dimension needs to be complemented by an internal dimension.To the extent that Western scholarship has focused upon an internal dimension to explain large-scale change, this has usually been in terms of the study of democratisation and the path to it.

Much of the earliest systematic study of democratization carried out in the 1950s and early 1960s focused upon the contextual factors for the emergence of democracy. This was manifested in a search for democratic prerequisites, chiefly identified in terms of levels of economic development.[2] This essentially static approach soon gave way to one which emphasised the role of 'modernization', of the development of modern industrial societies during the creation of which the prerequisites for democracy were established.[3] But this primarily structural approach was felt to be inadequate, not only because of its perceived Eurocentric bias, but because of the ambiguous role it allotted to political elites in the process. It was widely believed that neither the identification of prerequisites, such as development levels or cultural values, nor the emphasis upon the role of economic and social development in generating forces which burst

[2] For example, see Seymour Martin Lipset, 'Some Social Requisites of Democracy: Economic Development and Political Legitimacy', *American Political Science Review*, 53: 1 (Mar. 1959), 69–105. There has been renewed interest in this in the 1990s. For a selection, see Robert M. Marsh, 'Authoritarian and Democratic Transitions in National Political Systems', *International Journal of Comparative Sociology*, 32: 3–4 (1991), 219–32; Larry Diamond, 'Economic Development and Democracy Reconsidered', *American Behavioral Scientist*, 35: 4/5 (Mar./June 1992), 450–99; Seymour Martin Lipset, Kyoung-Ryung Soong, and John Charles Torres, 'A Comparative Analysis of the Social Requisites of Democracy', *International Social Science Journal*, 136 (May 1993), 155–75; and Mick Moore, 'Democracy and Development in Cross-National Perspective: A New Look at the Statistics', *Democratization*, 2: 2 (Summer 1995), 1–19.

[3] For example, Gabriel A. Almond and James S. Coleman, *The Politics of the Developing Areas* (Princeton, Princeton University Press, 1960); David E. Apter, *The Politics of Modernization* (Chicago, University of Chicago Press, 1965).

open the authoritarian regime, really explained what triggered the shift to democracy. Under the impetus of the large number of regime changes leading to the emergence of democratic systems in Southern Europe and Latin America in the 1970s and 1980s, what one observer has called the 'third wave' of democratization,[4] a new methodology for explaining democratic transition emerged. This 'transition literature' focused overwhelmingly upon political elites and their interactions, and although there has been some debate about whether this could be applied to the regime changes in the former communist world in 1989–91,[5] it has been used in an attempt to explain such developments.

In contrast to the structural focus of the earlier explanations of democratization, the transition literature emphasised the importance of political actors in explaining regime change. Central to this line of explanation were political elites. The basic explanation of regime change offered in this literature was clear,[6] and although different instances of democratization were acknowledged to have had variations in some of their aspects, these were seen as essentially variations on a theme. The starting point was the perception of a crisis or challenge (be it economic, social or political) to the authoritarian regime which required a response from that regime. In principle, two types of response were possible: a consolidation of rule though increased coercion, or an opening to the populace through a controlled process of liberalization.[7] This decision, whether to strengthen control or liberalise, may be made and reversed a number of times depending upon the balance of opinion within the political elite, but ultimately in the cases of democratization studied in the transition literature, a policy of liberalization was implemented. Usually this was accompanied by a split within the regime elite between those who favoured liberalization and

---

[4] Samuel P. Huntington, *The Third Wave. Democratization in the Late Twentieth Century* (Norman, University of Oklahoma Press, 1991).

[5] For example, see Philippe C. Schmitter with Terry Lynn Karl, 'The Conceptual Travels of Transitologists and Consolidologists: How Far to the East Should They Attempt to Go?', *Slavic Review*, 53: 1 (Spring 1994), 173–85; Valerie Bunce, 'Should Transitologists be Grounded?', *Slavic Review*, 54: 1 (Spring 1995), 111–27; Terry Lynn Karl and Philippe C. Schmitter, 'From an Iron Curtain to a Paper Curtain: Grounding Transitologists or Students of Postcommunism?', *Slavic Review*, 54: 4 (Winter 1995), 965–78, and Valerie Bunce, 'Paper Curtains and Paper Tigers', *Slavic Review*, 54: 4 (Winter 1995), 979–87.

[6] For the seminal work, see Guillermo O'Donnell, Philippe C. Schmitter and Laurence Whitehead (eds.), *Transitions from Authoritarian Rule: Prospects for Democracy* (Baltimore, The Johns Hopkins University Press, 1986).

[7] Liberalization involves an expansion of the sphere of public activity and a consequent roll back of regime control, but one which, in theory, does not alter the basic power distribution; the authorities retain the capacity to intervene to change an outcome they do not like. In contrast, democratization involves a fundamental change in the power relationship underlying the regime. See Adam Przeworski, 'Democracy as a Contingent Outcome of Conflicts', Jon Elster and Rune Slagstad (eds.), *Constitutionalism and Democracy* (Cambridge, Cambridge University Press, 1988), 61. Also Huntington, *The Third Wave*, 9.

those who opposed it. Part of the process of liberalization involves the reformist section of the elite seeking negotiating partners among the moderate elements of the opposition in society more generally. The search for such partners is propelled by the desire to keep liberalization under control by marginalizing more radical opposition, and to build some predictability into the process in order both to protect their own interests and deflect any possibility of military activity by hard-line regime opponents of liberalization concerned about their futures. Negotiations between regime reformers and opposition moderates may embrace three types of issue: the provision of guarantees to regime elites about protection of themselves and their interests when the regime relinquishes power (exit guarantees), the mechanism of the shift to democracy, and the types of social and economic measures required to meet the difficulties which brought on the regime's crisis. The first two issues featured in virtually all cases of negotiation, the third in only a few. At the conclusion of the negotiations, the mechanism for regime change agreed upon is implemented, leading to the installation of a democratic polity.

This sort of explanation has considerable explanatory power. Political elites have clearly played a major part in the shift to democracy in those countries experiencing such a regime change in the 1970s and 1980s. Indeed, the shift to democracy would hardly have been possible, at least in a relatively peaceful fashion, without such elite agreement. But this literature and this type of explanation have one considerable failing: at their best they underestimate the role of forces outside political elites, and at their worst they completely ignore them. Democracy is portrayed as a result of an elite compact, with non-elites having no independent part to play; they are to be manipulated and controlled by the elites. The achievement of democracy is a result of either elite commitment to those principles or, more usually, elite acceptance that there is little alternative to adoption of such a system. One author goes so far as to suggest that a democratic outcome is less likely if the masses are involved in the process.[8] Such a perspective can be reconciled with the notion of democratization only if a narrow, purely procedural, view of democracy is adopted—that what is important is the existence of the formal institutions of democracy (legislature, elections, parties), without any concern for the substantive considerations which are what distinguish democratic from other systems of government. This is a narrow, poverty-stricken, conception of democracy. But this elite perspective is also flawed in terms of its basic explanation.[9]

[8] Samuel P. Huntington, 'Will More Countries Become Democratic?', *Political Science Quarterly*, 99: 2 (1984), 212. This highlights the way in which the elite focus of this literature shares many of the assumptions of the elite actors themselves.

[9] The following argument is outlined in fuller form in Graeme Gill, *The Dynamics of Democratization: Elites, Civil Society and the Transition Process* (London, Macmillan, 2000).

By focusing upon elites and their activities, the transition literature emphasises the role of political actors, but without explaining either the context within
which those actors act or why particular actors are important in the process.
Consider the following questions, relating to the outline of the transition explanation sketched above: why is an opening to society through liberalization seen
by part of the regime elite as a possible solution to the regime's crisis? Why are
negotiating partners from outside the regime sought? What determines which
non-regime actors participate in negotiations? What currency do the non-
regime actors have in the negotiations, and why are they able to succeed? These
questions go to the heart of the process of regime change as envisaged in the
transition literature. Yet that literature has been unable to answer these questions because it remains within the elite paradigm. This paradigm effectively
excludes one of the chief sources of impetus for democratization, civil society
forces (see below). Elites do not operate in a vacuum; they are not disembodied
from society as a whole. Regime elites turn to liberalization because of fear of
how society will react to either doing nothing or tightening control. Non-regime
negotiating partners are sought because of the potential power they have at their
disposal, principally in the form of the popular support they can mobilise. This
is the currency they have, and it stems from the place they occupy as civil society forces which are operating in and are rooted in society at large. In this sense,
the whole elite approach assumes, even if it does not acknowledge, the operation
of non-elite civil society forces; they are intrinsic to the elite explanation because
the actions of the elites upon which it focuses can be explained only in terms of
the existence of these broader forces. This also makes them central in another
sense. Where civil society forces are not powerful and active (and both qualities
must be seen as relative to the regime), a democratic outcome is unlikely. The
elite approach assumes that elites agree to institute a democratic system and that
this then becomes embedded in the society. But why should elites choose
democracy? Democracy is a system which builds in a degree of uncertainty and
unpredictability.[10] Elite interests are more difficult to safeguard when basic decisions about power are in the hands of a mass electorate. Authoritarian ruling
elites will have little principled commitment to democracy. Their agreement to
a democratic transition, therefore, will be a function either of their belief that
this can be used as a tactical means of restabilizing their rule (in which case no
genuine transition will occur), or of the pressure imposed upon them by
circumstances, and the material form this takes will be pressure from pro-
democracy elements located in civil society forces. What this means for democratic transition is not just that any explanation of it must take account of civil
society forces, but that the success of the process of democratization itself is

[10] Przeworski, 'Democracy'.

dependent upon such forces. A democratic outcome is much less likely when the process is dependent purely upon elite preference than when civil society forces are active and powerful. The fate of the Soviet Union/Russia is a good illustration of this.

It is important to be clear about what we mean by civil society forces and their relationship to civil society. Civil society exists when groups autonomous from the state are able to act to project and defend the interests of their constituents, including against the state. This implies the existence of a public arena within which issues are discussed, and recognition by the state of a sphere within which those groups have a right to function largely unhindered; it also involves recognition by those groups that the state has a right to act unimpeded within certain spheres of competence. Crucially, a civil society must include state recognition of the right to act politically on the part of the autonomous groups. The projection and defence of interests means nothing unless they can be pursued within the political sphere and by political means. A civil society, therefore, does not exist in the absence of the right to pursue interests in the political sphere. This conception of civil society is underpinned by a hierarchy of forms of autonomous group activity. First order groups are those networks or organizations through which people structure their private lives (e.g., hobby and friendship groups). They are limited in their scope, usually local in their perspectives, and tend not to interact with the state or political authorities. Second order groups represent their members' interests in the broader public sphere. They are not specifically politically oriented, but may at times carry their members' interests into the political sphere. They constitute the main bulk of organizations of which civil society consists. Third order groups are those which are specifically political in their outlook and activities. The most important of this sort of group is the political party. Under authoritarian regimes, a wide range of first and second order groups is usually allowed to function (although that range was much more limited in communist than in other types of authoritarian regimes), but either no third order groups are tolerated or, if they are, it is under very tight restrictions. In such situations where third order groups are effectively prevented from operating, civil society does not exist, but those groups which are able to function constitute civil society forces. They are groups which seek to play the sort of representational role intrinsic to civil society even when that society does not exist because of restrictions upon political activity.

Under an authoritarian regime, it is these civil society forces which provide the impetus for democratic change. They are the major factor behind the successful shift in a democratic direction.[11] The course of democratic transition is

---

[11] See the argument in Gill, *The Dynamics of Democratization*.

therefore a function of the dynamic between regime elite and civil society forces, neither of which is likely to be homogeneous.[12] If we are to understand this dynamic, a longer-term perspective than simply the period of the transition (which is the focus of the transition literature) is required. Only through such a perspective can both the identity and importance of civil society forces and the nature of the regime elite be established. Such a perspective is also crucial to an understanding of the opportunities and constraints which face that elite at the time of the onset of regime crisis. It is the legacy of the past which defines these opportunities and constraints. In practice, what this means is that the strategic choices to be made by regime elites and by civil society forces are made within a range of possibilities set by the structural characteristics stemming in part from the past. So although the past does not ensure any particular outcome, it does make some outcomes less likely and others more so. In this sense, the inheritance from the past may best be seen as having helped to narrow the possibilities of certain avenues of development, or of making the following of such avenues difficult, without ruling them out altogether This path dependent approach[13] allows a degree of elite autonomy while recognizing the structural constraints imposed by the past, including the recent past. The question that arises is, what was the nature of the inheritance that confronted elite decision-makers in the Soviet Union of the mid-1980s? And were civil society forces sufficiently strong and active to press the course of change through to a democratic conclusion?

## The Soviet Inheritance

The basic structures inherited by the Soviet leadership in the 1980s stemmed from the state-building that occurred during the years of Stalinist rule. The sort of politico-economic structure which emerged at this time was unique, and although it was a conscious construction of the Stalinist elite, many of its implications were neither foreseen nor became evident during the Stalinist period. The Stalinist state that emerged in the early 1930s, was fired in the terror and the war and matured in the years following that conflict, was an

---

[12] Indeed, democratic transition almost always sees the regime split and greater involvement by some civil society forces than others.

[13] For one discussion of path dependency, see Terry Lynn Karl, 'Dilemmas of Democratization in Latin America', *Comparative Politics*, 23: 1 (Oct. 1990), 1–21. For an attempt to use this approach in relation to the post-socialist period in several East European countries, see Jerzy Hausner, Bob Jessop and Klaus Nielsen (eds.), *Strategic Choice and Path-Dependency in Post-Socialism. Institutional Dynamics in the Transformation Process* (Aldershot, Edward Elgar, 1995).

organisationally integrated structure in which the economic sphere was merged with the political sphere. While there are many problems with the totalitarian paradigm, its emphasis upon the organizational interlinking of the different structures of Soviet society was apposite. The imposition of the command economy meant that all economic decisions and priorities were essentially political, while the all-embracing nature of the economic plans meant that, in theory, there was no room for independent action throughout the economic structure. The merging of the political and economic meant that the structure was, at least in principle, highly integrated into one command and control system. This system embraced the whole country, cutting across the national boundaries that formally rendered the Soviet Union a federal state; the capacity for independent initiative on the part of republican or regional leaders was very limited within this command and control system. Furthermore, the focus of this system was its apex in the Soviet political elite, where supreme decision-making power resided. This integrated, centralized structure appeared in theory highly efficient, but in practice this was not the case.

This sort of structure as it emerged in the Soviet context had a number of major shortcomings which had serious implications for the way in which the Soviet system developed and for the legacy carried forward to those leaders who sought to save it. Two of these shortcomings are particularly important.

First, the system's organizational controls were insufficiently developed to ensure continuing close control or monitoring of the activities of officials at lower levels of the structure.[14] The struggle to create an efficient administrative system during the early years of the Soviet period was hampered by the technical difficulties of establishing a routinized and efficient form of communication and information flow between the centre and all parts of the country. The problem was the combination of low levels of technology and extensive distances to be covered. With telephone lines not always reliable and the major travel infrastructure (chiefly railways and all-weather roads) patchy in its coverage of the country, institutional mechanisms for exerting central control over all regions were weak. The centre was reliant overwhelmingly upon the network of party and other organizational cells dotted throughout the country, and yet this structure was only as strong as the sinews that bound these cells together, and often distance and technology combined to make those sinews very weak. In effect this meant that the command structure was somewhat disarticulated with the flow of communications frequently disjointed and difficult to monitor. It was not that sections of the apparatus were not in contact with the centre, because over time the flow of reports arriving in Moscow did become more regularised, but that the centre had few avenues

[14] For an argument which emphasises this for the pre-war period, see Graeme Gill, *The Origins of the Stalinist Political System* (Cambridge, Cambridge University Press, 1990).

for the independent verification of what it was being told from below. Such mechanisms as the party control commission, security apparatus, CC plenipotentiaries and the party press could function as a check on the veracity of local reports, but these were not always highly regularised and were often subject to the development of family groups (see below). The problems with this information flow were exacerbated, especially in the early period, by the poor state of the central administrative apparatus. These structures took some time to settle into the sort of routine which would enable them to deal efficiently with the volume of paper that began to flow into central offices in the 1920s and 1930s.

Second, the incentive structure embedded in the Soviet apparatus encouraged the systematic misleading of the centre by lower levels. Success was defined in terms of the fulfilment of plan targets and instructions from above rather than any considerations of social utility. If there was inconsistency between demands from above and considerations of social utility, or between those demands and formal rules, it was the demands which officials sought to meet. Almost anything was acceptable as long as the demands were satisfied. If those demands were not satisfied, responsible officials could be deemed to have failed in their duties and would suffer the consequences. Normally this meant demotion, movement sideways, or retirement, but during some parts of the Stalin period the consequences could be physical liquidation. There was, therefore potentially a high price to be paid if the centre was not satisfied. This sort of situation encouraged lower level officials to engage in a wide range of activities designed to satisfy demands from above, or at least give the appearance of doing so. For example, one widely used technique in the sphere of economic production was the acquisition of resources from outside formal channels to increase production levels while retaining the official input level stable and in accordance with plan directives. In this way officials could claim that the required production levels were being met despite the fact that official provision was not made for the resources necessary to achieve such levels.[15] But another common practice was to deceive the centre, to tell it that demands were being fulfilled even when they were not. Such false claims for achievement were the object of criticism throughout the entire Soviet period.[16]

This combination of weak organizational controls and a built-in incentive to mislead the centre was instrumental in the strengthening of the personalist

[15] For a discussion of the economy and some of the sorts of tactics used by responsible officials, see Alec Nove, *The Soviet Economic System* (London, Allen & Unwin, 1980), esp. ch. 4.

[16] See the discussion in Gill, *Origins*; and Graeme Gill and Roderic Pitty, *Power in the Party: The Organization of Power and Central–Republican Relations in the CPSU* (London, Macmillan, 1997).

principle throughout the Soviet structure. This principle took an organizational form through the emergence at various levels of the structure of so-called family groups. These were combinations of local leaders, often embracing the leaders of the local representative bodies of national organizations—party, soviets, control commission, security apparatus and press—and sometimes included the heads of the major productive enterprises (factories, kolkhozy) in the region. The essence of these was that they were mutual protection organizations, designed to bring together the local elite the better both to coordinate the running of local affairs and to defend themselves from potential attacks from above.[17] Where such family groups became dominant, and during the1930s this seems to have been most of the country, the official rules and regulations whereby the formal institutions were meant to function were secondary in importance to the norms and procedures of these informal cliques and cabals. They were the dominant powers in local affairs and the institutions which effectively structured much of Soviet political life.

The predominance of the family groups throughout Soviet life led to the growth of the personalist principle of organization, to acceptance of the view that, ideological rhetoric notwithstanding, the structuring of political relationships on the basis of personal ties was a legitimate form of organizing political life. The strength of this principle was reinforced by the weakness of bureaucratic procedures and thereby of the capacity of the system to rely overwhelmingly on the operation of those procedures to get things done.[18] If bureaucratic structures were ineffective, or at least uncertain, reliance upon personal connections was a sensible course to adopt. This has been recognised by many scholars in their emphasis upon the role of personal support in explaining Stalin's rise to power and his defeat of successive opposition groups in the 1920s,[19] but it was also important in explaining the way the whole system functioned. Reliance upon personal contacts and upon mutual obligations constituted the essential currency that made the system as a whole work; without it, the bureaucratic machinery would have been unable to cope with the demands placed upon it in the 1920s and 1930s.

But the presence of the personalist principle in the structuring of political life created a real tension in the Soviet state. Beside personalism, the Soviet

---

[17] On the family groups, see Gill, *Origins*; and Gill and Pitty, *Power*.

[18] This constitutes a weakness of the state's infrastructural power. On infrastructural and despotic power, see Michael Mann, 'The Autonomous Power of the State: Its Origins, Mechanisms and Results', in John A. Hall (ed.), *States in History* (Oxford, Blackwell, 1986), 113. Also Linda Weiss and John Hobson, *States and Economic Development. A Comparative Historical Analysis* (Oxford, Polity Press, 1995), ch. 1.

[19] For the classic statement, see Robert V. Daniels, 'Stalin's Rise to Dictatorship, 1922–29', in Alexander Dallin and Alan F. Weston (eds.), *Politics in the Soviet Union. 7 Cases* (New York, Harcourt, Brace & World Inc., 1966), 1–38. Also the classic biographies.

political apparatus was also characterised by pressures for the organizational routinisation of the structure. That structure, with its hierarchical ordering of bodies, was governed formally by a wide range of official rules: constitutions, regulations, administrative instructions, orders and rules proliferated over the growth of the Soviet state. These rules all sought to bring a sense of order and regularity to the functioning of the hierarchical structure. This aim was strengthened by the hierarchical structure itself; the essence of a bureaucracy is regularity, the component parts of the structure interacting in a predictable and regular fashion. The structure of committees and executive bodies attached to them generated their own pressures for such regularity and for the rules upon which that regularity could rest. This sort of emphasis upon organizational coherence, integrity and order, upon routinisation and procedure, ran directly counter to the personalist principle. Personalism rested upon principles which were not compatible with organizational regularity and routinisation. It rested upon extra-bureaucratic connections and personal linkages rather than the formal rules of hierarchical procedure; personalism had as its highest priority the achievement of particular (perhaps short term) political ends regardless of formal rules, while routinization embodied the priority of observance of rules and regulations. The tension between these two modes of operating was never fully resolved,[20] continuing to have a major impact upon the course of Soviet development until the system collapsed in 1991.

The presence of, and tension between, these two principles of functioning, the organizational and the personalist, vastly complicated the task of steering the state and of exercising continuing central direction and control. With these two principles of authority running the length of the hierarchical structure, two different patterns of activity and of relationship were validated within the Soviet structure. This coexistence of personalist norms and organizational principles gave the system's modus operandi an ambiguous character, and thereby built a sense of uncertainty into its operating procedures. During the Stalin period, this ambiguity and uncertainty was ameliorated by a combination of three factors.

1. The personal dominance of the dictator. The dominance that Stalin was able to exercise personally over the Soviet system gave that system a focus and a coherence that it would otherwise have lacked. This does not mean that the system was either highly focused or coherent, but that Stalin's position as the

---

[20] For an analysis of the importance of this tension in the decade following Stalin's death, see Graeme Gill, 'Khrushchev and Systemic Development', in Martin McCauley (ed.), *Khrushchev and Khrushchevism* (London, Macmillan, 1987), 30–45. Also Graeme Gill, 'Institutionalisation and Revolution: Rules and the Soviet Political System', *Soviet Studies*, 37: 2 (Apr. 1985), 212–26.

chief decision-maker at the centre[21] gave that system an ultimate arbiter which meant that policy issues could actually be brought to final resolution. Furthermore because of the unorthodox, or at least anti-official organizational, methods whereby Stalin operated, the interplay between personalist and organizational principles was less of a barrier than it would otherwise have been. Stalin's personal dominance, and the justification this provided for similar roles to be played by what one observer has called the 'little Stalins' at lower levels of the structure,[22] cut through the ambiguity by projecting personalist principles as the dominant paradigm for the structuring of political life.

2. The presence of extra-bureaucratic/organisational threat, principally in the form of the terror. Although the terror reached its most extreme forms in the latter part of the 1930s, the threat of extraordinary punishment for perceived wrong doing was present from the earliest years of Soviet rule. The continued rhetorical emphasis upon danger, both external and internal, and the search for opponents encouraged the regime to look to what were explicitly acknowledged to be extraordinary methods to deal with perceived opposition. This was given institutional form with the establishment of the Cheka in December 1917 and the prominent place that its successor organizations occupied in the regime over the following decades. This was the most visible institutional manifestation of an ethos which was deeply embedded in the structure: what was required was total loyalty, and anything less than that made one a legitimate target of the regime's coercive organs. The ever-present threat posed by the security organs and their brief to hunt out opposition (and the widening conception of what opposition meant during the 1920s and 1930s) reinforced the levels of uncertainty emanating from the personalist–organisational tension because of the consequences that it involved for those who were found deficient in their performance. What was important about this was that the threat was extra-bureaucratic, in the sense that there was a high degree of arbitrariness in its application. It did not operate according to the developing sets of administrative regulations and procedures which the structure was generating, but rather according to a logic far removed from that of systemic administrative efficiency. Part of the importance of this was its very lack of predictability, particularly in the late 1930s. But in operating in this way it also strengthened the personalist principle; in conditions of uncertainty, reliance upon personal contacts and patrons was widely seen as the best defence and protection against external threat.[23] Indeed, this was the essence of the family groups.

---

[21] On Stalin's role in decision-making, see Robert C. Tucker, *Stalin in Power: The Revolution from Above, 1928–1941* (New York, W. W. Norton & Co., 1990).

[22] Georg Lukacs, 'Reflections on the Cult of Stalin', *Survey*, 47 (Apr. 1963), 105.

[23] For an argument about Stalin's role as a patron in this way, see T. H. Rigby, 'Was Stalin a Disloyal Patron?', *Soviet Studies*, 38: 3 (July 1986), 311–24.

3. The generation of a sense of enthusiasm and commitment, principally through the ideology and its projection of the ideals which underpinned the regime. The massive changes initiated during the first five-year-plan period relied heavily upon mass enthusiasm, and although this was clearly complemented by significant inputs of force, the sense of building a new world and the commitment that engendered should not be underestimated. This was particularly true of those in responsible positions within the political structure, for whom the struggle to eliminate the old world and build a bright new future was the basic ideal which gave their lives its rationale. Reliance upon this sort of commitment was more consistent with personalist norms than with organizational principles. The ethos was one of breaking out of the shackles of the past and, through the enthusiastic application of commitment, overcoming the barriers to the construction of a new order; Stalin's aphorism 'cadres can decide everything'[24] reflects this ethos. Implicit in this was a rejection of bureaucratic priorities and adoption of those sorts of principles which involved a preference for achievement over obedience to official rules and regulations.

The combination of these three factors, personal dictatorship, extra-bureaucratic threat, and reliance upon enthusiastic commitment, helped during the Stalin period to moderate the effects of the ambiguity stemming from the two modes of operation, personalist and organizational. However, the death of Stalin created a fundamentally new situation.

At one blow, Stalin's death and the reaction to it by the new rulers significantly altered the formula whereby the system had been functioning. Stalin's death removed the personal dictator from the scene, a development confirmed by the public commitment on the part of his heirs to the principle of collective leadership. At the same time the new leadership sought to reduce the impact of extra-bureaucratic threat by bringing the security apparatus once again firmly under the control of the political leadership, thereby implicitly committing themselves to the abolition of terror as a mode of governance. The later campaign of destalinization spear-headed by Khrushchev confirmed both of these positions. The gradual disappearance of the third factor noted above, enthusiastic commitment, also became clear in the decade following Stalin's death. The decline of this had been evident in the post-war Stalin years, when the general level of exhaustion following the exertions of the last decade and a half and of the war and then of the drive to rebuild the Soviet Union and consolidate Stalinist control took their toll. But perhaps just as important, the idealism that had been evident throughout the earlier period was also tarnished by

[24] J. V. Stalin, 'Address Delivered in the Kremlin Palace to the Graduates from the Red Army Academies', 4 May 1935, in J. V. Stalin, *Problems of Leninism* (Peking, Foreign Languages Press, 1976), 772.

this time. Khrushchev tried to regenerate a sense of popular enthusiasm and genuine commitment through his policies on popular participation, the reinvigoration of the soviets, the encouragement of discussion and the criticism of Stalin, and although he did get a positive response it was shortlived. As the struggle to build communism became defined increasingly in terms simply of standards of living, the conception of building a new society qualitatively different from that which had existed before faded. As the system moved from a mobilizational phase to a consolidation phase,[25] life became more humdrum, programmatic commitments to the building of communism were increasingly empty, and the ethos of building the new through physical effort and commitment dissipated.

The effect of the removal of these three elements was profound. It enabled the tensions between the personalist and organizational principles to become the dominant force shaping regime development.[26] Under Khrushchev there was both a rhetorical and formal strengthening of organizational norms. Principles of collectivism were frequently invoked and they played a much more positive role in structuring the operations of political organs. The principal institutions of the system operated on a more regular basis, with the result that pressures for organizational institutionalization strengthened. Throughout the system there was a revival of political institutions and increased public emphasis placed upon regularity and adherence to formal rules and regulations. However the effect of this was significantly undercut by the way in which Khrushchev chose to play his leadership role. While acknowledging the importance of collectivism and of the formal organs of the system, Khrushchev sought to act as a leader little constrained by these considerations. Through a range of different measures, he continually attempted to side-step the limits which official bodies sought to place upon him. He overrode collective opinion when he thought this necessary and when he could get away with it, he tried to stack deliberative organs with his supporters in an attempt to get his way, and when he could do neither of these he tried to bully his leadership colleagues into agreeing with him. It was this mode of acting which was the source of the criticism levelled against him at the time he was overthrown in October 1964. Furthermore, Khrushchev also instituted a highly interventionist cadre policy, with the result that frequent changes of leaders at lower levels were brought about by central action. Although such leadership changes did not involve the same sinister consequences often evident under Stalin, they did inject a high degree of uncertainty into political life. Combined with the idio-

---

[25] For an early discussion of this, see Richard Lowenthal, 'Development vs Utopia in Communist Policy', in Chalmers Johnson (ed.), *Change in Communist Systems* (Stanford, Stanford University Press, 1970), 35–116.

[26] Gill, 'Khrushchev'.

syncratic behaviour of the leader, such personnel uncertainty did constitute a continuation of the sense of threat so evident under Stalin. It also sustained the personalist principle.

The result of this combination of pressures for increased institutional regularity and the continuation of the personalist principle is that the tension within the structure's organisational patterns remained. Although the improvement in communications technology during this period strengthened the infrastructure which could have underpinned increased institutionaliza-tion on an organisational basis, and therefore strengthened the state's infra-structural power, this was undermined by the reaffirmation of the personalist principle that Khrushchev's modus operandi constituted. Furthermore, in the localities, the centre's continuing apparent arbitrariness strengthened pres-sures for the creation and development of family groups. However, the elimin-ation of terror, and the weaker position that Khrushchev accordingly had compared with Stalin's, reduced the centre's capacity to enforce direction and control on the lower levels of the hierarchical machine. With the decline in ide-ological commitment, which Khrushchev's campaigns had been unable to reverse, appeal to idealism also offered little prospect of success for the centre. The centre's capacity to steer the state remained fundamentally flawed.

With the overthrow of Khrushchev, an opportunity was provided for the system to deal with the problems that the Khrushchev regime had bequeathed. But the new regime clearly failed this test. From the outset, its emphasis was on stability, and this became even more marked after the Czech experiment 'socialism with a human face' was seen to have exceeded acceptable limits and therefore had to be suppressed in 1968.[27] The new Brezhnev leadership strengthened the pressures for institutional regularity and organizational norms. There was increased emphasis upon formal rules and regulations, per-haps reflected most visibly in the adoption of a new state Constitution in 1977. At the centre, the political leadership emphasised a move away from the idio-syncratic personalist behaviour of Khrushchev towards a greater emphasis upon collectivist rule. This focus tried to incorporate strategic interests into the decision-making process,[28] thereby creating a structure at the centre within which the exercise of initiative, even by leading party officials, became very difficult. This was reinforced by an emphasis upon regularity of procedure in all matters, including personnel. The interventionist personnel policy of Khrushchev was abandoned in favour of one which emphasised 'trust in cadres' and which guaranteed political leaders almost unlimited tenure in the

---

[27] This was clearly seen in the winding-down of the Kosygin reforms at about this time.
[28] Leading some to see the regime in corporatist terms—e.g. Valerie Bunce, 'The Political Economy of the Brezhnev Era: The Rise and Fall of Corporatism', *British Journal of Political Science*, 13: 2 (1983), 129–58.

offices they held regardless of their performance. The sense of insecurity in the apparatus which had been evident under Khrushchev was thereby withdrawn.

The effect of the Brezhnev regime's approach was to consolidate a central decision-making system which operated on the basis of brokerage between interests and, for the most part, incrementalist politics. However, at lower levels the result was an entrenching of the personalist system as family groups were able to consolidate themselves in power. With the centre refusing to implement an interventionist personnel policy and with such structures already in place as a result of the dynamics of the Stalin and Khrushchev periods, there was nothing to stop the consolidation and spreading of the structuring of power on the basis of family groups,[29] nor of the growth of a sense of local/regional/republican identity on the part of local elites and pop-ulaces. With the centre taking a hands-off approach to much of what occurred at lower levels, its capacity to influence what happened at those levels weak-ened. In principle, had the centre sought to change what was happening in the regions, it could probably have done so, but given its preference not to inter-vene in a consistent or regular fashion, its capacity to assert effective central leadership was very limited. In effect, by eschewing threat, it had to appeal to the self-interest of lower level office holders if it hoped to achieve policy suc-cess. This had important implications for the future of the Soviet system.

This appeal to self-interest effectively justified activity which was interpreted both at the time and since in terms of the growth of corruption. While this took many forms, its essence, at least so far as we are concerned, involved the personal acquisition of state resources. This ranged from extravagant lifestyles based upon exploitation of the local economy (with Rashidov in Uzbekistan being the most extreme case of this), the use of local enterprises and produc-tive facilities for personal enrichment, through to the simple diversion of funds and resources into private pockets. While this had been occurring since the 1920s, when local clique control first became apparent, it seems to have reached a new height under Brezhnev. This sort of appropriation of state resources helped to create a layer of officials who, when circumstances permit-ted, were ready to enter into business legally. But during the time of Brezhnev, their chief importance was that they were one more indication of the centre's loss of the ability to both control the state at lower levels and to direct the econ-omy.

One important result of this sort of structure, with its emphasis upon satis-fying all interests and the resultant incrementalist style of politics, is that the system found it very difficult to take major decisions, especially if these involved significant policy change or alteration to the politico-economic struc-

---

[29] For an analysis of this phenomenon, see Gill and Pitty, *Power*.

ture. One of the boasts of the Soviet regime had been the way it had presided over massive economic expansion during its lifetime. The transformation of what was basically a backward agricultural country (albeit with some sectors of more advanced industrialism) into one of the world's superpowers within the space of some sixty years was an achievement of which Soviet citizens as well as the regime were rightly proud. Although the dimensions of this economic development may have been exaggerated in the official figures and the basis upon which it rested more fragile than it appeared, there was also real substance to this development. By the beginning of the 1970s the Soviet Union had become one of the economic giants of the globe. Despite continuing problems in the agricultural sector, reflected in Soviet reliance upon grain imports since the 1960s, the country had become a major producer of industrial goods and a significant source of technological development and innovation (reflected most clearly in military and space exploration sectors). But beneath this generalized picture of economic advance, the economy was actually far less healthy than it appeared.

The Soviet economy had for many years been experiencing reductions in levels of economic growth. According to official statistics reproduced by one scholar,[30] average annual rates of growth declined as shown in Table 1.1. According to the CIA, the decline was even greater: 1961–65 saw 5.1 per cent average growth of GNP compared with 1.9 per cent in 1981–85. Some even suggested there was negative growth at the beginning of the 1980s.[31] Increasingly industrial targets were not being met, while those production levels that were achieved were costing significantly more in terms of consumption of energy; unlike in other industrialized economies, energy and raw material

TABLE 1.1. *Soviet growth rates*

|  | Produced national income | Gross industrial production | Gross agricultural production | Labour productivity in industry |
|---|---|---|---|---|
| 1951–5 | 11.4 | 13.2 | 4.2 | 8.2 |
| 1956–60 | 9.2 | 10.4 | 6.0 | 6.5 |
| 1961–5 | 6.5 | 8.6 | 7.2 | 4.6 |
| 1966–70 | 7.8 | 8.5 | 3.9 | 5.8 |
| 1971–5 | 5.7 | 7.4 | 2.5 | 6.8 |
| 1976–80 | 4.3 | 4.4 | 1.7 | 4.4 |
| 1981–5 | 3.6 | 3.7 | 1.0 | 3.4 |

[30] Stephen White, *After Gorbachev* (Cambridge, Cambridge University Press, 1993), 104.
[31] Archie Brown, *The Gorbachev Factor* (Oxford, Oxford University Press, 1996), 134.

prices were rising. Furthermore much of what was produced did not con-
tribute substantially to the wealth of the country. The continuing emphasis
upon heavy industry allied to a failure to invest in new plant and equipment
throughout much of the Soviet industrial infrastructure meant that much production was wasted or of poor quality and added little to living standards. The
continued reliance on extensive as opposed to intensive development saw the
Soviet economy slip compared with its main rivals; national income fell from
67 per cent of that of the US in 1970 to 64 per cent in 1988.[32]

Declining overall growth levels were accompanied by declining living standards for much of the population. In the 1960s and early 1970s the lot of the
Soviet consumer seemed to be improving, with more goods becoming available and the hardships associated with post-war rebuilding in the past. Of
course, even at this time there were significant shortages of goods; the Soviet
economy remained a deficit economy. But the lot of the consumer was much
better than their parents' had been. However, by the late 1970s and early 1980s
popular expectations had been raised as a result of the promises of the regime,
people's experiences of the previous decade, and the greater familiarity within
sections of the Soviet population with comparable conditions abroad. With
the economic slowdown, the continuing emphasis upon heavy industry and
the increased economic and technological competition coupled with the threat
of renewed cold war, the situation of Soviet consumers declined. The growth
of the informal or black market so remarked upon by observers at this time was
in part a response to this. But although the informal market may have helped
people get by in the straitened circumstances, it was at the expense of their
faith in the official system. It was clear that, by itself, the official system could
not only not produce the standard of living to which they aspired, but in the
eyes of many could not even produce a standard that was tolerable.

Thus the economic slowdown at the national level was having significant
consequences. It was inhibiting the country's capacity to compete effectively
with the United States, and it was eroding confidence at home. But despite a
piecemeal attempt at economic reform in 1979, the Soviet leadership did nothing to meet this impending crisis. In retrospect it is clear that the Soviet economy needed significant reform if it was to overcome this challenge, but
guided by its incrementalist principles and unwilling to upset any major power
group in the system, the Brezhnev leadership eschewed any significant change.
The economic crisis continued to build.

---

[32] White, *After Gorbachev*, 105. For a short analysis of Soviet problems which focuses
broadly on economic matters, see Paul Kennedy, 'What Gorbachev Is Up Against', *The
Atlantic Monthly* (June 1987), 29–43. Also see Timothy Colton, *The Dilemma of Reform in
the Soviet Union* (Washington, Council on Foreign Relations, 1986).

The economic malaise was accompanied by a spiritual malaise. A feature of some of the earlier periods of Soviet rule had been the regime's reliance upon mass enthusiasm and commitment. By the 1970s, the popular reserves of this seem to have been expended. Although the Brezhnev regime sought to engender a sense of excitement and of building a bright future through the much-heralded BAM project, its efforts were doomed to failure. The regime itself had become grey and routine, and was unlikely to be able to evoke enthusiasm in even its most fervent supporters. But few among the Soviet population could have been counted as fervent supporters. The massive economic changes induced in the 1930s had had major social effects. Most important was the rapid large scale process of urbanization and, especially following the war, the development of a large Soviet 'middle class'.[33] By the 1970s, this group consisted mainly of people who had not struggled for the building of a new world in the October revolution or in the revolution from above of the 1930s, but may as children have experienced the trauma of the war and the hardships of post-war reconstruction. Their conception of the part they were to play in Soviet development and their expectations and aspirations were not likely to be associated with continuing difficult times. Growing up and maturing in the 1960s, they saw themselves as part of an increasingly confident world power characterized by improving standards of living. They were the real beneficiaries of the social changes wrought by the Soviet system, enjoying the best style and conditions of life of any Soviet generation. The sorts of ideological appeals that may have resonated with the populace in earlier decades evoked little popular enthusiasm from them, especially in the light of their disappointment at the failure of Khrushchev's attempt to reinvigorate the system. Indeed, there is some evidence to suggest that it evoked little popular response at all; the clandestine growth of religious observance and the increased popularity of Western fashions not only of dress but of cultural artefacts (including music and literature) suggests a search for values different to those officially promulgated by the regime.

The impact of economic slowdown was particularly important for this group of the community. The erosion of ideological belief noted by many observers and the regime's increasing reliance upon seeking legitimation through the provision of economic benefits meant that when the economic difficulties began to bite, the regime had little to fall back on in the way of sources of legitimation with this group. To the extent that this middle class

---

[33] This is a major theme in John Miller, *Mikhail Gorbachev and the End of Soviet Power* (London, Macmillan, 1993). Also see some interesting figures in Brown, *Gorbachev*, 18. In the Soviet context, we define the middle class principally in terms of that growing layer of educated, white-collar urban employees, the 'sluzhashchie', which came to dominate large Soviet cities in the post-war period.

chiefly sought from the regime improvements in their own living standards, that expectation was disappointed. As the beneficiaries of the massive Soviet educational effort, many of these people found themselves in jobs that were significantly below the qualifications they had achieved, a discrepancy that was particularly marked given the emphasis on technical education and upon the 'scientific and technical revolution' under Brezhnev. Furthermore, as the perception of growing corruption within the regime grew during the late 1970s–early 1980s,[34] a phenomenon connected with the increased strength of family groups throughout the political structure, the sense of betrayal on the part of the middle class is likely to have strengthened; while *their* aspirations were blunted, functionaries of the regime were perceived to be enriching themselves at society's expense.

The frustration that this situation engendered could not be alleviated through popular activism. The degree of control that the regime had exercised since Stalin's 'revolution from above' at the beginning of the 1930s ensured that civil society forces in the country were very weak. Sustained independent organization was possible for first order groups and for some second order groups,[35] but most of the latter and all third order, specifically political, groups were suppressed. Society was not completely flattened, as the totalitarian theorists suggest, but the capacity for autonomous organization to represent social interests was very weak. Given the impossibility of popular action, the response was social cynicism. Spiritual crisis was evident throughout the USSR.

This combination of a unitarist political system which lacked a central driving force but had significant fissiparous tendencies within its structure, impending economic crisis and broad-based spiritual malaise constituted a compelling case for major change. This does not mean that the system was about to fall. With increased discipline and some tightening of the screws, it is probable that the Soviet system could have continued for some years. However it is also clear, at least in retrospect, that unless major action was taken, the system would not survive in the long run. This was clear to many in the society at large, and to elements in the leadership. With Brezhnev's death on 10 November 1982, it seemed that a major barrier to reform may have been removed. But before looking at the fate of reform, we should enumerate the principal legacies from the old regime and its situation in the early 1980s

[34] On this see William A. Clark, *Crime and Punishment in Soviet Officialdom. Combating Corruption in the Political Elite, 1965–1990* (Armonk, M. E. Sharpe Inc., 1993), and Leslie Holmes, *The End of Communist Power: Anti-Corruption Campaigns and Legitimation Crisis* (Melbourne, Melbourne University Press, 1993).

[35] For a study which shows how such second-order groups could emerge to serve their members but were very weak, see Anne White, *Democratization in Russia Under Gorbachev 1985–91: The Birth of a Voluntary Sector* (London and New York, Macmillan & St Martin's Press, 1999), chs. 1–3.

which helped to structure initial reform efforts. This can be sketched baldly in a number of points:

1. The basic problem of the Soviet political system was structural, stemming from the tension between the personalist and organisational principles. With the political system torn between these different modes of functioning, both clear and decisive leadership and effective implementation were hamstrung. Any attempt at fixing the problems in the economic or social spheres were likely to fail unless this issue was resolved. But given this tension, it is probable that only the primacy of personalist over organisational principles, reflected in the dominance of an individual leader, could introduce such measures. However, this was likely to exacerbate the tension and generate high levels of conflict within the system.

2. The existence of a unitarist bureaucratic political system seeking with considerable success to penetrate all aspects of society ensured that a genuine civil society did not develop in the Soviet Union. While some may have discussed Soviet society in terms of an emergent civil society in the 1960s, 1970s, and early 1980s,[36] the sorts of structures that are normally associated with civil society (organizations autonomous from the state) could not become major features of the Soviet landscape. There were no organized bodies or fora of any size that were independent of the state, with the result that there were no real organizational vehicles for mobilising or structuring popular activity against the state. This means that if there was to be an impetus for reform, it was unlikely to originate from within society at large. The most likely source of reformist impetus was from within the regime itself, and given the weakness of those structures within the regime which some have seen as 'manifestations of an emerging civil society',[37] this could only come from the top.

[36] See e.g. Geoffrey Hosking, *The Awakening of the Soviet Union* (London, Heinemann, 1990), ch. 4.

[37] Moshe Lewin, *The Gorbachev Phenomenon: A Historical Interpretation* (Berkeley, University of California Press, 1989), 80. Discussion of an emergent civil society needs to be framed very carefully if it is to have any explanatory power. This is particularly so in those non-capitalist Soviet-type societies where the state's penetration of society is so extensive that the capacity for independent organization is highly restricted. Under such circumstances, the development of civil society may well take a different path to the classic situation in the West, even arising from the development of organizations within the state. However, if the study of the emergence of civil society under these conditions focuses solely upon structures within the state, it risks confusing the analytical distinction which is the essence of the concept 'civil society', that between society and state. If it focuses on groupings within society that 'do not necessarily oppose the state, but exist in contrast to outright state organisms and enjoy a certain degree of autonomy' (Lewin, 80), it is difficult to conceive of any form of human society that could not be classed as an emerging civil society. Both of these sorts of phenomena may be important in the development of civil society, but what needs to be established is their role in that development rather than simply assuming that, in themselves, they constitute civil society.

3. The unitarist political system contained within it currents of reformism which had been tapped by Khrushchev but then forced underground by Brezhnev. There had always been a strand of reformist thinking within the party,[38] but its significance had waxed and waned according to the scope given its development by successive leaders. Many of those who had been energized by Khrushchev's plans, including many idealists from the 1960s, not only remained in official positions in both the formal political structures such as the party but also the vast array of institutes and universities, but remained convinced that change of some sort was needed. Many of these people were of Gorbachev's generation, about which much was made at the time of his rise,[39] but many were older, already in positions of responsibility during the early Khrushchev period. They constituted a reservoir of potential energy and initiative in favour of reform. All they needed was the opening.

4. The unitarist political system was characterised by a weakness of infrastructural power, meaning that the centre had difficulty not only in reinvigorating the political and economic system, but also in continually monitoring and controlling events at lower levels of the hierarchy; initiatives taken at the centre were not always implemented in the regions. This was the reverse side of the dominance of family groups. Certainly the centre could intervene when it chose to change lower level personnel, but its capacity to be involved on a continuing basis was limited. The effect of this was reinforced by the non-interventionist personnel policy followed between 1964 and 1982, a policy which effectively ensured the dominance of the political structure at most levels by elderly office-holders. As a result of these two characteristics of the political structure, the dominance of family groups and the age of most responsible officials, the structure had in-built barriers to major change: such change would have threatened the local power of family groups and the positions of incumbent, especially elderly, officials.

5. The counterpart to the unitarist political system was the non-capitalist command economy administered by a privileged nomenklatura. This meant that economic change was closely intertwined with political and administrative change. It also denied the possibility of the development of a large, legal economic sector which could constitute both a potential power base from which to oppose the state and a possible independent source of economic

---

[38] For the most explicit statement of this, see Stephen F. Cohen, 'The Friends and Foes of Change: Reformism and Conservatism in the Soviet Union', *Slavic Review*, 38: 2 (June 1979), 187–202, plus subsequent comments by T. H. Rigby, S. Frederick Starr, Frederick Barghoorn, and George Breslauer. Also Moshe Lewin, *Political Undercurrents in Soviet Economic Debates: From Bukharin to the Modern Reformers* (London, Pluto Press, 1975).

[39] See e.g. Jerry F. Hough, *Russia and the West: Gorbachev and the Politics of Reform* (New York, Simon & Schuster, 1988), ch. 1.

innovation and change. But it did ensure that many of those in responsible administrative positions were able to gain personal control over significant resources, and thereby to constitute themselves (unknowingly at the time) as the basis for a future bourgeoisie. However for this to occur, there needed to be political and economic change, and the nature of the economy and the poverty of Soviet economic thinking ensured that this would occur in the absence of any real knowledge of the laws of capitalist development.

6. The poor state of the economy meant that any disruption that accompanied reform, and significant reform was bound to lead to some disruption, was likely to exacerbate economic difficulties. As a result the regime was not going to be able to buy public patience with improved economic performance and therefore better living standards in the short term. Increasing popular dissatisfaction was therefore likely to accompany reform unless other benefits were seen to outweigh the accompanying economic dislocation.

7. The structure of the Soviet Union itself was also significant. The construction of the union along national lines created a situation in which certain ethnic groups had their own political machines and constitutional vehicles which could be used to press national concerns, or elite concerns in nationalist guise. While most of the larger national groups had such constitutional vehicles in the form of republics, those which lacked republican status could appeal to the principle of national sovereignty and thereby exercise significant leverage on the system as a whole. The combination of suppressed national aspirations on the part of some groups and the existence of some organizational mechanisms to assert them, something which was seriously underestimated by the Soviet leadership, was to be an important factor in derailing the later course of reform.

These legacies were important in shaping the way in which events unfolded as the new post-Brezhnev Soviet leadership sought to come to grips with the challenges confronting the Soviet system. The actors and the structures, the entrenched patterns of behaviour and the assumptions which played a part in the unfolding of developments over the decade and a half following Brezhnev's death, were the products of the Soviet system. Furthermore, they were not the result of recent developments within that system, but stemmed from the whole course of its development beginning in 1917, but especially from the early 1930s. This was a legacy that was firmly entrenched, rooted as it was in the long-term structural development of the Soviet system. Although this historical legacy was not determinative, it limited the parameters within which a reformist leadership could manoeuvre.

# 2

# The Attempt at Liberalization

With the death of Brezhnev, preceded by that of his long-time supporter Suslov in January 1982, the barriers to more significant change at the apex of the system began to break down. However, the elite was divided between those who recognized that some change was necessary, and those who wished to retain things basically as they were, a harbinger of the classic divide between liberal reformers and conservatives that was to become crucial in the coming years. This division within the top elite was reflected in the course of political manoeuvring between Brezhnev's demise in November 1982 and Gorbachev's accession to the post of General Secretary in March 1985.

Brezhnev's death was followed by the election as General Secretary of former head of the KGB, Yury Andropov. As head of the KGB, Andropov had been in a position where he had become acutely aware of the Soviet technological lag compared with the West, especially in the military area, and was therefore someone who, it was believed, would foster change.[1] But Andropov's election was not a unanimous choice within the elite. He was supported by those who believed that some change was necessary, not because (contrary to some speculation in the West) he was someone of a more liberal disposition, but because his fostering of an anti-corruption campaign since 1979–80 had associated him with the spreading recognition that the ways that had prevailed under Brezhnev could not lead to a solution of the Soviet Union's mounting problems. But just as the anti-corruption campaign had been a sign of a potential force for change for some members of the elite, for others it was a real danger. Many of those who had been most closely associated with Brezhnev watched with concern as that campaign unrolled, increasingly coming closer to Brezhnev himself and his family.[2] Their personal positions were potentially

[1] For one view of the importance of Andropov's background and his period in the KGB, see Seweryn Bialer, *The Soviet Paradox: External Expansion, Internal Decline* (New York, Alfred A. Knopf, 1987), 82.

[2] On this campaign, see Konstantin Simis, 'Andropov's Anticorruption Campaign', *The Washington Quarterly*, 6: 3 (Summer 1983), 111–21; Zhores Medvedev, *Andropov: His Life and Death* (Oxford, Blackwell, 1983), ch. 9. Also see Archie Brown, 'Andropov: Discipline and Reform?', *Problems of Communism*, 32: 1 (Jan.–Feb. 1983), 18–24.

under threat as a result of this campaign and of the elevation of its patron. Andropov's KGB background, and the information that such a position was likely to bring him on their own personal circumstances, increased the worry. With many of these people in the twilight of their careers (see below), all they wanted was a peaceful time in which to see out their political lives. These people looked to the former assistant of Brezhnev, Konstantin Chernenko, as the preferred successor, because he promised the likelihood of little or no change.

Despite his advanced age at the time of his election (68), Andropov proceeded to realise the worst fears of his more cautious colleagues. The anti-corruption campaign was maintained, and it was supplemented by an attempt to improve labour productivity through heightened discipline both in the workplace and in society at large. In addition, Andropov began the process of leadership renewal, bringing new members into the Politburo and Secretariat[3] and replacing about 25 per cent of regional party first secretaries. But Andropov's approach was essentially technocratic in nature. His strategy of a tightening of discipline and some personnel replacement without structural change[4] was a traditional Soviet response to problems and unlikely to lead to sustained improvement. This was, however, enough to concern the old guard of the leadership, and when Andropov died in February 1984, Chernenko was elected as his replacement. But those opposed to change in the leadership were not unchallenged. Although Chernenko became the General Secretary, the youngest member of the Politburo, Mikhail Gorbachev, was established as the number two in the hierarchy and consequently the heir apparent. The Chernenko–Gorbachev arrangement was clearly a compromise, and this was shown by the stasis which gripped the leadership for the period of Chernenko's tenure. During this time, policy drifted; no more personnel changes were made at the top and no new policy initiatives announced. While the thrust of Andropov's policies was blunted, their substance was not rejected.

Gorbachev was elected General Secretary on 11 March 1985, the day after Chernenko died. Gorbachev's reformist credentials were by no means clearly established at the time of his election, although there were hints there for those who cared to look. His career within the party had been orthodox and he had

---

[3] There were three new full members of the Politburo (Vorotnikov, Solomentsev and Aliev—the latter two promoted from candidate status) and one candidate member of the Politburo (Chebrikov) and two new secretaries (Ryzhkov and Ligachev; a third, Romanov, was already a member of the Politburo): Timothy Colton, *The Dilemma of Reform in the Soviet Union* (Washington, Council for Foreign Relations, 1986), 74.

[4] And although Andropov did support some changes including the tying of wages to productivity, the introduction of labour collectives and some decentralisation of the economic structure, these had no real effect upon the way in which the system functioned. For a discussion of these measures, see Medvedev, *Andropov*, chs. 13–15.

been promoted to the centre under Brezhnev, a development which did not seem consistent with someone who would seek to bring about major change from the course that had been charted in the recent past. But as the Khrushchev experience of the arch-Stalinist becoming the deStalinizer suggests, past career was not an infallible guide to future positions. Indeed there were some elements of his career which are consistent with a more reformist approach. One was his membership of the post-Stalin political generation. Gorbachev's background was very different from that of those who had gone before him. Having been born in 1931, Gorbachev had no personal experience of the revolution and could have had only limited experience of the drive for agricultural collectivisation and the terror. He was not a participant in the war. For Gorbachev, the key formative event in his political life was deStalinization. This meant that unlike his predecessors, his personal career was independent from those key defining points in the life of the Soviet regime, with the result that a questioning of those structures, while perhaps personally painful, did not constitute a questioning of his life's struggle. This generation may thus have been far less emotionally entwined with the Soviet regime than its predecessors. Furthermore, Gorbachev's patron, and the person who was believed to have been instrumental in bringing him to the notice of Brezhnev, was Andropov, who saw in Gorbachev someone who seems to have agreed that there was a need for change. Indeed Gorbachev had publicly supported the introduction of reformist measures in what some saw as his policy speech at the end of 1984.[5]

Debate continues about the extent to which Gorbachev had a clear policy agenda in his mind when he was elected.[6] Those who believe that such an agenda existed argue that the cautious beginning and the zigzags that were apparent in his policy positions were simply reflections of the extent of the opposition he faced in elite ranks. In this view, he was continually manoeuvring to achieve the outcome he desired against the opposition of significant forces. Alternatively, many argue that while he recognised that there was a need for change, and as his December 1984 speech suggested that change had to be substantial, he did not have a clear idea about the substance or dimensions of that change or how it could be introduced. In this view the instability of his policy line was a function not only of the extent of opposition, but

[5] Mikhail Gorbachev, 'Zhivoe tvorchestvo naroda', *Izbrannye rechi i stat'i*, II (Moscow, 1987), 75–108. In the speech Gorbachev talked about democratisation, glasnost, equality before the law, self-government and the fostering of individual initiative. The speech introduced the notion of perestroika and foreshadowed political and economic reform, although this was not universally recognised at the time. Also see Archie Brown, *The Gorbachev Factor* (Oxford, Oxford University Press, 1996), 79–80.

[6] For one discussion of this question, see Brown, *Gorbachev*, 13–14.

also of this lack of clarity in his own vision. It is this latter view which is adopted here.

It is also important to recognise that, despite the claims made against him in some quarters in the post-1991 period, in 1985 Gorbachev did not set out to destroy, or even perhaps to fundamentally transform, the Soviet Union. Gorbachev's basic aim was to bring about only sufficient change to enable the system to work efficiently. He did not believe at the outset that the system had to be reformed root and branch, rather believing that a series of smaller-scale changes would be sufficient to restore the system to health. It was only when these did not bear fruit that his position began to radicalise and, from mid-1988, he was forced by the impetus of events he had unleashed, to take up even more radical positions than he had ever envisaged. But to the extent that he initially saw himself as embarking on a process of limited reform which would change neither major structures nor the locus of real power, he was engaged in a classic policy of liberalization.[7] Like most such policies when tried by authoritarian regimes elsewhere, the likelihood of success was remote.

## The Path Toward Liberalization

The initial approach adopted by the Gorbachev leadership was by and large a replay of the traditional means of approaching problems in the past: a combination of personnel change and increased discipline. This assumed that there was nothing wrong with the basics of the Soviet system, but all that was needed was a change in attitude and a tightening up of its processes. Whether Gorbachev and his immediate confidants believed this or whether they realised the need for more substantial change but were constrained by a more hostile majority in the leadership is not certain.[8] Throughout the initial year of Gorbachev's leadership, there was a continuing emphasis in the message coming from that leadership upon the need for a change in the way in which party members conducted themselves. This was reflected most clearly in the

---

[7] Liberalization has been discussed in many places. For example, see Samuel P. Huntington, *The Third Wave: Democratization in the Late Twentieth Century* (Norman, University of Oklahoma Press, 1991), 9 and Adam Przeworski, *Democracy and the Market: Political and Economic Reforms in Eastern Europe and Latin America* (Cambridge, Cambridge University Press, 1991), 54–66. For one application to the Soviet Union, see Graeme Gill, 'Liberalization and Democratization in the Soviet Union and Russia', *Democratization*, 2: 3 (Autumn 1995), 313–36.

[8] For a strong argument in favour of the latter, see Brown, *Gorbachev*, 95. For a good discussion of the early reforms, see John M. Battle, 'Uskorenie, Glasnost and Perestroika: The Pattern of Reform Under Gorbachev', *Soviet Studies*, 40: 3 (July 1988), 367–84.

publicity given to cases of corruption in different republics,[9] a state of affairs which in Gorbachev's view was associated with a personnel policy conducted on the basis of 'personal loyalty, servility and protectionism.'[10] Such a situation encouraged attempts by local party organisations to deceive the centre, to embellish reality, to engage in window-dressing and complacency and to hide abuses and speak only of successes.[11] Party organizations had to work in a new style, but this required a new approach by party officials. The key to this was to adopt a critical approach to their own and others' work and for party work to be characterised by greater openness, including the involvement of non-party people in party affairs.[12] This was a revival of the criticism-self-criticism campaigns of the past, and like earlier campaigns this was also associated with calls for collectivism and the increased responsibility of members of the collective for their actions.[13]

This theme of party discussion amounted to a demand 'for a profound reform in the psychology of cadres',[14] for the psychological restructuring of cadres in the spirit of the new demands and challenges, for making them think and work in new ways.[15] The problems could be overcome providing people escaped from the stereotyped ways of thinking of the past and thought creatively, using their critical faculties and their initiative to attack deficiencies and overcome the clear challenges the party faced. One problem with this call for psychological restructuring is that if it was to be successful, it would not bear fruit in a short period of time. The sort of change of patterns of activity envisaged by Gorbachev and his supporters would have involved a major dis-

[9] e.g *Pravda* 14 July 1985, 20 Jan. 1986, 27 Jan. 1986, 3 Feb. 1987. For discussions in English, see James Critchlow, ' "Corruption", Nationalism and the Native Elites in Soviet Central Asia', *The Journal of Communist Studies*, 4: 2 (June 1988), 142–61; and Peter Rutland, 'The Search for Stability: Ideology, Discipline, and the Cohesion of the Soviet Elite', *Studies in Comparative Communism*, 24: 1 (Mar. 1991), 47–50.

[10] Mikhail S. Gorbachev, 'O sozyve ocherednego XXVII s'ezda KPSS i zadachakh sviazannykh s ego podgotovkoi i provedeniem', *Pravda*, 24 April 1985. For a more extended discussion of the approach to personnel issues, see Graeme Gill, *The Collapse of a Single-Party System: The Disintegration of the Communist Party of the Soviet Union* (Cambridge, Cambridge University Press, 1994).

[11] 'O nedopustimosti iskazheniia fakticheskogo polozheniia del v soobshcheniiakh i informatsiiakh, postupaiushchikh v Ts K KPSS i drugie rukovodiashchie organy', 26 November 1985, *Izvestiia Ts.K. KPSS*, 2 (Feb. 1989), 39–41 and Mikhail S. Gorbachev, 'Politicheskii doklad Tsentral'nogo Komiteta KPSS', *Pravda*, 26 Feb. 1986.

[12] e.g. see the new party Rules adopted at the XXVII Congress, *Pravda*, 7 Mar. 1986, esp. section 4(b).

[13] Section 27 of the Rules, *Pravda*, 7 Mar. 1986.

[14] Shcherbitsky in *Pravda Ukrainy*, 1 June 1985, FBIS Soviet Union, 11 June 1985.

[15] M. S. Gorbachev, 'Nastoichivo dvigat'sia vpered', in M. S. Gorbachev, *Izbrannye*, II, 210–24 and M. S. Gorbachev, 'Korennoi vopros ekonomicheskoi politiki partii', *Pravda*, 12 June 1985.

ruption to existing routines and practices, and what they did not realise was that these were embedded not just in people's minds, but in the structures themselves. Yet no provision was made for the sort of structural reform which could have encouraged such independence. However this injunction to change was accompanied by something else which was often a feature of historical self-criticism campaigns, personnel turnover.

Gorbachev moved quickly in an attempt to reshape the upper echelons of the political system. He replaced those aides and personal advisers whom he had inherited from Chernenko, bringing into office a number of people who would exercise considerable influence on his thinking in subsequent years, including Andrei Grachev, Anatoly Chernyaev, and Georgy Smirnov.[16] This was a relatively easy task, because these jobs were within his own gift. However, changing the party leadership was more difficult. Nevertheless, Gorbachev also turned his attention to the leading organs of the party, bringing about a significant transformation within the first twelve months of his time in office. He was assisted in this by the sense of urgency that had been generated as a result of the last years when the sense of drift symbolised by the death of three elderly leaders created a widespread feeling that things could not go on as they had. This opportunity was reinforced by the age of many incumbents of official positions. This is reflected in the age profile of leading party organs at the time of Gorbachev's election. Table 2.1 shows the number of members in each elite party body by their age (figures for the Secretariat includes only those not also members of the Politburo, who are picked up in the Politburo categories).

TABLE 2.1. *Age of leadership*

|  | 50s | 60s | 70s | 80s | Approximate average age |
|---|---|---|---|---|---|
| Politburo full | 2 | 3 | 5 | — | 67.5 |
| Politburo candidate | 1 | 3 | — | 2 | 68.5 |
| Secretariat | 1 | 1 | 3 | — | 67.6 |

At Central Committee meetings during 1985 and at the time of the XXVII Congress in February–March 1986, membership of these leading organs was significantly renewed (see Table 2.2).

By the end of March 1986, some 61.5 per cent of the members of the Politburo and Secretariat had joined those bodies within the last twelve months, a rate of renewal at the top of the political structure unprecedented in

---

[16] For a discussion of this, see Brown, *Gorbachev*, 97–103. These advisers often tended to be more radical than leading Soviet politicians. For a discussion of one group of these, see Anders Aslund, 'Gorbachev's Economic Advisors', *Soviet Economy*, 3: 3 (1987), 246–69.

Table 2.2. Leadership change 1985–1986

| Central Committee | Politburo | | | | Secretariat | |
|---|---|---|---|---|---|---|
| | In (full) | Out (full) | In (candidate) | Out (candidate) | In | Out |
| April 1985 | Ligachev Chebrikov Ryzhkov | | Sokolov | | Nikonov | |
| July 1985 | Shevardnadze | Romanov | | Shevardnadze | Yeltsin Zaikov | Romanov |
| October 1985 February 1986 | | Tikhonov Grishin | Talyzin Yeltsin | | | |
| March 1986 | Zaikov | | Sliun'kov Solov'ev | Kuznetsov Ponomarev | Biriukova Medvedev Dobrynin Yakovlev Razumovsky | Ryzhkov Yeltsin Rusakov Kapitonov Ponomarev |

Soviet history. Furthermore, this seemed to constitute a significant strengthening of Gorbachev's position.[17] This was not only because he presided over the promotion of these people, but from the perspective of 1991, it is clear that many of these people supported the sort of moderate reform program Gorbachev was associated with at this time; the appointment of Ryzhkov as state premier in place of the elderly Brezhnevite Tikhonov in October 1985 was particularly important in this regard. Perhaps more importantly, two of his most significant allies, Shevardnadze and Yakovlev, entered the top leadership at this time; so too did Yeltsin. Also significant was the removal of Romanov, Tikhonov, Grishin, Kuznetsov, Ponomarov, Rusakov, and Kapitonov, all figures associated with a conservative approach to politics.

The personnel changes were not restricted to the apex of the party. In the CC elected at the XXVII Congress in March 1986, 44 per cent were new, compared with a figure of 28 per cent five years earlier. At the party's lower levels too there was significant change. In the eighteen months following Gorbachev's election, 57 of the 157 regional party secretaries were changed,[18] as were many party functionaries at lower levels. There was similar movement within the state structure; in the first twelve months of Gorbachev's leadership, more than one third of the membership of the Council of Ministers was changed. The levels of personnel change in all parts of the political structure were unprecedented in Soviet history, even in the time of the purges.

As well as the emphasis upon discipline and personnel change within the party, Gorbachev's initial reformist policy comprised two elements, uskorenie (acceleration) and glasnost (openness). These had first been advanced in his December 1984 speech to ideological workers,[19] where he suggested that they would lead to 'profound transformations in the economy and in the entire system of social relations'. But Gorbachev's view of the impact of these policies was exaggerated. The slogan uskorenie was associated with the promulgation of ambitious targets (including a doubling of economic output by the year 2000), the achievement of which relied upon massive increases in productivity, and the rationalization of the command administrative system, principally through concentrating power at the top and reducing the number of economic ministries.[20] The result of this was to be significant improvements in popular

[17] For the argument that he took over the client network of Kirilenko–Andropov, see Jerry F. Hough, *Democratization and Revolution in the USSR 1985–1991* (Washington, Brookings, 1997), 86–99.

[18] Richard Sakwa, *Gorbachev and His Reforms 1985–1990* (London, Philip Allan, 1990), 13.

[19] Gorbachev, 'Zhivoe'. Their changing meaning is discussed in Brown, *Gorbachev*, 122–6.

[20] For the official directives of the twelfth five-year plan which embodied these targets, see *Pravda*, 9 Mar. 1986. They are summarised in Stephen White, *Gorbachev and After* (Cambridge, Cambridge University Press, 1991), 104–5.

living standards and the availability of consumer goods and services (including housing, health and education), something clearly designed to appeal to the populace and to rally them behind his reform plans. However, no new mechanisms were introduced that had any hope of achieving the increase in productivity that was necessary. Uskorenie assumed the 'intensification' of production through the better use of resources, increased discipline and the sort of change in consciousness noted above. There was some short-term improvement in economic performance, but no means were introduced to achieve the better use of resources within the economy. Although the discipline campaign did have some impact on the life of Soviet workers, most particularly through the disastrous anti-alcohol campaign and the campaign against unearned income both launched by Gorbachev,[21] it had no substantial effect in improving economic performance; indeed the deeply unpopular anti-alcohol campaign had a disastrous effect on the economy by substantially cutting state revenues which had been heavily dependent on taxation of alcohol sales, thereby increasing the budget deficit which the government sought to meet by printing money, with a consequent contribution to high inflation rates and the collapse of the rouble in 1990.[22] As a disciplinary measure, the anti-alcohol drive proved counter-productive in the short term. While it does seem to have led to some improvement in work performance by workers and perhaps to decreased mortality rates, it also led to sugar shortages and the increased consumption of home brew (samogon), with resultant higher levels of alcoholic poisoning. Whatever the balance of its achievements, the anti-alcohol campaign had a negative impact on Gorbachev's popular standing, demonstrating that he was out of touch with the very forces he would need on side if he was to carry his programme through.

The notion of glasnost evident in this early period was also quite limited. While the ideas of honesty and accountability which became so prominent later in the decade were implicit in this term from the outset, its general tenor was really one which was much less threatening to traditional Soviet mores. It seems broadly to have been seen less as an invitation to criticism from below than as an opportunity for the elite to use the media to air issues which they believed should be discussed and to create a means for accurate information to be disseminated. This was designed to improve the quality of central decision-

[21] The best study of the anti-alcohol campaign is Stephen White, *Russia Goes Dry* (Cambridge, Cambridge University Press, 1996). Also see Daniel Tarschys, 'The Success of a Failure: Gorbachev's Alcohol Policy, 1985–88', *Europe-Asia Studies*, 45: 1 (1993), 7–25. For the measure against unearned income, see *Izvestiia*, 28 May 1986.

[22] See Rachel Walker, *Six Years That Shook the World: Perestroika the Impossible Project* (Manchester, Manchester University Press, 1993), 106–8. Although overall consumption seems to have fallen: Tarschys, 'Success', 22–3.

making, to stimulate a sense of accountability on the part of officials and thereby to combat 'bureaucratism', and, symbolically, to generate greater popular trust in and commitment to the system. Gorbachev argued from the outset that popular access to honest and reliable information was crucial to generating popular activism and support for the party and its programmes.[23] The impetus thus came from above, with the implication that the boundaries of such discussion could be set and the room for initiative from below was limited. Certainly editorial staff in some Soviet newspapers and magazines began to use the new freedom that this slogan seemed to imply, but in this early period the tone was still set by the political elite. The main tenor of this was the criticism of personnel performance associated with the substantial turnover of party figures at many levels, a process which created room for public criticism of the performance of political officials. The most important element of this was the criticism of privileges that appeared in the media in the lead up to the XXVII Congress in February–March 1986. This too was elite-initiated, symptomatic of the determination that the pace of liberalisation and the scope of popular input would be set by the party.

The development of such criticism of privileges reflects the emergence of what came to be substantial splits within the reform coalition. The origin of such splits was two-fold, the individual personalities involved and the consequences of the realisation in 1986 that the minimum reformist programme which had united the elite in 1985 was not having the desired effects. In terms of personalities, the crucial figure was Boris Yeltsin. Despite his strictly Soviet orthodox background, Yeltsin appears to have been the sort of person who could both question the established orthodoxy and step outside it if he believed this necessary. Furthermore it seems that his relationship with another leading figure in the elite, Yegor Ligachev, was always characterised by a certain degree of strain. This was manifested in early 1986 when, at the XXVII Congress, Yeltsin criticised the functioning of the CC Secretariat run by Ligachev and openly supported the criticism of leadership privileges that had appeared in a letter in *Pravda* just before the Congress. Ligachev responded, defending the Secretariat and criticising the way the question of privileges had been raised.[24] This exchange was the first public shot in a continuing conflict between what became a more radical and a more conservative wing of the reformist leadership. This was exacerbated by the second factor, the realisation that the reformist minimum programme had run into the sand.

---

[23] Gorbachev, *Izbrannye*, II, 131. This was his address to the March 1985 CC plenum.

[24] For the speeches by Yeltsin and Ligachev, see *XXVII s'ezd kommunisticheskoi partii sovetskogo soiuza 25 fevralia–6 marta 1986 goda. Stenograficheskii otchet* (Moscow, 1986), I, 140–5, 232–40.

Two factors were instrumental in the growth within sections of the political elite of the view that the reformist minimum programme had not had the sort of salutary effects Gorbachev had envisaged.[25] The first was economic performance. By early 1986 it was clear that sustained economic improvement was not under way. None of the structural impediments to economic improvement had been removed, while the campaign for increased discipline (which had actually begun in 1979) had lost its most potent quality, its shock value. Indeed, one aspect of the discipline campaign, Gorbachev's anti-alcohol drive, actually proved to be counter-productive in the short term. Rather than a stimulus to productivity, the discipline campaign was actually a drag on the economy.

The second factor which led to a re-evaluation of the programme within reformist elite circles was the nuclear accident at Chernobyl. The disaster which unfolded at the Chernobyl nuclear power plant in Ukraine, and more importantly the cover-up of the seriousness of it, acted as an important stimulus to the radicalization of glasnost. The Soviet delay in announcing what had happened at Chernobyl was much criticised in the West, but more important for the question of domestic reform was the cover-up conducted by local officials. The fact that the central leadership was not made aware of the seriousness of the situation for some days strengthened the conviction of some within that leadership, including Gorbachev, that what was needed was a means of checking on the presentation of misinformation by lower level officials. This had been a problem throughout the Soviet period,[26] and now the leadership chose the same solution that had been tried in the 1930s: encouragement of a more vigorous press and of popular activism.[27] Increasingly from mid-1986 glasnost became the vehicle for the expansion of the bounds of discussion of issues and a means whereby deficient office-holders could come under scrutiny and criticism. This was linked to an attempt by Gorbachev and his supporters to appeal to the Soviet intelligentsia for support, to use a somewhat freer media as an incentive for this group to come in behind the reform effort. Important in this was the appointment of new editors to a range of leading publications, including *Novyi Mir*, *Ogonek*, *Moscow News* and *Kommunist*. The censorship functions of Glavlit were restricted in June 1986, substantially leav-

[25] Archie Brown argues that from the outset Gorbachev's aim was much more radical reform than his earliest steps suggested, the early caution reflecting the extent of opposition within the leadership. For the view that from the outset he wished to move toward market socialism, see Brown, *Gorbachev*, 139.

[26] For one study of it in the post-Stalin period, see Graeme Gill and Roderic Pitty, *Power in the Party: The Organization of Power and Central-Republican Relations in the CPSU* (London, Macmillan, 1997).

[27] On the 1930s see Graeme Gill, *The Origins of the Stalinist Political System* (Cambridge, Cambridge University Press, 1990), chs. 5–8.

ing the shaping of what appeared in the press in the hands of individual editors; prepublication censorship disappeared and the CC's Propaganda Department no longer formally held editors accountable.[28] At the May Congress of the Cinema Workers' Union a new pro-reform leadership was elected, while at the VIII Congress of the Union of Writers in June 1986, a new more reformist leadership was elected and it publicly associated itself with the deStalinizing XXII Congress of the Party in 1961. In the theatrical world, a new, reform-leaning union was formed to ouflank the conservatives. Glasnost ultimately became a process that was highly erosive of Soviet legitimacy as its bounds expanded to embrace topics and to raise questions going to the heart of the Soviet system. However, in 1986 this process was only just beginning and it was largely supported by the reform-minded political elite, who effectively looked to the intelligentsia to voice popular opinion. But the intelligentsia could not provide a solid social base to sustain political reform, and ultimately proved to be the most unreliable of allies, as they lost faith in perestroika and turned against the Soviet system itself.

At this early stage another aspect of the reform programme became apparent: a new approach to international affairs, summarized in the term 'new thinking'.[29] From the outset, Gorbachev's accession to leadership was seen in some quarters in the West as the opportunity for a new opening and easing of relations with the USSR. This is reflected superficially in Margaret Thatcher's description of Gorbachev as someone with whom she could 'do business'.[30] More importantly, Gorbachev realised that any improvement in the Soviet domestic situation required the commitment of more resources to economic restructuring, and in the absence of an expanding domestic economy, these could only come by cutting elsewhere or by increasing the flow of resources (in the form of trade and/or aid) from the advanced Western economies into that of the USSR. The most obvious target, simply because of its size, was the defence budget;[31] according to Gorbachev in 1989, defence consumed 15 per cent of the budget.[32] But any reduction in the defence budget had to be

---

[28] Already some unusual and challenging material was appearing in the press, such as the publication of a poem by the anti-communist monarchist Gumilev in April 1986: John Miller, *Mikhail Gorbachev and the End of Soviet Power* (London, Macmillan, 1993), 94.

[29] For Shevardnadze's discussion of this, see Eduard Shevardnadze, *Moi Vybor. V zashchitu demokratii i svobody* (Moscow, Novosti, 1991), esp. ch. 3. Also M. S. Gorbachev, *Perestroika i novoe myshlenie dlia nashei strany i vsego mira* (Moscow, Politizdat, 1987).

[30] *Financial Times*, 22 Dec. 1984.

[31] Reduced assistance to third world and communist states was another potential area for cutting, with important political implications for improved relations with the West.

[32] Cited in Stephen White, *After Gorbachev* (Cambridge, Cambridge University Press, 1993), 89. The figure of 77.3 billion roubles used by White is given in Gorbachev's speech to the Congress of People's Deputies, *Pervyi s'ezd narodnykh deputatov SSSR. Stenograficheskii otchet*, I (Moscow, 1989), 435–71; the figure is on p. 449. According to

incumbent upon relaxation of international tensions, and Gorbachev set out to achieve this in 1985. He sought to move towards a reduction in nuclear tension with the USA, announcing in April 1985 (and renewing in 1986) a unilateral moratorium on nuclear testing and proposing a series of concrete measures aimed at arms reduction (including a proposal to reduce by 50 per cent all long-range nuclear weapons). In November 1985 he met US President Reagan at the first summit in a decade in Geneva, and in October 1986 at the Rejkavik summit he proposed the complete elimination of nuclear weapons by the end of the century. Gorbachev also sought to shift the Soviet focus away from its concentration on the USA by emphasising new initiatives elsewhere on the globe. In 1985 in a visit to Paris, he proposed the concept of the 'common European home', a conception which emphasised the commonalities rather than the differences between both sides of the post-war divide in Europe and envisaged a European community without American involvement but with closer ties between the Soviet Union and the European capitalist states.[33] In July 1986 he launched his Vladivostok initiative, which involved the projection of the USSR into the Pacific region in a peaceful and positive capacity, a region he also referred to as 'the Pacific, our common home.'[34]

These sorts of measures in the international arena were designed to revivify Soviet foreign policy and to blunt the sort of hostility that had confronted it in the wake of the decline of détente. In part they reflected the dead end into which foreign policy had drifted at the end of the 1970s and the increasingly dangerous international environment that seemed to be reflected in the rhetoric of the Reagan Administration and in its pursuit of the Strategic Defense Initiative. In particular the cost of the latter, reflecting as it did an American commitment to outspend the ailing Soviet economy in the defence area, heightened the need for Moscow to reduce its commitments in this area of activity. Gorbachev saw this, and aided by the replacement as foreign minister of the veteran Andrei Gromyko by his ally Eduard Shevardnadze in July 1985, was able to press ahead with initiatives in foreign policy designed to achieve this end.

Just as Gorbachev's initiative to eliminate nuclear weapons at the Rejkavik summit reflected a radicalisation of his foreign policy stance, so this sort of process was also evident in domestic policy.

Gorbachev's memoirs, military expenditure was 40% of the state budget. Mikhail Gorbachev, *Memoirs* (London, Doubleday, 1996), 215.

[33] M. S. Gorbachev, 'Vystuplenie po frantsuzskomu televideniiu' 30 Sept. 1985, *Izbrannye*, II, 441. He had actually used the term 'common home' on his trip to Britain in December 1984: Hough, *Democratization*, 193. In France, he used the term 'the same house'.

[34] For his speech in Vladivostok, see 'Rech' tovarishcha Gorbacheva M.S. na torzhestvennom sobranii, posviashchennom vrucheniiu Vladivostoku ordena Lenina', *Pravda*, 29 July 1986.

## The Radicalization of Official Policy

In the second half of 1986, Soviet policy shifted in a more radical direction.[35] In the economic sphere, the term 'perestroika', which had been used to refer to economic restructuring in Gorbachev's December 1984 speech, took on a more radical hue. In August measures were introduced providing for the creation of joint ventures with Western companies,[36] something which for the first time provided an opening for Western involvement in the Soviet economy, while in November legislation was passed enabling limited private entrepreneurial activity.[37] This Law on Individual Labour Activity created limited room for individual private initiative, principally in the service sector, and although the acceptable boundaries were reasonably narrowly drawn, official acceptance of the legality of private enterprise was a significant symbolic step in the process of economic restructuring.

The economic measures introduced in the second half of 1986 had little immediate practical impact on the overall functioning of the economy, but they were important symbolically in two ways. Firstly, on the public stage, they enabled the tentative emergence of private economic activity, principally in the form of the provision of goods and services and of small-scale restaurants. Not only did this help to improve the quality of life in some places, but it marked a public official questioning of the value of the collective economy. Secondly, these changes marked a recognition within the elite of the need for structural change in the economy. The policy of tinkering reflected in the slogan of uskorenie was replaced by a public commitment to perestroika, which was now projected in terms of a restructuring of the economy.[38] But this reconceptualization of perestroika did not only have economic effects. It also raised the issue of political reform. There were two aspects of this, the strategic and the tactical.

In strategic terms, the issue was whether there could be substantial economic reform without corresponding political change. With the Soviet politico-economic structure characterised by the intense interlocking of

[35] There were limits to how far Gorbachev was willing to go. Price reform was essential for economic reform, but Gorbachev opposed price rises at this time: Hough, *Democratization*, 125–6.

[36] This, and subsequent measures modifying its effect, are discussed in Anders Aslund, *Gorbachev's Struggle for Economic Reform* (Ithaca, Cornell University Press, 1987), 140–1, and Sakwa, *Gorbachev*, 285.

[37] 'Ob individual'noi trudovoi deiatel'nosti', *Pravda*, 21 Nov. 1986.

[38] For a discussion of some of the terminology used in the early Gorbachev period, see Klaus von Beyme, 'Economics and Politics in a Socialist Country: Gorbachev's New Concepts', *Government and Opposition*, 23: 2 (Spring 1988), 167–85.

political and economic institutions and imperatives, substantial economic reform was impossible without corresponding political change. If that economic change had involved principally a tightening up of control and re-imposition of discipline, no such political change would have been needed. However, when the course of economic reform involved the loosening of central control, as the measures introduced in the second half of 1986 did, there were bound to be political implications.[39] If there was to be an economy based less on central control and administrative fiat and more on the ebb and flow of private preference and initiative, popular enthusiasm and support had to be unleashed, and to do this adequate political institutions had to be either created anew or remoulded out of existing structures. In either event, successful decentralizing economic reform would require, sooner or later, political reform, regardless of the preferences of the political leadership. By late 1986 it was clear that Gorbachev and his supporters had realised this and moved to embrace political reform.[40]

In tactical terms, political reform was placed on the agenda by the need for the reformers to generate popular support. The recognition of the need for structural change increased the levels of opposition and resistance that was likely to confront such policies. Structural change of necessity involved an alteration to both established structures and patterns of power. It therefore provoked resistance not only from those who retained a fervent belief in the efficacy of the Soviet structure, but also from many of those who were located in its heart. Not only leading politicians and ideologues became concerned when the shift toward structural change occurred, but also many of those bureaucrats occupying administrative positions throughout the Soviet structure who had both power and position to lose should radical change be introduced. During 1986 Gorbachev criticised obstructionism and the failure to implement decisions on eliminating whitewashing and the false reporting of performance.[41] In the face of such opposition, Gorbachev turned more decisively to those in the populace who could expect to benefit from a modernizing reform: the younger, the better educated and the intelligentsia.[42] His support

[39] This is regardless of whether Gorbachev had, as Archie Brown argues, always wanted political reform.

[40] In this respect they charted a course markedly different from that of the Communist Party of China, which pursued economic reform while rejecting political reform, as events in Tiananmen Square in 1989 showed.

[41] See Gorbachev's speeches 'O piatiletnem plane ekonomicheskogo i sotsial'nogo razvitiia SSSR na 1986–1990 gody i zadachakh partiinykh organizatsii po ego realizatsii', *Pravda*, 17 June 1986; 'Pribavit' v rabote, deistvovat' initsiativno', *Pravda*, 18 Sept. 1986; and 'Rech' General'nogo Sekretaria TsK KPSS M. S. Gorbacheva na vstreche s partiinym aktivom Krasnodarskogo kraia', *Pravda*, 20 Sept. 1986.

[42] For an interpretation of Gorbachev's policies in terms of the construction of a social contract from which these groups in particular would benefit, see Peter Hauslohner,

for the changes in the cultural sphere noted above, his public support for 'responsible' glasnost in October[43] and his call in December for leading artists and directors to use glasnost to support perestroika,[44] were explicit appeals to the intelligentsia for support. But his greatest pitch for the support of this group came in December 1986 when he released long-time dissident Andrei Sakharov from internal exile in Gorky. However the most important element in Gorbachev's drive for political reform and lower level support was his policy of democratization initiated at the CC plenum in January 1987.

Gorbachev had been discussing the proposals he was to make to the CC plenum in January 1987 for some months prior to that meeting with party leaders throughout the country,[45] but not surprisingly there was little enthusiasm for the measures he was foreshadowing.[46] Lower-level opposition to change was brought home vividly on the eve of the plenum when the replacement of Kazakh first secretary Dinmukhamed Kunaev by the Russian Gennady Kolbin provoked popular riots in Alma Ata. These events were at least in part orchestrated by the Kunaev political machine and precipitated a purge of the Kazakh structure once Kolbin was in control. However, it was at the January plenum that Gorbachev's plan became known to all in the party, and that the strength of opposition to such changes was clear.

At the plenum Gorbachev criticised the state of the party,[47] and in particular the way it functioned on the basis of a lack of accountability and of a permissive attitude on the part of party leaders. His solution was to strengthen what he called democratisation within the CPSU, principally through emphasising the responsibility of the elected to the electors and by providing for competitive secret ballot multi-candidate elections for party secretaries from the district to union republican level. Moreover the nomination of candidates was not restricted to higher-level organs, as had been the practice, but participation in this by members of the committees to which the secretary was to be elected was to be encouraged. However, the effect of these provisions was

'Gorbachev's Social Contract', *Soviet Economy*, 3: 1 (1987), 54–89. See also Stephen White, 'Economic Performance and Communist Legitimacy', *World Politics*, 38: 3 (Apr. 1986), 462–82; Janine Ludlam, 'Reform and the Redefinition of the Social Contract under Gorbachev', *World Politics*, 43: 2 (Jan. 1991), 284–312; and Linda J. Cook, 'Brezhnev's "Social Contract" and Gorbachev's Reforms', *Soviet Studies*, 44: 1 (1992), 37–56.

[43] At a speech to an All-Union Conference of Directors of Faculties of Social Sciences, 'Rech' tovarishcha Gorbacheva M.S.', *Pravda*, 2 Oct. 1986.

[44] 'Vstrecha v TsK KPSS', *Pravda*, 5 Dec. 1986.

[45] See the interview with Krasnodar kraikom First Secretary Ivan Polozkov in *The Second Russian Revolution. III The Yeltsin File*, BBC Television, 1991.

[46] Opposition to his plans was responsible for the plenum being delayed three times. *Izbrannye*, IV, 428.

[47] M. S. Gorbachev, 'O perestroike i kadrovoi politike partii', *Pravda*, 28 Jan. 1987.

immediately blunted by Gorbachev's acceptance of the principle that the decisions of higher-standing bodies were to remain binding on those at lower levels (thereby enabling electoral competition to be thwarted by resolution of superior organs), by the failure to include the CC CPSU among the committees whose secretary was to be elected in this way,[48] and by the failure to make competitive elections mandatory. Gorbachev applied similar principles to the state electoral system, calling for greater popular involvement in all stages of the electoral process, and for competitive ballots in multi-member constituencies. These proposals constituted a classic attempt at liberalization; they did not change the fundamental power structure, because they did not make such changes mandatory. Entrenched leaders could circumvent the proposals if they wished, and in any case while they retained control over political life in their regions and continued to dominate a passive membership, even competitive elections could be rigged. In any event, the CC itself pulled the teeth from Gorbachev's proposal; the CC resolution emphasised democratization, accountability, criticism and self-criticism and other general principles that were both consistent with democracy and also with the rhetorical traditions of party life, but failed specifically to endorse those measures essential to the notion of democratization, competitive multi-candidate secret ballot elections. The extent of resistance within the CC was too strong; party secretaries at all levels feared the loss of control that competitive elections would bring. Gorbachev was caught in the classic contradiction of the liberal reformer; he was dependent on the very structure necessary to advance that reform, but which had most to lose from it.

Despite the blunting of this reform initiative from the top, the cause of change was given some, limited, impetus from below. Within two weeks of the plenum, reports occurred in the press of a competitive election by secret ballot for a local party secretary in Izhmorsky krai, Kemerovo oblast,[49] and although it was acknowledged that problems remained with the way this was handled, it was seen as a positive example for others to follow. During the remainder of the year, some 120 party secretaries were elected through competitive ballot, although none was for a post above the city level and candidates were still generally chosen from above rather than from below.[50] Despite the publicity these cases gained, most positions were still filled in the traditional way. At the end of March 1987 an experiment was announced, whereby in the forthcoming soviet elections a choice of candidates would be presented in a

---

[48] This may have been a result of tactical thinking on Gorbachev's part; he wanted to ensure that his own personal power was not eroded by making himself hostage to a non-reformist CC. Brown, *Gorbachev*, 167.

[49] *Pravda*, 10 Feb. 1987.          [50] *Partiinaia zhizn'* 11 (June 1988), 15.

series of enlarged constituencies each returning several members.[51] When the election was held, some 1 per cent of constituencies were formed on this basis and they returned 4 per cent of deputies elected in the June ballot.[52] Although the extent of the practice of competitive elections in both party and state was small in 1987, it did mark a sharp break with the past. Important at this stage too was the continuing discussion in the press of shortcomings in the way the party in particular but also various state organs had been functioning,[53] but it was the June 1987 plenum which gave the next fillip to reform.

While the plenum had been preceded by the beginning of competitive elections, this period also witnessed continuing signs of elite resistance to the course of policy Gorbachev was championing. In March, Ligachev warned against using glasnost to exaggerate the errors of the past and called for recognition of the successes that the revolution had brought in all fields.[54] In a conference of the CC in May called to discuss the failure to satisfy demands in the consumer goods field, both Ligachev and Biriukova argued that everything was in place to achieve the targets, all that was needed was discipline and application.[55] However, in contrast to this clear indication that at least a part of the ruling elite believed that the existing structures of the economy were appropriate to the tasks being faced, Gorbachev and his supporters were able to press forward with what they saw as a radical reconstruction of the economy. In February cooperatives for the production of consumer goods and services were legalised.[56] In early June the CC discussed a radical reconstruction of the administration of the economy, with CC Secretary Sliun'kov delivering a report. At the CC plenum on 25–26 June, a 'radical reform' of the economy was adopted, involving a partial dismantling of central economic control and of

---

[51] According to some memoirs cited by Jerry Hough, from the outset Gorbachev realized that the measures for democratization would lead to a multi-party system: Hough, *Democratization*, 150.

[52] Stephen White, Graeme Gill, Darrell Slider, *The Politics of Transition. Shaping a Post-Soviet Future* (Cambridge, Cambridge University Press, 1993) 23. Also Jeffrey Hahn, 'An Experiment in Competition: The 1987 Elections to the Local Soviets', *Slavic Review*, 47: 2 (Fall 1988).

[53] For a discussion of the sorts of charges, see Gill, *Collapse*, 39–44.

[54] Y. K. Ligachev, 'Navstrechu 70-letiu Velikogo Oktiabria', *Pravda*, 24 Mar. 1987. For a discussion of Ligachev's position, see Peter Reddaway, 'Resisting Gorbachev', *The New York Review of Books*, 18 Aug. 1988, pp. 36–41. For Ligachev's view, see Yegor Ligachev, *Inside Gorbachev's Kremlin: The Memoirs of Yegor Ligachev* (Boulder, Col., Westview Press, 1996), 284–97. For the argument that Ligachev was not an opponent of perestroika, nor even consistently more conservative on issues than Gorbachev, see Jeffrey Surovell, 'Ligachev and Soviet Politics', *Soviet Studies*, 43: 2 (1991), 355–74.

[55] *Pravda*, 23 May 1987.

[56] *Pravda*, 12 Feb. 1987. The first co-operative café opened in Moscow on 12 March. In September individuals and co-operatives were permitted to operate small shops and kiosks.

price subsidies. This 'Basic Provisions for the Fundamental Restructuring of Economic Management'[57] involved the substantial decentralization of the functioning of state industry and increased autonomy for both the republican governments and individual enterprises and production units. The most important part of this programme was the Law on the State Enterprise (Association) adopted in the Supreme Soviet on 1 July and to come into effect on 1 January 1988.[58] This provided for the elimination of precise targets and allocations set from above, and for individual enterprises to engage in wholesale trade with each other and to set their own prices. Enterprises were to be self-financing, and workers were given some powers to elect factory management, a small concession to popular initiative. On paper, these measures were a significant turn away from the centralized Soviet system of economic administration, and thereby constituted a direct rebuff to the positions being advanced by Ligachev in March and Ligachev and Biriukova in May, even if in practice enterprises remained significantly constrained.[59] By August markets functioning according to new private business laws were selling consumer goods in Moscow, while in September the Politburo authorised the operation of small kiosks and shops by individuals and cooperatives.

These structural changes in the January policy of democratization and the economic reforms in mid-year were alarming for many conservatives, and their concerns were hardly eased by three other types of domestic development during this year. First, Gorbachev's personal position within the leadership seemed to be substantially strengthened during the early part of 1987. At the January plenum, the disgraced Kunaev was formally removed from the Politburo, while future Gorbachev stalwart and CC Secretary Alexander Yakovlev was made a candidate member of the Politburo. Two new secretaries, Lukianov (a long-time Gorbachev friend) and Sliun'kov were appointed, while Zimianin was removed, meaning that only two party secretaries (Ligachev and Dolgikh) did not owe their positions to Gorbachev. At the June plenum, three secretaries who were all known to be Gorbachev associates, Sliun'kov, Yakovlev and Nikonov, were promoted to full membership of the Politburo, while the new defence minister, Dmitri Yazov, became a candidate member; his predecessor Sokolov was

---

[57] 'O zadachakh partii po korennoi perestroike upravleniia ekonomikoi', *Pravda*, 27 June 1987. According to Gorbachev, there was significant opposition to the changes proposed at the plenum, leading to the ultimate decisions being a compromise. He points to Ryzhkov, acting as the representative of the upper echelons of the state apparatus, in this regard: Gorbachev, *Memoirs*, ch. 11, esp. pp. 230 and 233.

[58] 'O gosudarstvennom predpriiatii (ob'edinenii)', *Vedomosti Verkhovnogo Soveta Soiuza Sovetskikh Sotsialisticheskikh Respublik* 26 (2412) 1 July 1987, 427–63.

[59] Although enterprises could draw up their own plans, the broad parameters of them continued to be set by the state, which also was to provide a significant part of the demand for the enterprise's production through state orders.

removed.[60] These changes meant that the party leadership overwhelmingly owed its position to Gorbachev, and although in retrospect not all were willing to support Gorbachev on his trajectory of deepening reform, at the time those resistant to him can hardly have taken heart at these personnel moves.

Second, Gorbachev gave a significant boost to the radicalizing power of glasnost by his call for the elimination of 'blank spots' in history and his references to 'socialist pluralism'. In a speech on 13 February 1987[61] in which he emphasised the importance of glasnost in helping people to understand and support perestroika, Gorbachev called for the review of Soviet history and the elimination of all 'blank spots' from it. This call for historical truth, which was a call to extend the already increasingly critical evaluations of the Brezhnev period to other areas of Soviet history[62] and the spur for Ligachev's comments the following month noted above, legitimized the radical rewriting of Soviet history. This process actually pre-dated Gorbachev's speech, with the potential for a revolutionary rewriting of the Soviet past becoming apparent in January 1987 with the release of Abuladze's anti-Stalinist film *Pokayanie* (*Repentance*). As if the intent of Gorbachev's actions was not clear enough, Gorbachev also announced the establishment of a commission to investigate the repressions of the 1930s, 1940s and 1950s,[63] a development which ultimately led to the rehabilitation of large numbers of victims of the Stalinist terror, including all of the leading figures except Trotsky. Gorbachev also explicitly criticised the terror of 1937–38.[64] Although his speech on the seventieth anniversary of the revolution on 2 November was a disappointment to many in that his evaluation of Stalin was far less negative than many had hoped it would be, it was also a disappointment for those who did not wish to see the Stalin years tarnished. However, it did provide a further stimulus to the radicalisation of history writing and the consequent reconceptualisation of the Soviet past.[65] Once again,

[60] Sokolov bore responsibility for the Matthias Rust affair, when the German penetrated Soviet airspace and landed a light plane on Red Square.

[61] For the report of the meeting, see *Pravda*, 14 Feb. 1987.

[62] Criticism of the Brezhnev period as an era of stagnation and lost opportunity became increasingly hard-hitting over 1986 as economic performance continued to disappoint. For a discussion see White, *Gorbachev and After*, pp. 73–5.

[63] *Pravda*, 14 Feb. 1987.

[64] M. S. Gorbachev, 'Prakticheskim delami uglubliat' perestroiku', *Pravda*, 15 July 1987. The beginning of the serialization of Rybakov's *Children of the Arbat* in March was also significant.

[65] On history writing, see R. W. Davies, *Soviet History in the Gorbachev Revolution* (Bloomington, Indiana University Press, 1989); Stephen Wheatcroft, 'Unleashing the Energy of History, Mentioning the Unmentionable and Reconstructing Soviet Historical Awareness: Moscow 1987', *Australian Slavonic and East European Studies*, 1: 1 (1987), 85–132, and 'Steadying the Energy of History and Probing the Limits of Glasnost': Moscow July to December 1987', *Australian Slavonic and East European Studies*, 1: 2 (1987), 57–114.

through his campaign to lift the lid on the Soviet past, Gorbachev was making an overture to the intelligentsia and, through them, the populace. But exposing the crimes of Stalin had the opposite effect from that intended. Rather than bolstering support for perestroika, it sapped it, hastening the erosion of the legitimacy of the Soviet system, as the conservatives feared.

Also disconcerting for conservatives was Gorbachev's references to 'socialist pluralism'. Gorbachev's first reference to this occurred in his speech to media executives in July 1987.[66] Although most references to socialist pluralism referred to a pluralism of opinions rather than of actions or organizations, the introduction of this concept was disturbing for a number of reasons. One is that it seemed to be introducing into the Soviet lexicon a concept which for long had been decried as bourgeois and resonant of capitalist society. Furthermore, by accepting that a range of opinions was possible on any particular topic, it seemed to be legitimizing the view that had been creeping into Soviet public life, that there could be a diversity of interests in Soviet society.[67] Thus not only was it promoting public debate and disagreement, but it was challenging the basic unity of interest of the society as a whole. Recognition of different interests also seemed to imply a right to promote those interests and, therefore by definition, a right to independent organization. The notion of 'socialist pluralism' could thus be interpreted as signalling a tolerance for independent activity and organization.[68] Although Gorbachev did at times argue that Leninist socialism made room for 'pluralism of opinions, interests and needs' and that the pluralism of opinions should be directed at strengthening the cause of socialism,[69] this sort of conception of society was clearly at odds with that held by conservative elements throughout Soviet society. This was given clear expression in the Andreeva letter.[70] But in reality, many reformers shared the conservatives' wariness of independent activity outside the bounds of the party. Nevertheless it was on the rise.

Third, for the first time 1987 witnessed the emergence on a more widespread basis of an informal politics of the streets. In early February, daily

[66]  *Pravda*, 15 July 1987.

[67]  This had been acknowledged before, but not universally accepted. See 'The Novosibirsk Report', *Survey*, 28: 1 (Spring 1984), 88–108. Also Yury Andropov, 'Leninizm—neischerpaemyi istochnik revoliutsionnoi energii i tvorchestva mass', *Pravda*, 23 Apr. 1982.

[68]  On this see M. Steven Fish, *Democracy from Scratch: Opposition and Regime in the New Russian Revolution* (Princeton, Princeton University Press, 1995), 32.

[69]  Respectively M. S. Gorbachev, 'Cherez demokratizatsiiu—k novomu obliku sotsializma', *Pravda*, 11 May 1988 and 'Na novom etape perestroiki', *Pravda*, 25 Sept. 1988.

[70]  On pluralism, see Thomas Remington, 'A Socialist Pluralism of Opinions: Glasnost and Policy-Making under Gorbachev', *The Russian Review*, 48: 3 (July 1989), 271–304. On the Andreeva letter, see below.

protests were held on the streets of Moscow in support of the Jewish dissident Yosif Begun, resulting in clashes between security police and demonstrators on 12 February. In May, the anti-semitic organization Pamiat' launched a public demonstration in Moscow, after which its leaders were met by Moscow First Secretary Boris Yeltsin. More importantly, in July Crimean Tatars launched a three week vigil in Moscow, protesting against the authorities' refusal to allow them to return to their homeland.[71] The result was the establishment of a commission to investigate their complaints, an unprecedented show of flexibility on the part of the Soviet authorities. In August, thousands demonstrated in the Baltic capitals in protest at the 1939 non-aggression pact between Germany and the Soviet Union which resulted in the incorporation of the Baltic states into the USSR. As a result of these popular demonstrations, new regulations were introduced to control rallies and demonstrations in Moscow. In the same month, the first conference of independent political activists, attended by activists from 47 organizations,[72] was held in Moscow. This sort of gathering was significant because it was part of the growing wave of development of the so-called 'informals', groups which emerged without legal sanction but with official toleration, uniting people of like mind around particular areas of interest (ranging from stamp collecting to environmental protection) and designed as vehicles to help further those interests. Informals began to emerge in 1986–87 and really mushroomed in 1988.[73] For conservatives, this gradual growth of public protest, while still on a small scale and lacking any overall organization, was profoundly worrying, especially given that the government seemed intent on handling it with kid gloves. Despite the emergence of these second-order manifestations of civil society (see Chapter 1), there was no real attempt on the reformists' part to channel the energy of the 'informals' into their reform project.

[71] They had been removed from the Crimea in 1944, allegedly for supporting the Nazis. Although exonerated of this charge in 1967, they had not been allowed to return home. On their case, see Robert Conquest, *The Nation Killers* (London, Macmillan, 1970) and Alexander M. Nekrich, *The Punished Peoples* (New York, Norton, 1978).

[72] The conference was organised by four groups, the Club of Social Initiatives, Moscow Perestroika Club, Commune, and the Foundation of Social Initiatives. John B. Dunlop, *The Rise of Russia and the Fall of the Soviet Empire* (Princeton, Princeton University Press, 1993), 73–4.

[73] For discussion of the informals, see M. V. Maliutin, 'Neformaly v perestroike: opyt i perspektivy', Yu. Afanas'ev (ed.), *Inogo ne dano* (Moscow, 1988); White, Gill, and Slider, *Politics*, ch. 8; Vladimir Brovkin, 'Revolution from Below: Informal Political Associations in Russia 1988–1989', *Soviet Studies*, 42: 2 (Apr. 1990), 233–57; Judith B. Sedaitis and Jim Butterfield (eds.), *Perestroika from Below* (Boulder, Westview, 1991); and Judith Devlin, *The Rise of the Russian Democrats: The Causes and Consequences of the Elite Revolution* (Aldershot, Edward Elgar, 1995), ch. 5.

Meanwhile, some of Gorbachev's international initiatives were alienating key sectors of the Soviet elite. For the first time in July 1987, Gorbachev declared that the Soviet Union would withdraw its forces from Afghanistan without the sorts of qualifications that formerly had attended Soviet discussion of disengagement from this region. Although the Geneva Accords were not signed until April 1988 and the actual withdrawal was not completed until February 1989, the public acknowledgement of this in 1987 caused major concern in some military and security circles; indeed, the protracted nature of the process was in part due to foot dragging and delaying tactics by senior military figures.[74] A second cause for concern was the signature at the December 1987 Washington summit of the INF Treaty, which eliminated intermediate and shorter range missiles from Europe.[75] This involved asymmetrical cuts in weaponry, with the Soviet Union eliminating four times as many weapons as the USA, something which rang alarm bells in some conservative circles and left Gorbachev open to charges of mishandling Soviet foreign relations.

The radicalization of the political agenda that all of this constituted placed immense strains on the fragile unity of the political elite, undercutting elite consensus and making it more difficult to reach agreement on the problems confronting them and the means of resolving them. In October 1987, elite unity snapped. The key figure here was Boris Yeltsin. Since his elevation to national office in Moscow, Yeltsin had been an unorthodox leader. His populism, while less evident than it was to become, was nevertheless already a characteristic of his political style and clearly set him apart from all other members of the leadership, including Gorbachev. Furthermore he seems to have had difficult personal relations with Ligachev, and their differences had already been publicly aired at the XXVII Congress. At the October CC plenum at which Gorbachev presented the draft of his October revolution anniversary speech (to be delivered on 2 November) to the Committee, Yeltsin launched a bitter attack on Ligachev, accusing him of being responsible for the poor way in which the apparatus operated, upon the slow speed of reform, and upon the increasing glorification of Gorbachev.[76] Yeltsin's assault was vigorously rebutted by Ligachev, and rejected by a whole string of speakers who followed Ligachev to the microphone, including both Gorbachev and Yakovlev. Gorbachev made no attempt to save Yeltsin, and he was subsequently removed as candidate member of the Politburo[77] and as Moscow First

[74] Brown, *Gorbachev*, 234–5.
[75] In July Gorbachev had called for the elimination of all intermediate-range nuclear missiles.
[76] *Izvestiia Ts.K. KPSS*, 2 (1989), 239–41.
[77] At the February 1988 CC plenum. Aliev was removed at the same time, while two new candidate members were appointed, Razumovsky and Masliukov, and one new secretary, Baklanov.

Secretary.[78] Yeltsin's removal was a significant event because it removed from the leadership a radical force favouring change (although he was at this stage nowhere near as radical as he was to become), thereby strengthening those more conservative elements.[79] It also exposed Gorbachev's hesitant centrism. Gorbachav saw his role as that of a balancer between two forces, unable to throw his lot in completely either with those who favoured a more rapid pace of change or those who wanted to slow down that pace. But this setback to reform did not deter Gorbachev, and the pace of change picked up substantially during 1988.[80] However this increased pace was not all due to the elite; in this sense, 1988 was a crucial year for the nature of reform in the Soviet Union.

## From Liberalization to Democratization?

During 1988, the stakes of the reform programme were raised significantly, as those pressing for reform pushed through changes which, in the long term unleashed forces which the reformers were unable to control, and opposition to the radicalization of reform mounted, especially in the party leadership. Important too was the strengthening of the pressure for change from below which had initially stirred in 1987, but which Gorbachev never seriously sought to mobilise. This combination of increasing pressure from above and below, although in no sense synchronized, combined to force the trend of change in a direction which ultimately led to the collapse of the system. This dynamic showed that the basic principle upon which Gorbachev rested his reform strategy was flawed. This was the belief that the reform process could be controlled through a combination of guidance from above and pressure from below, with that pressure from below itself being contained and channelled by the political leadership, principally Gorbachev.[81] In conception, this

[78] For a stenographic report of the plenum, see *Izvestiia Ts.K. KPSS*, 2 (1989), 209–87. For Yeltsin's side of the story, see Boris Yeltsin, *Ispoved' na zadannuiu temu* (Moscow, 1990), 79–90. For Gorbachev's, see Gorbachev, *Memoirs*, 242–8.

[79] His replacement as Moscow party first secretary by the defence industry representative Lev Zaikov was symptomatic of this.

[80] For the (unconvincing) argument that Gorbachev pursued what he terms a 'strategy of political liberalization' in order to defeat his conservative opponents, see Christopher Young, 'The Strategy of Political Liberalization: A Comparative View of Gorbachev's Reforms', *World Politics*, 45: 1 (Oct. 1992), 47–65. This exaggerates one element of the dynamic of reform and enables explanation of Gorbachev's motives only in terms of a quest for power.

[81] Its contradiction is clearly reflected in Gorbachev's injunction to the press: 'Publish everything. There should be pluralism of opinions. But the thrust should be such that the

was a classic case of a strategy of liberalization. At most there had been a tepid encouragement of second-order elements of civil society such as the 'informals', but the reformists remained reluctant to deepen this process by giving full-blooded support to the transformation of these into independent political parties.

Initially, despite the fall of Yeltsin, the course of events seemed to be running in favour of further reform. The Law on the State Enterprise (Association) which had been introduced in 1987 went into effect on 1 January, while in May a Law on Cooperatives was introduced, legalizing small and medium-sized businesses and enabling them to set their own prices, wages and production levels. Although in practice the cooperatives found their activity heavily constrained,[82] in principle this constituted a radical shift away from the command economy in the direction of private enterprise. In February Nikolai Bukharin, who reformers associated with the ideological justification of NEP and therefore of a private sector in the economy, was rehabilitated (along with Alexei Rykov). In the cultural sphere, in January the monthly journal *Novyi Mir* began to serialize Pasternak's Nobel Prize winning novel, *Dr Zhivago*.[83] Throughout the year this trend of increased openness in the press continued (with one hiccup—see below), maintaining the practice that had begun in 1987 of discussing the range of social problems that affected Soviet society. Issues that had formerly been left unremarked, such as crime, prostitution, drugs, declining health levels, strikes, poverty, and the abuse of psychiatry, were now openly discussed in the media.[84] In February mass demonstrations occurred in Nagorno-Karabakh and in Armenia itself, demanding the return of that part of Azerbaijan to Armenia; at the end of the month ethnic rioting and a pogrom of Armenians occurred in the Azeri town of Sumgait. Although this particular sort of popular activism was an ominous threat to reform, it did reinforce the view that society was no longer passive and that forces were there to take advantage of the new room for public activity Gorbachev's changes were creating. For the conservatives, this combination seemed to bode ill for the future; a rolling back of the state economic sector, the publication of critical literature, and the emergence of mass politics in the streets. The conservative response came in March.

line of perestroika and the cause of socialism are defended and strengthened.' M. S. Gorbachev, 'Na novom'.

[82] By January 1990 there were 193,100 co-operatives throughout the USSR: White, *Gorbachev and After*, 113.

[83] For details about the publication of other formerly prohibited works, including Solzhenitsyn's *The Gulag Archipelago* (in August 1989), see White, *Gorbachev and After*, 86–8.

[84] Television in particular became important in this regard; investigative, and at times even muck-raking, journalism became common.

On the eve of Gorbachev's state visit to Yugoslavia (and Yakovlev's to Mongolia), on 13 March the conservative newspaper *Sovetskaia Rossiia* published a letter purportedly from a chemistry teacher in Leningrad, Nina Andreeva.[85] This letter criticised the way in which the Soviet past was constantly being criticised and its achievements denigrated. It was an open defence of the old Soviet order and a rebuttal of the Gorbachev reform programme. The letter was warmly praised by Ligachev (parts of it were written in the CC apparatus, probably under Ligachev's supervision[86]), and it was widely interpreted as a semi-official warning to those who supported reform not to go too far. Certainly the press seemed to see it in this light, because upon its appearance a new sense of caution and reserve was evident in the way issues were discussed. Upon Gorbachev's return from Yugoslavia, he set about trying to deal with the effect of the Andreeva letter, which involved overcoming the substantial support it had in the Politburo.[87] It was not until 5 April that *Pravda* printed an official rebuttal.[88] While the response to Andreeva sent a signal to pro-reform elements that the reformist section of the elite was still broadly in charge, the appearance of the letter and the time it took to get an official response showed that the reformists were not having it all their own way in elite circles.[89]

The key event in the political calendar in 1988 was the XIX Conference of the CPSU held in June–July. The Conference had been announced at the June 1987 plenum, and it was seen by both reformers and opponents as a potentially significant event. The last conference had been held in 1941, and these events were therefore highly unusual in party life. For Gorbachev and his reformist supporters, who had seen their reform proposals swept under the carpet in January 1987, this was seen as an opportunity to out flank their opponents at middle and upper levels of the apparatus by appealing over their heads to the rank-and-file who, they believed, would support democratisation. It was also seen as a means of getting rid of some of their opponents through bringing

[85] Nina Andreeva, 'Ne mogu postupat'sia printsipami', *Sovetskaia Rossiia*, 13 Mar. 1988.

[86] See the discussion in Brown, *Gorbachev*, 172–3. For Ligachev's side of the story, see Ligachev, *Inside*, 298–311.

[87] Those supporting the Andreeva position were Ligachev, Gromyko, Solomentsev, Vorotnikov, Chebrikov, Nikonov and Lukianov. Those supporting Gorbachev were Yakovlev, Shevardnadze, Ryzhkov and Medvedev: Brown, *Gorbachev*, 173–4. Also see Reddaway, 'Resisting Gorbachev', 40.

[88] 'Printsipy perestroiki: revoliutsionnost' myshlenniia i deistvii', *Pravda*, 5 Apr. 1988. According to Gorbachev, a draft was initially written by *Pravda* editor Afanas'ev, and substantially rewritten and strengthened by Yakovlev, Medvedev, and Gorbachev's aides: Gorbachev, *Memoirs*, 253.

[89] Gorbachev later said that in the first half of 1988, the reformers in the leadership were himself, Yakovlev, Medvedev, Shevardnadze, Ryzhkov, Sliun'kov, and perhaps Zaikov and Razumovsky: Gorbachev, *Memoirs*, 254.

about changes in the leadership. For opponents of the radicalization of reform, this was seen as a good opportunity to use a high party podium to slow down the impetus for change. That both sides saw the importance of the conference is reflected in the struggle that took place to gain advantage in the preparations for it.

The twelve months between the announcement of the conference and its opening were a time of vigorous political conflict. The radical attack mounted by Yeltsin in October and his (and its) rejection by the more conservative leadership have already been mentioned. But this period also saw the significant radicalization of the political agenda. Throughout the period, but especially during the latter part of 1987, a wide-ranging debate on party reform unrolled in the pages of the press, stimulated by the officially sponsored discussion of issues leading up to the Conference. While much of this was concerned with the implementation of measures to make the party and its functioning more democratic, the control exercised in it by the nomenklatura or by the apparatus (and both terms were used) also came under strong criticism.[90] The agenda of change contained in the various proposals that were floated in the debate would, if implemented, have transformed the Soviet political system. When the culmination of the debate was reached with the publication of the CC Theses for the Conference in May 1988,[91] these theses did constitute a programme of significant change, although they also pulled back from some of the more radical proposals that had surfaced during the debate: while they called for competitive elections in the party these were not made compulsory, they enabled the nomination of candidates by the rank-and-file (instead of higher level officials) without making this mandatory, and bureaux and secretaries were not made subject to direct election by congresses or conferences. Moreover, the Theses did not draw the logical conclusion which flowed from their authorization of competitive elections; they made no provisions for the right to organize factions within the party. The Theses were a clear compromise between radical and more conservative forces,[92] because while they provided for the introduction of radical departures from the status quo in how the party functioned, they were permissive rather than mandatory. This meant that the fate of these proposals would rest upon the power dispositions at all levels of the party in the regions of the USSR. And there was no evidence that proponents of radical reform were in a majority throughout the country. As the election of delegates to the Conference shows, conservative elements were

[90] For a discussion, see Gill, *Collapse*, 55–7.

[91] 'Tezisy Tsentral'nogo Komiteta KPSS k XIX Vsesoiuznoi konferentsii (Odobreny Plenumom Ts.K. KPSS 23 maia 1988 goda')', *Pravda*, 27 May 1988. They are discussed in Gill, *Collapse*, 56–7.

[92] See the comments on this by Tatiana Zaslavskaia, *Izvestiia*, 4 June 1988.

usually able to use their positions to buttress their power and blunt more radical forces. Unless the party's electoral procedures could successfully be democratized, the conservatives would remain able to stymie further party reform.

The method of selection of delegates to the Conference was structured in such a way that the middle and upper levels of the party apparatus were able to prevent undesirable candidates from appearing on the ballot paper, and thereby weed out potentially troublesome would-be delegates. Throughout most of the country the selection of delegates proceeded in accordance with established Soviet procedures: the leaders handed down lists of candidates equal in number to the number of positions to be filled, and the electors voted these people into office. However, in some isolated instances, this practice was rejected by the rank-and-file. In Moscow, Sakhalin, Omsk, and Yaroslavl, the electors rejected the choices given them by higher-ranking party authorities and engaged in public mass demonstrations to get their way.[93] These instances gained nationwide publicity, and generated significant discussion in the press of the way 'the apparatus' was manipulating the delegate-selection process to achieve safe delegates. It was accused of subverting the democratic process and undermining Gorbachev's preference for the way delegates should be chosen.[94] Despite such criticism, officially the selection process was evaluated positively,[95] and although calls had been made to ensure that the Conference was not dominated by old-style apparatchiks,[96] the way the selection of delegates was organised ensured that the Conference would be dominated by delegates acceptable to those who dominated the apparatus. Given this pedigree, it is even more surprising that the Conference turned out as it did.

The Conference broke the mould that had set around official Soviet gatherings from the late 1920s. Instead of the stultifying pro forma speeches greeted by ritualized applause, the high level of formality and the unanimous adoption of resolutions and decisions, the Conference was a disputatious assembly in which diverse opinions were aired and a real process of debate occurred, leaders were criticized to their faces, the course of events was not scripted, and many of the decisions adopted were momentous in the consequences they involved for the future of the Soviet structure. The Conference was set on a reformist course right from the outset. The Conference Theses published in May[97] sketched out a programme which, if implemented, would have meant a

---

[93] For details, see Gill, *Collapse*, 58.

[94] For discussion of the elections and their conduct, see Aryeh L. Unger, 'The Travails of Intra-Party Democracy in the Soviet Union: The Elections to the 19th Conference of the CPSU', *Soviet Studies*, 43: 2 (1991).

[95] *Pravda*, 13 June 1988.　　　　　　　　　[96] e.g. *Sovetskaia Kul'tura*, 21 Apr. 1988.

[97] *Pravda*, 27 May 1988.

major restructuring of the contours of Soviet political life. Chief among these were measures for the substantial democratization of the party, its withdrawal from the administrative life of the state, and the restructuring of the major organs of the state. All of these measures were taken up by Gorbachev in his address to the Conference,[98] and in resolutions adopted by that body.[99]

The decisions of the Conference constituted a major stimulus for reform. The main resolution[100] called for a reanimation of internal party life by the energising of the rank-and-file and their participation in party bodies, the reconfiguring of the CC Secretariat, a higher level of responsibility of party bodies to those who elected them, the filling of positions by multi-candidate elections and secret ballot, nomination from below, strict time limits on tenure of elected positions, and stricter monitoring by the centre over lower-level party affairs. The resolution also provided for a new state structure based upon enhanced democracy and the rule of law, as reflected in the call for a 'law-gov-erned state'. The new structure was to consist of a sovereign Congress of People's Deputies which was to decide the most important questions in annual sessions. The Congress would in turn elect a smaller 'standing legislative, exec-utive, administrative and supervisory body', the bicameral Supreme Soviet. It was also to elect by secret ballot the Chairman of the Supreme Soviet. The unlimited nomination of candidates, their free and extensive discussion, the listing of more candidates than there were seats to be filled and a democratic electoral procedure were also seen as important. So too was the view that the local party secretary should chair the soviet, although s/he would have to be confirmed in office by popular election. The resolution also noted that the recent emergence of several new public associations and alliances was a pos-itive development in the democratisation of Soviet society. This resolution was a clear rejection of the so-called command style of work and a positive stimu-lus for Gorbachev's cause of democratisation. This effect was confirmed in res-olutions on glasnost, on combating bureaucracy, and on legal reform.[101]

The decisions of the XIX Conference constituted a clear expression of a pro-gramme of political change that Gorbachev hoped would overcome the defi-ciencies in the Soviet system. This programme shows that by early 1988 at the latest, Gorbachev had ceased to believe that the problems of the Soviet Union were not structural; he was now openly convinced that only structural change

---

[98] M. S. Gorbachev, 'O khode realizatsii reshenii XXVII s'ezda KPSS i zadachakh po uglubleniiu perestroiki', *Pravda*, 29 June 1988.

[99] For the Conference resolutions, see *Pravda*, 5 July 1988.

[100] 'O demokratizatsii sovetskogo obshchestva i reforme politicheskoi sistemy', *Pravda*, 5 July 1988.

[101] 'O glasnosti', 'O bor'be s biurokratizmom', and 'O pravovoi reforme', *Pravda*, 5 July 1988.

to the system would enable it to survive. The structural changes he sought, contained principally in the decisions of the Conference (the shift in favour of industrial democracy had been contained in the Law on the State Enterprise which had come into effect at the start of the year), involved the reanimation of political structures through competitive elections, the strengthening of state legislative institutions (the soviets) as organs of popular self-government and of supervision over the executive, the transformation of the party from a command-administrative structure into an organ able to exercise leadership by virtue of the moral authority it gained from popular support and commitment, and the primacy of law. If realised, these principles would have undercut the bureaucratic control of the command-administrative apparatus which Gorbachev now believed to be at the heart of the Soviet Union's problems; the Conference marked the shift in the programme from renovation of the existing political structure to transformation of it, even if this was not publicly acknowledged at the time.

The decisions taken at the Conference were a charter for the transformation of Soviet political life, but it is not clear that all at the time saw them this way. The call for competitive secret ballot elections to replace what was seen as the nomenklatura style of personnel policy and the right legislative organs gained to ratify appointments to leading positions in the state posed a direct challenge to the established structure of power and privilege in the party by robbing the apparatus of the power to determine the identity of leading officials. The construction of a new legislative state structure resting on popular election, combined with the withdrawal of the party from the day-to-day management of administrative affairs and the strengthening of legal norms, threatened the dominant position the party had enjoyed for so long by creating a new structure of power with its own independent mandate; the 'leading role' of the party was completely incompatible with notions of the rule of law. The strengthening of public criticism and the opening up of the party even more to the public gaze was even more alarming given the possibility that the party might have to compete for support in the electoral arena. Although some radical proposals had been watered down in the face of hostile opposition—competitive elections and rank-and-file nomination remained possible rather than mandatory, the call for a review of all party members' qualifications was dropped (and there were no changes to the leadership) and the provisions on press freedom were weakened—the combined effect was still significant. Right at the end of the Conference, Gorbachev introduced a timetable for the rapid implementation of these changes,[102] and managed to ram it through to general assent. If

---

[102] Constitutional changes were to be made at the next meeting of the Supreme Soviet, the new legislature was to be in operation by April 1989, and reductions were to be made to the party apparatus before the end of the year.

the conservatives had hoped that such measures would have no effect, they were very wrong.

Gorbachev and his supporters lost no time in pushing home the advantage they had gained through the decisions of the XIX Conference. At a CC plenum at the end of July, party organisations were called upon to operate on the basis of the decisions of the Conference without waiting for those decisions to be translated into formal amendments to the party Rules.[103] The plenum scheduled the new report and election campaign within the party which the Conference had announced for the end of the year, and the way in which this was discussed showed that for the reformists this election campaign was a crucial weapon in the battle against those within the apparatus who opposed change. In the words of Georgy Razumovsky, who was soon to take over leadership of cadre policy, the democratic resolution of cadre questions through real election from below 'changes the very concept of the "nomenklatura" about which there are so many arguments at present. The party's cadre corps will henceforth be determined not by membership of some kind of "list", but by the free, totally unrestricted expression of the communists' will and the effective functioning of the democratic institutions of our political system.'[104] The election was seen as a means of transforming the traditional power axis in the party, the system of appointment through the nomenklatura. But the conservatives were still in a position to thwart such measures.

When the rules governing the election were promulgated,[105] they contained provisions which enabled a more democratic process, but there were also clear limitations on this, reflecting remaining levels of caution about the course of reform. The regulations did not eliminate the possibility of either prior-arranged lists of candidates being presented to the meeting or of co-optation from above, much of the nomination process took place in the open, multi-candidate competition was possible but not mandatory, and election required support by only 50 per cent of voters which in a party election seemed well within the grasp of members of the apparatus. These restrictions on the unrolling of democratism through the electoral process were reflected in the campaign when held towards the end of the year. Although there were some cases of competitive elections, these seem to have occurred predominantly at lower levels of the party structure and were not a country-wide phenomenon; no gorkom or raikom secretary was elected by competitive ballot.[106] The 1988

[103] The plenum resolutions were 'O prakticheskoi rabote po realizatsii reshenii XIX vsesoiuznoi konferentsii KPSS', 'Ob otchetakh i vyborakh v partiinykh organizatsiiakh', and 'Ob osnovnykh napravleniiakh perestroiki partiinogo apparata', *Pravda*, 31 July 1988.

[104] *Pravda*, 18 Aug. 1988.

[105] 'Instruktsiia o provedenii vyborov rukovodiashchikh partiinykh organov', *Partiinaia zhizn'*, 16 Aug. 1988, pp. 30–5.

[106] *Izvestiia Ts.K. KPSS*, 4 (1989), 38.

election campaign in the party seems in practice to have differed little from earlier such campaigns despite the rhetoric and high hopes that were invested in it.[107]

In the six months following the Conference, the decision on the reconfiguring of the Secretariat was carried out. This involved the introduction of six commissions and the reduction in both the number and staff of CC departments, with corresponding changes taking place at lower levels.[108] These changes were meant to make the central party apparatus more accessible to lower levels of the party and to make it operate in a more democratic fashion. However, there is no evidence that the operation of these commissions either made central party affairs more democratic or more efficient. The effective weakening of the central party apparatus that the replacement of the Secretariat by the commissions constituted weakened the centre's control over lower-level party bodies even more than had been happening as a result of the centrifugal tendencies that were already in place within the party. The party's control over state policy, including its capacity to direct the economy (virtually all departments exercising economic oversight were abolished), was also completely undercut by this change. It also weakened the nucleus of apparat opposition to further reform and change. Indeed, the Secretariat effectively ceased to exist; in Ligachev's words, 'The Party was deprived of an operating staff for its leaders'.[109] A major focus of opposition to Gorbachev was thereby removed, but so too was the ability of the party centre to give impetus and direction to the reform process.

Later that year the Constitution was amended to include the new state structure that had been outlined at the XIX Conference,[110] and a new electoral law promulgated.[111] Like the party electoral regulation, this one made provision for competitive elections without making them mandatory, but it is clear from the rhetoric surrounding its introduction that competition was the preferred option.

---

[107] See the discussion in Gill, *Collapse*, 70–2.

[108] For the decision on the commissions, see 'Ob obrazovanii komissii Ts.K. KPSS i reorganizatsii apparata Ts.K. KPSS v svete reshenii XIX vsesoiuznoi partiinoi konferentsii', *Pravda*, 1 Oct. 1988. These changes are discussed in Gill, *Collapse*, 72–4; Gordon M. Hahn, 'The First Reorganisation of the CPSU Central Committee *Apparat* under *Perestroika*', *Europe-Asia Studies*, 49: 2 (Mar. 1997), 281–302; and Alexander Rahr, 'The CPSU in the 1980s: Changes in the Party Apparatus', *The Journal of Communist Studies*, 7: 2 (June 1991), 161–9.

[109] Ligachev, *Inside*, 110.

[110] 'Ob izmeneniiakh i dopolneniiakh Konstitutsii (Osnovnogo Zakona) SSSR', *Pravda*, 3 Dec. 1988.

[111] 'O vyborakh narodnykh deputatov SSSR', *Pravda*, 4 Dec. 1988. For details, see White, *Gorbachev and After*, 30.

The measures introduced at the Conference generated significant opposition. A vigorous exchange of views between Yeltsin and Ligachev culminated in overwhelming support from the delegates for the latter, and was reflected in the rejection of Yeltsin's appeal for political rehabilitation. Ligachev hinted openly in his speech at Gorbachev's reliance upon more cautious elements in the leadership (specifically Chebrikov, Solomentsev, Gromyko, and himself) for retention of his position. While other speakers supported change, that support was not always full blooded, while the drive for change was moderated in some regards compared with the positions adopted during the lead up to the Conference.[112] The absence of personnel changes at the Conference may also reflect the strength of opposition. At the Politburo and CC meetings following the Conference, at which practical measures were adopted to implement the Conference decisions, high-level opposition was again strongly expressed as opponents of the changes worked to blunt their effect.[113] At this time Ligachev again publicly stated his reservations about the course of reform in speeches at Gorky and Tula on 5 and 31 August.[114] By the end of 1988, conservative worries had considerably strengthened;[115] they were to grow in 1989.

However, there appeared to be a strengthening of the reformist side of the leadership at the September 1988 CC plenum. Some cautious members of the leadership were removed (Gromyko and Somomentsev as full members and Dolgikh and Demichev as candidate members of the Politburo), Ligachev was downgraded through the shifting of his secretarial responsibilities[116] and the elimination of the Secretariat, and Gorbachev supporters Medvedev and Yakovlev were promoted.[117] In addition, in October Gorbachev replaced

[112] In particular see the change in position on the need for a review of the qualifications of the party membership and on press freedom.

[113] For Gorbachev's discussion of one case, that of the constitutional amendments, see Gorbachev, *Memoirs*, 269.

[114] See the reports in *Pravda*, 6 August and 2 September 1988. The text of the former speech will be found in E. K. Ligachev, *Izbrannye rechi i stat'i* (Moscow, 1989), 281–91. For Gorbachev's reaction, see Gorbachev, *Memoirs*, 261–2. Also see the discussion in Ellen Mickiewicz, 'Mobilization and Reform: Political Communication Policy Under Gorbachev', *PS: Political Science and Politics*, 19: 2 (June 1989), 201.

[115] In the international sphere the signature of the Geneva Accords on ending involvement in the Afghan conflict in April and the beginning of the troops returning home the following month, and Gorbachev's speech to the UN in December, when he announced a unilateral reduction in Soviet military force and of its deployment in Eastern Europe, and when the rhetoric of Marxism was clearly displaced by that emphasizing universal human values ('Vystuplenie v organizatsii ob'edinennykh natsii', *Izbrannye*, VII, 184–202) were not designed to set conservative fears at rest.

[116] He had lost responsibility for the press to Yakovlev in the wake of the Andreeva affair. He was now given responsibility for agriculture.

[117] The former straight into full membership of the Politburo, the latter in the secretarial hierarchy.

Gromyko as Chairman of the Presidium of the Supreme Soviet, or effective Soviet President, thereby placing him favourably for when a constitutional president would be elected by the Congress of People's Deputies. His long-time friend, Lukianov was chosen as his deputy. The only apparent contrary element in this reformist consolidation was the appointment of Chebrikov as a CC Secretary.

The XIX Conference stimulated a new spirit of political life in the country. Much of the Conference was televised, and it made compulsive viewing. Viewers saw individual leaders, including Gorbachev, criticised by name and to their faces. Many aspects of contemporary political life came under scrutiny and intense questioning, while for the first time since 1925 a major party forum witnessed a form of genuine debate. The message that this projected was one of a political culture that was far removed from Soviet traditions, one characterized by questioning, criticism and debate, and one in which the word of the leadership was not taken at face value. The implication was, of course, that independent political initiative was to be valued and that the stylised formulae of the past should be overthrown. But few specific mechanisms or measures were put in place to ensure that this new spirit affected the structures of power. Further, the unrolling of debate in the media on all aspects of Soviet society and its reform was not without cost. Gorbachev's attempts to mobilize the intelligentsia had initially borne fruit as reformist intellectuals publicly came out in support of perestroika. However, many of these intellectuals became increasingly critical of the reform programme and the Soviet past as a whole, and they now had the means to voice their criticisms and thereby drive the public agenda beyond the bounds envisaged by that programme,[118] further widening the gulf between the reformers and the conservatives. This provided a significant stimulus to the politics of the streets that began to gather pace during 1988, but not in the direction the reformers around Gorbachev desired.

Popular mobilization grew in 1988, but it remained largely focused around specific issues. Early in the year, the Nagorno–Karabakh question pushed itself onto the political agenda with the vote by that region's Supreme Soviet to leave Azerbaijan and rejoin Armenia. The pogrom of Armenians in the Azeri town of Sumgait later in February provoked mass demonstrations in the Armenian capital Erevan, as citizens in that republic came out onto the street to demonstrate in support of their brethren in Nagorno–Karabakh. As the official position remained one of support for the status quo, the growing activism in Armenia (including a general strike and clashes with troops in which

[118] For one discussion, see Joel C. Moses, 'Democratic Reform in the Gorbachev Era: Dimensions of Reform in the Soviet Union, 1986–1989', *The Russian Review*, 48: 3 (July 1989), 235–69.

individuals died) was reflective of a continuing process of erosion of the authority of the party. It was at this time too that organizations which seemed to represent the shoots of a civil society became increasingly prominent. 'Informals' continued to multiply in number, with political clubs becoming increasingly prominent; by the end of 1987 there were said to be 30,000 and by early 1989 more than 60,000 informals in the USSR.[119] These remained over-whelmingly small, involved in debate and discussion, with very little activity of a mass-based organized character.[120] However during 1988 political issues did come increasingly to the fore for many of these bodies, and there were some attempts to unite on a broader basis. The middle of the year saw the emergence of an important form of such activity, front organizations for the defence of perestroika.[121] Encouraged by reformist figures in the party,[122] these were umbrella organizations that sought to unite popular elements in an attempt to defend the reform programme from the attacks upon it emanating from the apparatus. They provided a means for the bringing together of some of the political clubs, but they became effective as political actors only when they were focused on national issues, reflecting the limited nature of the discus-sion/political club format. The most important cases were in the Baltic republics; in June, the Estonian government gave official recognition to the Popular Front of Estonia. In May, in Moscow the establishment of the first independent political party since the early 1920s was announced, the Democratic Union.[123] This was a stridently anti-communist party and was officially illegal, but little attempt was made to break it up.

In August, the demonstrations that had occurred in the Baltic republics in 1987 were repeated, and this time the demands had expanded; as well as calls for recognition of the illegality of the incorporation of these republics into the Union in 1940,[124] demonstrators now demanded economic and political

[119] *Pravda*, 27 Dec. 1987 and 10 Feb. 1989.

[120] For a discussion of some clubs, see Devlin, *Rise of Russian Democrats*, ch. 5.

[121] On popular fronts see Devlin, *Rise of Russian Democrats* ch. 6; Mike Urban, 'Popular Fronts and Informals', *Détente*, 14 (1989), 3–8.

[122] e.g. T. Zaslavskaia, 'O strategii sotsial'nogo upravleniia perestroikoi', Afanas'ev, 9–50.

[123] For discussion of the Democratic Union, see Fish, *Democracy*; Michael McFaul and Sergei Markov, *The Troubled Birth of Russian Democracy. Parties, Personalities and Programs* (Stanford, Hoover Institution Press, 1993); Vera Tolz, *The USSR's Emerging Multiparty System* (New York, Praeger, 1990); Geoffrey A. Hosking, Jonathan Aves and Peter J. S. Duncan, *The Road to Post-Communism: Independent Political Movements in the Soviet Union 1985–1991* (London, Pinter, 1992); Michael Urban, with Vyacheslav Igrunov and Sergei Mitrokhin, *The Rebirth of Politics in Russia* (Cambridge, Cambridge University Press, 1997).

[124] The secret protocols providing for the incorporation of the Baltic states into the USSR were published in an Estonian newspaper on 17 August 1988. White, *Gorbachev and After*, 153.

sovereignty, citizens' rights, and the return of the inter-war flags. This activity soon took an organized form, with the creation of popular fronts in the three Baltic republics by October.[125] These fronts added organizational strength to the demand for sovereignty, providing an organizational basis to add to the symbolism of flag, anthem and language. In September, Gorbachev gained first-hand experience of popular activism when, during his visit to Krasnoyarsk, he was confronted by popular anger at the poor material rewards that perestroika had thus far produced;[126] by the end of 1988 rationing had been introduced in parts of the country on a range of basic items.

During 1988 popular mobilization remained an isolated as opposed to a mass phenomenon, except in some specific cases of nationalist agitation, most particularly in Armenia and the Baltic republics. It was the nationalist issue rather than the policies of perestroika which gave most focus to popular organization. Among urban intellectuals there were moves to organize in order to support reform, as reflected in the Popular Front for the Defence of Perestroika, but such bodies were relatively insulated from the vast mass of the population. For the ordinary people in the street, political organization was not seen as a viable form of activity, and their impact on reform and upon the debates among the elite was small. It was not until they were provided with the opening that the election for the Congress of People's Deputies constituted that the populace could have a major effect on the course of elite politics and of the reform programme. The failure of the reformists to channel popular, and in particular nationalist, sentiment behind perestroika was to prove a major factor in its undoing.

The institutional changes that flowed from the XIX Conference revolutionised the conduct of Soviet politics. They constituted the shift of Gorbachev's programme from one of political reform to one of transformation of the political system, a shift that would be realized in practice in subsequent years. In the short term, this entailed the radical restructuring of political life, as Gorbachev had intended, but in the longer term its effects fed through to lead to the fundamental change of the entire Soviet socio-economic system. Not only did the changes introduced at the Conference create new institutional arenas within which new patterns of politics and new political actors emerged, but they created openings into the Soviet political structure which, as they widened, ultimately burst that structure asunder. The tightly

[125] On the Baltic popular fronts, see references cited in nn. 121 and 123. Nils R. Muiznieks, 'The Influence of the Baltic Popular Movements on the Process of Soviet Disintegration', *Europe–Asia Studies*, 47: 1 (1995), 3–25 discusses their influence elsewhere in the Union.

[126] For a report of his visit, see *Pravda*, 13 Sept. 1988. For his reflections, Gorbachev, *Memoirs*, 263–5.

intertwined nature of the political and economic structures, meant that to relax control in the former threatened loss of control in the latter. The motor power for this was principally through the electoral process, which opened up the chief axis of power within the Soviet structure (the nomenklatura system of appointment to office) to challenge from outside that system. Gorbachev had undermined the authority of the Communist Party, the major obstacle to reform but paradoxically the only vehicle he had to promote it. Its full effect was to become evident in 1989 when the process of reform began seriously to unravel.

# 3

# From Reform to Transformation

The dynamics of the whole process of change were to alter fundamentally in 1989–90, shifting from one of reform within the system to transformation of the system.[1] Increasingly the public agenda was driven in a more radical direction, seeking substantial change to both the structures of the Soviet socio-political system and the way that system functioned. The radicalization of the public agenda was in part a function of the response of the central elite to the exacerbation of the problems confronting the Soviet state, but also important was the entry of new political actors from outside that elite into the main arenas of Soviet politics. Indeed, increasingly during this period, central elite preferences became subordinated to forces from outside that elite that acted as the main drivers of change. Nevertheless the dynamic of elite politics remained pivotal to the course of Soviet development.

Up until this time Gorbachev had followed a path of seeking to maintain a consensus within the leadership about the course of reform, and thereby retaining all sections of that leadership within a coalition behind the changes that were being introduced. The problem was that this was a consensus located at the edge of policy acceptability within the leadership, and each time that edge was moved in a more radical direction, more sections of that coalition found the new position unacceptable. As the agenda radicalized, the extent of opposition increased, and this could not be totally offset by the movement into the elite of forces supporting radical reform. This is because, following the Yeltsin experience, Gorbachev seems to have been unwilling to appoint really radical elements to the leadership who might have alienated more conservative figures and because there was a real shortage of such people in the areas within which Gorbachev looked for candidates to fill top leadership positions. Certainly many of Gorbachev's own advisers had the sort of radical policy

---

[1] For the argument that 'the reforms [of perestroika] built up to a critical mass for the transition from quantitative changes to qualitative ones', and that perestroika was 'revolutionary evolution', see Vladimir K. Yegorov, *Out of a Dead End into the Unknown* (Chicago, edition q, 1993), 67 and ch. 6. Yegorov was an assistant to Gorbachev in 1990–1, and in 1998 was named Minister of Culture.

profile needed, but while Gorbachev retained his faith in the party and its ability to change, he remained constricted by its traditions and procedures, and these prevented him from moving his personal staff into party leadership positions. As a result, Gorbachev was forced to look for new blood in the leadership from those traditional sources of Soviet leaders, the upper ranks of the party-state hierarchy, and most of those who had gained prominence here had done so for reasons other than their policy radicalism.

Consequently when these people were appointed to the inner councils of the leadership, for most of them the leadership coalition was already at the edge of policy acceptability. When that edge moved, it moved away from their positions, so that their support for the reform effort soon became problematic. While Gorbachev remained wedded to the party and while the party retained a central place in the Soviet structure, there was a structural barrier to the formation of a really reformist leadership which could radically deepen the reform. As events were to show, there were also limits to how far Gorbachev could make the conceptual leap to radical change.[2] This situation had two important consequences. First, as the process of change evolved, the meaning of reformism and conservatism changed with it; as events were to show, what was radical in 1988 could well be conservative in 1990. Second, a divided elite was bound to result from the radicalization of policy, and Gorbachev's task of maintaining consensus was certain to fail. What made this inevitable was the decisive entry of new forces, many associated with civil society, into the political dynamic. It was in 1989 that such forces became the principal stimulus to policy radicalization; if up until the end of 1988 Gorbachev and those around him can be said to have been guiding the course of change, from February to March 1989 they were principally reacting to change and developments initiated elsewhere.

The principal forces promoting change from below in this year were varied, including nationalist groups, trade unions, citizens' groups and emergent political parties. At first sight, this tapestry of various types of group appears to represent the emergence of a powerful civil society in the Soviet Union, but this was not the case. The problem is that these groups were largely specifically oriented and narrowly based, with little interaction or cooperation between them; despite attempts to foster unity through national front organizations, these were successful in only a few cases where they were focused overwhelmingly on nationalist issues. There was therefore not that web of inter-relations

---

[2] For an argument that utilises collective learning theory harnessed to notions of borrowing from the West and the importance of institutional constituency to explain economic policy and the divergences that were to develop, see James Clay Moltz, 'Divergent Learning and the Failed Politics of Soviet Economic Reform', *World Politics*, 45: 2 (Jan. 1993), 301–25.

and connections that is so vital for the sustenance of a civil society, as opposed to a congeries of different groups each pushing their own types of interests. This fragmentation of effort had two important consequences. First, it weakened the force of pressure from below by diffusing it onto a broader front. At this stage, this may not have been a bad thing because a concentration of pressure from below may have increased the stakes dramatically in the eyes of those elements who ultimately supported the August 1991 putsch, and thereby have encouraged them to act before events had so escaped their control that they could not be opposed. So the diffusion and consequent weakening of pressure from below may have ensured the continuing possibility of such pressure. Second, the diffusion of pressure geographically and across a wide issue area ensured that regardless of what the authorities did, it was unlikely that they would be able to satisfy all of their critics. As a result, frustration was bound to continue from below regardless of the elite's actions.

The initial entry of mass actors into the political process came about with the nomination procedures for election to the Congress of People's Deputies in February 1989. The Congress was a classic creature of attempted liberalization; its structure reflected an attempt to build into it a guarantee of continuing party dominance designed to reassure conservative elements worried by the changes. There were three aspects of this. First, conduct of the election in each constituency was to be controlled by the local electoral commission, which in turn was dominated by the local party apparatus. The nomination process could thus be manipulated to increase the chances of the election of a candidate favourable to the party. Second, of the 2,250 seats in the Congress, 750 were to be filled by representatives of certain public organizations, each of which had specific numbers of seats set aside for them. Such organizations were under general party supervision, and it was assumed that the party would dominate the candidate selection process in these organizations. Third, the remaining 1,500 seats were to be filled by direct popular election. According to the electoral law, a candidate needed to gain 50 per cent plus one of the votes cast, a requirement which it seemed inconceivable in late 1988 that someone supported by the party apparatus could fail to attain. But in practice both of these assumptions proved to be false.

In the nomination process in the public organizations, open competition was not always in evidence. For the 100 seats allocated to the CPSU, the CC named 100 candidates, with Gorbachev, who had publicly championed competition, even refusing to face a competitive contest.[3] In those organisations

---

[3] This list was selected from a larger list of 312 potential candidates. Peter Lentini, 'Reforming the Electoral System: The 1989 Elections to the USSR Congress of People's Deputies', *The Journal of Communist Studies*, 7: 1 (Mar. 1991), 87. Gorbachev argued that if the party list had contained more than 100 names (the same as the places allotted to the

where there may have been some competition, non-establishment candidates often found it difficult to gain nomination. The case of Andrei Sakharov was the most celebrated. Despite being nominated by sixty scientific organizations for one of the positions on the Academy of Sciences' list, those who controlled the process in the Academy denied Sakharov a position. This was only reversed following popular mobilization of members of the Academy, who forced the calling of another meeting at which a number of liberals (Sakharov, Nikolai Shmelev and Roald Sagdeev) gained nomination. In the popular constituencies, in some areas local party leaders were able to ensure that only the same number of candidates were nominated as there were seats to be filled: in 385 seats (most particularly in Ukraine and Central Asia) there was only one candidate, in 953 seats there were two candidates, and in the remaining 162 seats there were three or more candidates.[4] Once again, anti-establishment candidates often experienced difficulty navigating the electoral process, with Boris Yeltsin's experience in a Moscow constituency being a case in point.[5] But despite the evident manipulation to blunt the effect of popular support for anti-establishment candidates, the election result was a major shock for conservative elements within the party and the elite.

The election was held on 26 March, with the second round in those constituencies where no candidate received 50 per cent being held on 9 April and 14 May. While in many constituencies, traditional candidates were elected in traditional ways, the overwhelming impression of the election result was one of the rejection of the traditional style of candidate. Overall, some 20 per cent of party officials standing failed to gain election, while 10 per cent of those who stood unopposed were unable to get the 50 per cent vote necessary for success at the polls.[6] A wide range of prominent party figures were defeated, including the mayors of Moscow and Kiev, party first secretaries in Kiev, Minsk, Kishinev, Alma Ata and Frunze, the prime minister of Latvia, the president and prime minister of Lithuania, almost the entire leadership in Leningrad

party), reformist figures such as Yakovlev would not have been elected to the Congress as party representatives. Gorbachev, *Memoirs*, 279.

[4] Richard Sakwa, *Russian Politics and Society*, 2nd edn. (London, Routledge, 1996), 136. For a discussion of the nomination and election processes, see Stephen White, *Gorbachev and After* (Cambridge, Cambridge University Press, 1991) 41–8 and Stephen White, 'The Soviet Elections of 1989: From Acclamation to Limited Choice', *Coexistence*, 28: 4 (Dec. 1991), 513–39.

[5] On Yeltsin's difficulties, see Michael E. Urban, *More Power to the Soviets. The Democratic Revolution in the USSR* (Aldershot, Edward Elgar, 1990) 105–7.

[6] Sakwa, *Russian Politics*, 138. Of the 191 party secretaries standing for election, 153 were successful; only 6 of the 126 secretaries who ran unopposed were defeated, while in contested elections 32 of the 65 secretaries were successful. Cited in Jerry F. Hough, *Democratization and Revolution in the USSR 1985–1991* (Washington, Brookings, 1997), 166.

(including Politburo candidate member Solov'ev, who had stood unopposed), and some 38 regional and district party first secretaries. In the Baltic republics, candidates gained election generally only if they supported the local popular front movements. The routing of traditional candidates was demonstrated most spectacularly by Boris Yeltsin's victory with 89 per cent of the vote in a Moscow constituency over an apparat-supported local factory director.

The election results were a major shock to many in the party. The basic response was to interpret this setback as evidence that the party was out of touch with developments in society, or at least parts of the party were out of touch, and this had been recognized and punished by voters.[7] This enabled party leaders to adopt the sanguine view that the election showed that the vast majority of the people supported the party's policy of perestroika. However not all sections of the party found this view convincing. At a meeting of the CC on 25 April,[8] at which 110 members of the CC and Central Auditing Commission reluctantly retired,[9] leading party figures were less inclined to see the vote as a vote for the party's policy. Some sought to blame individual laggards in the party or the press for the electoral outcome, but others placed the responsibility squarely on the central party leadership and its policies. Glasnost was being used to drag the party's name through the mud and to pin responsibility for crimes upon current incumbents of party offices. The policy of democratization was said to have opened the way for 'demagoguery, egoism, nationalism and anti-Sovietism', and for attacks upon all that was worthy about the Soviet experience. Speakers also criticised the lack of leadership by the party apex. The Politburo and CC did not give clear and decisive leadership, while the party apparatus continued to perform in a deficient, overly bureaucratic, fashion with, in the view of one speaker, the recent reorganization only just beginning to bear fruit. The single most prominent theme in the discussion was the failure of adequate leadership from the centre, with one speaker (Ivan Polozkov) openly calling for the resignation of those comrades who had allowed the party to get into this situation.

The CC plenum gave clear evidence of the extent of opposition within leading party ranks to the policies which were seen to have been responsible for the electoral setback. Further strong evidence was forthcoming at a meeting of regional party leaders held on 18 July 1989.[10] At this meeting, Gorbachev came

---

[7] *Pravda*, 13 Apr. 1989.          [8] See the report in *Pravda*, 27 Apr. 1989.

[9] See the discussion in Graeme Gill, *The Collapse of a Single Party System: The Disintegration of the Communist Party of the Soviet Union* (Cambridge, Cambridge University Press, 1994), 80–5.

[10] *Pravda*, 19 and 21 July 1989. A transcript was published separately: *Perestroika raboty partii—vazneishaia kliuchevaia zadacha dnia* (Moscow, 1989). Also see Jeff Gleisner, 'The Lessons of March: The Apparatus Fights Back', *Détente*, 15 (1989), 19–24.

under sustained attack, albeit at times obliquely, both for the perceived destruction of the party apparatus and for the state into which Soviet society had fallen. Speakers urged the reversal of the measures taken in September 1988 to restructure the central party apparatus, arguing that this had contributed substantially to the party losing control over both policy and personnel matters. Particularly striking was the hostility of many speakers to what they saw as 'extremist groups', including those nascent parties and movements that had been emerging in recent years, and to the tolerance being granted these groups by Soviet authorities. There were calls for a restoration of 'law and order', the reassertion of firm central control, and the withdrawal of many of those legal provisions which made possible freer public activity (including the laws on cooperatives and the state enterprise). The depth and extent of the opposition to the path Gorbachev was pursuing was clear in the course of the meeting, with the majority of speakers from the regional party apparatus being highly critical; Gorbachev's Politburo colleagues Ligachev, Ryzhkov, Zaikov, and Vorotnikov also expressed significant criticism. The comments in July were much more negative and hard-hitting than they had been in April.

But there was no clear alternative policy line suggested by Gorbachev's conservative critics to that being followed which might have given some hope of averting a further deterioration of the party's situation. In this sense, the opposition to a continuation of perestroika had no viable alternative to offer.[11] This lack of a clear alternative policy meant that the opponents of reform were unable to unite to check the reformist elements around Gorbachev. But even those reformist elements soon found themselves lagging behind the course of developments. Crucial in this was the opening of the Congress of People's Deputies.

The Congress was crucial for the unrolling of the process of change for two main reasons: its institutional form, and the content of its activity. The institutional form of the new organs[12] was significant in a number of ways. As indicated below, the new legislative organs constituted official state fora within which the authorities could come under vigorous and wide-ranging criticism with those critics constitutionally immune to official action.[13] They were thus a legitimate platform from which those critical of contemporary developments could make their views known. But perhaps more important, they constituted

[11]  Nor, it must be said, did the leadership have a decisive view of future policy lines. See the bland document issued at the end of the April plenum. 'Programma deistvii po itogam aprel'skogo (1989g) Plenuma Ts.K. KPSS', *Izvestiia Ts.K. KPSS,* 7 (1989), 7–13.

[12]  Although the practical relationship between Congress and Supreme Soviet was never clearly defined.

[13]  It is significant that radical deputies from Moscow and the Baltic seem to have been given the right to speak by Gorbachev much more frequently than their numbers would have warranted. Archie Brown, *The Gorbachev Factor* (Oxford, Oxford University Press, 1996), 191.

a rival centre of power to the traditional institution of Soviet power, the party. By acting as fora for the discussion and resolution of major issues, the legislative bodies effectively challenged the party's traditional supremacy within the system. Moreover, by resting that challenge on a constitutional basis (through the amendments to the Constitution introduced in December 1988), that challenge could not easily be dismissed by defenders of the old order. This image of the new institutions as a rival centre of power was highlighted by the creation of the post of chairman of the (new) Supreme Soviet and the election of Gorbachev to it by the Congress in May. This was a stark illustration of the way in which the party General Secretary was now no longer institutionally dependent upon the party to sustain him. Now as head of the executive arm of the state, he not only had an alternative institutional structure upon which to stand, but he was rendered immune from removal from high political office by the party. If as General Secretary he could be removed by vote of the CC, much of which was clearly opposed to the course he was charting, as Supreme Soviet chairman, he could only be removed by the national legislature, which the party no longer formally controlled. Thus these institutional innovations constituted an important restriction of the party's power and position and potentially marginalised it from the centre of policy-making while providing the opportunity for other forces to seize the initiative.

In terms of its activity, the Congress provided a significant stimulus to the opening up of the political system. Although some 87 per cent of deputies were members of the party (an even higher proportion than in the Soviet era Supreme Soviet), the number of professionals had increased and of workers and apparatchiks had decreased.[14] Furthermore, following the instruction from Gorbachev that they were to think and vote for themselves, these members no longer considered themselves as having slavishly to follow the party line, with the result that the Congress was not the sort of obedient assembly that former Soviet legislatures had been. From the outset, its proceedings were unpredictable, and although Gorbachev was able through force of personality and some bullying tactics usually to get his way on issues, the televising of this body's proceedings (and of those of its standing organ, the Supreme Soviet) projected into Soviet homes a forum far more fractious and critical than any they had seen before. During sessions, party leaders often came under vigorous attack and criticism, both for the mistakes of the past and the mismanagement and perceived timidity of the present. The open discussion of issues, criticism of authorities, and condemnation of mistakes gained a popular legitimacy they had never before possessed, and thereby fed into the

[14] Sakwa, *Russian Politics*, 138. Also see the analysis by Hough, who argues that the Congress was conservative in its outlook because of the high proportion of moderate and conservative elements among party representatives. Hough, *Democratization*, 166–7.

radicalization of debate and the cracking open of the system. Furthermore the image of the deputies vigorously questioning and even rejecting some candidates presented by Prime Minister Ryzhkov as ministers in his government reflected a sense of accountability never before evident in Soviet history.

An important aspect of the emergence of open debate and discussion in the Congress of People's Deputies and Supreme Soviet was the crystallisation of two distinct strands of opposition to the existing structure of Soviet rule.[15] The first was the civic strand, represented most clearly by the emergence of a series of small, nascent political parties.[16] While these had begun to emerge in 1988, they were symbolised most clearly by the emergence in the Congress of the so-called Inter-Regional Group of Deputies, which had been established on 28 July 1989.[17] This was a loose grouping of more radical deputies (388 of the 2,250 announced their adherence to this group[18]) including Yeltsin, former dissident Andrei Sakharov, Yury Afanas'ev, Gavriil Popov and Viktor Pal'm. This grouping came to symbolize what would later be called the radical 'democrats', but whose demands for change were wider than just the democratisation of the system, although this was clearly central to their purpose. This strand of opposition saw the democratisation of the Soviet Union and the development of a genuine civic culture as being the key aim to be achieved through the perestroika process. In this sense, this group began by accepting the starting point of perestroika and then pressing it much further than Gorbachev and his colleagues had envisaged. However, neither the Inter-Regional Group nor any other organized faction in the legislature developed into a coherent and organized political party playing a positive role in the assembly.[19] The principal importance of the Inter-Regional Group is that it gave rise to the Democratic Russia movement which was to prove significant in the emergence of an independent Russia (see Chapter 4).[20]

---

[15] For a discussion of political divisions within the Congress, see Giuletto Chiesa with Douglas Taylor Northrop, *Transition to Democracy: Political Change in the Soviet Union, 1987–1991* (Hanover, University Press of New England, 1993).

[16] On these, see Vera Tolz, *The USSR's Emerging Multiparty System* (New York, Praeger, 1990); Michael E. Urban, 'The Soviet Multi-party System: A Moscow Roundtable', *Russia and the World*, 18 (1990), 1–6.

[17] On this see John B. Dunlop, *The Rise of Russia and the Fall of the Soviet Empire* (Princeton, Princeton University Press, 1993), 81–5.

[18] For a range of figures, see Judith Devlin, *The Rise of the Russian Democrats: The Causes and Consequences of the Elite Revolution* (Aldershot, Edward Elgar, 1995), 138; for discussion, 136–42.

[19] See e.g. Neil Robinson, 'Parliamentary Politics under Gorbachev: Opposition and the Failure of Socialist Pluralism', *The Journal of Communist Studies*, 9: 1 (Mar. 1993), 91–108.

[20] The stance adopted by Democratic Russia and the role it played reflects the fact that the distinction between these two strands of opposition, the civic and the nationalist, although clear in principle was less distinct in practice.

The second strand of opposition was nationalist. This too had emerged earlier, but the new legislative organs gave it a new prominence by providing a platform from which its demands could be declared. The nationalist opposition principally took the form of popular fronts, which gained representation in the Soviet legislative organs. But where this differed from the civic opposition is that rather than seeking change within the Soviet Union, ultimately these groups sought the dissolution of that entity. They were interested in democratization principally in an instrumental sense, in order to further their most fundamental demand, initially greater national autonomy and then national independence. This assumed the break-up of the Soviet Union, at least in its current form.

The activity of these legislative bodies opened up the political agenda to inputs from below in a way that had been impossible before, leading to a significant radicalization of that agenda. But that agenda was also radicalised by activity outside the new institutions. One source of this was the continuing growth of civic opposition within society through the growth of civil society forces, which provided a basis upon which civic opposition in the parliamentary organs could rest.[21] Informals continued to function and to press for a range of changes in the areas of their particular concern. Sometimes these were harmless pursuits, like chess clubs and sporting organizations, but they also ranged through bodies whose interests could have political implications (like environmental groups) to those with specific political aims. Regardless of the specific areas of concern of such organisations,[22] their very emergence and mushrooming constituted a challenge to the dominance of the party. They meant that ordinary citizens could now look to unofficial organizations as possible means of fulfilling their wishes, that they no longer had to rely upon the official bodies of the party-state as the vehicles for pursuit of their interests. Given that the regime did not move to crush such independent organizations, although some were subjected to significant state pressure, their very existence stimulated both further organization and the citizens' quest for autonomous organization. But although 1989 witnessed a flourishing of their activity, with much wider public discussion of political issues, a wave of public meetings and demonstrations, and attempts to foster closer relations between them through conferences and meetings,[23] the

---

[21] The effect of the Tiananmen Square incident in China in April–May 1989, just after Gorbachev's visit, on conservative opinion may also have been important.

[22] For a discussion of those in the voluntary sector, see Anne White, *Democratization in Russia Under Gorbachev 1985–91: The Birth of a Voluntary Sector* (London and New York, Macmillan & St Martin's Press, 1999).

[23] M. Steven Fish, *Democracy from Scratch. Opposition and Regime in the New Russian Revolution* (Princeton, Princeton University Press, 1995), 35–41.

existence of these bodies did not represent the presence of a mature civil society. Most of these organizations remained weak, and they were tolerated rather than encouraged by the regime as a whole. As noted above, they remained fragmented and were not part of a web of interactions and relations which constituted an arena of activity which the party-state acknowledged as theirs by right; rather they had to carve out niches in Soviet society against the general hostility of the party apparatus.

The emergent political parties remained weak. They usually lacked a developed organizational structure, established rules and procedures, and a stable membership. They were for the most part notable-centred bodies, whose existence was heavily dependent upon the continuing drive, energy and enthusiasm of their leading group, and often of the individual leader by whose name they became known. In most political systems they would not have been considered major threats to a dominant party like the CPSU, but what increased their apparent challenge was the barrenness of the landscape before 1985; no other parties had even been allowed to exist prior to the Gorbachev period, and no alternative forms of political organization were tolerated. The continuing existence of these bodies thereby in itself constituted an important structural change to the political system and a challenge to the ruling party's monopoly of power.[24]

A more serious challenge emerged in the middle of the year with the outbreak of strike activity on the coalfields of the Kuzbass, Donbass and Vorkuta. This also spread to Pavlodar and Karaganda in Kazakhstan.[25] The strike activity, which paralysed the coal industry, was highly organized, and as well as being motivated by immediate economic concerns, took on a distinctly political dimension. While the strikers demanded improvement in their immediate living and working conditions, including increased pay, decreased hours and better provision of housing, medical care and supplies, they also made a major political demand. In calling for the abolition of the party's leading role in Soviet society enshrined in Article 6 of the state Constitution, the miners were demanding an end to the constitutional basis which underpinned the party's continuing dominance of Soviet society. They were also giving voice to a demand which was to swell over coming months and which reflected the tension within Gorbachev's programme made evident by the March election: even if the people voted against communist candidates, they could not remove

---

[24] This is notwithstanding the suspicion that a number of the new parties were actually fostered from within the CPSU in an attempt to contain this challenge.

[25] On these strikes see Theodore Friedgut and Lewis Siegelbaum, 'Perestroika from Below: The Soviet Miners' Strike and its Aftermath', *New Left Review*, 181 (1990), 5–32, and Donald Filtzer, *Soviet Workers and the Collapse of Perestroika. The Soviet Labour Process and Gorbachev's Reforms 1985–1991* (Cambridge, Cambridge University Press, 1994), 94–122.

party control. Importantly, the miners also formed their own independent organizations to press their case. The strike was ended only when the government gave in to the strikers' socio-economic demands, although in practice the promises made at this time were not kept. But the miners' strike activity was particularly important because it was the first case of a group of citizens organizing and pressing political activity on a non-national issue, and because it was this group which was quintessentially working class, and which therefore posed a direct challenge to the party's ideological rationale of being the party of the working class. It was a challenge not only to the party's position in society, but also to the ideological underpinning of its very existence. The failure to win over this powerful constituency meant that the reformers missed an opportunity to strengthen the process of change and left the way open for others to rally these forces for their own purposes.

The other source of the radicalization of the political agenda was the growth of nationalist opposition, which escalated considerably during 1989 reflecting Gorbachev's failure to take steps to reform the federal system or to even acknowledge that there was a problem in the federal distribution of power. There was a real heightening in tension and level of nationalist issues during this period. This was marked by events in Georgia early in the year. In February a large demonstration marked the sixty-eighth anniversary of the incorporation of Georgia into the union. In March, Abkhaz separatists called for autonomy for Abkhazia, but more importantly, on 9 April a demonstration by nationalists in Tbilisi was broken up by troops with the death of twenty demonstrators and injuring of more than two hundred. This heavy handed action, which was initiated by the local party and military leadership, inflamed nationalist sentiment across the country, sending the clear message that the centre was unwilling to countenance a questioning of the Soviet federal structure. But the most important nationalist developments occurred in the Baltic republics.

The seeds of nationalist agitation had been bearing fruit for some time in these republics, ever since the emergence of popular front organizations in 1988. The electoral victories of the Baltic republican popular fronts in the March election to the Congress of People's Deputies have already been noted, and the deputies thus sent to Moscow made a point of pressing demands for greater local autonomy through the Congress of People's Deputies and Supreme Soviet. New language laws, giving primacy to the republican language over Russian, were introduced in Estonia and Lithuania in January and Latvia in May. Later in May, the Lithuanian Supreme Soviet declared the sovereigny of Lithuania (thereby asserting the primacy of the republican government over the Soviet government in Moscow) and amended the constitution accordingly, while in Estonia legislation was adopted asserting republican sovereignty.[26] The Latvian legislature did likewise in July. In the middle of the year, Lithuania and Latvia introduced a form of republican citizenship. These acts were a direct challenge to continued control by Moscow. The response from the centre was restrained; the Supreme Soviet passed a resolution on 27 July supporting the moves in Lithuania and Estonia towards free market economic systems, while in August the Politburo supported limited economic autonomy for the republics; on 27 November the Supreme Soviet formally granted such autonomy to the Baltic republics,[27] but they were not given ownership of their resources and fixed assets, which remained in Moscow's hands and rendered such autonomy ethereal. But it is clear that Baltic nationalists were not interested merely in constitutional provisions. In early August the Estonian Supreme Soviet established minimum residency requirements for voting and holding office, action which prompted a strike among Russian residents of the republic and which was declared illegal by the Soviet Ministry of Justice. On 22 August the Lithuanian Supreme Soviet declared that the Soviet incorporation of Lithuania in 1940 was illegal,[28] and on the following day massive demonstrations occurred on the fiftieth anniversary of the pact which led to the annexation of the Baltic republics by the Soviet Union. This included a 400 mile long human chain stretching from Vilnius to Tallinn, which gained maximum television coverage. By the end of the year, secession from the union was being actively canvassed within the popular front movements. On 6 December the Lithuanian Supreme Soviet voted to abolish the CPSU's political monopoly and, on the following day, legalised opposition parties. A fortnight later the Lithuanian Communist Party decided to break with the CPSU and become an independent communist party, a development which prompted large demonstrations in Vilnius in support of the new party. A day later, on 28 December, the Latvian Supreme Soviet voted to delete references to the party's 'leading role' from the Constitution. In the Baltic republics, the nationalist movements were increasingly making the political running at the expense of the local communist parties.

Elsewhere in the union also nationalist sentiment was moving to the centre of the political stage. There was ethnic conflict in Uzbekistan between Meskhetian Turks and native Uzbeks, with more than 100 people killed. New language laws were adopted in Kirgizia and Moldavia on 24 and 28 August

---

[26] Already on 16 November 1988 the Estonian legislature had amended the republic's constitution to enable officials to ignore USSR laws that conflicted with those of Estonia. This was nullified ten days later by the Soviet authorities.

[27] *Pravda*, 2 Dec. 1979.

[28] Four days earlier, on 18 August, the Soviet authorities had for the first time publicly acknowledged the secret protocols of the Molotov–Ribbentrop Pact which had led to the incorporation of the Baltic states: *Pravda*, 18 Aug. 1989.

respectively and in Uzbekistan and Ukraine on 21 and 28 October. In Ukraine in early September, the nationalist movement Rukh held its first meeting and demanded the transformation of the USSR into a confederation of autonomous republics and the removal of republican party leader Volodymyr Shcherbitsky (he was removed on 28 September). Throughout the year the Nagorno-Karabakh dispute continued to build, resulting in vigorous military action in Baku in January 1990.

As well as this nationalist challenge, the Soviet structure was also under threat from the widening scope of glasnost, a development propelled in significant measure by the intelligentsia. Under their influence, glasnost was becoming increasingly erosive of Soviet legitimacy. Both through cultural outlets (literature in particular) and investigative reporting/historical research, the Stalinist past was being laid bare and its unsavoury aspects publicised.[29] Khrushchev's secret speech attacking Stalin's rule was published in March 1989,[30] while mass graves of the victims of the terror were unearthed at various locations in the USSR. But particularly important was the way this process of historical revision reached back to the Lenin period and began to question the very basis upon which the regime stood; the revolution and the state constructed by Lenin. As the Lenin era came increasingly under the spotlight, and some commentators began to link Leninism and Stalinism,[31] the legitimacy of the regime was called increasingly into question.

This questioning of the regime's origins and the so-called 'socialist choice' made in October 1917 was also reflected in the way in which the currency of discussion of contemporary developments was undergoing fundamental change. Development and future options were no longer being presented as being possible only within socialist bounds. Socialism as embraced in the Soviet experience was changing in the public sphere from being the paradigm within which change must take place to the site from which escape must be had. Although few were willing to use the terms 'capitalist' and 'capitalism' publicly in a positive fashion before the August putsch, the shift toward a new paradigm is reflected in the gradual expansion of use of the term 'market', initially qualified in the form 'socialist market' or 'regulated market', then unqualified, and finally qualified again as 'free market'. Parallel changes

---

[29] For a survey of the treatment of Stalin, see Devlin, *The Rise of Russian Democrats*, 60–9. Also R. W. Davies, *Soviet History in the Gorbachev Revolution* (Bloomington, Indiana University Press, 1989), and Alec Nove, *Glasnost in Action: Cultural Renaissance in Russia* (Boston, Unwin Hyman, 1989), chs. 2, 4.

[30] *Izvestiia Ts.K. KPSS*, 3 (1989), 128–70.

[31] For an early and important case of this, see Vasily Seliunin, 'Istoki', *Novyi Mir*, 5 (1988), 162–89. For discussions, see Nove, *Glasnost in Action*, Davies, *Soviet History . . . Gorbachev Revolution*, and R. W. Davies, *Soviet History in the Yeltsin Era* (London, Macmillan, 1997).

occurred with the term 'property'. This change in terminology and conceptualization was becoming evident in 1989, but really gathered pace in 1990 and
1991, and by rapidly becoming the dominant discourse, undercut the validity
of the conceptual basis upon which the regime stood.

The multi-faceted assault on the traditional Soviet structure left the elite
with few answers. The announced withdrawal of the party from a direct
administrative role following the XIX Conference and the failure of Gorbachev
and his leadership colleagues to articulate a new vision for the party helped to
generate increasing confusion in party ranks about what the party's real role
might be. The forceful suppression of the Georgian protesters had only served
to underline the absence of any effective response on the part of Moscow to
nationalist dissent. It also helped to discredit the centre in the eyes of many of
its subjects. The growth of nationalist disturbances in the middle of the year
prompted Gorbachev to criticise ethnic violence in a nationally televised
speech[32] and to refer to the 'enormous danger' it posed to perestroika. There
was a hint that Gorbachev actually realised that the problems were more deep-
seated than simply ethnic difference, with his admission in the July meeting
with regional party leaders that there had been a popular loss of confidence in
the party.[33] Five days later he publicly supported many of the demands of the
striking coal miners.[34] But the absence of any realistic policy which could hope
to meet the popular demands was reflected when, at the CC plenum called to
discuss the national question, Gorbachev condemned republican separatists,[35]
refusing to countenance suggestions that the USSR might become a confederation, and the platform adopted at that plenum, despite some concessions to
nationalist concerns, fell far short of the radical demands emanating from
some republican capitals.[36] Gorbachev maintained this position throughout a
visit to Lithuania in January 1990 when he went to Vilnius in an attempt to
persuade the Lithuanian party leader Algirdas Brazauskas to rescind the decision making the LCP independent of the CPSU. Gorbachev's reluctance to
countenance an independent LCP cost it any chance it may have had of plac-

[32] *Pravda*, 2 July 1989.
[33] For the report of the meeting, see *Pravda*, 19, 21 July 1989.
[34] For the report of the session of the Supreme Soviet where he made these comments,
see *Pravda*, 25 July 1989.
[35] M. S. Gorbachev , 'O natsional'noi politike partii v sovremennykh usloviiakh', *Pravda*
20 Sept. 1989. In the view of knowledgeable observers of the Soviet scene, Gorbachev was
under considerable pressure on the Baltic issue, and it would have placed him in a position
of considerable danger had he compromised with the nationalist leaderships: Jack Matlock
Jr., 'Gorbachev: Lingering Mysteries', *The New York Review of Books*, 19 Dec. 1996, p. 36.
[36] 'Natsional'naia politika partii v sovremennykh usloviiakh (platforma KPSS)', *Pravda*,
24 Sept. 1989. This platform did include the idea of a new union treaty. The platform
replaced a set of 'theses' issued in November 1988, which also lagged far behind opinion in
the Baltics.

ing itself at the head of the nationalist movement and swinging it in behind perestroika, and was a costly error of judgement. Recognition of the leadership's failure to articulate a clear vision, or even a coherent strategy to deal with the mounting problems, was evident in the wave of criticism at the December 1989 plenum. This wave was so strong, that Gorbachev was able to quell it only by threatening to resign.[37]

On the defensive, the leadership now made concessions on a number of issues. On 9 October the Supreme Soviet approved a decree which granted the right to strike, although workers in transportation, communications, defence, electric power, coal mining and oil and gas were excluded from its provisions. As noted above, economic autonomy was granted to the Baltic republics. There was also high-level discussion of, and considerable argument about, the issue of the abolition of the party's constitutional monopoly of power enshrined in Article 6 of the Constitution.[38] In early December an editorial in *Pravda* asserted that Article 6 could be the subject of re-evaluation, modernization or even removal, but not under political pressure and only in the context of a balanced consideration of the Constitution.[39] At the CC plenum soon after, Gorbachev repeated this position and hinted that Article 6 might not be essential; this position was then taken up by other party figures.[40] That the leader of the party could contemplate the removal of the constitutional underpinning of the party's dominance cannot be explained only by the growing strength of public opinion (which on this issue was led by the Inter-Regional Group), although this was clearly important. It may be that he believed what he said, that the party could survive with its leading role intact because of the strength of the popular support which it enjoyed. But his recognition earlier that year that people had lost confidence in the party is not consistent with such a view. Important here was probably recognition that, with the establishment of the new legislative structure and his election as chairman of the Supreme Soviet, his personal primacy no longer depended solely on the party. This was to be even more the case when he assumed the executive presidency in early 1990. But for many in the party this undercutting of the party's position was a source of deep concern. So too was was the erosion of the Soviet position in Eastern Europe, long regarded as a defensive bastion paid for with Soviet blood in the Great Patriotic War.

[37] *Izvestiia Ts.K. KPSS*, 4 (1990), 25–112.

[38] At the time of the discussion of this issue, according to Gorbachev the Politburo was divided between conservatives (Ligachev, Nikonov, Shcherbitsky), 'active advocates of reform' (Medvedev, Shevardnadze, Yakovlev), and 'centrists' (Ryzhkov, Vorotnikov, Sliun'kov, Chebrikov): Mikhail Gorbachev, *Memoirs* (London, Doubleday, 1996), 317.

[39] 'Ob avangardnoi roli KPSS', *Pravda*, 8 Dec. 1989.

[40] 'Vystuplenie M. S. Gorbacheva na Plenume Ts.K. KPSS po voprosam II S'ezda narodnykh deputatov SSSR', *Pravda*, 10 Dec. 1989. Also Gill, *Collapse*, 99.

One of the principal developments in 1989 was the fall of communist regimes throughout Eastern Europe. The course of this development does not need to be analysed here. What is important for current purposes is the speed with which these regimes collapsed and the fact that Gorbachev was instrumental in this development. As early as 1986 Gorbachev had privately told the leaders of the region that Soviet troops would not intervene to ensure that they stayed in power, while in 1987 talks proceeded about the reduction of Soviet troops in the region. Gorbachev also made it clear that he believed that the countries of Eastern Europe should follow a similar course of reform to that in the Soviet Union, and that each country had the right to choose its own path and style of development independent of outside influence. The removal of Soviet troops from the region had begun in April 1989, but more important was the visit of Gorbachev to East Berlin in October. During this visit he urged reform and made it clear that the Soviet Union would not step in in order to reverse any changes that were made. This stimulated the developing popular ferment in the GDR, which led to the fall of the government and the dismantling of the Berlin Wall. The actions in Germany encouraged change elsewhere in the region, leading to the quick fall of communist governments in most of the countries of Eastern Europe. Shevardnadze's acknowledgement of the right of Warsaw Treaty Organisation (WTO) members to political independence, the condemnation of the invasion of Czechoslovakia in 1968 at a WTO meeting, and Gorbachev's rhetoric about the 'common European home' further stimulated the erosion of communist rule. By the end of the year, established communist governments had been replaced throughout most of the region. The psychological impact of this on the broad Soviet elite was profound, further undermining their confidence by calling into question the survivability of a Soviet style political structure, while the position Gorbachev adopted internationally of supporting the right of countries to determine their own futures could not fail to give impetus to nationalist sentiment within the USSR. The collapse of communism in Eastern Europe thus both weakened the elite defenders of the regime while strengthening those forces favouring change, particularly those who were coming to believe in the need for a decisive break with the Soviet system.

The speed (and relative ease) of this process that Gorbachev had unleashed infuriated many in the upper levels of the party.[41] The loss of this part of the communist patrimony was further evidence of, at best, the stupidity of the

---

[41] Although according to memoir material, as early as 1985 or 1986 the Politburo had adopted a decision not to use Soviet force in Eastern Europe, a position which rendered such a development likely. However it is not clear that they had fully thought through the implications of this: See Hough, *Democratization*, 199.

course Gorbachev and his supporters were engaged on, or at worst the treasonous acts of the reformist faction in the party. Regardless of whichever of these positions individuals tended towards, the result was a strengthening of opposition to Gorbachev and his supporters. But this occurred against a background of seeming consolidation of the reformist position during 1989. By acceding to chairmanship of the Supreme Soviet in May, Gorbachev had seemingly made himself invulnerable to removal from the political stage by his opponents within the party. Further changes to the leadership were made during 1989 at the September CC plenum with the promotion of Kriuchkov and Masliukov as full members of the Politburo at the expense of Shcherbitsky, Chebrikov and Nikonov; two new candidate members (Primakov and Pugo in place of Talyzin, Solov'ev and the promoted Masliukov) and four new secretaries (Stroev, Manaenkov, Usmanov and Girenko) rounded out these changes. In December Ivashko became a full member of the Politburo and Frolov a secretary. While in hindsight these appointments did not bring steadfast allies to Gorbachev's side, their effect meant that by the end of 1989 the entire membership of Politburo and Secretariat had been appointed since Gorbachev came to power. Given the role of the General Secretary in making such appointments, this should have meant a leadership much more closely aligned to Gorbachev's way of thinking than was in practice the case. By this time Gorbachev could still rely on the full blooded support of only Shevardnadze, Yakovlev and, with some reservations, Medvedev. The remainder of the leadership was characterized by different degrees of scepticism about or opposition to the reform course being charted by the General Secretary. Why was the leadership split in this way?

One reason that has been advanced for this is that Gorbachev was not a good judge of character. On many occasions Gorbachev either appointed or acceded to the promotion of people who were to turn on him. While perhaps the most egregious cases of this were still to come, this pattern replayed itself throughout the entire perestroika period. But more important was the dynamic of change itself, something which was particularly influential during 1989. During this year as the pace of change quickened, the likelihood of finding people who could be brought into the leadership whose views could move as fast as that change was reduced. As a result, people who supported the reforms as understood at the start of the year found themselves greatly out of step with those changes by the end of the year. They had been left behind; the radicalization of the agenda turned many reformists into conservatives. Gorbachev himself was much more flexible in his thinking than many of his colleagues, and although he was slow to accept some of the changes coming from below (such as the demands for autonomy/independence coming from the Baltic republics), usually he could be brought around to accept and ultimately support the changes. In 1989, Gorbachev became a reactive leader instead of setting the agenda as he had done in earlier years.

The fact that most of his colleagues could not adjust to and support the changes and the increased speed at which they were occurring was a major problem for Gorbachev in his continuing attempt to maintain the unity of the elite. He had to try to pull his more conservative colleagues along with him, both because he believed that the party which they controlled retained an important role in the Soviet future, and because he understood the damage that the high-level opponents of change could do were they left to their own devices. Both of these were reasons why Gorbachev did not entirely desert the party and throw in his lot with the growing constituency openly favouring transformation. But the growth and development of this constituency itself posed a further problem for Gorbachev. As this constituency, seizing the initiative, pushed the bounds of reform further in a radical direction, dragging Gorbachev with it, his links with the conservative elements became more attenuated. But also his public image as a leading reformer became somewhat tarnished, as he was seen to lag behind others pressing for more radical change. This was reflected in his declining public approval ratings during 1989. An important element of this was the way that these more radical elements rested on bases other than the party, and thereby gave a growing sense of popular legitimacy to other types of organizations. With people like Yeltsin and Sakharov (until his death in December 1989) championing the cause of change and appealing to a popular constituency, the party appeared even more irrelevant to the ordinary Soviet citizenry. And with this development went the undermining of the legitimacy of Gorbachev's power base. For example, the popular demonstrations in Moscow in support of Yeltsin on 5 and 19 March 1989, and popular threats of a national strike on 29 May when it appeared that Yeltsin would be denied a seat in the Supreme Soviet illustrated not just the popularity of Gorbachev's former supporter, but also the way the more radical reformers were developing a popular support base which threatened to overwhelm any reformer who sought to remain rooted in the structure of the party. This was to become even more evident during 1990.

Indeed 1990 proved to be a watershed year in the course of change in the Soviet Union. This was the year when the process of reform unambiguously became one of transformation.[42] As reform was increasingly radicalised in ear-

[42] The fact that the Soviet Union was undergoing a 'thorough going systemic transformation' in Michael Urban's words, raises questions about the appropriateness of the word 'reform', which implies a gradual improvement of the system from above, to describe this process. Perestroika certainly fits this description, at least in its early years, but it is less clear that the transformation that has taken place in the 1990s does. When we employ the term 'reform', it is usually because it has entered common parlance. It should be understood that

lier years, especially 1988 and 1989, both in terms of the type of solution sought to problems and the identity of the actors playing a part, it more and more pressed against the boundaries between change within the system and change of the system. This dynamic occurred in both the political and economic spheres, each of which fed off the other, but in 1990 in both spheres a significant break occurred with what had gone before. In the political sphere, the introduction of an executive presidency and the abolition of the Communist Party's formal monopoly of power associated with the growing conceptualization of it in social democratic (as opposed to communist) terms, prefigured the shift to a different type of system to that to which the programme of perestroika had been applied. In the economic sphere, debate openly embraced the market in a much more substantial form than it had earlier, coming to see market forces as the primary mechanism of the economy rather than one subsidiary to state regulation. Similarly with regard to the actors involved, 1990 saw the open split of the state as increasingly central authorities were opposed by those heading the republics. This shift from reform to transformation, while not acknowledged in these terms, was recognised at the time by the elites, and led ultimately to the crisis of Gorbachev's 'turn to the right' in the autumn.

## The Fragmentation of the System

The unity of the Soviet polity became increasingly frayed during 1990, with both nationalist and civic pressures increasing the tensions within the elite and making it more difficult for Gorbachev to retain elite unity while continuing the momentum of change. Shifts in Gorbachev's personal position during the first part of this year show a continuing ability to change with the changing circumstances, although the stance he adopted later in the year seems to reflect a limit to that adaptability, at least temporarily. Both the nationalist and civic pressures were acute early in the year, with the former appearing to conservatives to be the more dangerous.

we recognise the limitations of it. Michael E. Urban, 'Boris El'tsin, Democratic Russia and the Campaign for the Russian Presidency', *Soviet Studies*, 44: 2 (1992), 187. For a critique of the term 'reform' and an argument that what is occurring is a revolution, see David M. Kotz with Fred Weir, *Revolution From Above: The Demise of the Soviet System* (London and New York, Routledge, 1997), 163. For an argument that this fundamental overturning amounts to a rolling back of the social legacy of the October Revolution and therefore amounts to a 'counter-revolution', see Roger D. Markwick, 'A Discipline in Transition?: From Sovietology to "Transitology" ', *The Journal of Communist Studies and Transition Politics*, 12: 3 (Sept. 1996), 269.

At the start of the year, nationalist pressures appeared principally in two guises. One was the violent exacerbation of the Armenian–Azeri differences over Nagorno-Karabakh, with the anti-Armenian pogroms in Azerbaijan in the middle of January followed by the Soviet army smashing its way into Baku which had been blockaded by Azeri nationalists. These events constituted the effective beginning of civil war within the Soviet Union, as neither the Armenian nor the Azeri government was willing to compromise on the territorial issue. The Soviet government had lost control in this region, a fact most clearly reflected in the outbreak of conflict, but also symbolically by the assertion on 11 January by the Armenian legislature of the right to veto Soviet laws. It was also clear in the adoption of a resolution by the Georgian Supreme Soviet condemning the forced incorporation of the republic into the USSR in 1921. Throughout the year unrest also occurred in some of the republics of Central Asia—Tajikistan in February, Uzbekistan and Kyrgystan in June.

But if the loss of control by the Soviet centre was starkly evident in the conflict in the Caucasus, it was no less serious in the Baltic region and, from March, in other parts of the country. As noted above, Gorbachev visited Lithuania in January to try to head off the split of the Lithuanian party from the CPSU and the general push toward independence. He was unsuccessful in this, but his visit does seem to have been instrumental in a change in position on his own part. He seems to have gained some appreciation of the depth of feeling within Lithuania on the issue of independence, and henceforth when he discussed this issue with regard to the Baltic region, the debate seemed to focus not on whether secession would be possible, but how this could be achieved. The answer was given in April, when the Supreme Soviet adopted a Law on Secession, but the conditions of this were such that nationalists rejected it as nothing more than a further attempt to place a barrier in their way.[43] While this may have been the immediate intent, by providing a mechanism for realising the right of secession provided for in the Constitution, this measure stimulated nationalist pressures for independence. This was given further encouragement by the republican elections.

With the exception of Georgia, Armenia, and Azerbaijan (which voted in October, May, and September respectively), republican and local elections were held throughout the country between December 1989 and March 1990.[44]

---

[43] This was to involve a referendum yielding a two thirds vote in favour of secession, a cooling-off period of five years, a further referendum, and approval by the Congress of People's Deputies.

[44] These occurred under revised electoral laws: *Izvestiia*, 23 Dec. 1989. For a discussion, see Hough, *Democratization*, ch. 9 and White, *Gorbachev and After*, 54.

At the republican level, where the elections were generally freer, more democratic and more competitive[45] (they were characterised by a higher level of
organised partisan activity, although the process was still not structured
through the activities of the parties) than they had been for the Congress of
People's Deputies in 1989, the results were often striking, with a significant
increase in the number of radical and nationalist deputies elected in a number
of republics including Russia. Such radical candidates did much better in the
large cities than in the smaller towns and the countryside, and they became a
major force on the political scene. The elections enabled opposition groups to
gain parliamentary majorities in Lithuania, Latvia, and Georgia (with a near
majority in Estonia), while in Russia, Ukraine, Belorussia, Armenia,[46] and
Moldavia they gained sufficient support to be able to influence subsequent
decision-making without gaining a parliamentary majority; in the Central
Asian republics, Kazakhstan, and Azerbaijan, the elections served to consolidate the power of the existing elites in new institutions.[47] Radical opponents
gained control of many of the major Soviet cities, including Moscow,
Leningrad, and Kiev. In Lithuania, the popular front organization Sajudis won
a majority in the Supreme Soviet (90 of 141 deputies), which a week later
declared Lithuanian independence from the USSR and elected Vytautas
Landsbergis as president. For the first time, a non-communist coalition government was formed in Vilnius. In Estonia, the Popular Front won 46 of 105
seats, but with allies and other groups was able to provide the prime minister
(the communist party won 55 seats, but some members supported the front).
At the end of March the new government declared that it no longer recognized
the force of the Soviet Constitution. In Latvia the popular front won 111 of the
210 seats, with allies taking another 20, and on 4 May the new government officially restored its 1922 Constitution, while providing for a timetable for negotiations to lead to ultimate independence. Most dramatically, in late May in
Russia, Yeltsin was elected on the fourth ballot as chairman of the Supreme
Soviet, and on 9 June the Russian government declared sovereignty over its

---

[45] For some figures on the degree of competition, see Stephen White, Graeme Gill, and
Darrell Slider, *The Politics of Transition: Shaping a Post-Soviet Future* (Cambridge,
Cambridge University Press, 1993), 32.

[46] Opposition forces were able to get Ter-Petrossian elected President in August.
Further elections were held in October 1990, won by Ter-Petrossian's Armenian Pan-
National Movement.

[47] For a discussion of the elections, see Kathleen Montgomery and Thomas F.
Remington, 'Regime Transition and the 1990 Soviet Republican Elections', *The Journal of
Communist Studies and Transition Politics*, 10: 1 (Mar. 1994), 55–79. On the elections in the
Baltic republics, see Rein Taagepera, 'Baltic Elections, February–April 1990', *Electoral
Studies*, 9: 4 (Dec. 1990), 303–11.

territory and resources. Similar action was taken by other republics in suc-
ceeding months.[48]

In the months following the republican elections, the power of the centre
fragmented as republican governments refused to implement the decisions of
the Soviet authorities in Moscow; federal laws were impotent unless ratified by
republican authorities.[49] The CPSU was effectively sidelined as new, popular
governments emerged. Although the aggressive drive for independence on the
part of the Baltic republics and spearheaded by Lithuania had the most immediate impact, the declarations of sovereignty by the other republics, and above
all Russia, were no less crucial for the ultimate break up of the political structure, because they constituted direct rejections of Moscow's right of control
over the republics. Henceforth republican governments pressed for, at minimum, a reworking of the federal compact involving a significant reduction in
the size and power of the centre. Furthermore, this represented the emergence
into positions of authority at the republican level of people who began to see
their best interests as lying with the republics rather than with the centre, and
with satisfying the wishes of their domestic constituencies rather than their
former political masters in Moscow. This constituted the horizontal fracturing
of the Soviet political apparatus and the beginning of the differentiation of the
political elite on a wide scale. The fact that sovereignty was declared even in
those republics which did not have governments run by radical oppositionists
shows that the basic division was horizontal and national rather than vertical
and policy/political. And in the elevation of Yeltsin, the independence movement gained a high-profile spokesman democratically elected and in charge of
the largest and most powerful republic in the union. He was to be crucial in
giving leadership to the nationalist push, and in taking some of the heat off the
leaders of the Baltic republics, particularly Landsbergis. And finally the election of republican legislatures in many parts of the country on more democratic lines than the Soviet Congress, convinced many democratic reformers
that it would be politically more advantageous to focus their activity at the
republican level than at the centre. This meant a meshing, in some cases
uneasy, of the democratic/civic and nationalist strands of opposition.

This fragmentation along republican lines was matched by a similar process
within many union republics. As the elections formally brought to power soviets at all levels containing people who owed their positions to the electors
rather than the nomenklatura, the link which the nomenklatura had provided

[48] Uzbekistan, 20 June; Moldavia, 21 June; Ukraine, 16 July; Turkmenistan, 22 August;
Armenia (declaration of independence), 23 August ; Tajikistan, 24 August ; Kazakhstan, 25
October; Kyrgyzstan, 12 December; Georgia had announced its sovereignty in April.
[49] Rachel Walker, *Six Years That Shook the World: Perestroika—The Impossible Project*
(Manchester, Manchester University Press, 1993), 180–2.

between the levels of the Soviet hierarchy was broken. Individual soviets (and therefore local governments) increasingly began to go their own way; the political cement of the system was disintegrating.

The centre's response to the growing territorial disintegration of the state was confused. On the one hand, significant pressure was brought to bear on the Baltic states to get them to withdraw from the positions they had occupied. Gorbachev publicly attacked the Baltic decisions. There was a show of force as military convoys rolled through Vilnius on 22 March, the headquarters of the Lithuanian Communist Party was seized by Soviet paratroopers on 25 March, and Lithuanian 'deserters' were arrested. Fuel supplies were cut off to Lithuania, and legal measures were enacted to make void the decisions of some of the Baltic governments.[50] But on the other hand, the centre was more responsive to the demands emanating from the republics. On the occasion of his election as Soviet President (see below) on 15 March, Gorbachev called for the drafting of a new union treaty,[51] symbolising a commitment to working out a new relationship between the constituent parts of the USSR; talks between federal and republican (minus the Baltic republics) authorities to draft such a treaty began on 30 July 1990. He also established a Council of the Federation, comprising representatives of all of the republics, to give him advice on issues relating to the federation. In early April a measure was enacted regularising economic relations between the centre and republics, and the Law on Secession discussed above was introduced. On 24 May Gorbachev told Lithuanian officials that the question of secession could be considered in 1992 providing the declaration of independence was suspended. The Soviet response was thus a combination of pressure designed to at least slow down the push toward independence and a somewhat begrudging acceptance of this push, including concessions to it. This mixed message not only had no chance of quelling nationalist pressures, but it also could not produce unity within the elite. A similar result emanated from the pressures for civic resistance.

Throughout 1990 the levels of political activity in the streets continued to build. As the ripples of glasnost continued to spread, embracing ever-more sensitive political and historical topics, and freedom of discussion grew, Soviet citizens increasingly found a public voice. No longer did they have to bite their tongues and discuss matters only with trusted friends. Now every citizen could openly participate in public discussion, and many did. Unfortunately for Gorbachev, as perestroika continued and the economic return remained

---

[50] It was at this time that Shevardnadze is reported to have had fears about the possibility of a putsch against Gorbachev to free the hands of the hardliners to deal with the Lithuanians: Jack Matlock Jr., 'Success Story', *The New York Review of Books*, 25 Sept. 1997, p. 67.

[51] *Pravda,* 16 Mar. 1997.

sparse, popular sentiment shifted decisively away from Gorbachev and his policies and placed a question mark in the minds of some over the continuing viability of the Soviet system as a whole.[52] People did not generally support a wholesale return to the former system, although clearly there were elements who wanted just that, but rather wanted to show their frustration and resentment at what they had. Here was a potential reservoir waiting to be mobilised against the CPSU. Popular demonstrations escalated. In early February, at the start of a momentous CC plenum (see below), more than 300,000 people demonstrated in Moscow in favour of the elimination of the party's constitutionally enshrined monopoly of power, while later that month pro-democracy demonstrators marched in more than thirty cities across the country. On May Day, the official parade was disrupted by independent and unofficial organizations which had been given permission to march but which displayed virulent anti-Soviet posters.

In addition to such popular demonstrations, the growth of independent party-type organisations continued apace. The republican and local elections in the spring acted as a powerful stimulus to such party development, particularly given the success that some of the umbrella groups had at the polls in places such as Moscow and Leningrad. In Moscow, 292 of the 465 seats in the city soviet were won by Democratic Russia (DemRossiia), while in Leningrad the Election 90 coalition won 355 of the 400 seats.[53] On the streets of the big cities, newspapers, news-sheets and leaflets multiplied enormously as all sorts of political groups emerged and sought to win converts. By 1990 there were at least twenty parties active at the federal level with a further 500 in the republics.[54] All of these nascent parties were very weak organizationally. Often they consisted of little more than a group of intellectuals in the large cities, with little or no mass following or organizational structure to sustain their activity. While some groups did try to create a broader organizational structure, such as DemRossiia which held its first congress in Moscow in mid-October,[55] few party activists had the experience, knowledge or skill to be particularly effective as party-builders. While representation in various legislative fora (Congress of People's Deputies, Supreme Soviet, local soviets) did provide some impetus for organization, at least within the legislative cham-

[52] This was clearly true, for example, for many among the so-called 'radical democrats' who were supporting Yeltsin at this time.

[53] Sakwa, *Russian Politics*, 141.

[54] Walker, *Six Years*, 142. For discussions of some of these, see Dunlop, *The Rise*, 97–102; Devlin, *Rise of the Russian Democrats*, ch. 9; and Fish, *Democracy*.

[55] It had been set up in January 1990 and was a direct product of the Inter-regional Group of Deputies: Dunlop, *The Rise*, 92–5, 102–6. By April 1991 it claimed to have 400,000 members, organizations in 72 of the 73 regions of Russia, and to publish 50 newspapers with a circulation of 1.5 million: ibid., 105. Also see Devlin, *Rise of the Russian Democrats*, 214–18.

ber,[56] this generally proved chimerical and did not extend into the society at large. Furthermore the new parties often found it difficult to gain access to the sorts of resources they needed (such as printing facilities, halls in which to hold meetings) because these usually were controlled by the local organizations of the CPSU, which were rarely willing to make them available to potential competitors. Generally dominated by the intelligentsia,[57] the parties remained weak as vehicles of popular mobilization and as political actors in their own rights, with the result that the populace was not mobilised in an organized fashion. However, they were significant in adding their voice to the process of radicalization of the political agenda that was continuing during 1990; the demands from the popular sector became increasingly radical during 1990 as, with the amendment of Article 6 of the Constitution,[58] the elimination of the CPSU altogether began to appear a realistic goal.

The issue of the leading role of the Communist Party was an important factor in the growth of other political parties. The development of pressures in the latter part of 1989 in favour of eliminating the party's constitutionally entrenched leading role has already been noted. Such pressures gathered strength in early 1990, culminating in the February plenum at which Gorbachev rejected the constitutional embedding of the party's leading role, declaring instead that the party should compete for the position of being ruling party without any legal or political advantages. He also acknowledged the growth of political pluralism, which he said could lead to the creation of political parties.[59] The CC ratified this position, and in March the Congress of People's Deputies amended the Constitution to do away with the party's leading role. In one fell swoop, Gorbachev and those around him had eliminated the legal basis upon which the party's dominance rested, placed it squarely in competition with other political forces in society, and thereby created a legitimate arena within which diverse political forces could operate. Henceforth there was scope not only for legitimate opposition in the Soviet political

[56] This was more developed in the Russian legislature than the Soviet one: Hough, *Democratization*, 298–304.

[57] Marcia A. Weigle, 'Political Participation and Party Formation in Russia, 1985–1992: Institutionalizing Democracy?', *The Russian Review*, 53 (Apr. 1994), 257.

[58] The new wording read: 'The CPSU, other political parties, trade unions, youth, social organisations and mass movements participate in shaping the policies of the Soviet state and in running state and social affairs through their representatives elected to the Congress of People's Deputies as well as in other ways.' The former article had referred to the CPSU as 'The leading and guiding force of Soviet society and the nucleus of its political system, of all state organisations and public organisations'.

[59] *Pravda*, 6 Feb. 1990. For the argument that Gorbachev had believed this since 1988, see Brown, *Gorbachev*, 194. For a broader view expressed by one of Gorbachev's closest supporters at this time, see Aleksandr Yakovlev, *Muki Prochteniia Bytiia. Perestroika: nadezhdy i real'nosti* (Moscow, Novosti, 1991), 87–129.

system, but also for the emergence of third-order manifestations of civil society which could articulate popular political opinion, including that of a nationalist hue. The question was, would this breakthrough of civil society forces re-energize Soviet reform or rupture it, opening the way to the overturn of the Soviet system? Already it was looking increasingly like the latter.

The breaking of the monolithic mould of Soviet politics which the amendment of Article 6 represented had a counterpart within the party itself, where there were pressures to represent the diversity of views which had become clearly evident within that institution. During 1989 pressures emerged within the Baltic parties in particular favouring the replacement of the unitary nature of the party by some sort of federal arrangement.[60] This culminated in the declarations of independence from the CPSU by the Lithuanian and Estonian parties in December 1989 and March 1990; in April the Latvian party split into pro- and anti-independence wings, as the Lithuanian party had done in December. The issue of a federal party was also addressed by the republican parties in a number of other republics, with mixed results. Beside these pressures for federalisation, there also emerged pressures for the establishment of a separate party within the CPSU for the Russian Republic. Such pressures had been growing in late 1989, and despite Gorbachev's attempt to head them off through the compromise of the creation of a Russian Bureau instead of a full party,[61] they proved irresistible. A Russian Communist Party was established with its founding conference in June (see below).

But as well as these pressures pluralising the party along national lines, there were also pressures favouring the explicit recognition of political differences within the party. The official position as expressed by Politburo member Vadim Medvedev in mid-1989 was that while there may be differences of view and ideological struggle within party ranks, there could be no organized tendencies.[62] This was little more than a restatement of the position that had prevailed since 1921. However, there was also strong support for the protection within the party of the rights of dissident minorities to maintain their views regardless of the position of the majority.[63] At the February 1990 plenum this view was accepted, with the Draft Platform adopted at that meeting providing for 'pluralism of opinions, freedom of criticism, diversity of approaches and platforms . . . and the minority's right to uphold its views subject to mandatory fulfilment of decisions made by the majority', although this should not lead to 'the formation of factions with their own internal organisation and dis-

---

[60] For details see Gill, *Collapse*, 92–3.

[61] Ibid., 93–4. Pressure for a Russian communist party was one element in a broader resurgence of Russian national feeling. For a discussion of this, see Dunlop, *The Rise*.

[62] *Le Monde*, 25 May 1989.          [63] Gill, *Collapse*, 95.

cipline.'[64] However, this injunction about organised factions was already being overtaken by events, with the emergence of two major factions in the party early in 1990. The first was the Democratic Platform, which emerged out of a Moscow Party Club 'Communists for Perestroika' organized in April 1989[65] and which, during 1990, was able to assume an organizational structure which penetrated the party in many parts of the country. It held meetings, published its own newspaper,and concentrated upon internal party reform; its main goal was the transformation of the CPSU into a social democratic parliamentary party that was characterised by a diversity of interest and outlook. The second faction was called the Marxist Platform. Also emerging out of the Moscow Party Club, the Marxist Platform consisted of a federation of party clubs situated across large areas of the USSR.[66] Its main concern was to apply a Marxist style of analysis to the problems facing the country. Its view was thus broader than that of the Democratic Platform, but it lacked a natural constituency; for that growing number of people who were rejecting Marxism, its basic *raison d'être* drove them away from it, while for those who remained true to traditional Soviet Marxist precepts, the Platform's support for a transition to a socialist market economy was unpopular.

But if the Marxist Platform seemed to lack a constituency, the same could not be said of the Democratic Platform. Its call for the transformation of the party into a social democratic parliamentary party, with the consequent jettisoning of much of what the CPSU had stood for, must have seemed to many disgruntled party members to be one answer to the impasse into which the party was drifting. Gorbachev himself was to prove sympathetic to this view. The Democratic Platform's call for the party to compete on its merits, and their recognition of its inability to be able thus to compete unless it underwent change, was forcefully emphasised by many of the republican election results in spring 1990, and by the fact that in a series of party organizations early in the year unpopular party leaders were ousted as a result of popular pressure; in such places as Tiumen, Voroshilovgrad, Donetsk, Kostroma, Cheboksary, Sverdlovsk, Ufa, Chernigov, Tomsk, Volgograd and almost one third of obkoms in Ukraine, unpopular leaders were forced from office.[67]

The organisational fragmentation of the party destroyed the principle of monolithic unity which had been its chief characteristic since 1921, and transformed it into an ideological battleground; by 1991 there were said to be at

---

[64] 'K gumannomu demokraticheskomu sotsializmu', *Pravda*, 13 Feb. 1990.

[65] For one discussion, see Michael McFaul and Sergei Markov, *The Troubled Birth of Russian Democracy: Parties, Personalities, and Programs* (Stanford, Hoover Institution Press, 1993), 94–5. Also Gill, *Collapse*, 122–4; and Devlin, *Rise of the Russian Democrats*, 190–5.

[66] See Gill, *Collapse*, 124–5.                                              [67] Ibid., 98.

least ten[68] different tendencies in the party. The disintegration of party unity was matched by growing disillusionment among rank-and-file party members. One symbol of this was the fact that for the first time since 1954 the party shrank between 1989 and 1990; this followed minimal growth in 1988.[69] In 1990 and the first half of 1991, the party shrank by 25 per cent, losing 4.2 million members.[70] More people were leaving the party than were joining, while many of those who remained formally within its ranks had lapsed into passivity or were even engaged in anti-party activity; non-payment of party dues became chronic, and by mid-1991 party income was less than half expenditure.[71] Especially in the more nationalistic republics, large numbers of party members were supporting nationalist organizations that were rejecting the continuation of Soviet rule. In some regions where strike activity had broken out, party members had been prominent in its organization. Party organizations in various parts of the country lapsed into disuse as members ceased to attend meetings or carry out their party responsibilities. The declining utility of the party in the eyes of many was reflected in the decreased circulation levels of the party press. Popular opinion polls also registered the decline in the authority of the party in the eyes of the Soviet people.[72] The party, the chief control mechanism of the system and the organizational basis upon which the political elite rested, was disintegrating. With it went the last shreds of the unity of the system as a whole.

The political elite had no answer to this problem. In response to the growth of intra-party factions, in April 1990 the CC issued a letter entitled 'For Consolidation on a Principled Basis'.[73] While acknowledging the wide diversity of views that existed within the party, this letter called for organizational action against those who had attacked the party's ideological and organizational foundations and Lenin and Leninism, including the Democratic Platform. Those who seek to split the party from within and deny the socialist choice of the Soviet people (by wanting to turn the party into a social democratic entity) must be removed from the party.[74] This call for the use of organisational measures against those who questioned the party's organizational and ideological foundations found some support among party officials at various levels of the party, but it can hardly have appealed to those who were

---

[68] *Krasnaia zvezda*, 16 Mar. 1991, FBIS Soviet Union, 27 Mar. 1991. Also see the comments of Alexander Yakovlev, *Predislovie, Obval, Posleslovie* (Moscow, 1992), 161–8.

[69] For the figures, see Gill, *Collapse*, 101.

[70] *Pravda*, 26 July 1991. Also see Stephen White, 'The Failure of CPSU Democratization', *The Slavonic and East European Review*, 75: 4 (Oct. 1997), 683–4.

[71] *Pravda*, 29 July 1991. This was also due to other factors, including the drop in circulation of party publications.

[72] Gill, *Collapse*, 105. On press circulation see ibid.

[73] *Pravda*, 11 April 1990.           [74] Also see the editorial in *Pravda*, 16 Apr. 1990.

already becoming disillusioned with the party and its message. These people were looking for positive leadership rather than threats and punishment, and it was this which the leaders were unable to give.

The first six months of 1990 leading up to the convocation of the XXVIII Congress of the party in July should have been a perfect opportunity for the party leadership to seek to restore its position by enunciating a clear and direct programme of action to rescue the party and the country from the morass into which it seemed to be slipping. CC plena were held in February and March to discuss the party's draft Platform and Rules, which were to be adopted at the Congress. The Draft Platform[75] contained many broad formulae about economic reform, democratization and legal reform, including the amendment of Article 6, but it did not satisfy those who had hoped for a sense of guidance and leadership.[76] At the plenum the draft was accused of failing to give adequate leadership, of being unclear, superficial, trite and failing to give any sense of how its goals might be achieved. It was seen as a compromise document, confusing and contradictory, and designed to paper over the differences within the leadership's ranks. It showed that the leadership was out of step with both the rank-and-file and what was happening more broadly within the country. These sorts of criticisms showed the draft to be highly inadequate as a means of energizing the party and of rekindling the commitment that had been cooling. Instead of uniting the party around its leadership, the draft was perceived to have merely highlighted the differences within that leadership and to have shown how far it (and the party) was out of touch with reality.

At the March plenum approval was given for the amendment of Article 6 of the Constitution, Gorbachev was nominated as Soviet President (see below), and the new draft party Rules were discussed. Because of the way the plenum was organized (sessions were held on 11, 14, and 16 March), the discussion never gained any momentum or sense of flow. Nevertheless this did not stop severe criticism of the failure of the party leadership to offer real guidance and leadership to the party as a whole.[77] There was said to be a sense of drift, of ambiguity about goals and a real confusion of identity in the party as it seemed to be forsaking terms like 'communist' and 'marxist', while the classic formula of 'democratic centralism' was missing from the draft Rules. Again the absence of any sense of guidance from the centre was a prominent theme, and this seemed to be confirmed when the precise method of choosing delegates for the forthcoming Congress was left up to lower-level party organs to decide. The Congress was formally the supreme policy-making body of the party, but here too the absence of decisive and clear leadership was evident. The course of

---

[75] 'K gumannomu . . .' Also see Gill, *Collapse*, 106–7.
[76] *Pravda*, 6–9 Feb. 1990 for the speeches from the plenum.
[77] For the speeches see *Pravda*, 12, 17, 18, 19, 20 Mar. 1990.

pre-congress debate had done nothing to clear up the growing problems of
party organizational incoherence and party identity. The complaint made at
the February and March plena that the central leadership was not giving adequate leadership continued to be heard during the pre-congress discussions,
including at the founding conference of the Communist Party of the RSFSR.[78]
Indeed, this conference was a major platform for conservative opposition to
the course of reform to be openly expressed (see below). At the Congress,
Gorbachev's main report, which should have been expected to give the lead in
setting out a clear programme for the party for the immediate future failed to
achieve this. The view of the party which he offered[79] was one which seemed
to lack any of the organizational principles which had characterised the party
in the past and which was devoid of any firm ideological commitment; the shift
in emphasis from traditional communist rhetoric towards social democratism
was evident in his speech.[80] As a result, the way the party was presented meant
it seemed to lack any intellectual raison d'être or sense of direction. Gorbachev
was followed by a string of speeches which bemoaned the party's loss of
authority, and which attributed this largely to the reform course being pursued
by the General Secretary and those immediately around him.[81] But although
conservative, anti-reform sentiments dominated in the early days of the conference, their proponents were as unable as Gorbachev to offer a coherent
vision of what the future should be like and how the party should fit into it.
This problem of the lack of clear and decisive leadership was clearly illustrated
by the way in which the Congress adopted a much-revised version of the CC
Platform presented to the February plenum,[82] but it was adopted not as the
new party programme much heralded in recent months, but as a 'policy statement' to remain in force until a new programme could be produced. The document was clearly a compromise, even if its basic ethos was social democratic

---

[78] For a discussion of this, see Gill, *Collapse*, 126–37.

[79] *Pravda*, 3 July 1990. On the congress, see E. A. Rees (ed.), *The Soviet Communist Party
in Disarray: The XXVIII Congress of the Communist Party of the Soviet Union* (London,
Macmillan, 1992); Giuletto Chiesa, 'The 28th Congress of the CPSU', *Problems of
Communism*, 39: 4 (July–Aug. 1990), 24–38; John Gooding, 'The XXVIII Congress of the
CPSU in Perspective', *Soviet Studies*, 43: 2 (1991), 237–54; Ronald J. Hill, 'The Twenty-
eighth CPSU Congress', *The Journal of Communist Studies*, 7: 1 (Mar. 1991), 95–105.

[80] For an analysis of the way references to communism disappeared from Gorbachev's
speeches, see John Gooding, 'Gorbachev and Democracy', *Soviet Studies*, 42: 2 (Apr. 1990),
195–231.

[81] For a flavour of some of the speeches, see White, 'The Failure', 685–94. For
Gorbachev's interpretation of the Congress, which he sees in strict reformist-conservative
terms, see Gorbachev, *Memoirs*, 359–71.

[82] 'K gumannomu demokraticheskomu sotsializmu', *Pravda*, 13 July 1990. See Mark
Sandle, 'The Final Word: The Draft Party Programme of July/August 1991', *Europe–Asia
Studies*, 48: 7 (Nov. 1996), 1131–50.

rather than marxist in tone. After six months debate, the party was unable to come up with a single, clear programmatic document outlining what it stood for and where it was going. The fracturing of elite opinion and the resultant failure of leadership were palpable.

This lack of effective leadership was sharply highlighted by the way in which institutional changes made during 1990 seemed to strengthen Gorbachev's individual position of leadership while weakening the potential counter posed by the party. Important here was the establishment in March of a new position of executive presidency and the election of Gorbachev to this by the Congress of People's Deputies (by a vote of 1,329 to 495). This new position was significantly strengthened compared with that of Chairman of the Supreme Soviet which Gorbachev had formerly occupied, formally investing in him a wide range of executive powers. In the face of the growing confusion at the top of the Soviet system, with no regularized relationships between the political organizations established in 1988–89, this was an attempt to exert a powerful central executive authority. The symbolism of the creation of this position was important because it came about at the same session of the Congress of People's Deputies in which Article 6 was amended. Thus at the same time as the party's constitutionally entrenched position of dominance was eliminated, a new seemingly powerful state presidency was established. Gorbachev hoped that the presidency would provide him with the executive structure to implement policy which formerly the party had provided for the General Secretary but which was now unable to perform that function because of the disarray within the party itself. Later the same month Gorbachev set about building up the presidential apparatus with the creation of a new Presidential Council designed to advise him on the main lines of domestic and foreign policy (and thereby to replace the Politburo which, with the new membership structure to be instituted at the XXVIII Congress, was to become moribund as an effective continuing organization); an advisory Federation Council consisting of the heads of the union republican governments was also created. But this apparent strengthening of Gorbachev's personal position had some clear defects; the authority of the new post stemmed from the authority vested in the Soviet organs which established it (principally the party and the Congress of People's Deputies), but as the authority of those institutions began to erode with the decline in prestige of and commitment to the system as a whole, the position of the presidency was undercut. Gorbachev may have been able to offset this development had he stood for popular election to the presidency, but this he chose not to do.[83] This problem of the declining authority of the position is

---

[83] For a sophisticated discussion which seeks to explain why Gorbachev chose not to stand for popular election, see Brown, *Gorbachev*, 203–4.

reflected in the fact that in mid-May the Supreme Soviet felt it had to draft a law which prohibited public insults directed at the President and imposed jail sentences for those who engaged in such activity. The power of the presidency was also compromised by the absence of a new state constitution, with the result that the demarcation of powers between executive and legislature was never made clear, and by the absence of clear and effective administrative structures through which Gorbachev could project his power; the Presidential and Federation Councils were of little use in this regard. In practice, he was left largely to exhortation, and although he tried to overcome this through some institutional reconfiguration and personnel changes (see below), the presidency could never overcome the lack of institutional structures extending into society at large.

This strengthening of the institution of state President further weakened the capacity of the party. The amendment of Article 6 has already been mentioned. But perhaps just as important were the changes to the party structure made at the XXVIII Congress.[84] The nature of the Politburo was changed by altering its membership to make the republican party leaders ex officio members, and thereby ensuring that that body could not meet on a regular basis and could therefore not play a key role in decision-making.[85] The fact that only the General Secretary was also a member of the Presidential Council meant that the link between the party's leading body and what was envisaged as the leading executive body of the state was attenuated. Furthermore, the republican parties were given the power to demand a CC review of any decision made by the Politburo, thereby further undermining that body's capacity to play any effective decision-making role. A new style of CC Secretariat was also introduced, with the instruction that new commissions were to be formed because the existing ones had failed to perform satisfactorily. The powers of the CC were also downgraded. Henceforth the General Secretary and the new post of Deputy General Secretary were to be elected by the Congress rather than the CC, while membership of this latter body was to be based on a formal quota system. The CC was being turned into a representative parliament of the party, a fact reflected in the reduction in the number of officials who were members of that body and a rise in the number of rank-and-file members. In the party more generally, although organised factions remained outlawed, 'platforms' and 'horizontal structures' were now allowed, while republican parties were given the right to work out their own programmes, normative documents, and

---

[84] For details of these changes see Gill, *Collapse*, 139–41.

[85] The ex officio nature of much of its membership, the General Secretary, Deputy General Secretary, and republican leaders, also means that the Politburo ceased to be a useful measure of the balance of reformist–conservative forces at the top of the Soviet political structure. As well as the ex officio members, seven were elected by the CC.

resolution of issues. The main effect of the organisational changes ushered in at the XXVIII Congress was to reduce the power of central direction within the party, withdraw the party from state administration, and increase the likelihood of incoherence in the party's internal life. Combined with the creation of the executive presidency, this seemed like a significant shift of power in favour of the state presidency and of Gorbachev in particular. But this apparent concentration of power still did not enable him to exercise effective leadership.

The establishment of the executive presidency and Gorbachev's ascension to it, and thereby his creation of an institutional power base separate from the party, plus the strength of the conservative pressure within the party, has caused some commentators to question why Gorbachev did not leave the party and seek to push through reform from his new power base.[86] In this view, Gorbachev was now ideally placed further to sideline the party conservatives and to use his new institutional standing to reach out to those more radical reformers like Yeltsin and press the reform path more vigorously. Furthermore, his retention of both posts seemed to compromise both his stated belief in the need to remove the party from power and himself personally because it directly tied him to what many saw to be the main barrier to reform, the party. This is a logical position, but fails to appreciate two factors. First, Gorbachev seems to have remained convinced until the aftermath of the August 1991 putsch of the reformability of the party. Along with this went a conviction that the party had a positive role to play in the new Soviet Union that he hoped was emerging, but also the realization that if he did not stay in the party, his ability to drag it in a social democratic direction was going to be compromised. Second, and linked with this, was his realisation that, should he leave the party, the likelihood was that it would be taken over completely by those opposed to such a course.[87] It was already widely suspected that those leaving the party included a significant number who supported the radicalization of the public agenda that a move in a social democratic direction constituted, but were disappointed by the continuing opposition to it by wide sections within the party; most significantly at the XXVIII Congress this included Boris Yeltsin, the mayors of Moscow and Leningrad—Gavriil Popov and Anatoly Sobchak—and members of the Democratic Platform. Given that the party remained the only organization with its tentacles extending into all parts of the country (even if in some areas those tentacles had become significantly weakened), if it was dominated by oppositionist forces, Gorbachev believed it could still actively undermine the new course towards which he was moving. By remaining in the

---

[86] See e.g. Jonathan Steele, 'Why Gorbachev Failed', *New Left Review*, 216: 3–4 (1996), 148–9, and John Miller, *Mikhail Gorbachev and the End of Soviet Power* (London, Macmillan, 1993), 147–8.

[87] See Brown, *Gorbachev*, 196, 205–7.

party, Gorbachev believed that he could keep this conservative force at least somewhat under control.

This second factor reflects the continuing divisions within the Soviet political elite. Throughout the first six months of 1990, the political elite around Gorbachev remained unchanged, with no changes being made at either the February or March plena. However, the XXVIII Congress did change the leading organs of the party quite significantly, especially the Politburo. Given the new structure of the Politburo, with all republican first secretaries now ex officio members, only Gorbachev and his deputy Ivashko remained of the pre-congress membership. However of the former Politburo members, Kriuchkov, Medvedev, Primakov, Ryzhkov, Shevardnadze, Yakovlev, and Yazov were members of the new Presidential Council. Of these, Kriuchkov and Yazov later proved themselves to be hostile to the course reform took, and Ryzhkov and Medvedev had reservations. Only Yakovlev and Shevardnadze were ardent supporters of the new course, and they were to leave Gorbachev by the end of the year (see below). So within the political elite, there was still a division over the course of change, and as the pace of that change accelerated, this division could only widen.

But at least as important as this continuing division at the top was the growing evidence of polarization at the second level of the elite. Major champions of nationalism and the market were attaining positions of power in many of the union republics. Boris Yeltsin was the most important of these,[88] but also among this group were Lithuanian leaders Landsbergis and Brazauskas, and their counterparts in Latvia, Estonia and Georgia. Those most closely associated with Gorbachev had difficulty reaching out to these people because they represented ultimately the disintegration of the USSR, something which was abhorrent to Gorbachev and those closest to him. There was also the emergence of a more identifiable conservative force within the political, and especially party, structure. The XXVIII Congress was characterized by the strength of the conservative reaction to what they perceived as the perestroika-inspired disintegration of the country. Not only were many of the speeches highly critical of Gorbachev and his policy of perestroika, but when supporters of reform tried to present their case, they were greeted with abuse and howled down. Those like Ligachev who tempered their support for perestroika by criticism of recent mistakes received a warm reception. This sort of situation is explained by the nature of the delegates to the Congress: 45 per cent were party officials and 20 per cent managers in the economy, a result largely due to the manipulation of the selection process by the party apparat. The conservative disposition of the Congress was evident in the significant levels of votes cast in the

---

[88] On Yeltsin's role, see Dunlop, *The Rise*, esp. chs. 1 and 2.

election for CC membership against those who were most supportive of Gorbachev and his changes. The strength of the conservative showing was hardly dented by the announcement at the Congress that Ligachev was retiring from politics.

The strengthening of the conservative elements in the party at the secondary, sub-national, elite level was also evident in the establishment of the Communist Party of the RSFSR in June 1990, on the eve of the Congress.[89] Much of the impetus for this had come from Leningrad. While the case for a Russian party had been strong for some time, what made it compelling in the eyes of conservative forces in the middle of 1990 was the increasingly assertive position being adopted by the Russian Congress of People's Deputies and the Russian government, and in particular the election of Yeltsin as Chairman of the Russian Supreme Soviet. An explicitly Russian conservative counterweight was seen as being necessary to check the aspirations of the new Russian state authorities. Conservatives also seem to have seen a powerful Russian party as a potential counter to Gorbachev and the reformists around him. The conservative disposition of the new party was evident from its founding conference, where 42.3 per cent of delegates were workers in the party apparatus.[90] The conference (which was transformed into a congress in order formally to establish the new party) was dominated by conservative speeches critical of the effects of perestroika, and it elected the conservative Krasnodar party boss Ivan Polozkov first secretary of the new Russian party. The creation of the new Russian party had two important effects. First, it increased the exodus from the CPSU of liberal elements, especially among the Moscow intelligentsia, and thereby in a *de facto* sense strengthened conservative forces. Second, the creation of a conservative party comprising more than half of all members of the CPSU threatened fundamentally to change the balance of forces within the party. There was no reason why many of the functions of the central party apparatus could not be transferred to the new party, in line with the pressures prevailing in other republics, with the possible result that the central party could be stripped of much of its power and functions. Indeed, the establishment of a Russian party raised in acute form the question of the powers exercised by the central party apparatus *vis-à-vis* republican parties, thereby adding to the uncertainties surrounding the future of the party apparatus that arose from the changes that flowed from the XIX party Conference.

[89] For a discussion of this, see Gill, *Collapse*, 126–30; Robert W. Orttung, 'The Russian Right and the Dilemmas of Party Organisation', *Soviet Studies*, 44: 3 (1992), 445–78; and Joan Barth Urban and Valerii D. Solovei, *Russia's Communists at the Crossroads* (Boulder, Westview, 1997), 37–46. Many of the other republican party leaders, especially in Central Asia, were also clearly in the conservative camp.

[90] *Pravda*, 21 June 1990.

The split in the party was a formal and public division that had significant implications for the course of political development in the last stages of the Soviet period. But for the long-term structuring of Russian development, perhaps even more important was the differentiation that was occurring within Soviet administrative, economic and intellectual (mainly in the research institutes) officialdom. While it is clear that the oppositionist stance to the continuing radicalization of reform adopted by some leading politicians was solidly supported by sections within the Soviet intelligentsia and administrative apparatus, it is also clear that other sections became supportive of the trend espoused by those around Gorbachev. The growth of these supporters of change within the interstices of the Soviet regime itself was crucial because it created a constituency that controlled resources that could be influential in shaping the contours of that change, and it prevented the Soviet apparatus from wielding the sort of unalloyed power that could have seriously hindered the transmutation of reform into transformation. It also created a crucial group able to take personal advantage of the Soviet collapse, and in so doing help to shape the course of post-Soviet development.

One source of the support for transformation of the Soviet system by these people was intellectual: many knew the problems of the Soviet (especially economic) system and had come to believe that movement in a democratic and market direction was essential if the country was to survive. This was certainly the view of many reform economists who came to prominence in 1990–91, and there is no reason to believe that similar convictions were not shared within the administrative apparatus. But also important were the opportunities for personal gain that were involved in the shift to the market.[91] Given the increasingly disjointed economic situation and the continuing question marks over the legitimacy of private economic activity, those best placed to take advantage of the new opportunities were those with the connections and insider knowledge that came from holding responsible office in the Soviet bureaucracy. A number of elements were important in this:[92]

[91] For a general argument along these lines, and some examples, see Kotz and Weir, *Revolution*, esp. ch. 7. It is striking in this context that, through his policies, Gorbachev provided little incentive for officials to support change. Rather he threatened them with punishment for failure to support it.

[92] For discussion of this issue, see Kotz and Weir, *Revolution*, and Olga Kryshtanovskaia and Stephen White, 'From Soviet *Nomenklatura* to Russian Elite', *Europe–Asia Studies*, 48, 5 (July 1996), 716–21. For the argument, paradoxically quoting Trotsky, that Soviet bureaucrats were from the beginnings of the regime exercising a form of ownership over the state's resources and sought to transform this into private ownership, see Yegor Gaidar, *Gosudarstvo i evoliutsiia* (Moscow, Evraziia, 1995), 103–40, esp. 126. He also refers to those who functioned in the 'bureaucratic market' that was the Soviet system as a ' "pre-civil" society'.

a) Foreign contacts facilitated the development of opportunities for trade and speculative gain, especially given the low world prices for Soviet natural resources. Such international opportunities were a crucial stimulant to the development of joint stock companies, legalised in 1986.

b) The conversion of paper assets into cash was something which, after 1987, could only be carried out by the Centres for the Scientific and Technical Creativity of Youth. These were bodies created by the Komsomol to provide commercial services to enterprises, and by expanding their activities, they developed a fully-fledged so-called 'Komsomol economy'.[93] In the absence of commercial banks, these Centres became potentially significant profit generators.

c) Access to favourable rates of credit was available only to those with personal contacts into relevant sectors of officialdom.

d) Access to state property was monopolised by officialdom. Those with inside knowledge were able to purchase state property at nominal prices, or to get a cut from the rental of such property to foreign and other entities.

e) Privatization of assets for which they were officially responsible. There was a variety of ways in which such privatization could occur,[94] but the effect was the same: public assets were appropriated by officials long before any official privatization policies were introduced. This occurred in all spheres of activity, including state ministries, state banks, retail trade and industrial enterprises.[95] State assets and premises were turned into private concerns by their former administrative controllers.

Through the exploitation of these sorts of opportunities, many state bureaucrats were able to turn administrative control into private ownership and themselves into entrepreneurs. This process of the transformation of power into property proceeded by stealth, behind the back so to speak of civil society which had not developed the means to scrutinise let alone forestall this process.

The dimensions of this process are not clear, but it seems to have been extensive.[96] It was stimulated by the legislation freeing up economic activity,

[93] Kryshtanovskaia and White, '*Nomenklatura*', 716, 718.

[94] See e.g. Simon Clarke, 'Privatization and the Development of Capitalism in Russia', *New Left Review*, 196: 11–12 (1992), 3–27, and Simon Johnson and Heidi Kroll, 'Managerial Strategies for Spontaneous Privatisation', *Soviet Economy*, 7: 4 (1991), 281–316.

[95] Kryshtanovskaia and White, '*Nomenklatura*', 720–1. For a discussion of how commercial banks emerged from state structures, see Joel S. Hellman, 'Bureaucrats vs Markets? Rethinking the Bureaucratic Response to Market Reform in Centrally Planned Economies', in Susan Gross Solomon (ed.), *Beyond Sovietology: Essays in Politics and History* (Armonk, M. E. Sharpe Inc., 1993), 53–93.

[96] For a suggestive but by no means conclusive study of elite attitudes which bears upon this question, see Judith S. Kullberg, 'The Ideological Roots of Elite Political Conflict in Post-Soviet Russia', *Europe–Asia Studies*, 46: 6 (Sept. 1994), 929–53.

especially the legalization of joint ventures and cooperatives and the law on the state enterprise. The influence of this pro-market force cannot be unambiguously identified, but it may be evident in the radical nature of the economic debate in 1990–91, the time when many officials were leaving the party and concentrating their activities in state bodies (which could, unlike party structures, generate commercial structures) or commercial structures. The economic debate of these years (see below) reflected a division between different economic sectors. The programme of a measured shift to a market economy with a central role maintained by the state was favoured by managerial and industrial interests—that is, those sectors most dependent upon continuing state support. The defence industry and more conservative bureaucratic interests were also to be found here. In contrast, the 500 Days rush to a market economy involving the replacement of state distribution by commodity exchanges and wholesale firms, the withdrawal of state subsidies for industry, the demonopolization of the fuel and energy sectors, and the decollectivisation of agriculture, was favoured by the new financial-commercial concerns active in trade, export-import and currency speculation.[97] The 500 Days Programme was also vigorously supported by radical members of the economic intelligentsia. Furthermore, this policy was seen to be linked to the destruction of the power of the central Soviet state, and was therefore embraced by Yeltsin. This was the link between the Russian leader and pro-market elements of the central Soviet bureaucracy that was significant in eroding the positions of both the conservative opposition and Gorbachev.

The radicalization of the public agenda by elements outside the Soviet leadership and the strengthening of conservative opposition in the party was also reflected in the policy domain. Particularly important here was economic policy. By spring 1990, it was clear that the economic reforms introduced in previous years had not had a beneficial effect on the economy; in fact, Soviet economic performance had deteriorated.[98] The main problem was that many of the links between different parts of the Soviet economic system had broken down, and replacements had not yet emerged. The result was that various parts of the country were imposing economic blockades on their neighbours, including for a short time the blockade of Moscow by its surrounding regions as local administrations refused to export goods from their areas.[99] Widespread shortages and increasing popular dissatisfaction occurred; by mid-1990 only 7 per cent of people expressed full trust in the country's leadership.[100] Furthermore, from the middle of 1990, republican governments, and in particular that of Russia, began to wrest control over taxation powers

---

[97] This analysis follows Urban and Solovei, *Russian Communists*, 66.

[98] For a discussion and some figures, see White, *Gorbachev and After*, 116–18, 127.

[99] *Pravda*, 14, 16 June 1990.                              [100] Walker, *Six Years*, 206.

and revenues away from the centre, thereby significantly weakening the capacity of the centre and exacerbating economic dislocation.

In response to the growing economic difficulties, in the first half of 1990 there was increased debate around economic policy and a radicalization in its nature. This marked the decisive shift to transformation in the economic sphere. In December 1989 Prime Minister Ryzhkov had outlined a plan for a staged economic reform which was to last until 2000 and was to involve the strengthening of market elements.[101] Although not particularly radical in the light of what was to come, this proposal was important because it reflected high-level official acceptance of the need for the introduction of market forces into the economy. In February 1990 the CC plenum approved a programme of 'radical economic reform' which involved a market economy and the possibility of the private ownership of the means of production.[102] It is clear that radical, pro-market economic reform was high on the political agenda at this time. However, Gorbachev's spokesman Nikolai Petrakov made clear in late April Gorbachev's opposition to any attempt at the introduction of a shock therapy style of reform in the USSR. On 24 May Prime Minister Ryzhkov introduced a new reform proposal which provided for the transition to a 'regulated market' in three stages up to 1995.[103] This was to involve the ultimate denationalization of most state enterprises, with only the 'commanding heights' remaining in state hands, but the method of regulating the new market economy remained unclear. This seemed to be a proposal for some kind of public-private hybrid economy.

At the same time more radical thinking was taking place on this question. With the active encouragement of Boris Yeltsin, a number of economists including Grigory Yavlinsky were working on an economic reform proposal that was to result in the 500 Days Programme, which envisaged the transformation of the USSR into a full market economy within 18 months. During the summer, negotiations had been taking place between federal and republican (excluding the Baltic) representatives to draft a new union treaty which was to redefine the relationship between the republics and the centre and, hopefully as far as Gorbachev was concerned, head off the push to republican independence.

---

[101] This included most of the elements of a plan put forward by Deputy Prime Minister Abalkin in November. For the programme, see *O merakh po ozdorovleniiu ekonomiki, etapakh ekonomicheskoi reformy i printsipal'nykh podkhodakh k razrabotke trinadtsatogo piatiletnogo plana* (Moscow, 1990). For one discussion, see Hough, *Democratization*, 349–52. For Ryzhkov's discussion of this question, see Nikolai Ryzhkov, *Perestroika: istoriia predatel'stv* (Moscow, Novosti, 1992), 295–342.

[102] *Izvestiia*, 13 Feb. 1990.

[103] It was the projected increase in prices that this involved which led to panic buying in Moscow and regional refusal to export goods noted above. For the background and discussion, see Hough, *Democratization*, 358–61.

In this endeavour, Gorbachev worked in particular with Yeltsin in an attempt to achieve a satisfactory outcome. At the end of July these two leaders also agreed to cooperate in working out an appropriate approach to economic reform involving a transition to a market economy. This was to resolve the economic issues which were the analogues of the political issues to be resolved by the new union treaty. This agreement resulted in the formation of a working group headed by Soviet Presidential Councillor Stanislav Shatalin and comprising economists from both Gorbachev's and Yeltsin's circles; one member of Ryzhkov's government team also participated. By September two rival plans were on the table: the 500 Days Programme which involved massive and rapid privatization and a strict financial policy[104] sponsored by Shatalin, and the more measured Ryzhkov plan. Gorbachev was now under enormous pressure from conservative elements of the leadership; Ryzhkov and much of his government, the economic ministries, the military and the KGB all opposed the 500 Days Programme. In the middle of the month, in an attempt to bridge the gap between these two proposals, Gorbachev unveiled a 'Presidential Plan', worked out by Abel Aganbegyan as an alternative to the Shatalin and Ryzhkov proposals.[105] Gorbachev also acquired emergency powers to issue decrees on economic reform and law and order issues. During the late summer Gorbachev was trying to achieve some sort of compromise between the radical 500 Days sponsored by Shatalin and Yavlinsky and the more moderate Ryzhkov proposals, although his initial inclination seems to have been to support the more radical proponents of economic reform.

However in mid-October in what has been called 'the turn to the right', Gorbachev threw his weight behind the Presidential Plan, to the dismay of Yeltsin and Shatalin;[106] a week earlier the Russian government had authorized implementation of the Shatalin plan within Russia. This conjunction of events showed up the lack of direction in economic policy and the real problems that were emerging in the relationship between the centre and the republics, but it also highlighted the way in which Gorbachev seemed decisively to have thrown in his lot with more conservative elements in the leadership. Why did Gorbachev act in this way? [107] One reason is that during this period the levels

[104] Its official name was 'Transition to the Market: Conception and Programme'.

[105] It was called 'Guidelines for the Stabilisation of the Economy and the Transition to a Market Economy'.

[106] For Shatalin's view, see *Komsomol'skaia Pravda*, 4 Nov. 1990. For one discussion that emphasizes Gorbachev's tactics and sees him both as very powerful and highly Machiavellian, see Hough, *Democratization*, ch. 11. For Gorbachev's view, see Gorbachev, *Memoirs*, ch. 17.

[107] See Brown, *Gorbachev*, 273–4 for an explanation of this shift. Also see the discussion in Jeffrey Surovell, 'Gorbachev's Last Year: Leftist or Rightist?', *Europe–Asia Studies*, 46: 3 (1994), 465–87.

of pressure being exerted by conservatives on Gorbachev seem to have increased while the radical forces had become much more critical of him. Conservative concerns about the future of the Communist Party and of the Union more broadly had been significantly fuelled in the first half of the year; the sidelining of the party associated with the development of the presidency and the shift in rhetoric in the direction of social democratism (and away from Soviet Marxism) were both significant here. The concerns had been stimulated by a number of measures introduced in the summer and autumn. Particularly important were measures increasing civic freedoms; a law on the press which effectively allowed the private operation of media organs (12 June), the removal of the party's monopoly on radio and television (17 July), laws on religious education in schools (26 September) and the freedom of religious observance (1 October), the rehabilitation of the victims of Stalinism (13 August), and a law legalizing political parties (9 October),[108] added to the creation of the first nationwide independent union by coal miners (26 October),[109] created an image of the opening up of a new and more open political sphere than had existed before. In addition, ethnic disturbances continued to wrack the country, in the Caucasus, Kyrgyzstan and Moldavia. Economic difficulties were continuing, with the fragmentation of the Soviet economic space becoming increasingly apparent. Furthermore the more radical solutions suggested for the economy (especially the 500 Days Programme) were well received in the West and appeared to be consistent with demands on the part of such bodies as the G7 and the IMF for substantial marketization and privatization as the cost of loans the Soviet government was currently seeking. This fed into the suspicion that the government was acting at the behest of capitalist interests in the West. In foreign affairs, conservative concerns about the replacement of notions of class struggle by the primacy of universal human values, about the warmth of the relationship with the West (especially the USA), and about the loss of Eastern Europe, were heightened by Gorbachev's agreement to the unification of Germany and the possible incorporation of German forces into NATO, and by Soviet support for the USA in the Gulf War against long-time Soviet ally Iraq. Gorbachev stood guilty in their eyes of betraying Soviet interests to the West. But the conservatives realised that they could not do without Gorbachev because they had no one who could replace him. With the situation seemingly spinning even further out of control, and having gained a new, better organized and articulate voice in the parliamentary faction Soiuz and its

---

[108] This was much opposed in leading circles, having to go through four drafts before it was adopted: *Pravda*, 16 Oct. 1990.

[109] The miners also demanded Gorbachev's resignation and the removal of CPSU organizations from the workplace.

leader Viktor Alknsis,[110] conservative elements increased their pressure on Gorbachev, even urging him to use military force to restore central control.[111]

Although Gorbachev did not endorse the use of force, he did succumb to conservative pressure. Why was this? It may be that he remained uncertain about how far and how fast systemic change could be pursued, and the adoption of a programme designed to lead to a fully-fledged market economy was a major departure from what had existed in the past. But probably more important was his belief that he still needed to act in a way which would keep the conservatives in the game. This would prevent them from adopting the sorts of measures which either would have destroyed the process of change or would have led to civil war, and it would have blunted their attacks on him and thereby shored up his personal position as President. There had already been rumours about a conspiracy to seize power and the likelihood of an armed crackdown by conservative elements.[112] Given his belief in the need to draw the more conservative elements behind the shift to a market economy and the levels of pressure being exerted by those elements, plus the rapid radicalization of the public agenda during 1990, Gorbachev may have felt that he had little option but to lean toward the hardliners in autumn 1990.

In November, Gorbachev enacted a change to his governing arrangements designed to move the system more completely to a presidential one. He obtained Supreme Soviet approval for the reworking of the Federation Council comprising the heads of the fifteen union republics (this may in part have been an attempt to give the centre some power over the implementation of policy in the republics), the abolition of the Presidential Council, and the creation of a new position of Vice-President. A new Security Council responsible for defence and public order was also created, while the Council of Ministers, nominally responsible to the legislature, was replaced by a Cabinet of Ministers responsible to the President. This reorganization was criticised by republican leaders and by democrats, especially Yeltsin, as being an attempt to expand presidential power at the expense of the republics and to create a basis for dictatorship. Shortly after this a proposed new draft union treaty to structure the

---

[110] Soiuz was initially formed in February 1990, and became prominent in November–December 1990 when Alksnis emerged as an articulate and effective critic of Gorbachev. In November he publicly, albeitly implicitly, threatened Gorbachev with removal: Dunlop, *The Rise*, 147–51.

[111] See e.g. the call to Gorbachev by RCP leader Ivan Polozkov 'to take the most decisive measures to create order in the country' in *Sovetskaia Rossiia*, 16 Nov. 1990. Also the comments by former Chief of the General Staff Sergei Akhromeev in *Sovetskaia Rossiia*, 14 Nov. 1990 and by Viktor Alksnis in *Sovetskaia Rossiia*, 21 Nov. 1990 and *Izvestiia*, 24 Nov. 1990. Also see Miller, *Mikhail Gorbachev*, 166–71.

[112] e.g. on 26 November Defence Minister Yazov had to publicly deny that there was a connection between military manoeuvres and a conspiracy to seize power.

relations between centre and republics, with the republics having responsibility for their territory, economic affairs and natural resources, but with federal primacy over republican laws and federal control over foreign affairs and defence was published with Gorbachev's support. This was unacceptable to republican governments because of the control the centre retained over their economies, the primacy of federal laws, the assertion of Russian as the state language, and the absence of any acknowledgement of a right of secession.[113] At this time a secret decree was adopted enabling joint army–police patrols as a measure against unrest. In December, conservative rhetoric about the threat to the Soviet order increased. Gorbachev made a number of significant personnel changes at this time: on 2 December the liberal Vadim Bakatin was replaced as Minister of Internal Affairs by Boris Pugo, on 27 December the Gorbachev-nominated Gennady Yanaev was ratified as Vice President, and on 14 January 1991 Valentin Pavlov became Prime Minister; five days later the liberal Nikolai Petrakov resigned as Gorbachev's adviser. In addition, on 20 December long-time Gorbachev ally Eduard Shevardnadze resigned as foreign minister, warning of the approach of a dictatorship.[114] This move, added to the withdrawal of Yakovlev following Gorbachev's rejection of the 500 Days Programme (which he had supported) and abolition of the Presidential Council (upon which he sat), removed the last high profile proponent of radical transformation from Gorbachev's side. Gorbachev's apparent turn toward the hardliners who wanted to shore up the centre and maintain social order was accompanied by the strengthening of conservative forces around him and the desertion by key allies.

Gorbachev was not wholly captured by the conservatives, nor did the shift toward system transformation end. Formally at least the policy remained one of a transition to a market economy, and the commitment to a new union treaty seems to have been undiminished. A presidential decree on 5 January provided for the distribution of farmland to individuals and cooperatives (although it did not mention private property). However, the real symbol of the conservative ascendancy in Moscow seemed to be the military activity in Lithuania and Latvia in January 1991. At least partly in response to continuing popular agitation, Soviet security troops seized various facilities in the capitals, Vilnius and Riga, killing a number of people in the process. This activity raised a storm of protest among the radical democrats and many other more moderate groups, and although Gorbachev may have had no prior knowledge of the

---

[113] A new draft was published in March 1991 providing a highly restricted right of secession within a much looser federation. See below.

[114] For his discussion of this, see Eduard Shevardnadze, *Moi vybor. V zashchitu demokratii i svobody* (Moscow, Novosti, 1991), 320–30.

decision to use force in Vilnius,[115] his failure publicly to condemn the actions of his troops condemned him in the eyes of many in the USSR. In the initial months of 1991, as those favouring reform deserted Gorbachev, rumours became stronger about the possibility of a conservative crackdown. Despite continued popular demonstrations in support of reform (including one of more than 100,000 people in Moscow on 20 January 1991 protesting against events in the Baltic and one of 400,000 on 2 February sponsored by Democratic Russia), the warnings about the coming dictatorship that emanated from reformist circles seemed to be closer to catching the reality of Soviet life. The contrast seemed stark in late March 1991 when a large popular demonstration in support of Yeltsin and opposed to those in the Russian Congress of People's Deputies who sought to depose him, prompted Gorbachev to call troops onto the streets of Moscow. While the public confrontation between troops and citizens led eventually to the withdrawal of the troops and the shifting of the demonstration from the centre of the city (and was therefore a compromise outcome), for many Gorbachev was cast in the guise of a hard-line defender of a dying order. Perhaps more importantly, his use of troops united the majority of the Russian Congress of People's Deputies behind Yeltsin as an anti-centre force. The differences within the Russian legislature were thereby largely subordinated to the struggle against Gorbachev's centre.

The major source of organized opposition to the more conservative course being followed by Gorbachev came from Yeltsin and the Russian government. Beating his populist drum, Yeltsin used whatever public fora he could to criticize Gorbachev and the conservatives and to press for a radicalisation of the reform programme; on 19 February he publicly called on Gorbachev to resign, while on 9 March he called on his supporters to 'declare war' on the Gorbachev leadership. This line was supported by popular demonstrations[116] and by strike activity among the miners in various parts of the country in early March. There was also significant support from within the ranks of the civic opposition, although the effect of this was muted by the continuing splits and fragmentation within these organizations,[117] and from some of the republican governments.[118] Early in March, Gorbachev nominated a new Security

---

[115] Brown, *Gorbachev*, 279–83. Although Gorbachev's tough language threatening martial law a few days earlier did help to set the scene. Many believe Gorbachev was involved in the planning: See Hough, *Democratization*, 396–8. For Gorbachev's view, see Gorbachev, *Memoirs*, 578–81.

[116] For some figures on the pro- and anti-Yeltsin demonstrations at this time, see Dunlop, *The Rise*, 32, 33.

[117] Fish, *Democracy*, 49–50.

[118] Of the 15 republican presidents at this time, six were independants with links to national fronts or non-communist organizations, three were nominally Communist Party

Council consisting of Yanaev, Pavlov, Bessmertnykh, Pugo, Kriuchkov, Yazov, Primakov, and Bakatin, a majority of whom were clearly in the conservative camp. At this time negotiations were still continuing around the proposed union treaty, a draft of which was published early in March.[119] Later that month a crucial strengthening of Gorbachev's position seemed to occur with the national referendum scheduled to pass judgement on whether the USSR should be preserved. Despite the refusal to participate by the Baltic (earlier republican-sponsored plebiscites in Estonia and Latvia had overwhelming majorities in favour of independence), Armenian, Georgian, and Moldavian governments, the referendum showed a clear majority of those who voted favoured the maintenance of the Soviet Union.[120] Within Russia, the referendum also supported the institution of a directly elected presidency, a development which was to greatly strengthen Yeltsin compared with Gorbachev when later in the year he used this to gain a popular mandate. The date for such an election was tentatively set for July.

In April, a crucial turn around in the process occurred. With political tension growing, widespread strike activity continuing, and the Yeltsin-led Russian government taking the lead among the republics in pushing back renewed attempts by the conservative Soviet government to reassert central power, on 23 April the USSR Supreme Soviet adopted an 'anti-crisis programme' proposed by Pavlov, which included a ban on strikes. However, on the same day the Pavlov programme was introduced, it was announced that negotiations between Gorbachev and the leaders of nine of the republics (excluding Estonia, Latvia, Lithuania, Moldavia, Armenia, and Georgia) had led to the signature of what came to be called the Novo-Ogarevo agreement. This involved a commitment to a new union treaty which would effectively have stripped most power away from the centre and vested it in the republican capitals.[121] The agreement also recognised the right of republics not to enter

leaders who worked closely with such fronts and organisations, and six were considered pro-Moscow. Donald R. Kelley, 'Gorbachev's Democratic Revolution: Coping with Pluralism in Soviet and Post-Soviet Politics', in Gary D. Wekkin *et al.* (eds.), *Building Democracy in One-Party Systems. Theoretical Problems and Cross-Nation Experiences* (Westport, Praeger, 1993), 174.

[119] *Izvestiia,* 9 Mar. 1991.

[120] Despite the failure of six republics to participate, 80 per cent of the adult population of the Soviet Union voted, with 76.4 per cent supporting the maintenance of the federation. This figure did not fall below 70 per cent in any republic. *Pravda,* 27 March 1991.

[121] There had been four drafts of this treaty, each successive one making the centre weaker and the republics stronger. The first one had been strongly centralist, and diluted the power of the union republics by making virtually no distinction between them and the autonomous republics. The final one was unveiled on 14 August. Negotiations had begun in August 1990. See the discussion in Hough, *Democratization,* ch. 12.

the union[122] and that the union had to be reconstituted by way of a new union treaty and constitution between sovereign states. If implemented, this would have turned the country into a confederation with a very weak centre. The new union treaty was to be signed on 20 August following further negotiation on some of its features. Gorbachev had seemingly swung away from the conservatives and back into the camp of those insistent on transformation of the system.

The response at the CC plenum on 25 April to Gorbachev's swing away from the conservatives was predictable; Gorbachev came under bitter attack. Once again he blunted this by threatening to resign; the conservatives recognised that they had no leader of national standing who had any hope of keeping the union together, and buckled. Just as Gorbachev continued to believe that the reform process needed the conservatives, so they realised that they would be unable to achieve their aim of a continuation of the USSR without Gorbachev.

Throughout the first half of 1991, radical and conservative tendencies continued to struggle for dominance within the disintegrating Soviet polity. In economic policy, the conservative tenor of the Pavlov programme, which reflected his opposition to a rapid shift to the market, was tempered. In April a law on entrepreneurship effectively legalised private enterprise and recognized the equality of private property with other forms of ownership.[123] On 1 July a timetable was established for the removal of enterprises from state control and the passing of them into non-state hands.[124] But more important than economic reform, was the continuing problem of federal relations. Increasingly some republican governments, especially those of the Baltic republics and Russia, flexed their muscles, encroaching ever more on federal prerogatives; Yeltsin's banning of Communist Party organizations in workplaces in June was particularly inflammatory here. The Russian government in particular moved to extend its control over virtually all areas of the economy to the exclusion of the Soviet authorities; the assertion of Russian control over the mines was also important, coming as it did with an end to strike activity in these regions. Ethnic tension and conflict continued out of control in the Caucasus while border tensions and clashes occurred in the Baltic. At the same time, continuing discussion was taking place around the draft union treaty, while public organizations in a number of republics (including the Baltic, Armenia, Georgia and Moldavia) continued to mobilise to press their cases for full independence in the lead-up to the proposed signature of that treaty. In

[122] Procedurally the USSR would have to be dissolved and a new union constituted.

[123] 'Ob obshchikh nachalakh predprinimatel'stva grazhdan v SSSR', *Izvestiia*, 10 Apr. 1991.

[124] 'Ob osnovnykh nachalakh razgosudarstvleniia i privatizatsii predpriiati', *Vedomosti S'ezda narodnykh deputatov SSSR i Verkhovnogo Soveta SSSR*, 32: 7 (Aug. 1991), 1324–35.

Russia, preparations and campaigning for the popular election of the President took place against a background of growing sentiment for independence. When the election was held on 12 June, Yeltsin won with 57.3 per cent of the vote;[125] at the same time the radicals Popov and Sobchak were elected mayor respectively in Moscow and Leningrad. Importantly, and in contrast to Gorbachev, Yeltsin now had a popular mandate. In the face of these obvious advances, in mid-June Soviet Prime Minister Pavlov persuaded the Supreme Soviet to grant him emergency powers, but Gorbachev was able to persuade this body to reverse its decision. Had Pavlov's move been successful, it would have constituted a putsch against Gorbachev. This move was buttressed by heightened rhetoric about attempts by Western countries to undermine the Soviet Union. In July a letter in the press signed among others by two members of the government, Gromov and Varennikov, obliquely threatened military action against Gorbachev,[126] while in the July CC plenum Gorbachev again came under strong conservative attack; many members were enraged by the draft party programme which Gorbachev presented, which was clearly much more social democratic in tone than it was communist.[127] At the same time, Gorbachev was becoming more supportive of an economic reform pro-gramme championed by Yavlinsky and Harvard scholar Graham Allison, a plan which, had it been implemented, would have been as radical in its impact on the economy as the 500 Days Programme of 1990. In the summer of 1991, Gorbachev was moving even more firmly in favour of the market, of a social democratic party, and of a new type of federal structure for the state. His posi-tion on the state was reflected in the new draft of the union treaty made pub-lic on 14 August, which rendered the Soviet authorities dependent upon the republics for their revenue and therefore virtually economically powerless. This alarmed the conservatives, a feeling heightened by the proposed timetable for the signature of the union treaty on 20 August 1991. But this was short cir-cuited by the attempted putsch mounted on 19 August.

## The End of the Old Regime

The attempted putsch was directed at preventing the signature of the union treaty and the consequent break up of the USSR. The conservative forces,

---

[125] For a discussion of the background and circumstances, see Hough, *Democratization*, ch. 13.

[126] *Sovetskaia Rossiia*, 23 July 1991.

[127] For the plenum resolutions and the draft programme, see *Pravda*, 27 July 1991.

represented by the so-called State Committee for the State of Emergency,[128] seem to have hoped that by exerting even more pressure on Gorbachev, they could persuade him to abandon his course and switch back to the conservative side. They may have had some grounds for believing that such action would bring a change in Gorbachev's position. Throughout the course of perestroika Gorbachev had oscillated between reformists and conservatives, and in the months leading up to the putsch there had been some discussion at high levels of the need to clamp down, and Gorbachev had seemingly not dissented from this; indeed, he had failed to respond vigorously to the use of force in Lithuania and Latvia in early 1991 (he had actually threatened the Lithuanians with martial law), action subsequently seen by some as a dry run for the August putsch.[129] But there is no evidence, as some have argued, that Gorbachev was complicit in the putsch attempt.[130]

In structural terms, the putsch was a move by various components of the central political elite against another component of that elite, which would also have had the effect, had it been successful on the conspirators' terms, of reducing the influence of republican political elites. But although the initial activity was based in the Soviet elite, using sections of the mobilized armed forces as the weapon, resolution of the issue was not a function purely of that elite. The failure of the putsch was due to a range of factors, including incompetence and the poor planning of the conspirators and the lack of firm commitment on the part of the military. It was a rearguard action on the part of an increasingly demoralized Soviet elite on the defensive. But three other factors were crucial. First, Gorbachev's refusal to buckle and go along with the putsch. Had Gorbachev agreed to the plotters' proposal that he feign illness and then be brought back as President of a newly consolidated conservative regime, the putsch would not have collapsed as quickly as it did because part of the reason for the mobilization against it was the perception that Gorbachev had been illegally deposed. The absence of any legal justification for Gorbachev's removal also helped to divide the military and KGB because Gorbachev's

---

[128] This consisted of Vice President Yanaev, Prime Minister Pavlov, KGB chief Kriuchkov, Interior Minister Pugo, Defence Minister Yazov, Defence Council First Deputy Chair Baklanov, Peasants' Union head Starodubtsev, and state defence industry figure Tizyakov. All except Starodubtsev and Tizyakov had been appointed by Gorbachev. For an extensive discussion of the putsch, see Dunlop, *The Rise*, ch. 5. For Gorbachev's interpretation, M. S. Gorbachev, *Avgustovskii putch. Prichiny i sledstviia* (Moscow, Novosti, 1991), and *Memoirs*, ch. 30.

[129] On this see Brown, *Gorbachev*, 294.

[130] See the exchange between Jack Matlock, Amy Knight, Archie Brown, and Donald Jensen in ' "The Gorbachev Factor" An Exchange', *New York Review of Books*, 27 Mar. 1997, pp. 48–9 and 'Gorbachev and the Coup: An Exchange', *New York Review of Books*, 26 June 1997, p. 67

refusal to play his part denied the putsch plotters any semblance of legitimacy. Second, the leadership given by Boris Yeltsin. With his popular mandate barely two months old, the Russian President was perfectly placed to provide the leadership and focus for opposition to the putsch attempt. Unlike many other republican leaders, Yeltsin did not hesitate to come out against the putsch and to present himself as a public symbol of opposition. He was able to crystallize the opposition and concentrate it in Moscow where it could have the most effect. Third, the popular opposition to the putsch from among the Moscow citizenry. In fact, a very small number of people across the country mobilized in opposition to the putsch (there was little response to Yeltsin's call for a general strike), but what was important was that most of those were to be found in Moscow. The popular opposition that emerged, and the focusing of it around the White House where Yeltsin was to be found, undermined the morale and sense of purpose of the young troops upon whom the conspirators relied, and significantly increased the costs of any military action to press the putsch home. Ultimately this was a cost which those mounting the putsch (or at least those in control of the troops) were unwilling to pay.

This means that the intra-elite conflict at the centre was resolved principally by action initiated by a section of the elite in the Russian republic. This was a significant development, because its effect was to sideline much of the central Soviet elite from the main action in the political process. Central actors were diminished and republican ones (and especially Yeltsin) boosted, as the future of the USSR was decided principally by republican leaders. When Gorbachev returned to Moscow to be publicly humiliated by Yeltsin, he was a leader without a power base. On 24 August he resigned as party General Secretary,[131] but not before Yeltsin had suspended the party throughout Russia and nationalised its property; at the end of the month, the party was suspended throughout the entire USSR, while on the eve of the anniversary of the revolution, Yeltsin formally banned the party. In any case the party was haemorrhaging internally as members now left in large numbers. The demise of the party and his resignation from it now left Gorbachev with only his state office, but this was an office with a disintegrating foundation. Between the putsch and late September, eleven republics declared their independence: Estonia, Latvia, Ukraine, Belarus, Moldavia, Georgia, Azerbaijan, Kyrgyzstan, Uzbekistan, Tajikistan, and Armenia (Lithuania had declared her independence on 11 March 1990), although only the Baltic states received international recognition. The Soviet government was being left a government without a state to govern. Furthermore, republican governments, and especially the Russian,

---

[131] But not before publicly restating his earlier position that the renewed party still had an important part to play in the Soviet future. His position was clearly out of touch with contemporary reality.

stepped up their efforts to take over parts of some of the central state ministries and to give them a republican jurisdiction.[132] The central Soviet government was disintegrating.

While the Soviet structure was disintegrating around them, the political elites were manoeuvring. Many of those who had come to oppose Gorbachev's course and who were left without a political organization because of the suspension of the Communist Party now joined other small political groups, retired from political life, or simply waited in the hope that the party would be restored. Those members of the nomenklatura who had been taking advantage of the Soviet disintegration to acquire state assets and thereby set themselves up, continued to do this. They were joined by many newcomers who could see that the future lay with a freed-up market economy, and that to prosper in it, they needed to control economic assets. Some of those who had surrounded Gorbachev remained with the former leader, finding an institutional home in the newly founded Gorbachev Foundation. Others sought to enter republican politics, especially joining those administrations of a more reformist tendency. Others simply retired.

Gorbachev himself continued to try to conduct negotiations with republican leaders in an attempt to maintain the union.[133] He pressed for a new union treaty, and by mid-November seemed to have the agreement of seven republics. However, some republican leaders were also negotiating among themselves, and in December they made a deal which both excluded Gorbachev and ended the USSR, the Belovezha Accords; on 8 December the leaders of Russia, Ukraine and Belarus agreed to the establishment of the Commonwealth of Independent States, while two weeks later the CIS was formally established with all former republics as members except for those in the Baltic region and Georgia. The CIS was a loose confederation, and could in no sense be seen as an institutional extension of the USSR. Gorbachev had been rendered irrelevant; he resigned as President of the USSR on 25 December, and the Soviet Union ceased to exist, being replaced by 15 independent states.

In Russia, Yeltsin was the big victor from the failure of the putsch. His personal authority, already substantial as a result of his popular election in June, was increased enormously by his role in foiling the putsch. He used this authority to eliminate the Communist Party from the political scene, to take over central Soviet governmental institutions, and to announce the introduction of a radically pro-market economic policy in October, to come into effect

---

[132] For details and a discussion of the situation within the Yeltsin camp, see Hough, *Democratization*, ch. 14.

[133] For a discussion of this period by someone close to Gorbachev, see Andrei S. Grachev, *Final Days: The Inside Story of the Collapse of the Soviet Union* (Boulder, HarperCollins, 1995).

at the beginning of 1992. It was his activism which was chiefly responsible for the failure of Gorbachev's attempts to keep alive the union concept. His personal authority and support by his democrat allies enabled him to push through these measures despite reservations about aspects of them among other elements in the Russian legislature. These reservations were to have a significant impact in structuring developments in 1992–93.

## The Gorbachev Heritage

The fall of the Soviet regime opened the way for the construction of a new set of political arrangements in the former republics of the USSR, including Russia. However the construction of a new system could not occur *de novo*; it could work only with the material left it by the former system. But it is important to realise that the nature of that material was fundamentally shaped by the momentous events which had run their course in the USSR between 1985 and 1991. It was essentially the legacy of the perestroika period of Soviet rule that provided the material from which a new system had to be constructed. This inheritance was crucial for setting the broad parameters within which subsequent development could take place. Important in this was the basic dynamic of the course of reform under Gorbachev.

When Gorbachev set reform in progress in April 1985, he was surrounded by a leadership team which was balanced firmly in favour of moderate reform, but with a few holdovers from the past who would have been more content with a quiet life than the sort of disruption to their world which change would signify. However within a short space of time Gorbachev was able to get rid of these people and bring in new supporters of reform, some of whom would prove to be able to keep pace with the growth of radicalism of reform and some who would not. While the nature of reform remained moderate, the initial reform coalition of some older members of the leadership (represented most importantly by Gromyko) and some newer entrants (most importantly Gorbachev's nominal second in charge, Ligachev) remained intact. But as the course of reform became increasingly radicalized, initially from early 1987 and then with increased impetus in subsequent years, the unity of this coalition frayed. Leadership conflict became the hallmark of elite relations as the programme of change moved increasingly away from that upon which the elite had initially combined. This dynamic continued throughout the period; as the speed of radicalization increased from mid-1988 on, the capacity of members of the elite to remain abreast (even if not ahead) of it was reduced. Because Gorbachev was constrained to choose leadership colleagues from broadly traditional sources of leadership recruitment and because he wished to retain conservative support for the reform process, he could not seek leadership colleagues from among those more radical sections of society, even had he wished to do so. Consequently the pool of people from whom fellow leaders were chosen was unlikely to throw up significant numbers of those with the flexibility and openness of mind to be able to cope with the radicalization of reform. Thus as reform became more and more radical, the opposition would gain new adherents and thereby in part modify its shape. The clearest evidence for this is the identity of the August 1991 putsch leaders; none were among the leading opposition figures in 1989.[134] Continuing splits within the leadership were therefore the inevitable consequence of the course reform took, and was something which, despite his best efforts, Gorbachev could not avoid.

The split in the leadership was a significant factor in structuring both the course of politics during the Gorbachev period and the way the General Secretary himself acted. If Gorbachev could not eliminate leadership conflict, he had to find a way of reconciling this with the continuation of the reform process. The policy positions Gorbachev adopted were generally at the edge of policy consensus within the elite. While there were certainly occasions when Gorbachev either opposed or retreated from more radical positions, he was usually to be found towards the more radical end of the spectrum on most issues. However, Gorbachev seems in most cases to have been willing to trim his sails in an attempt to retain as much of the support of the conservatives as possible. The political strategy he adopted was to seek to establish and maintain a leadership consensus which would lock in both conservative and more radical elements behind the advancement of the reform programme.[135] But this sort of strategy had two consequences. First, in order to avoid the extremes, Gorbachev had to moderate and weaken many policy proposals before they were implemented. This led to the appearance of his support for a range of half-measures and the projection of him as a weak and indecisive leader. Second, his record of tacking between extremes and of supporting measures which satisfied neither side ultimately discredited him in the eyes of both conservatives and reformers. Neither trusted him, forcing him increasingly to seek new political allies in the quest to remain in power and at the head of the reform process.

[134] It is also a measure of the decline of the party that the leaders of the putsch held high state rather than party office, although some had been members of the Politburo before it was changed at the XXVIII Congress in 1990.

[135] In this sense Gorbachev was playing out the classic role of the centrist politician, trying to keep both conservatives and radicals on board while pushing the reform programme forward. To be a centrist Gorbachev did not have to be in the precise middle of the spectrum as Archie Brown argues; all that was needed was for there to be both more conservative and more radical forces which he was trying to conciliate—see Brown, *Gorbachev*, 273.

These leadership dynamics were crucial for the outcome of the attempt to reform the Soviet Union and for subsequent development. The discrediting of Gorbachev, the changing contours of both reformists and conservatives, and the way in which the process of change escaped from his control (see below) robbed him of any ability to construct agreements with opposition forces whereby they could leave politics and in return have their interests protected. No such pact, often present in transitions elsewhere, could be constructed because Gorbachev lacked the authority to guarantee protection of the inter-ests of powerful forces opposed to reform. The inability to reach such an accommodation and thereby to gain elite unity condemned the Soviet centre; with its elite divided, it could not combat the pressures emanating from some of the republican capitals, with the result that the construction of the post-Soviet future was guided overwhelmingly by people who were not part of the central Soviet elite. The Soviet centre collapsed because its elite was too divided to be able to fight successfully to sustain it.

Important in understanding this is the question of the source of the increas-ing radicalization of the reform programme and its transformation into a process of systemic change. Initially it was Gorbachev himself and his imme-diate supporters who provided the main impetus for the radicalization of reform. In this sense, the main drive came from the reformist wing of the polit-ical elite. This remained the principal dynamo of reform until early 1989. Of course it did not do this alone. From 1987 onwards, there was continuing sup-port from within society as a whole, support which Gorbachev made some efforts to foster although he never really trusted it. One effect of much of the early programme of reform was to create space precisely for civil society forces to emerge and to play a political role. While we can see a general process of development and growth of those social forces, from political clubs through fronts to parties, those organizations of civic opposition never became the leading forces for reform. They certainly contributed to the radicalization of the political agenda through their publications, demonstrations and meetings, and the involvement of their representatives in the new parliamentary organs established during this period, but they remained overwhelmingly individu-alised and predominantly narrowly focused. The weakness of the parties is rel-evant here. These were chiefly loose groupings around individual notables, with little effective organisational structure or substantive membership. The under-development of the parties was due to a number of factors: the dom-inance of the CPSU, the holding of elections before the parties were well estab-lished and their consequent inability to take advantage of the opportunities the electoral campaign offered, state pressure, the weakness of potential sources of material support for party development (this is linked to the absence of private property), the fact that parties (as opposed to legislative institutions) did not appear to be the path to political prominence (and therefore for ambitious people perhaps not worth investing time and effort), and the fact that they tended to be organized by members of the intelligentsia or Communist Party figures, both of which were isolated from the mass of the populace, were all significant.[136] Although the numbers of independent organizations continued to grow significantly over this period and although they were an important radicalizing force on the public agenda, they did not develop as effective mechanisms linking populace with polity; they did not constitute vehicles for the representation of popular interests, they did not represent clear constituencies, and they were not effective means of mobilizing the populace into politics in a structured way. Despite their numbers, parties and other civic opposition groups were not leading players in the progress of reform. This meant that, almost by default, the major players in the political process were regime elites.

This raises the issue of civil society. If civil society is defined in terms of a network of autonomous, self-organising bodies, whose existence is accepted and recognized by the state, interacting in regularised ways to place limitations on government,[137] the range of civic oppositional groups which emerged did not constitute a civil society.[138] While many of them were autonomous from the state (see below) and were self-organizing, many were tolerated rather than accepted, the sphere of public activity was ambiguous and weak, and the myriad of groups can hardly be said to have been interacting in any meaningful fashion. There was no real network of public activity which could underpin the development of a vigorous public sphere. Most groups pursued their aims in relative isolation from others, with little of the interchange between groups that is characteristic of a developed civil society. Perhaps the best illustration of this is that the most politically significant groups which emerged were the national fronts in the Baltic republics. Unlike the groups of the civic opposition, they were able to utilise the federal structures of the Soviet system itself and to sink their roots deeply into the respective populations. Rather than seeking to regulate relations between state and society, a major thrust of classic notions of civil society, what these groups sought to do was to establish their own independent states and societies on a national basis. They did not want to construct new types of power relationships within existing society; they wanted a new society.

Another problem with the attempt to interpret the events of 1985–91 in terms of a civil society is that while many of the groups were autonomous, many others were in a more ambiguous relationship with the state. It was a common tactic on the part of conservative elements in the party to foster sup-

---

[136] See the discussion in Fish, *Democracy*, 73–7, 133–4.
[137] See John Keane, *Democracy and Civil Society* (New York, Verso, 1988), 14.
[138] See the argument in Fish, *Democracy*, ch. 3.

posedly independent groups in an attempt to sow discord and confusion among genuinely independent groups and their supporters. The proliferation of groups with very similar names was due in part to this. The presence of such stalking horses in the public realm greatly increased the appearance of the diversity and organizational strength of the informal sector. But even many of those organizations which were not front organisations for conservatives but were genuine independent voices in the political landscape, were often dependent upon official state structures, at least in the early years.[139] Some relied upon official organizations for protection and material support, with pro-reform party secretaries being prominent in such activities as making premises available for meetings, providing access to printing facilities and other sorts of support. In other cases, official bodies were taken over by supporters of reform and turned into major forces pressing the reform agenda; the best cases of this were some of the official publications (including *Moskovskie Novosti*, *Ogonek* and at times even *Kommunist*) who were led by reform-minded editors. Even given this sort of institutional ambiguity, it is possible that a true civil society could have developed in the Soviet Union, that these state or semi-state bodies could have separated themselves off from the state and, in conjunction with emerging autonomous organizations, have grown into that sort of complex network of relations which underpins a mature civil society. But this clearly had not happened by the time of the putsch. Thus to talk of the development of civil society in the Soviet Union is premature. Certainly it was more developed in some parts of the country (the Baltic states) than others (Central Asia), but nowhere was it firmly entrenched and powerful. This is reflected in the fact that there were no prominent leading public activists who did not hold official office and were acknowledged as leaders of the opposition forces; the civic opposition remained weak. There was therefore no representative of society with whom the reformist elite could seek to conduct meaningful negotiations in any attempt to democratise Soviet power. In the course of this transition, the civic opposition was a vocal but essentially minor participant. This is one reason why civil society posed little organisational constraint on the state and the political elite (and was therefore also in a weak position to do so at the start of the post-Soviet period), and why the major source of influence on the course of reform emanating from outside the central political elite was nationalist.

---

[139] This follows Ding's notion of 'institutional amphibiousness': X. L. Ding, 'Institutional Amphibiousness and the Transition from Communism: The Case of China', *British Journal of Political Science*, 24: 3 (1994), 293–318. For Zhang, the nature of communist systems, and of the oppositions that were able to emerge in them, meant that there was no viable opposition for regime leaders to seek to reach a pact with: Baohui Zhang, 'Corporatism, Totalitarianism, and Transitions to Democracy', *Comparative Political Studies*, 27: 1 (Apr. 1994), 108–36. Also see White, *Democratization*, 165.

In recognising the importance of nationalist forces both in radicalizing and redirecting reform and in structuring the outcome, it is important to see that what gave this its real power was less the actions of an aroused national population (although this was significant in giving moral authority) or of national front organizations, but the role played by republican elites, and particularly that of Russia. Initially it was the Baltic governments which radicalized the agenda by pressing for national sovereignty and then independence, and then the Russian government added economic radicalism to national sovereignty and, ultimately, independence. It was this pressure on the part of the republican governments, buttressed by popular support, which transformed the whole reform process, stimulated the conservative backlash of August 1991, and determined the break-up of the Soviet state. It is important to recognize that this was effectively the second rung of the Soviet elite, those in office in the union republican capitals, which was pressing for change; even in the Baltics, the post-March 1990 governments included significant elements who had held responsible office within the Soviet system. So the pressures for reform and for change emanated less from society at large than from within the broad official structure itself. This had significant implications.

One implication is that the issue of reform became inextricably intertwined with the question of national independence. From early 1990, as Gorbachev struggled to bring about change in the political and economic structures of Soviet society, and as those changes became even more far reaching with the shift to a non-party presidential system and discussion about rapidly moving the economy onto a free market basis, power tilted away from the centre in the direction of the republics. Had the governments in all of the republics been willing to remain within a reconstituted Soviet Union, and wholeheartedly supported the drive for change at the centre, it may be that a potent coalition could have been constructed to drive the process through to a democratic and market-oriented conclusion. But the republican governments were unwilling to act in this way. Most of those which wanted to remain within the union were sceptical about some aspects of the course being taken, especially the governments of the Central Asian republics. The governments of the Baltic republics were, from their election, intent on gaining independence from the USSR regardless of the success or otherwise of Gorbachev's attempt to reconfigure the union. But they were so small that, apart from the symbolic aspect, their drive to go their own way had little practical effect. The main player was Russia. Once Boris Yeltsin gained the leadership of that republic, he used it to drive change from reform towards transformation and to seek the independence of Russia. These two aims became fused, especially after Gorbachev's turn to the right in autumn 1990: for Yeltsin and his supporters, a market economy could be achieved only in an independent Russia, liberated from the constraints of the old Soviet centre. This was implicit in the 500 Days Programme, which envisaged the effective destruction of the centre's economic powers. In this context and given Gorbachev's history of temporizing compared with Yeltsin's apparent decisiveness,[140] it should not be surprising that radical democrats flocked to Yeltsin's banner and deserted Gorbachev. In doing so, they accepted the linkage of change with national independence. Once Yeltsin was set upon this course,[141] meaningful compromise was impossible; there was no way both Gorbachev and Yeltsin could achieve what they stood for. This means that while society threw up no leaders with whom Gorbachev could reach a pact to negotiate a shift of power which protected the interests of more conservative elements, those leaders which emerged on the second rung of the Soviet power structure were not interested in any form of pact which protected the interests of the centre. Their aim was independence, and this required the destruction of that centre. When the centre was fatally weakened in the wake of the putsch, Yeltsin took the opportunity to destroy it, rendering real negotiation irrelevant.

This inability on the part of Gorbachev to negotiate a pact to defend the interests of those embedded within Soviet power structures meant that they had to defend their interests themselves. This reinforced the shift into market activity on the part of many high- and middle-level bureaucrats during the last years of the Soviet period. This experience is likely to have impressed upon them the realization that their political masters would seek their own interests regardless of the consequences for them (the embracing of market principles by politicians clearly had significant implications for Soviet bureaucrats and the likelihood of continuing employment) and therefore they should actively seek to further their own interests as best they saw fit. But they would also have been aware that their political masters could profoundly affect the likelihood of success in these efforts, and that they should therefore do all that they could to keep powerful politicians on side. This was part of the dynamic which explains the shift of allegiance by many of these people from Gorbachev to Yeltsin. The basis was thereby laid for continuing close cooperation in the new

---

[140] Although in this case appearances were deceptive.

[141] Yeltsin's decision to follow this course was not because he was an ardent Russian nationalist. He had shown no signs of such views before 1989–90. He may have been a believer in the principle of Russian independence, he may have believed that the Soviet centre was a drag on development and needed to be eliminated, and he may have become a vigorous anti-communist. All of these could have been behind his adoption of the position he took. But also important was surely his personal antagonism toward Gorbachev; an attitude which was reciprocated. This assumes that, even had the August putsch not taken place, both Yeltsin and Gorbachev could not have agreed upon a draft union treaty. The last draft published prior to the putsch suggests that negotiations were moving very strongly in the direction of satisfying Yeltsin's demands at the expense of the centre and Gorbachev.

Russia between those who moved into the commercial sphere and those who remained in the politico-administrative structures.

The dynamics of the course of reform were important for the state structure of the emergent Russian Federation not only by creating incentives for state functionaries to exploit their state positions for personal gain by moving into the commercial sphere, but also in terms of what it meant for state capacity. Although the capacity of the Soviet party-state apparatus had in practice been significantly less than envisaged by those who labelled it totalitarian,[142] it was nevertheless a powerful state with capacity to intervene in society at any point and at any time. The capacity of the central apparatus was significant, and the confidence of central apparatchiks in their ability to utilise that power effectively was high. However, the course of reform under Gorbachev undermined both that capacity and that confidence. Two aspects of the dynamic of reform affected capacity. First, a major key to the success of the Soviet party-state apparatus, internal discipline, was largely destroyed by the radicalization of reform. A continuing theme of the reformers was the way in which their reform efforts were constantly being blunted by the opposition encountered in the apparatus. Instead of being the obedient tool of a united leadership, the political structure mirrored the divisions at the top, with conflicts over the course of reform occurring at all levels. Furthermore the personalist norms entrenched in the Soviet political structure and discussed in Chapter 1 proved impervious to attempts to overcome them, with the result that the political structure remained resistant to central policy directives. The capacity of the institutional structure to carry out central instructions was thereby further eroded. This was exacerbated by the collapse of the party as a coherent institution. As this occurred, the institutional cement which had held the Soviet structure together disintegrated. By the time the putsch finally shifted the balance of power and undercut the authority of the central Soviet organs, many of those organs had already lost the capacity to govern. Filled with demoralized functionaries and internally deadlocked by the reform–anti-reform conflict, they were easily taken over by the republican governments. However, this did not solve the problem; the new masters in Russia inherited an administrative apparatus whose capacity for effective functioning remained distinctly problematic.

The second aspect of the reform dynamic affecting state capacity was the nature of the reform itself. Central to the whole reform project was a winding back of state involvement in all aspects of life. This became even more pronounced as reform shifted to transformation of the Soviet politico-economic

---

[142] For one study emphasising the limits of control exercised by central authorities, see Graeme Gill and Roderic Pitty, *Power in the Party: The Organization of Power and Central-Republicans Relations in the CPSU* (London, Macmillan, 1997).

system. It was assumed that if the project was to be successful, it had to involve a reduction in the size and functions of the state. This was the case in all areas of life, but it was particularly marked in the economic sphere, where the attempt to shift to a market system was explicitly anti-statist. But the reform process was not only one which attempted to reduce state involvement; it was one which, particularly in its pro-market theme reflected most strongly in the 500 Days Programme, was virulently anti-state. For many of the more enthusiastic advocates of the market who gained the ascendancy in the Russian government following the putsch, the state was not something which was essentially neutral and needed to be trimmed back, but was a major malign force whose influence needed to be eliminated. Their misguided trust in the capacity of market forces and civil society to immediately grow and fill the gap created by the destruction of the state and to thereby structure all aspects of social life encouraged them to denigrate the state and refuse to see that it could play a positive role in structuring future development. As the Russian government set about seeking to create the bases of a market economy, the state was therefore not seen as central to this task.

The weakness of the state inherited by the post-Soviet leaders should not only be seen in terms of its implementation functions. The state was also weak in terms of the contribution it could make to the construction of a democracy. Under Gorbachev, the institutional arena for the transition to democracy was not firmly established. The absence of effective institutional mechanisms linking the public with the political sphere (principally parties) has already been noted. But also important was the institutional configuration of the state which was emerging under Gorbachev. While a new Soviet state structure had been created in 1989–90 and in the republics in 1990, the new institutional arrangements had not become firmly embedded within the polity. The clearest evidence for this is the continuing changes made to the institution of the presidency in both the USSR and Russia right up to the eve of the putsch. In the Soviet sphere, the new legislative institutions were developing procedures for structuring their internal functioning, but in the absence of effective party groups, they remained overwhelmingly more suited to responding to initiatives from the government or President than to being active law-making bodies. This means that from the outset, they lacked real power. But this was even more marked when seen in the broader context of the overall institutional structure. In the new structure of Soviet power, the legislature was less powerful than the presidency; while this was less clear in the Russian case (and was to be worked out violently later), following the establishment of the executive presidency in 1990, there could be no question in the Soviet case even if precise constitutional relationships had still to be worked out. This means that the lore inherited by the post-Soviet polities was one of an activist and powerful

President and a less powerful legislature. While many argued that such a presidency was crucial to overcoming the problems confronting the society, comparative studies show that the prospects for the successful establishment of democracy are greater under a parliamentary system than under one in which the President in paramount.[143] But it was this latter type that was the ultimate Soviet legacy. One further problem with this is that although the lore was one of a powerful presidency, when it came to the republican level, the constitutional position remained distinctly unclear. This was to be the cause of subsequent problems (see Chapter 4).

It is clear, then, that the post-Soviet regimes carried with them a significant legacy into the future. This was a legacy not only in terms of a daunting agenda of public policy issues: an economy in ruins, an untried political system, and doubts over the nature of the national unit (aspirations for independence on the part of autonomous republics within Russia and the question of Russian national identity) to mention only the most pressing; but also of the capacity to deal with these problems. With a regime that was internally fractured, both within the central elite and between the central and regional elites, and where there were only weak civil society forces, the main dynamic of change lay in elite relations, with those civil society forces exercising some influence from the margins. The failure of Soviet reform to result in a negotiated settlement through an elite compact rather than the seizure of power by the second rung of that elite had significant implications for future politics. The weakness of the elite political arena and institutions and the weakness of civil society actors were the major parameters within which the transformation of Russian society and state had to be carried out.

---

[143] For example, see Alfred Stepan and Cindy Skach, 'Constitutional Frameworks and Democratic Consolidation: Parliamentarism vs Presidentialism', *World Politics*, 46: 1 (Oct. 1993), 1–22; and Juan J. Linz and Arturo Valenzuela, *The Failure of Presidential Democracy* (Baltimore, Johns Hopkins University Press, 1994).

# 4

# The Struggle for a Hegemonic Presidency

With the collapse of Soviet power, the Russian political elite had to fashion a new state apparatus in order to come to grips with the range of problems confronting them. This apparatus could not be constructed *de novo*. It had to involve many of the existing institutions inherited from the Soviet period. But those institutions could not remain unchanged; they had constituted the essential elements of an authoritarian political system serving a state socialist economy, but what was now needed were institutions suitable for a democratic polity and a capitalist economy. It is clear, then, that the moulding of new institutions of state would be a major arena within which shifting elite relations would be played out. In this sense, the attempt to overcome the state weakness inherited from the Soviet period fused with the fluid nature of elite relations to create an unstable political situation.

An important factor conditioning the course of political development during the first two years following the Soviet fall was the uncertainty and ambiguity in the rules governing political life. The general question here concerned the relevance of those institutions, rules, norms and procedures developed during the Soviet period to the structuring of political life in the post-Soviet period. Were bodies that were integral parts of the Soviet authoritarian political structure appropriate to a political system that aspired to democracy? Were the informal norms and practices that had emerged to structure Soviet politics consistent with the shift to a more transparent and open political system? These sorts of concerns injected into political life a significant level of ambiguity as political actors, while they groped for new patterns of politics, disagreed over what to retain from the past and what should be rejected.

This problem was symbolised most clearly during this period by the state Constitution. The Constitution inherited by the Russian authorities was that of the RSFSR introduced in 1978. It had been designed for a constituent unit of a federation (and a highly centralised one in practice), but was now the Constitution of an independent state. Furthermore, in the period between its introduction and when it was superseded at the end of 1993 (see below), it was amended on more than 300 occasions without any substantial redrafting. As a result, the document was internally inconsistent and contradictory. An important case of this concerns that institution which was to be central to the course of post-Soviet development, the presidency. When the presidency was introduced and the Constitution accordingly amended in April 1991, this office was welded onto a structure that was parliamentary in form. But those who drafted the legislation establishing the presidency had seen that office as being less powerful than the parliamentary organs; in the words of Sergei Shakhrai, chairman of the Supreme Soviet's Committee on Legislation which drafted the documents, 'I assume that in the composition of the highest organs of power in the Russian Federation, the superior role belongs to the Congress and Supreme Soviet.'[1] The Congress of People's Deputies was 'the supreme organ of state power', the Supreme Soviet was 'the standing legislative, administrative and supervisory organ of state power', while the President was 'the supreme official and head of executive power in the Russian Federation.'[2] The President was to be popularly elected, had the power of legislative initiative, directed the Council of Ministers and appointed the Prime Minister and the ministers of defence, foreign affairs, security and internal affairs with the consent of the Supreme Soviet. He was to report to the Congress annually. He also headed the Security Council, but the powers of this body were set by the parliament. The President could veto legislation but this veto could be overridden by a majority of deputies, he could declare a state of emergency but only with the agreement of the 'supreme organs of state power', and he could neither dissolve nor suspend the activity of legally elected organs while the Parliament could initiate impeachment proceedings against him. He had the power to issue binding decrees, but these could be vetoed by the parliamentary organs. The distribution of powers seemed clearly to place the presidency in a subordinate position to the legislature. However, three factors served to obscure such clarity. First, the designation of two institutions as 'supreme' raised the spectre of ambiguity. Second, the adoption of the principle of separation of powers, which seemed to underpin much of the discussion at this time, appeared to be antithetical to a notion of a presidency which was subordinate to the legislature. And third, popular election would give the president an independent popular mandate at least the equal of that of the Congress. Yeltsin was to make much of these in 1992–93.

---

[1] Cited in Timothy Frye, 'A Politics of Institutional Choice. Post-Communist Presidencies', *Comparative Political Studies*, 30: 5 (Oct. 1997), 536. For other studies of the presidency, see Stephen White, 'Russia: Presidential Leadership under Yeltsin', in Ray Taras (ed.), *Postcommunist Presidents* (Cambridge, Cambridge University Press, 1997), 38–66; John P. Willerton and Aleksei A. Shulus, 'Constructing a New Political Process: The Hegemonic Presidency and the Legislature', *The John Marshall Law Review*, 27 (1995), 787–823.

[2] See *Kto est' chto. Politicheskaia Moskva 1993* (Moscow, Satallakhu, 1993), 15, 77, 93.

## The Moulding of the Presidency

As shown above, the phase of Russian politics from March 1990 until December 1991 was dominated by a tug of war between the Soviet and republican authorities, with the latter seeking to undermine, displace and ultimately supplant the Soviet party-state. At the core of this process was Boris Yeltsin. Resting on the electoral bloc DemRossiia,[3] Yeltsin seemed to symbolize the struggle of the democrats for the displacement of communist power. United only by their determination to break the Communist Party's stranglehold on power, the democrats rallied around the slogan 'All Power to the Soviets!' This demagogic, pseudo-radical slogan became symbolic of the impression that the democrats had come to power in Russia.[4] However, in reality, power fell into the hands of neither the soviets nor the Russian Congress of People's Deputies (CPD). It was seized from the CPSU and the Soviet centre by RSFSR President and former Chairman of the Supreme Soviet of Russia, Boris Yeltsin and his circle.[5]

Yeltsin had been elected Chairman of the Russian Supreme Soviet on 29 May 1990, but it is evident that he saw this merely as a stepping stone to an executive presidency. He insisted that there was an acute crisis of executive authority. Yeltsin's opponents in the Russian CPD were wary of a presidential system because they realised that, given his position as Chairman of the Supreme Soviet, he would be the front runner to fill such an office were it to be established; they realised that the establishment of the Russian presidency was a 'political act inseparable from the issue of who would fill the office.'[6] The opportunity to resolve this issue in Yeltsin's favour came with the March 1991 referendum on the shape of the new Union. Almost 70 per cent of Russians voted in favour of a popularly elected President. On 5 April, the Russian CPD now not only acceded to elections for a President, but it also accepted Yeltsin's demand for immediate powers to issue presidential decrees within the existing

[3] For a contemporary analysis of the component parts of DemRossiia, see *Argumenty i fakty*, 46, 1990.

[4] A. Kol'ev, *Miatezh nomenklatury: Moskva 1990–93* (Moscow, Intellekt, 1995, 2nd corrected edn.), 12, 14. In their programme DemRossiia called on the First Congress of People's Deputies of the RSFSR to 'take *complete state power in the RSFSR*, having failed to do so at an all-Union level' (emphasis in original).

[5] Roger D. Markwick, 'An Uncivil Society: Moscow in Political Change', in Vladimir Tikhomirov (ed.), *In Search of Identity: Five Years Since the Fall of the Soviet Union* (Melbourne, University of Melbourne, Centre for Russian and Euro-Asian Studies, 1996), 41.

[6] Michael E. Urban, 'Boris El'tsin, Democratic Russia and the Campaign for the Russian Presidency', *Soviet Studies*, 44: 2 (1992), 187.

legislative framework to further Russian 'reform'. On 12 June 1991 Yeltsin was elected President of Russia with 57 per cent of the votes in the first round.[7] Yeltsin's election as President was seen as far more than a mere change of leadership title. It was seen as symbolic of the birth of a new Russia.

It is clear that Yeltsin saw the presidency as a means of advancing his personal ambitions. But the question remains as to why Russia opted for a presidential form of government as opposed, for example, to a Westminster style prime ministership (support for a presidency came even from Communists of Russia, at least until they saw Yeltsin could well occupy that post).[8] Could not Yeltsin's ambitions have been satisfied as Chairman of the Russian Supreme Soviet? Plainly there is more at issue here than ambition. It suggests that very early in the piece Yeltsin recognised that if he was to lead a decisive break with the legacy of Soviet state socialism, then he could not do so without establishing an institutional platform entirely separate from existing Soviet-era institutions. In this regard there was the precedent of Gorbachev becoming Soviet President. But Yeltsin made it clear that his administration, unlike that of Gorbachev, would not be deterred from a final reckoning with Soviet socialism and the radical transformation of Russian politics and society. To achieve this, Yeltsin required a kind of Bonapartism[9]—a regime more or less independent of particular interests, especially popular interests, that might well resist the kind of fundamental changes that market measures would necessarily entail. The necessity for a regime which could break decisively with the old Soviet order was implied in the comment by a director of Yeltsin's May 1991 presidential election campaign: 'We are facing an economic crisis and we need presidential action immediately'.[10]

It was intended that the president and his administration would form the nucleus of a new state apparatus with which to oversee the transition from a state socialist system to a capitalist system. The problem facing the new Russian leaders was, as RSFSR State Counsellor Sergei Stankevich succinctly put it,[11] that they were faced with two simultaneous tasks. They needed to establish a 'strong and effective state', while at the same time using that state 'as a tool for accelerating reforms'. In other words, the new Russian apparatus of state, which it was intended should oversee the introduction of the new democratic capitalist order, could only be built from the remnants of the old Soviet state-socialist apparatus. Moreover, this transformation of state and society was not being conducted in the most propitious conditions. The 'reserve of

---

[7] Richard Sakwa, *Russian Politics and Society* (London and New York, Routledge, 1996, 2nd edn.), 140–1.

[8] Urban, *Boris El'tsin*, 188.          [9] Sakwa, *Russian Politics*, 56.

[10] Cited in Urban, *Boris El'tsin*, 190. See *Izvestiia*, 5 Dec. 1991.

[11] 'The Traps that lie in Wait for Us', interview with Sergei Stankevich in *Megapolis-Express*, 12 Dec. 1991, Current Digest of the Soviet Press, XLIII, 50 (1991), 22.

social patience was almost exhausted before the real reforms began', thus threatening a 'social explosion'. In these circumstances, Stankevich concluded, 'the government has only one significant reserve at its disposal—the personal popularity and authority of the president'.

Symptomatic of the pivotal role of Yeltsin personally and of his determination that he should not be beholden to any one particular interest is his passage to power. He rode to power on the back of DemRossiia (and militant miners) and then abandoned it.[12] While Yeltsin had relinquished membership of DemRossiia prior to contesting the election for Chairman of the Supreme Soviet in 1990, he remained its symbolic leader. He closely identified with its call for the dissolution of the Soviet state and the 'departification' of Russia's public institutions (that is, the exclusion of the Communist Party from state institutions and enterprises).

DemRossiia mobilised its 150,000 members for Yeltsin's presidential election campaign in April 1991. But Yeltsin refused to acknowledge that he had any obligations to the movement that had supported him. On 23 April he signed Gorbachev's Novo-Ogarevo 'nine-plus-one' agreement on the future of the Union, to the dismay of DemRossiia leaders. Nor were they consulted when Yeltsin chose Rutskoi to be his vice-presidential candidate in the elections. Moreover, while using his informal alliance with DemRossiia to promote his candidature, Yeltsin pursued the tactic of campaigning without campaigning—conducting himself as if he was already president and promoting his personal authority to the detriment of institution-building.[13] As we shall see, projecting himself as a personality above politics was to be a hallmark of Yeltsin's presidential style. In effect, to invoke Weber, Yeltsin pursued a judicious combination of charismatic and legal rational legitimation of the Russian presidency. Such an approach was to weigh heavily in his favour in his 1993 showdown with the Russian legislature. Indeed, Yeltsin's crucial role as legitimator of state authority was to be key to his very survival as President, despite the odds of ill health and unpopularity.

Support for the notion of a presidential 'strong hand' was widespread among those who regarded themselves as democrats. Before the victory of the Russian 'shadow state' over the Soviet centre in August 1991, several leading democrats, such as Gavriil Popov and Anatoly Sobchak, respectively the mayors of Moscow and St Petersburg, were extolling the virtues of the elevation of executive power above legislative control.[14] With Yeltsin's triumph over the

---

[12] Sakwa, *Russian Politics*, 48. On the miners see below Chapter 6.

[13] Urban, *Boris El'tsin*, 191–2.

[14] V. Sogrin, *Politicheskaia istoriia sovremennoi Rossii 1985–1994: ot Gorbacheva do Yeltsina* (Moscow, Progress-akademiia, 1994), 113. See also Gavriil Popov, 'Dangers of Democracy', *New York Review of Books*, 16 Aug. 1990, pp. 27–8.

CPSU, proponents of economic reform were quick to advocate a 'strong hand' in politics as a necessity for driving the reforms through. A 'strong hand', it was argued, was required to overcome the inevitable elite and popular resistance to traumatic social and economic changes. Timing was crucial too. It was necessary to act decisively and expeditiously while Yeltsin still enjoyed popular support—the classic shock therapy scenario:

Only a strong state, having the confidence of the people, is capable of effecting the decisive and extremely unpopular measures without which it is impossible to stabilise and reform the economy, since the struggle with inflation demands the further reduction of the real income of the population and the curtailment of a number of social programmes. Structural reform will become the cause of mass unemployment—an inevitable cost for past mistakes in investment policy. Privatisation will entail the distribution or sale to the citizens of state property, but also the actual limitation of the rights of those social groups that previously controlled this property. The strong state already exists in a number of republics, though no longer at the centre. In particular, the president of Russia, B. Yeltsin, of Kazakhstan, N. Nazarbaev, and of Armenia, L. Ter-Petrossian, possess a high degree of legitimacy. [At present] the people concur with the temporary decline of 'their' standard of living. Popularity and legitimacy, however, are not permanent attributes of politicians. After the collapse of the August putsch, any reforms were open to the president of Russia. But already two months have elapsed and nothing has been achieved. Another five or six months and scarcely a trace of this immense popularity might remain. The recent history of the Soviet Union provides a glaring example of the diminished standing of the head of state in only a couple of years. The conclusion follows: reforms are required immediately, while the credit of confidence is still not exhausted. Above all, the reforms must be effected by those who have this credit.[15]

More generally, several commentators raised the possibility that extraordinary circumstances might justify, even necessitate, recourse to authoritarian presidential rule. Prominent among them was Andrannik Migranian. In August 1989 he, together with Igor Kliamkin, had argued that it was impossible to proceed directly from totalitarianism to democracy without an intermediate stage of authoritarianism.[16] Writing in November 1991,[17] Migranian argued that a Yeltsin dictatorship might be a guarantee against the disintegration of Russia and in favour of radical reform. Such a 'strong, stable state' might be required by Western states and businesses to undertake aid and

[15]  *Nezavisimaia gazeta* (henceforth *Ng*), 12 Nov. 1991.

[16]  See Jonathan Steele, *Eternal Russia: Yeltsin, Gorbachev and the Mirage of Democracy* (London and Boston, Faber and Faber, 1994), 268–9.

[17]  *Ng*, 14 Nov. 1991. As early as 13 November 1991 *Nezavisimaia gazeta* was warning that the victory of democracy in August 1991 had been short-lived. The 'new oligarchy' which was emerging correctly presumes that in conditions of growing chaos 'democratic methods of administration will produce few dividends'.

investment. In the situation facing Russia in late 1991 where, according to Migranian, there was no basis for a 'truly functioning democratic regime', two authoritarian scenarios were possible. Either a Yeltsin dictatorship moving towards the market and democracy with Western aid, or, should the reform collapse, a populist-nationalistic Yeltsin dictatorship as the basis of a 'national-socialist regime'. Migranian's first scenario proved to be closer to the mark than the second, which approximated more to the aspirations of Zhirinovsky's Liberal Democratic Party of Russia.

Yeltsin's public stature had reached heroic proportions due to his dramatic defiance of the August putsch, atop an armoured vehicle. Already, after his 10 July 1991 inauguration as President, he had reshaped the Russian government and further weakened the CPSU by proscribing political parties in executive bodies. Now, with the defeat of the putsch, Yeltsin was able to exploit his popular standing to justify his resort to extraordinary measures to drive through his economic and political programme. The last bastions of Soviet central authority were soon to succumb to a putsch by the Russian President, with his suspension and later banning of the party and expropriation of its property. In pursuing these measures, he was actively supported by the Russian Supreme Soviet, which had granted him emergency powers to deal with the situation.[18] On 1 November the reassembled Fifth CPD endowed the president with further extraordinary powers for one year. Under these powers, Yeltsin could appoint ministers and issue decrees to accelerate the transition to a market economy without consulting the Supreme Soviet. In addition, elections for provincial heads of administration, which Yeltsin had begun appointing by decree on 22 August, were postponed until 1 December 1992.[19] Four days later, he assumed the post of Prime Minister. On 8 November, Gennady Burbulis, Yegor Gaidar and Aleksandr Shokhin were appointed Deputy Prime Ministers of what on 15 November was declared a 'government of reforms'.

The fact that all of these measures were willingly acceded to by the Parliament reflects the degree to which differences within the elite were subordinated to the immediate task at hand. For the time being the democrat politicians, from the President to the chair of the Supreme Soviet, Ruslan Khasbulatov, were united by their opposition to the Soviet party-state and their commitment to shift towards an independent, capitalist Russia. It is

[18] For a summary of the events of 19–21 August see Sakwa, *Russian Politics*, 14–16. See also Richard Sakwa, 'A Cleansing Storm: The August Coup and the Triumph of Perestroika', *The Journal of Communist Studies*, 9: 1 (1993), 131–49.

[19] For a discussion of this policy, see William A. Clark, 'Presidential Prefects in the Russian Provinces: Yeltsin's Regional Cadres Policy', in Graeme Gill (ed.), *Elites and Leadership in Russian Politics* (London, Macmillan, 1998), 24–51. Also Irina Busygina, 'Predstaviteli prezidenta', *Svobodnaia mysl'*, 4 (1996), 52–61.

evident that at this stage Yeltsin felt no need to take advantage of his enhanced political stature to force the Parliament to new elections, let alone overturn a legislative body bequeathed from the Soviet era.[20]

With the President rapidly accumulating power, the unity of the political elite was not to last long. Already signs of the tensions that were subsequently to erupt into outright war between President and Parliament were evident. On 7 November the Supreme Soviet abrogated Yeltsin's declaration of a state of emergency in Chechnya, leading Yeltsin, in uncharacteristically chastened mood, to acknowledge his 'mistake'. Furthermore Yeltsin was able to gain the postponement of local soviet elections for a year only under threat of his resignation. As yet, however, such tensions did not jeopardise relations between President and Parliament. Nevertheless there were already those who were calling in question the very existence of Soviet-style legislative institutions. Moscow mayor Gavriil Popov was a particularly vehement proponent of dispersing the system of soviets on the grounds that it was incompatible with democracy.[21] Yeltsin's closest adviser at the time, Burbulis, argued in favour of strong executive power. In current conditions soviets 'could become a major obstacle to the course of reform', due to their composition, purpose and structure.[22] It seems likely that Burbulis and Popov were voicing what Yeltsin could only think privately about the soviets. Having defended the Russian Supreme Soviet in August 1991, Yeltsin was hardly in a position to advocate the elimination of the soviet system—at least until he had completely discredited it. His first steps, therefore, were directed at marginalising the soviets by concentrating real decision-making power in the presidency.

The key to this was the construction of a hegemonic presidency. Yeltsin needed to build upon the basis provided by the Constitution and to stabilise and consolidate the extraordinary powers granted to him by the Parliament. Part of this involved the struggle for a new Constitution, discussed below in terms of the relationship with the legislative organs. But also crucial to the creation of a strong presidency were personnel issues and the creation of institutions designed to support an activist president.

In terms of personnel, it was clear soon after the failure of the putsch that the elite 'Moscow group' of radical democratic activists was being shunted aside. Under the banner of a democratic Russia, the democrat intelligentsia

---

[20] Several commentators have raised the question of why Yeltsin failed to take advantage of his unchallenged authority to bring about a clean sweep of Soviet era political institutions. Clark, 'Presidential Prefects', 27, 48 n. 11, argues that Yeltsin 'missed a fine opportunity in the autumn of 1991 to disband the Russian parliament and call for new elections . . . In suspending the activities of the communist party . . . Yeltsin took only one of two necessary steps.'

[21] *Izvestiia*, 3 Oct. 1991.

[22] *Argumenty i fakty*, 41 (1991), in Sakwa, *Russian Politics*, 169.

had fought for a place in Yeltsin's political pantheon. The leaders of the anti-Gorbachev 'democratic opposition', such as Yury Afanas'ev, who had collaborated with Yeltsin since his election as chair of the RSFSR Supreme Soviet, saw Russian constitutional reform as their vehicle for Union-wide political dominance. They looked set to dominate the Russian political scene. It was not, however, the radical democrats such as Afanas'ev who came to the fore in 1991 (he finally broke with DemRossiia in January 1992) but the hitherto unknown Burbulis, who had commanded the successful election campaign to make Yeltsin President of Russia. He was part of the so-called 'Sverdlovsk mafia' which came to dominate Yeltsin's apparatus as early as August 1991 and he consolidated his position through his role in the Belovezha Accords of 8 December 1991 which abolished the Soviet Union.[23]

The Sverdlovsk group was drawn from former associates of Yeltsin in Sverdlovsk region, where he had been First Secretary of the obkom before being brought to Moscow by Gorbachev. Burbulis, State Secretary of the Russian Federation and First Deputy Prime Minister in 1991–92, had been a lecturer in Marxism-Leninism at a Sverdlovsk metallurgical institute.[24] Yury Petrov, the first head of the Presidential Administration, had succeeded Yeltsin as Sverdlovsk obkom First Secretary. Petrov distinguished himself during the Russian Federation's onslaught on Soviet institutions and property in the dying days of the Union. It was Petrov who oversaw the transfer of Soviet property to Russian control, who put in place the system of presidential representatives in the provinces, prepared the decrees on the transfer of Soviet ministries to Russian jurisdiction, secured the remaining gold reserves of the country, 'privatised' the Kremlin, and rescued the system of secret communications.[25]

Petrov's deputy in Sverdlovsk, Oleg Lobov, became chairman of the Expert Council, initially under the government and later the President.[26] Viktor Iliushin, a graduate of the Urals Polytechnic Institute and the CPSU Academy of Social Sciences, was appointed head of the president's secretariat in July 1991. The following year he was appointed to the crucial post of chief personal assistant to Yeltsin.[27] The presence of such former members of the Sverdlovsk provincial elite led to accusations of a 'nomenklatura underground' in the president's entourage and calls to remove 'odious pro-communists' such

---

[23] *Ng*, 31 Mar. 1992. According to Aleksandr Korzhakov, an 'active role' was played in the Belovezha Accords by Burbulis, together with Andrei Kozyrev and Sergei Shakhrai: Aleksandr Korzhakov, *Boris Yeltsin: Ot rassveta do zakata* (Moscow, Interbuk, 1997), 127.

[24] Kol'ev, '*Miatezh*', 79; Korzhakov, *Boris Yeltsin*, 465.     [25] *Izvestiia*, 2 July, 1994.

[26] *Kto est' kto v Rossii: 1997 goda* (Moscow, Olymp, 1997), 391–2.

[27] Sakwa, *Russian Politics*, 144–5; Kol'ev, '*Miatezh*', 79; Korzhakov, *Boris Yeltsin*, 465, 468; and *Kto est' kto*, 272–3.

as Petrov.[28] Such accusations, despite the rhetoric, had some substance. It was members of the 'partkhoznomenklatura', the former party-state elite overseeing the economy against whom the democrats had railed bitterly since early 1991, who were to be the silent partners and beneficiaries of Yeltsin's consolidation of power.

Burbulis was the key to the inclusion of another group which played a crucial role in the early years, the young economists headed by Yegor Gaidar, a former economics editor of both *Kommunist* and *Pravda*. At the insistence of Burbulis, on 7 November Yeltsin decreed Gaidar, who with his group had been the principal architects of shock therapy (see below), Minister of Economics and a Deputy Prime Minister.[29] In turn, Gaidar was responsible for the promotion of a grouping that would become extremely important in shaping the new Russia: the so-called 'St Petersburg team' of economists, led by Anatoly Chubais.[30] One other figure who was to emerge as very influential later, especially after the 1993 election, was Aleksandr Korzhakov, who had been Yeltsin's personal bodyguard since 1985.[31]

The role of the 'Sverdlovsk mafia' was important during this early period because their long association with Yeltsin encouraged him to trust and rely upon them. But at least as important as the identity of these people, and more so in terms of the development of the presidency, was the creation of institutions designed to support the President and to implement his will.[32] A State Council had been established in July as a consultative body to the President. Consisting mainly of prominent persons rather than active politicians (although Burbulis was its first head), this body had little impact on decision-making, but it presented the President as open to advice from what one observer called 'the great and the good'[33] in Russian society. This body later changed its name, first to Presidential Consultative Council (30 November

---

[28] This was the substance of a report presented in early 1992 to the President by the thinktank 'RF-Politika', in conjunction with a Supreme Soviet subcommittee on political reform: *Ng*, 22 Feb. 1992.

[29] Kol'ev, '*Miatezh*', 79. Burbulis also introduced Andrei Kozyrev, who was appointed Foreign Minister, to Yeltsin. Pat Willerton distinguishes between Yeltsin's 'proteges' and 'clients'. 'Proteges' have longer-term personal relations with Yeltsin, dating from before his election as President in 1991. 'Clients' are politicians who have achieved at least two career promotions since he was elected President, mainly drawn from lower rungs of the Soviet political or bureaucratic establishment. The Sverdlovsk grouping and survivors of the Gaidar team, such as Chubais, respectively fit these categories. John P. Willerton, 'Post-Soviet Clientelist Norms at Russian Federal Level', in Gill (ed.), *Elites*, 60–2.

[30] Roi Medvedev, *Chubais i vaucher: Iz istorii rossiiskoi privatizatsii* (Moscow, Impeto, 1997), 6.

[31] *Kto est' kto*, 328–30.     [32] For a schematic diagram of this, see *Kto est' kto* 99.

[33] Sakwa, *Russian Politics*, 144. Compare the treatment of this body in Sakwa with that in *Kto est' chto*, 98.

1991) and then in February 1993 to Presidential Council. More important was the Presidential Administration, headed until January 1993 by Petrov, who was then replaced by Sergei Filatov. He lasted as chief of staff until January 1996, when he was replaced by Nikolai Yegorov. The Presidential Administration did the basic housekeeping for the President, including the vetting of documents before they went to Yeltsin. This was clearly a very significant body, providing much of the sort of infrastructural support without which Yeltsin could not have functioned. It also exercised a key information filtering role.

One of the most significant parts of the Presidential Administration was the State-Legal Administration (GPU) established on 27 December 1991. The pretext was to ensure uniformity of laws—a 'single legal space'—throughout the fledgling Russian Federation in order to preempt any repetition of the 'war of laws' that had accompanied the Union's disintegration.[34] In this sense, the GPU might be seen as legal reinforcement for the President's plenipotentiaries in the regions. From its inception the GPU was charged with primary responsibility for drafting and vetting legislation on the President's behalf.[35] But its writ has run larger than this, encompassing law-making in general and, increasingly, executive rule-making through the issuing of decrees and instructions in particular.[36]

The GPU was the child of Sergei Shakhrai,[37] and remained so, despite his resignation as GPU chief in mid-1992. Almost from its inception there was intense rivalry between the GPU and other players for access to the President. This led to particular rivalry with the head of the presidential administration, Petrov, which resulted in Shakhrai's resignation.[38] This saw the successive

[34] Eugene Huskey, 'The State-Legal Administration and the Politics of Redundancy', *Post-Soviet Affairs*, 11: 2 (1995), 118.

[35] Ibid. 118. Among other responsibilities the GPU was 'authorised to present Russian draft laws to the President of the Russian Federation, to give its imprimatur to the texts of laws already adopted by the parliament and of presidential and government decrees before they are signed, and to issue official interpretations concerning the application of laws currently in effect'—*Izvestiia*, 29 Jan. 1992.

[36] Huskey, 'State-Legal Administration', 126–7.

[37] For biographical details of Shakhrai and his successor Aleksandr Kotenkov, see ibid. 118–19. In an interview Kotenkov claimed that while Shakhrai was the 'ideologue' who had fathered the GPU, he (Kotenkov) was its first real head. *Ng*, 26 June 1992.

[38] When Shakhrai resigned as State Adviser on Legal Policy in May 1992 he singled out 'differences of opinion' with Petrov as the main reason for his resignation: *Rossiiskaia gazeta*, 26 May 1992. Shakhrai clearly felt the GPU was marginalised as an overseer of legal norms. Following his resignation he complained that he had seen 'barely half' of the decrees Yeltsin had signed. In this regard he singled out the 'entire package of documents concerning the Security Council' which, he alleged, 'was pushed through by its secretary, Yury Skokov, without our knowledge, virtually without any official stamps of approval at all': *Komsomolskaia pravda*, 8 Aug. 1997, in *Current Digest of the Post-Soviet Press*, XLIV, 32 (1992), 23.

installation of two of Shakhrai's proteges: Kotenkov (sacked by Yeltsin in December 1993) and then Kotenkov's replacement, Ruslan Orekhov.[39] As GPU director accountable only to Yeltsin, Shakhrai was the lynchpin in the GPU's pivotal role within the Presidential Administration. Combined with the other offices Shakhrai then held (deputy prime minister, state adviser on legal policy, people's deputy, member of the Supreme Soviet), he was accused of concentrating in one official the 'three branches of power—legislative, executive and judicial'.[40] If this was not the reality, it was certainly an aspiration. From the start Shakhrai was determined that there should be no rival power centre to that of the presidency. His immediate concern here was not so much the legislature as the government. As GPU head, Shakhrai even went so far as to draft a proposal to eliminate the office of Prime Minister and bring the ministries directly under presidential competence. This proposal failed, but Shakhrai envisaged that duplication between the governmental and presidential apparatuses would eventually be eliminated through 'competitive struggle', no doubt in the latter's favour.[41] Not surprisingly, the GPU was seen as a presidential usurpation of governmental authority. Justice Minister Nikolai Fedorov saw it as 'an unusual entity in the system of state power', the activities of which, judged by some of its draconian draft legislation, threatened a 'paralysis of power'.[42] Fedorov's apprehensions proved well founded (see Chapter 5).

Yeltsin sought to strengthen his position not only by the development of institutions designed to sustain him administratively, but also by giving him control over the means of coercion. Among the first proposals put forward by Yeltsin, following the defeat of the August 1991 putsch, was to establish a Russian National Guard, presumably as an independent alternative to the Soviet security forces.[43] Nothing came of this particular proposal. Rather, it was a matter of Russia incorporating the erstwhile Soviet security structures into its new ones. Thus in late December 1991 control of the Alpha Group, Gorbachev's personal security detachment, passed to Yeltsin.[44] The apparatuses of surveillance too were quickly put in place. In swift succession, by presidential decree, followed the transformation of the Russian KGB into the Federal Security Service and then the attempt to consolidate all former Soviet and RSFSR police and security agencies, including the interior ministries, into a 'super' security ministry.[45] As one commentator put it, 'the president's act should be viewed in the context of efforts aimed at strengthening executive

---

[39] Huskey, 'State-Legal Administration', 119.     [40] *Izvestiia*, 29 Jan. 1992.

[41] Huskey, 'State-Legal Administration', 116.     [42] *Izvestiia*, 29 Jan. 1992.

[43] *Izvestiia*, 22 Aug. 1991. This task was allotted to Vice President Rutskoi.

[44] *Rossiiskaia gazeta*, 19 Dec. 1991.

[45] The decree was 'On the Formation of the RSFSR Ministry of Security and Internal Affairs', *CDSP*, XLIII, 51 (1991), 10.

power, which, in turn, are designed to ensure the implementation of economic reforms—including the measure for introducing a free market and uncontrolled prices, which are not very popular with the public. It is clearly no accident that the new agency was created on the threshold of expected manifestations of discontent—hunger riots, strikes and mass disturbances.'[46] And in the words of then Minister of Security and Internal affairs in January 1992, 'The people are fed up with perestroika. The way things stand now, the president's only support is the Armed Forces and the security and internal affairs agencies . . .'[47]

Yeltsin's attempt to create a super security ministry provoked one of the first rifts between the President and the Russian Parliament. On 24 December 1991 five parliamentary committees denounced both the new unified security ministry and the covert way it was decreed 'under pressure from structures that have been hidden from the public and are now going out of existence.'[48] This statement clearly implied that there had been collusion between the President, as head of government, and former Soviet security bodies. Credence for this was given by the revelation that neither State Counsellor Yury Skokov nor Deputy Prime Minister Sergei Shakhrai, who dissented from Yeltsin's decision, was apprised of the decision beforehand. This suggests that even at this stage, decision-making on crucial issues of state was taking place within Yeltsin's most inner circle, bypassing formal institutions.

The proposed superministry also put the presidency on a collision course with the Constitutional Court. In January 1992 Yeltsin's decree to create an amalgamated Ministry of Security and Internal Affairs was rebuffed by the court on the grounds that it violated the principle of the separation of powers.[49] The President complied with the ruling. The combined ministry reverted to a separate Ministry of Security under Viktor Barannikov and a Ministry of Internal Affairs (MVD) under Viktor Yerin. In reality these were little more than Soviet institutions transformed into Russian ones. Their organization and the bulk of their personnel remained the same.

The President's desire for control over the means of coercion was also reflected in the establishment of the Security Council. Soon after he was elected in June 1991, Yeltsin established a Security Council, but this was dissolved when he became Prime Minister in November 1991. The Security

---

[46] Professor Igor Petrukhin, chief research associate Institute of State and Law, Russian Academy of Sciences: *Kuranty*, 20 Dec. 1991, *CDSP*, XLIII, 52 (1991), 14.

[47] *Izvestiia*, 29 Jan. 1992. See also the reference to the Ministry's Order No. 5 for suppressing possible unrest in the wake of price liberalization.

[48] *Rossiiskaia gazeta*, 25 Dec. 1991. The decree was seen as violating the principle that there should be no combining of the 'functions of state security and public safety in a single agency.'

[49] *Izvestiia*, 15 Jan. 1992; *Rossiiskaia gazeta*, 20 Jan. 1992.

Council of the Russian Federation was re-established with the adoption of the Law On Security of 5 March 1992.[50] Given the sinister connotations of 'security' in the Soviet era, Yeltsin moved to allay fears that this body posed any threat to the constitutional order. At its first session he personally guaranteed, as President, that it would abide completely by the spirit and letter of the law.[51] The original intention was to ensure that the Security Council would not become a creature of the coercive apparatuses of the state. To this end it would be an advisory, not a decision-making, body, most of the members of which would be appointed by the President and approved by the legislature.[52]

Nevertheless others were apprehensive about the Security Council's role. It was feared it might supersede both executive and legislative authority.[53] Headed by Skokov, who was closely identified with the defence industries,[54] the Council was even viewed as the 'new guiding and directing force of our society.' With the Council allegedly possessing unlimited authority, concern was expressed that the President might find himself reduced to a mere 'formulator' of the decisions of the Council.[55] These initial fears proved unjustified. Yeltsin and his advisers continued to have the decisive say over the Council, but this was at the expense of the legislature rather than the power ministries. Despite the provisions on parliamentary confirmation, only two members of the Council, its secretary Skokov and non-permanent member Deputy Prime Minister Shakhrai, were confirmed by the legislature.[56] This was a clear breach of the Law On Security.

Power in the Security Council lay with its secretaries, initially Skokov, who was sacked in May 1993, and then Oleg Lobov (Yeltsin's friend from

---

[50] *Rossiiskaia gazeta*, 6 May 1992.                [51] Ibid. 21 May 1992.

[52] 'O bezopasnosti', ibid. 6 May 1992. See also J. William Derleth, 'The Evolution of the Russian Polity: The Case of the Security Council', *Communist and Post-Communist Studies*, 29: 1 (1996), 45. For a list of its permanent and non-permanent members as of April 1993, see p. 46. The permanent members were the President, Vice President, First Deputy Chair of the Supreme Soviet and Security Council Secretary. The Prime Minister was, of course, appointed by the President and confirmed by the Parliament; so too was the Security Council Secretary. All of the non-permanent members were also to be appointed by the President and approved by the Parliament.

[53] *Ng*, 17 June 1992.

[54] Skokov was appointed by decree in April 1992. He made his name before perestroika as the general director of a Moscow-based association of defence-energy producers. In May 1991 he became Yeltsin's official economic adviser and later, RSFSR State Adviser on Security Questions. In this capacity, his criticism of Gaidar's government earned him the reputation as the 'undisputed leader of the anti-market lobby'. As Security Council Secretary, Skokov was in a position to shape the upper echelons of the Defence Ministry as well as influencing military doctrines and policies. *Moskovskie novosti*, 19 July 1992, *CDPSP*, XLIV, 28 (1992), 4.

[55] *Ng*, 31 July 1992.                [56] Derleth, 'Evolution', 46.

Sverdlovsk) who was appointed in the critical month of September 1993.[57] Presidential decrees amplified the already wide-ranging authority of the Security Council Secretary. Decrees adopted on 4 June and 7 July 1992 effectively elevated the Council above the government and made Skokov the 'No. 2 man.'[58] Hitherto, under the Law On Security, it had had a consultative role. Now, however, implementation of the Security Council's decisions was to be made 'mandatory'. Further, the Council was granted virtually unlimited discretion on the range of questions on which it could coordinate executive agencies.[59] There was certainly no constitutional provision for such powers, which threatened the prerogatives of both government and legislature: 'A constitutional body with unconstitutional powers ha[d] come to power without tanks.' Russia, some feared at the time, was on the road to presidential dictatorship.[60]

This certainly seemed to be the case, if judged by the powers vested in Security Council Secretary Skokov. He could give direct orders to Security, Interior Ministry and military forces through local commissions of the Council which were to be set up throughout Russia. These commissions also meant Skokov could bypass and overrule local government authority. Skokov's hand was also strengthened during 1992 by a series of appointments to other bodies concerned with national security. In April he was appointed Deputy Chairman of the Russian State Commission responsible for creating a Russian Defence Ministry. In May he became chair of a committee responsible for Defence Ministry personnel. In December he was appointed chairman of the new Interdepartmental Foreign Policy Commission. This commission, it has been suggested, stripped the Foreign Ministry of real control over foreign policy, which fell into the hands of Skokov (and subsequently, of Lobov).[61]

The immediate cause of Yeltsin's quiet coup reflected in this strengthening of the role of the Security Council seems to have been the impasse between Yeltsin's government and the April Sixth Congress of People's Deputies. As part of a deal struck at the Congress, Yeltsin resigned as Prime Minister. But he retained decisive executive power by transferring responsibility for security,

---

[57] Ibid. 56. For a portrait of this staunch, technocratic 'Yeltsinite', and like the President an engineer, see *Izvestiia*, 13 May 1995.

[58] *Moskovskie novosti*, 19 July 1992, *CDPSP*, XLIV, 28 (12 Aug. 1992), 2–3.

[59] *Kommersant*, 6–13 July 1992, *CDPSP*, XLIV, 28 (12 Aug. 1992), 1.

[60] *Moskovskie novosti*, 19 July 1992.

[61] Derleth, 'Evolution', 50 and n. 24. Rivalry between the Russian Security Ministry and the Foreign Ministry probably prompted the remark by Minister of Foreign Affairs Andrei Kozyrev about the threat of a coup from a 'war party' that has formed in Russia's 'structures of force'—the former KGB, the army and security forces: *Izvestiia*, 30 June 1992. The Russian Security Ministry took issue with these remarks, denying the threat of a coup: *Izvestiia*, 9 July 1992.

defence and foreign affairs from the government to the Security Council.[62] In so doing, Yeltsin had created 'a shadow cabinet', as Shakhrai called it.[63] The centrality of the Security Council to presidential power had become apparent. It provided a convenient mechanism for bringing together the traditional security, military and industrial bureaucracies, free from oversight by either the legislature or the government, but under the tutelage of the President's administrative staff. Concerns remained, however, about the Security Council's weight within the presidential apparatus, and indeed its augmentation of presidential power.

The Security Council proved not to be a rival to presidential authority, as many feared.[64] Ultimate authority always rested with the President. His aides always attended Security Council meetings and in May 1993, after Skokov's dismissal, then head of the presidential administration Filatov set the Council's agenda.[65] The Security Council was not even mentioned in the draft constitution in mid-1993.[66] After the October 1993 showdown, however, the Security Council was formally brought under the authority of the President. The new Constitution gave sole responsibility for the Security Council to the President. Under an amended Law on Security, he chaired the Council, the decisions of which were to be issued as presidential decrees and instructions.[67]

The fate of the Security Council after it reached its peak of power in mid-1992, when it was superseded in importance by the Presidential Administration, reflects one of the key characteristics of the structure of presidential power as it emerged under Boris Yeltsin: the continual rivalry and jockeying for position by both institutions and individuals. The GPU, for example, tried to depict its rivalry with other executive agencies, especially the government, as one of 'reform' versus 'conservatism'. Accusations and counter-accusations of anti-reformist motivation and sentiment between the GPU and

[62] Alexander Rahr, 'The Roots of the Power Struggle', *RFE/RL Research Report*, 2: 20 (14 May 1993), 10.

[63] *Komsomolskaia pravda*, 8 Aug. 1992, *CDPSP*, XLIV, 32 (1992), 23. In the course of this interview, Shakhrai made the point that the Security Council was in a position to effect a coup covertly by changing the 'correlation of forces within the shadow cabinet'. The Security Council, he argued, had emerged to fill the 'power vacuum' left by the collapse of the old party-state.

[64] For example, *Ng*, 31 July 1992.

[65] Derleth, 'Evolution', 56–7. June–August 1993 saw a brief interregnum with Marshal Yevgeny Shaposhnikov replacing Skokov, who had apparently fallen foul of the power ministries, as Security Council Secretary. Shaposhnikov himself resigned in mid-August when it became apparent that his first priority was supposed to be 'political loyalty to the President' rather than coordinating national security. This occurred when the heads of the Ministries of Security and Internal Affairs had resigned. It was evident that Yeltsin would rely on the army and Minister of Defence, Pavel Grachev: *Ng*, 12 Aug. 1993.

[66] Derleth, 'Evolution', 52, 53, 55.          [67] Sakwa, *Russian Politics*, 146.

other executive agencies masked institutional rivalries fuelled in good part by personal ambition. The career machinations of elite Russian politicians demonstrate the importance of informal personal relations in structuring a newly emerging state apparatus—or more precisely, in the post-Soviet case, restructuring an existing state—in the absence of well-established formal institutions. However, such conflict between different institutions has masked shared commitment to the implantation of private property and the market, though the means and motivation might vary. On the one hand, under the banner of an 'anti-nomenklatura revolution' a layer of the erstwhile Soviet nomenklatura has been able to ensconce itself in the new post-Soviet order (see below). On the other hand executive institutions, such as the GPU, in the name of 'democratic reform' have provided a place where a young layer of the educated post-Soviet elite have been able to pursue well-rewarded careers.[68] This is no small issue in a society where employment opportunities and career paths virtually disappeared over night. It is not surprising then that by 1994–95 the GPU, like other presidential agencies such as the Security Council, should be perceived as a bulwark of bureaucratic conservatism.[69]

It is important to see the broader political significance of the development of a substantial independent presidential apparatus. By building such an apparatus upon which to stand, and thereby seeking to insulate himself to some degree from the daily political tussle, in the eyes of one observer[70] Yeltsin risked 'political weightlessness.' Therefore he looked to a 'third force' in order to offset the threat to his popularity resulting from the economic difficulties, the lack of a presidential party and the fragmentation of Democratic Russia. In his quest for a firm basis for strong presidential power, it was said Yeltsin turned to the 'corporative solidarity of yesterday's Party nomenklatura and the military-industrial establishment.' Amid rumours of a military coup Yeltsin is said to have concluded that 'he had to be on good terms with the Army.'[71] Hence the Security Council came to the fore. The Yeltsin regime thus demonstrated many of the attributes of classical Bonapartism: an authoritarian figure casting around for a base of social support and, failing to find one, turning to the coercive apparatuses.

---

[68] According to Huskey, 'State-Legal Administration', 120, the pay and conditions of the 220 staff in the employ of the GPU compared to the rest of the state bureaucracy were 'very handsome indeed.'

[69] Ibid. 135.

[70] *Moskovskie novosti*, 19 July 1992. In July 1992, on the eve of the anniversary of the August putsch, Moscow abounded with rumours of an impending coup from various high-placed quarters. Such warnings, however, seemed to be more about the personal agenda of those who made them, than recognition of a definite threat: *Rossiiskaia gazeta*, 11 July 1992.

[71] *Moskovskie novosti*, 17 July 1992.

## Shock Therapy

This strengthening of presidential executive powers had preceded the escalation of the confrontation with the parliament in 1992–93, and had occurred against a background of fears about possible popular unrest. The source of such fears was the policy of shock therapy.

The move to the market was high on the list of Yeltsin's priorities from the outset. On 28 October 1991, in a speech reputed to have been written by Gaidar,[72] Yeltsin presented his programme for radical economic reform to the Russian CPD: 'The period of progress by small steps is over', he declared. 'A large-scale reformist breakthrough is needed.' Inspired by Western monetarist economics, shock therapy had a number of ingredients. These entailed the liberalisation of retail and wholesale prices, strict control over money and credit, severe reduction of the budget deficit, opening up the economy to the world market, and the privatisation of state property. Although Gaidar gave a lower priority to privatization, shock therapy was tantamount to a complete, more or less simultaneous, overturning of the Russian economic system.[73] Based on a fundamentalist reading of monetarism, shock therapy aimed to replace state regulation of the economy with market regulation. The state would vacate the field of social and economic support, and the private market would move in to fill the space. In what still remained a highly statised economy, such an abrupt deregulation of economic life could only entail extraordinary social dislocation.

Although shock therapy was soon to become central to the conflict between executive and legislature, it was endorsed almost unanimously, 876 votes to 16, by the Fifth CPD at its second session in October 1991. Coming as it did with the imprimatur of the International Monetary Fund (IMF) and Western monetarist economists such as Jeffrey Sachs, few Russian politicians publicly questioned Gaidar's course. Khasbulatov, soon to repudiate shock therapy, enthusiastically endorsed it at the time.[74] The optimistic scenario presented by Yeltsin, who promised the economy would stabilise and life would improve within six months, played an important role in garnering political support. The deputies, swept along by the tide of euphoria that followed the defeat of Soviet communism, unhesitatingly gave Yeltsin the authority to implement his programme.[75]

---

[72] David M. Kotz with Fred Weir, *Revolution from Above: The Demise of the Soviet System* (London and New York, Routledge, 1997), 166.
[73] Kotz and Weir, Revolution, 161–3.                                    [74] Ibid. 167–8.
[75] Vladimir Inozemstev, 'Na pereput'e', *Svobodnaia mysl'*, 13 (1992), 20–1.

On 2 January 1992 Gaidar's price liberalisation went into effect. State controls were lifted on 80 per cent of wholesale prices and 90 per cent of retail prices. The consequences were catastrophic. Living standards plummeted over night, as did production, especially of consumer goods. Prices rose astronomically in the first month. According to official Russian statistics, which probably underestimated the situation, in January consumer prices and the cost of services increased 3.5 times. The price of foodstuffs increased four-fold, while non-foodstuffs rose 2.5 times. Consumption contracted abruptly, as demand switched to essential items such as food. Nevertheless, demand for staple commodities, such as milk fell to 24 per cent and meat and meat products to 14 per cent of that in December 1991. Half the budget of the average family was spent on food. Production contracted sharply, especially in consumer goods, ferrous metals and oil extraction. The total volume of production for the first two months of 1992 was 85 per cent of that for the corresponding period in 1991. Meanwhile, mutual indebtedness between banks and enterprises accelerated from 39 billion roubles at the beginning of January to 650 billion at the end of March. Hundreds of enterprises and tens of banks were teetering on the edge of bankruptcy.[76]

The objective of a minimum budget deficit (in accordance with the IMF endorsed memorandum on Russian economic policies issued in February 1992)[77] looked to be on track. In the first quarter the budget was actually slightly in surplus, despite a sharp decline in receipts, outlays for miners' wages, who were on strike, and massive export subsidies to industry. It was achieved by slashing expenditure by 40 per cent. But attempts to control credit and the money supply were initially less than successful. The volume of credit and money actually grew in the first two months of 1992, thanks to the policies of the Russian Central Bank.[78] Nevertheless during the first half of 1992, shock therapy was ruthlessly applied, though there was some easing of policy in the second half of the year in order to ease social tensions.

Overall, however, in the course of the next six years, the fiscal and monetary prescriptions of shock therapy and the IMF were generally adhered to. Prices remained unregulated, state orders were reduced, government spending continued to be reduced, industrial subsidies declined, the rouble was made convertible, the economy was opened up to foreign investment, most controls on exports and (especially) imports were eased. Moreover, the second ingredient of shock therapy, wholesale privatization of state enterprises, was

---

[76] Reported by Mikhail Zadornov, 'Sostoianie ekonomiki i blizhaishie perspektivy', *Svobodnaia mysl'*, 6 (1992), 56–60, 62–3.

[77] On 1 June 1992 Russia officially became a member of the IMF.

[78] Zadornov, 'Sostoianie', 61–2.

implemented. By mid-1994, barely two years after privatisation began, two-thirds of state and municipal enterprises had been privatised.[79]

The economic and social costs of shock therapy were extremely high, reflecting the imposition of a monetarist model that took little account of Russian reality. Price liberalization, instead of encouraging production as intended, produced an abrupt contraction of the economy. Foisted on a highly monopolised economy, producers reacted by limiting production and raising prices. An already crippled economy now found itself in free fall. Inflation was rampant in 1992. Consumer prices rose by 2,500 per cent. Inflation slowed over the next three years, but was still running at an annual 63 per cent at the end of 1995. By that time consumer prices had risen by a factor of 1,411.[80] Industrial production, already in a trough in 1991, rapidly contracted thereafter. In 1992 production was 75.4 per cent of the level of 1990. Thereafter the rate of decline slowed, but in 1997 it was only 47.9 per cent of its 1990 level. Crucially, investment suffered a near collapse. In 1992 it was 51 per cent what it had been in 1990. Over the period 1990–97, investment fell 77.2 per cent. By 1997, the Russian economy measured by GDP, was a mere 59.2 per cent of its 1990 level.[81] In the years 1991 to 1998 Russia's GDP was estimated to have contracted by three times the amount the Soviet Union lost in the Second World War. Russia was in a major depression, unprecedented in the twentieth century.[82]

Such a situation could not but have a fundamental bearing on political developments. Already by mid-1992 Yeltsin's government had lost control over the economy. Strong external support from Western governments and financial institutions, and the unexpected forbearance of the population, within which there was still considerable confidence in Yeltsin personally, were the saving graces for the government.[83] Nevertheless, it found itself increasingly lacking any active social support. The dashed expectations of the politicians' promises left the Russian people as a whole bewildered in the face of scorched earth economic policies.[84]

## Conflict with the Legislature

The implementation of shock therapy shattered the initial unity of the political elite, turning the Parliament against the government and eventually the

---

[79] Kotz and Weir, *Revolution*, 168–72.          [80] Ibid. 177.

[81] The figures are from *Russian and Euro-Asian Bulletin*, 6: 8 (1997), 10; and 7: 4 (1998), 6.

[82] Kotz and Weir, *Revolution*, 173–7; *Argumenty i fakty*, 22 May 1998.

[83] Zadornov, 'Sostoianie', 63.          [84] Inozemtsev, 'Na pereput'e', 20.

President himself. But even before the rupture over the course of economic policy, there were inauspicious rifts between executive and legislature over their political prerogatives.

From the outset the soviets were under siege from democrat ideologues such as Anatoly Sobchak and Gavriil Popov who saw them as an obstruction to the radical transformation of Russia, and who explicitly called for the 'desovietisation' of the country. Yeltsin refrained from openly endorsing such a call until mid-1993, when the confrontation with the Supreme Soviet heated up. Then he declared that soviets and democracy were 'not compatible'.[85] But it had been clear since his appointment of plenipotentiaries to the regions that he was determined to marginalize the soviets and eventually make them redundant. The soviets, led by the Moscow-based Supreme Soviet and its ambitious chairman Khasbulatov, were determined that they should have the final say in government. This was increasingly the case, as the pernicious effects of shock therapy became apparent to all. The short-lived unity within the regime founding coalition soon gave way to a struggle between executive and legislature for institutional supremacy, which would culminate in outright physical confrontation.[86]

At the heart of the struggle between the President and the legislature were two different conceptions of government. Yeltsin aspired to a presidential regime whereby ultimate governmental authority devolved from himself as head of state. Khasbulatov, following the Soviet conception whereby the Supreme Soviet exercised both legislative and executive functions, aspired to a parliamentary style of government with himself as Prime Minister. In effect however, in November 1991 the CPD and the Supreme Soviet had temporarily surrendered to the President their right of oversight of the executive, by allowing Yeltsin to appoint himself head of government and to issue economic decrees. In early 1992, as shock therapy bit hard into the Russian economy and society, the legislature fought to re-establish its authority over government. Constitutional ambiguity undoubtedly exacerbated institutional rivalry. But as social tensions rose, competition gave way to conflict, fuelled by the personal ambitions of the President and the Chairman of the Supreme Soviet. Yeltsin and his allies were not entirely wrong when they viewed the ensuing struggle as one of incompatible 'dual power'.

[85] Clark, 'Presidential Prefects', 15. Speech by Yeltsin, 5 June 1993, opening the Constitutional Assembly, cited in Elizabeth Teague, 'Yeltsin Disbands the Soviets', *RFE/RL Research Report*, 2: 43 (29 Oct. 1993), 4.

[86] For an interpretation of these developments that puts the primary responsibility for the conflict on Khasbulatov and Rutskoi and the ambiguity of the Russian Constitution, see Yitzhak M. Brudny, 'Ruslan Khasbulatov, Aleksandr Rutskoi, and Intraelite Conflict in Postcommunist Russia, 1991–1994', in Timothy J. Colton and Robert C. Tucker (eds.), *Patterns in Post-Soviet Leadership* (Boulder, Westview, 1995), 75–101.

Early tensions over Yeltsin's declaration of a state of emergency in Chechnya and his attempt to create a super security ministry have already been noted. The lead-up to the April 1992 Sixth CPD saw a quickening of these institutional rivalries around a variety of issues: the structure of the Russian Federation,[87] the overall course of economic and political policy, and a new Constitution. Yeltsin's government was increasingly under fire for the consequences of shock therapy. It was not only from Khasbulatov and the parliament; it issued from within the executive itself. Vice President Rutskoi, angered at the marginal role to which Yeltsin had relegated him, was a vociferous critic of shock therapy and its architects, Gaidar and his group—the 'boys in pink shorts'. In the face of such criticism, some observers[88] believed the Yeltsin regime was facing its 'first serious internal crisis' and the real danger of the collapse of the Russian Federation, just like its Soviet predecessor. Given the extreme unpopularity of the current government, the old structures appeared incapable of holding the country together. In this context, it was argued, it was necessary to introduce 'presidential government and a regime of personal power' which could, among other things, finally rid Russia of the ideology of 'state paternalism with a socialist hue.' Confidence that such a presidential regime could be put in place with little or no popular resistance was drawn from the generally passive response to the recent draconian price rises.

There was also concern about the President's popular support due to the corrosion of the democratic movement.[89] At a confidential meeting between Yeltsin and sympathetic democrat leaders held in late March 1992, a number of measures were proposed to enhance the President's popular standing. The proposals included encouraging the development of a layer of petty and middle entrepreneurs, and a programme of social guarantees to broaden the President's support. Some Yeltsin supporters apparently urged him to relinquish his direct control over the government in order to save his reputation,

---

[87] For example, in mid-March 1992 Yeltsin indicated to his critics, such as Rutskoi and Travkin, his readiness to support the 'gosudarstvenniki' in the Congress of People's Deputies: those who advocated Russia as a multinational power. The aim was to give local elites some say in the central leadership. This opened the prospect of Yeltsin gaining a stable majority for his government's policies in the forthcoming Congress of People's Deputies among those who had been most critical of the methods used to introduce the market, amongst them the People's Party of Free Russia (NPSR) and the Democratic Party of Russia: *Ng*, 14 Mar. 1992.

[88] Ibid.

[89] Some erosion of personal support for Yeltsin was registered in a telephone poll of Moscow residents in February and March 1992. Among respondents, 'positive' support for Yeltsin had dropped from 38% to 30% (though it rose in April, after the CPD, back to 39%), while a 'negative' assessment for the same period rose from 9% to 15% (dropping back in April to 10%): *Kto est' chto*, 97.

but he refused to do so.[90] Some democrats, doubtful of their ability to reassemble their forces, had pinned their hopes on the President himself, even entertaining the possibility that he might head up a new movement in the lead-up to the Congress. But as one commentator observed, and as Yeltsin has generally maintained throughout his presidency, such a move would deprive him of one of his 'trump cards: . . . his position as head of state, rising above all political squabbles and having the possibility from his exalted station to speak as an arbiter in relation to the entire spectrum of Russia's problems.'[91]

For Yeltsin, resolution of Russia's multifarious problems hinged on putting a new Constitution in place. This question was a priority for him in the lead-up to the Sixth Congress. He proposed putting his own Constitution before the Congress on 4 April, dismissing as 'socialist' the constitution drafted by the CPD's own Constitutional Commission. In turn, Rumiantsev, the responsible secretary of the commission, saw Yeltsin's threat to introduce his own Constitution as due to the influence of politicians who had an 'in' with him, particularly mayors like Sobchak and, especially, Popov.[92] According to Rumiantsev, on the eve of the Sixth Congress there had been a tremendous struggle at the summit of Russian politics, with the 'seizure of the initiative by the Popov-Sobchak group.' The proposal for an alternative constitution to that of Rumiantsev was a 'counter-offensive' by Popov and Sobchak—the 'Moscow group'—who since late 1991 had been side-lined by the Burbulis 'Sverdlovsk group'. They had to convince Yeltsin of the need to push his constitutional alternative before the Congress. But this also made Sobchak a potential rival to Burbulis and even Yeltsin. This competition between groups to influence the President, in this case using the Constitution to advance their cause, Rumiantsev labelled as 'insider' politics (vkhozhest'), a feature of Russian politics since the boyars.[93] In short, Yeltsin's threatened rejection of the proposal of the Constitutional Commission threatened, in Rumiantsev's words, a 'coup within the limits of constitutional reform.'[94]

The alternative constitutional proposals being put forward by Yeltsin's supporters, if not by the President himself, threatened to eliminate the existing legislative branch of government. Sobchak[95] proposed a strengthened presidential form of government, similar to that of the French Fifth Republic, and the complete desovietisation of the country, substituting municipal and federal forms of government for the structure inherited from Soviet times. Moreover, proposing an 'uncompromising' Constitution that inevitably would

---

[90] *Ng*, 6 Mar. 1992.   [91] *Ng*, 5 Mar. 1992.

[92] *Ng*, 28 Mar. 1992. Rumiantsev viewed the President's proposal with alarm, because the commission's Constitution represented the basic document worked out with Yeltsin's own participation in autumn 1990.

[93] *Ng*, 3 Mar. 1992.   [94] *Ng*, 31 Mar. 1992.   [95] Ibid.

be rejected by the Congress would provide a trigger for an 'unprecedented radical reform of the state and its personnel.' A similar manifesto for such a 'reform' was advanced by the think-tank 'RF-Politika' on the eve of the Congress.[96] Again the target was the entire system of soviets that, it was argued, reproduced 'in new historical conditions' the 'political omnipotence of the nomenklatura'. Accordingly, the immediate 'dismissal and re-election of the soviets at every level' was as vital as the prohibition on the CPSU. For this reason too the outcome of the Sixth Congress was seen as crucial. It allegedly threatened to become a 'forum for nomenklatura revenge'. It would try to bring the President under its control, withdrawing his plenary powers, especially those enabling him to form the government. The memorandum linked its call for the revamping of the soviets to putting the Russian Federation on a firm constitutional foundation. The 'integrity' of the Russian state was threatened by an 'avalanche' of separatist tendencies. An uncompromising, 'presidential' variant of the Constitution should be thrown down before the Congress. Its guaranteed rejection by the Congress would open the way for Yeltsin to make a dramatic appeal to the people concerning the impossibility of Russia's renewal in the face of the 'aggressive' resistance of the nomenklatura and their 'bulwark', the 'entire soviet system.' It would also open the way to putting the new constitution to a referendum and the declaration of pre-term, that is before autumn 1992, elections for representative institutions.

However, Yeltsin took a less belligerent, though no less unequivocal, stance than his democrat ideologues. Addressing the Citizens' Assembly of the Russian Federation, a body set up to give a semblance of popular support to his constitutional aspirations, he had bluntly posed the choice facing Russia: a parliamentary or presidential republic? His answer was unambiguous: 'In the present distribution of political forces . . . a move to a parliamentary government is extremely undesirable and even completely unacceptable. As President I will never agree to this form [of government]. In the current situation for the next 2–3 years only a presidential republic is possible.' He softened his challenge, however. 'This does not signify, of course, granting the President unlimited rights . . . If the parliament has the necessary instruments of control, then the balance of power will not be upset. We favour a strong judiciary—especially a constitutional court.'[97] Yeltsin was not prepared to force events. While he wanted the April Congress to adopt a new constitution, he rejected the calling of elections before they were due, ignoring the anxieties of some (including the People's Party of Russia) that without elections by the end of the year 'the steam will blow the lid off the cauldron'. It was suggested that Yeltsin had in mind a plan of definite steps for a 'symbolic act to achieve the political unity

[96] *Ng*, 9 Mar. 1992.        [97] *Ng*, 7 Apr. 1992.

of the Russian people'.[98] There seems to have been a general sentiment among the politically active in Russia that an act of national unity, similar to that which they believed had healed the wounds of the civil war in Spain, was necessary to bring an end to political discord.[99] Yeltsin shared this desire for national unity, but saw the strong presidential figure as the means to bring this about.

Such encouragement for a strong presidential regime casts light on several facets of this phase of the Russian transition. There was increasing recognition that Soviet era legislative institutions were an obstacle to thoroughgoing marketization of the economy. The CPD and its Supreme Soviet provided a platform of resistance for those who were opposed to shock therapy. More than three-quarters of the deputies who had been elected in March 1990 had a managerial background.[100] They represented the traditional Soviet industrial sectors that were hurting so badly under shock therapy. Increasingly, the primary objective of the self-styled democrats was to eliminate the political and economic legacy of the old Soviet regime, not democratize it. In place of the current parliamentary-presidential hybrid some advocated a fully-fledged presidential regime.

Confrontation loomed on the eve of the Sixth Congress. Yeltsin tried to head it off. On 2 April he moved to safeguard his closest allies from the people's deputies. The 'eminence grise' Gennady Burbulis, then the 'most influential politician in Yeltsin's circle',[101] was relieved of the post of First Deputy Prime Minister but remained State Secretary, while Sergei Shakhrai also lost his ministerial status. Responsibility for the entire presidential apparatus, including the administration and the domestic and foreign security services, was transferred to Burbulis' authority. Simultaneously, Gaidar relinquished the finance ministry, but his position was actually strengthened because he was now the sole Deputy Prime Minister, and therefore in effect Prime Minister.[102]

At the Congress, the main issue turned out to be not the Constitution but the plenary powers of the President and the formation of the government. The main opposition to Yeltsin came from the conservative nationalist Smena faction and from Russian Unity, the recently formed patriotic-communist bloc.

---

[98] *Ng*, 9 Mar. 1992.

[99] One aspect of this was the interest shown in the Spanish experience, especially the Pact of Moncloa. For example, Vladimir Alpatov, 'Vozmozhen li Rossiiskii "Pakt Monkloa" ', *Svobodnaia mysl'*, 13 (1993), 67.

[100] Sakwa, *Russian Politics*, 120, 442, nn. 15, 16.

[101] *Ng*, 4 Apr. 1992. As head of the State Council, Burbulis changed the title of his position five times in 18 months. According to Sakwa, he was dismissed 'from all his substantive posts' on 26 November 1992. Note, however, that he became 'adviser without title' on 14 December 1992: Sakwa, *Russian Politics*, 144 and n. 17.

[102] *Ng*, 4 Apr. 1992.

In the face of this, Yeltsin pursued a more conciliatory course, as did the Congress leaders, despite all the sabre-rattling in the lead-up to the Congress. There was some retreat from complete price liberalization and some offsets to harsh monetary restrictions. For example, 50 billion roubles were made available to alleviate the wage crisis; 70 billion to placate the agrarian lobby, described as 'one of the most powerful groups',[103] and a wooing of the industrialists by offering tax concessions and a presence in the cabinet.

Nevertheless, Yeltsin refused any concession that would imply a fundamental change of direction. He refused to surrender his plenary powers, to sacrifice anybody else from his ministry, or to countenance the subordination of the government to the Parliament, as the Congress was demanding. Yeltsin's conception of the presidency rejected the view that its functions should be restricted to mere Head of State coupled with an independent government responsible for policy.[104] In fact Gaidar called the bluff of the Congress: threatening to resign in the face of the threatened deprivation of the President's plenary powers, arguing that this would make it impossible to realise the economic reforms.[105] Faced on the one hand with strong criticism from within the Congress of economic policy and demands for the subordination of government to parliament and for Yeltsin to step down as Prime Minister, and on the other the hard line by the President and government, Khasbulatov, who had initially supported the Congress's position,[106] sought a compromise solution. In the end it was agreed that the President would present to the Supreme Soviet a law on the formation of the Council of Ministers. The only requirement was that the President should 'concur' with the parliament on the Prime Minister and members of the government, a formulation so vague, one commentator noted, that the proposed law strengthened Yeltsin's right to 'form a government unilaterally'.[107]

The expected confrontation at the Congress had been defused by concessions on both sides, but especially from the legislature. In the end, far from calling for the government's removal or the curtailment of Yeltsin's plenary powers, Khasbulatov had merely called for 'correctives in the strategic line of reform' and for 'strengthening state regulation'. Moreover in a comment that reflected his basic commitment to economic change, Khasbulatov argued that Yeltsin's 'global reforms required popular support, otherwise they will not be irreversible.' Khasbulatov's apparent change of heart indicated a reluctance to

---

[103] *Ng*, 8 Apr. 1992.

[104] *Ng*, 9 Apr. 1992. Yeltsin's conception was certainly more presidential than the 'three-quarters presidential republic' advocated by the Constitutional Commission, which at least allowed Parliament to remove individual members of the government: *Ng*, 10 Apr. 1992.

[105] *Ng*, 10 Apr. 1992.

[106] See the discussion in Brudny, 'Ruslan Khasbulatov', 87.     [107] *Ng*, 10 Apr. 1992.

drive Yeltsin into a corner that might be fraught with unknown consequences[108] for the political elite as a whole.

The absence of a clear outcome from the Sixth Congress left a vacuum of authority in Russian politics. The Congress did not want to vote either 'confidence' or 'no confidence' in the government; the government made no commitment to fulfil the Congress's decisions, while the President maintained silence on the government's resignation.[109] It was this impasse that Yeltsin was determined to overcome, but not immediately. The question of a referendum was to the fore both in Yeltsin's mind and in Russian politics more generally in mid-1992. For Yeltsin and his supporters, including DemRossiia, the question of the future institutional shape of Russian politics should be decided by the people as a whole. Yeltsin wanted to put to popular referendum the basic principles of a new Constitution, and the question of whether the parliament should be dissolved (its term was not due to end until March 1995) and new elections held.[110] DemRossiia went a little further; they wanted a constituent assembly. Equally, the leaders of the Supreme Soviet were determined that the Congress of People's Deputies, as the representative organ of popular opinion, should have the final say.[111] At issue here were irreconcilable views about the relative weight of the legislature and the executive. Popov posed the question even more sharply: at stake was 'dual power', that is, the reform process itself.[112] However at this juncture, Yeltsin was not certain he could win a referendum for a presidential republic.[113] In any case, he needed the assent of the Supreme Soviet before any referendum could be held, and given the questions he wished to ask, this was unlikely.

In the wake of the Congress and under attack from many sides, not least the Parliament, government policy began to shift. The first indicator of this was a cabinet reshuffle. It saw the entry into the government of major representatives of the industrial 'directors corps', who already occupied high positions in the legislature. In May–June three new Deputy Prime Ministers were appointed: Viktor Chernomyrdin, former Gazprom director, who also took over responsibility for energy, Vladimir Shumeiko became responsible for industrial administration, and Georgy Khizha.[114] Some saw these appointments as

---

[108] *Ng*, 3 Apr. 1992.                    [109] *Ng*, 14 Apr. 1992.

[110] *Ng*, 28 May 1992. For strenuous opposition to this by Viktor Sheinis, see *Ng*, 23 May 1992.

[111] Although Burbulis was accused of going behind Khasbulatov's back in order to organise a 'fifth column' of democratic deputies in favour of a referendum on the constitution: *Ng*, 21 May 1992.

[112] *Ng*, 15 May 1992.                    [113] *Ng*, 16 Apr. 1992.

[114] At this time too the head of the Central Bank, Georgy Matiukhin, resigned, to be replaced by Viktor Gerashchenko. Matiukhin had supported the policies of tight credit advocated by Gaidar and opposed by the industrial lobby and many deputies.

Yeltsin's attempt to establish closer links with Parliament.[115] Others saw it as a retreat from economic reform,[116] as the government then adopted a Programme for the Deepening of Economic Reform. Despite the title, it was more about pulling back from the brink of economic catastrophe. It involved some concessions to the industrialists and to the Supreme Soviet, which had proposed a reduction in the onerous taxes on industry. Moderate inflation, support for industry, retreat from harsh budgetary constraints and avoiding unemployment were the aims. These concessions, however, were soon qualified by a number of measures intended to further weaken state control over the economy (for example, raising energy prices, ending central state procurement of agricultural products, and introduction of a convertible rouble). This put the government immediately on a collision course with the industrialists' parliamentary bloc Civic Union, formed in June 1992.[117]

On 15 June Gaidar became acting Prime Minister, a step that served to distance the President from direct responsibility for government policy and thereby to deflect some of the policy-based criticism away from him. However, the government, while making some overtures to the industrialists, did not fundamentally veer from its course, thus precluding any possibility of establishing strong social support from this key sector of Russian society. Relations with the democrats were also becoming strained. Tensions between Yeltsin and the democrat movement manifested themselves at a meeting with a group of parliamentary deputies who had generally supported the President. The democrats expressed 'deep concern' about the failure of the President to consult them when making appointments to the so-called 'power ministries'[118] and reminded Yeltsin that he owed his position to the vote of the democrats. Nevertheless, though Yeltsin expressed concern about the lack of a social base of support for his reform, he was not prepared to tie himself to the democrat bandwagon, because, he emphasised, he considered himself 'representative of

[115] *Ng*, 5 June 1992.

[116] *Ng*, 4 June 1992. Popov apparently felt that the reform process had stalled politically. In June he resigned as mayor of Moscow in order to tackle the soviets which, according to the editor of *Nezavisimaia gazeta* Vitaly Tretiakov, remained bulwarks of communist opposition despite the ban on the Communist Party. Nevertheless, Tretiakov expressed considerable satisfaction about the achievements of Yeltsin's administration in his first year. He endorsed Yeltsin's recourse to a traditional imperial system of plenipotentiaries, subordinate to the centre, as a means of circumventing the soviets. And he applauded the speed with which Yeltsin's dictatorial methods had re-established order in the state and put in place an administrative apparatus. Nevertheless, he considered that there was a crisis at hand. Yeltsin had yet to build a new political or economic system. But he saw no alternative to the Yeltsin-Gaidar team: *Ng*, 5 June 1992; 11 June 1992.

[117] Inozemstev, 'Na pereput'e', 24; Sakwa, *Russian Politics*, 81–2.

[118] The colloquial name given to the Defence, Security and Interior Ministries, and sometimes the Foreign Ministry.

the entire nation'.[119] In the face of increasing opposition to its policies within the Parliament and society, and bereft of any solid social base, the Yeltsin administration found itself in a situation of unstable equilibrium.

Despite opinion polls that, even at this early stage, suggested a decline in Yeltsin's popular standing,[120] overall the most striking feature of this period was the continuing centrality of the presidency as an institution. Political apathy meant there was no popular, organised anti-government opposition. Yeltsin's unrivalled political stature in mid-1992, even if by default, made it highly unlikely that he would be subject to any of the few legal measures open to removing him, such as impeachment, let alone illegal measures, such as a military coup.[121] This situation was not to last; within six months he faced a threat of impeachment (see below).

The pivotal role of the presidency in the transformation process is illustrated by the indulgence that the deputies exhibited towards the President, as opposed to his government. At the fifth session of the Supreme Soviet, which opened on 21 September 1992, there was much more hostility towards Gaidar than there had been at the April Congress of People's Deputies. In particular the Industrial Union, reacting to the collapse of production, turned against his government.[122] But this hostility did not extend to the President. On the contrary, many deputies looked to the presidency as a bulwark of stability in the face of the threatening economic and social crisis brought on by shock therapy. A leading member of Civic Union, for instance, argued that the President could rally the populace and reform politicians around the reform process.[123] Yeltsin realised the political importance of this view, and recognised the need to maintain a distinct separation in the public mind between the presidency and government policy. As the political temperature rose in late 1992, with an increasing number of reform politicians moving into opposition and with his popularity already declining, Yeltsin sought to distance himself somewhat from Gaidar's policies. In a speech on 6 October to the Supreme Soviet he declared, 'I am not head of government but head of state'.[124] In the same speech Yeltsin emphasised the need to decentralise executive authority. It was apparent that he was seeking support from the heads of Russia's constituent regions. A week later it was reported that Yeltsin had established a powerful Council of the Heads of the Republics of the Russian Federation.[125]

---

[119] *Ng*, 4 Aug. 1992.

[120] Among Muscovites surveyed in 1992, the percentage with a 'positive' view of Yeltsin declined from 54% in February to 45% in June: *Kto est chto*, 97.

[121] *Ng*, 20 Aug. 1992.     [122] *Ng*, 23 Sept. 1992.     [123] *Ng*, 25 Oct. 1992.

[124] *Ng*, 7 Oct. 1992.

[125] The Council was linked to the Security Council, providing Moscow with what was described as 'harsh control' over the nationalities and another opportunity for Yeltsin to demonstrate to the Parliament just who was boss in Russia: *Ng*, 16 Oct. 1992.

But Yeltsin was not yet master of the Parliament. His attempts to have the Seventh Congress postponed to allow for amendment of the constitution[126] were rebuffed. The Congress was due to convene on 1 December, the date set for Yeltsin's plenary powers to expire. The scene was thus set for a clash with the Congress. But again, this was a clash both executive and legislature wished to avoid. In September Yeltsin agreed to drop threats to prorogue Parliament in return for an agreement from Khasbulatov to postpone scheduled elections for regional Heads of Administration.[127] It was apparent that Yeltsin was not yet willing to use force to intimidate the Parliament.[128] But behind the scenes there was reported to be activity which could now be seen to constitute dress rehearsals for October 1993. Yeltsin's administration was allegedly manoeuvring to remove the Supreme Soviet.[129] A recent session of the Security Council had discussed what was called a 'soft dismantling of the Supreme Soviet' and even a 'presidential administration'. On 26 October Yeltsin stripped Khasbulatov of his authority over the Parliament's 5,000 strong security force, subordinating it instead to the Ministry of the Interior.[130] The next day Yeltsin outlawed the National Salvation Front, a measure that was seen by a leader of Civic Union as a warning to the Supreme Soviet: 'Postpone the [December 1992] Congress or the parliament will be dispersed.'[131]

It is apparent that political tensions in the lead-up to the Seventh Congress were causing considerable alarm within the political elite. Most of them were anxious to defuse the situation. Vitaly Tretiakov, editor of *Nezavisimaia gazeta*, called for open collaboration between the various branches of government.[132] Defence Minister Grachev, while concerned about the growing political confrontation, reaffirmed the continued apolitical role of the army, while Gaidar expressed concern about the threat to the 'balance of forces.'[133] However, other politicians were evidently intent on a confrontationist course. Burbulis and Mikhail Poltoranin, Deputy Prime Minister for information, encouraged Yeltsin to confront the Supreme Soviet over the issue of postponing the Congress of People's Deputies.[134] Khasbulatov was accused of preparing a

---

[126] *Ng*, 17 Oct. 1992.          [127] Steele, *Eternal Russia*, 285.

[128] *Ng*, 22 Oct. 1992.          [129] *Ng*, 27 Oct. 1992; 29 Oct. 1992.

[130] Brudny, 'Ruslan Khasbulatov', 89. Khasbulatov had set this force up without any constitutional standing and probably as a counter to Yeltsin's security guard.

[131] *Ng*, 30 Oct. 1992; 28 Oct. 1992. On the formation of the NSF, in late October 1992, and its eventual banning immediately after 3 October 1993 see Jeremy Lester, *Modern Tsars and Princes: The Struggle for Hegemony in Russia* (London and New York, Verso, 1995), 156–9.

[132] *Ng*, 27 Oct. 1992. Tretiakov was also worried by the way in which the press could get dragged into the conflict. Khasbulatov had used his guard to seize control of the daily *Izvestiia* (this is what had prompted Yeltsin to remove the security force from his control). Ultimately this matter was to go before the Constitutional Court.

[133] *Ng*, 30 Oct. 1992.          [134] Ibid.

'creeping coup'. At a private briefing for foreign correspondents in late October, Poltoranin declared that the forthcoming Congress planned to oust the government and introduce elections for judges to the Constitutional Court: 'This would enable them to declare most of the President's decrees unconstitutional, get rid of the executive presidency itself and turn the President into an icon.'[135]

In November, in the lead-up to the Congress, Yeltsin, who had acknowledged he had been mistaken 'not to go down to the parliament',[136] sought to cement alliances with 'centrists' in order to head off confrontation with 'extremists' in the Congress. In particular he courted Civic Union, the enterprise managers' party led by Arkady Volsky who was critical of Gaidar's monetarism and called for an examination of the Chinese experience.[137] It was a mutual attraction. Volsky made overtures to the government for an accord amongst the centrist forces.[138] This was an attempt to create, in the absence of tight party structures or allegiances, some kind of stable majority for Yeltsin's government in the Congress (of the kind, it was suggested, that had facilitated Mitterand's 'co-habitation').[139] Yeltsin also sought to enhance his standing outside the parliament. He signed a number of decrees designed to elicit popular sympathy and support among industrialists, with a view to switching the debate from the 'anti-people policies' of the government to one of its economic competence.[140]

The Seventh Congress threatened to be a showdown between the executive and the legislature. In the end, however, the Congress was a compromise between them, though a compromise in which Yeltsin came out on top. It was not reached, however, without considerable drama. At the opening session on 1 December, Yeltsin offered to relinquish his emergency powers if the Congress gave him the right to form the government. In the view of many this was no compromise at all; in effect Yeltsin was saying 'Give me what I want, then I will not ask for it.'[141] In response, the Congress sought to amend the Constitution in order to give the Parliament the right to appoint the Prime Minister and

---

[135] Cited in Steele, *Eternal Russia*, 285–6. As well as Poltoranin, then State Secretary Burbulis, Foreign Minister Kozyrev and Deputy Prime Minister in charge of privatization Chubais were present at a dinner for foreign correspondents. Steele interpreted the ministers' 'unusual invitation' as 'designed to elicit foreign support against the Congress, and prepare the ground for sympathetic coverage if Yeltsin chose to impose presidential rule to close the Congress.'

[136] *Ng*, 29 Oct. 1992. Analysis of every deputy's voting behaviour between May 1990 and December 1992 showed extraordinary erosion of support for the President in the Parliament. 'Had Yeltsin been a more skilful leader, he should have been able to increase his support' argues Steele in *Eternal Russia*, 278.

[137] *Ng*, 4 Nov. 1992.     [138] *Ng*, 13 Nov. 1992.     [139] *Ng*, 11 Nov. 1992.

[140] *Ng*, 13 Nov. 1992.     [141] Steele, *Eternal Russia*, 286.

other leading ministers, but it failed to secure the two-thirds vote required. However it rejected Gaidar's nomination for the post of Prime Minister on the grounds that 'not one of his government's promises were fulfilled, while all the basic economic and social indicators were negative.' The Gaidar period, it was said, had 'used up the sources of August democratism and revived the total-itarian temptation, the essence of which is the systematic search for enemies of society . . . and public declaration of war on them.'[142]

The open declaration of war came on 10 December in the form of a pres-idential address to the Congress.[143] In his speech, drafted by Burbulis and Poltoranin, Yeltsin denounced the Congress as a 'bulwark of conservative forces and reaction' and demanded that a referendum be held in January to decide who should have power: President or Parliament. Referring to 'two irreconcilable forces', he appealed to the people over the heads of the deputies for a polarization of forces, thereby raising the spectre of civil war. After his speech, Yeltsin strode from the chamber, calling on the deputies who sup-ported him to follow suit. The intention was to deprive the Congress of a quo-rum, forcing its closure. Drama turned to farce as Yeltsin, having failed to alert his supporters of the plan, took with him only 150 deputies, less than half of those who had voted for Gaidar.[144]

Yeltsin certainly raised the political stakes at the Congress, but the crucial players in his administration were not yet prepared for confrontation. The Ministries of Defence, Security, Internal Affairs, the General Secretary of the Security Council and the Procurator of the Republic all resiled from the 'bar-ricade' option.[145] The heat was taken out of the situation by the direct inter-vention of the head of the Constitutional Court. On 10 December Valery Zorkin declared that in the event of the failure of the President and the Chairman of the Supreme Soviet to compromise, the Constitutional Court, 'on its own initiative would consider the constitutional positions of the heads of the legislative and executive branches of the state.' The compromise came in the form of an agreement to hold a referendum on 11 April 1993 on the basic provisions of a new constitution, viz. whether Russia should be a parliamen-

---

[142] *Ng,* 11 Jan. 1993. As at November 1992 'Gaidarnomiks' had achieved 'practically nothing'. Privatization in retail trade, services and catering was a mere 7.7%, 6.5% and 2.7% respectively, while 'big' privatization had come to 'nought'. Meanwhile, coupled with a rad-ical reduction in living standards the overall downward demographic trends had dramat-ically worsened.

[143] Steele, *Eternal Russia,* 287.

[144] *Ng,* 11 Jan. 1993. Yeltsin omitted to mention that his meeting with deputies who sup-ported him would take place 'during the break'. Many of his potential supporters, not understanding his plan, and 'still stunned' by Yeltsin's speech, remained in their places: Steele, *Eternal Russia,* 287–8.

[145] *Ng,* 11 Jan. 1993.

tary or presidential republic, and agreement to extend Yeltsin's special powers for a four-month period (until the referendum).[146] In return, Yeltsin agreed that the Congress of People's Deputies could vote on his nominees for Prime Minister. Zorkin's initiative, declared Nikolai Travkin, leader of the Democratic Party of Russia, marked 'the birth of civil society in Russia'.[147]

As a result of this compromise, Congress delegates voted on the list of nominees for Prime Minister proposed by Yeltsin. Gaidar was relegated to third of five. Yeltsin was accorded the last word on the appointment of the new premier; he could choose whichever of the top three supported by the Congress he wished. He chose Chernomyrdin. On the surface this was a concession. After all, Yeltsin had vowed before the Congress that he would never accept any other candidate for premier than Gaidar. Gaidar now declared he was leaving the government and would not return. Again, some observers were aghast. Tretiakov editorialized that Chernomyrdin's appointment was Yeltsin's 'biggest political defeat' in 1992. It would mean, Tretiakov warned, a much larger role for the state sector and encourage inflation. Yeltsin was personally culpable for this U-turn. Similarly, others saw Gaidar's departure as a mortal blow to the reforms, depriving them of a 'theoretical basis'. It was a 'victory of politics over economics'.[148] Others, however, welcomed Chernomyrdin's appointment, notably, Travkin's Democratic Party of Russia.[149] Others noted what had not changed: Yeltsin had kept his promise to preserve the old Gaidar leadership. Thus he retained Chubais, Shokhin, and Foreign Minister Andrei Kozyrev. The real winner from this 'weakened' cabinet, it was suggested, would not be the Parliament but the President, who had also retained one of his closest advisers, Sergei Shakhrai.[150] The subsequent course of events was to prove the optimists right. Under Chernomyrdin there was to be no fundamental retreat from the course set by Gaidar. Nor, despite tactical feints, was there any pulling back from settling accounts with the Parliament.

Travkin's contention about the birth of civil society was over-optimistic, as October 1993 would demonstrate. In fact the proposed referendum simply

---

[146] *Izvestiia*,14 Dec. 1992.

[147] Similarly, the head of the secretariat of the Constitutional Commission Andrei Gol'tsblat, welcomed the forthcoming 11 April referendum on the Basic Law, as a step towards social stability. The existing Constitution, he argued, gave the Congress of Peoples Deputies too much scope to resurrect the 'omnipotence of the Soviets'. At issue was not how much power the President had in relation to the Supreme Soviet, but the potential of the Congress not to observe the Constitution or other laws: 'This is the path to the destruction of the state', Gol'tsblat argued. The way was now open for Yeltsin to rectify the constitutional weakness of his position: *Ng*, 29 Dec. 1993. The response in some quarters bordered on hysteria: 'There has been a coup. A junta has come to power: Yeltsin, Khasbulatov and Zorkin!' exclaimed a Kadet deputy: V. Todres, *Ng*, 15 Dec. 1993.

[148] *Ng*, 16 Dec. 1992.      [149] *Ng*, 22 Dec. 1992.      [150] *Ng*, 24 Dec. 1992.

meant that the intra-state struggle took on legal forms. Having resiled from dispersing the Congress in December 1992, Yeltsin resorted to 'soft' methods: his campaign for the 11 April 1993 referendum. Pending the referendum, the Supreme Soviet had agreed not to upset the existing balance of power between the three branches of government.[151] Whatever the outcome of the referendum, given the nature of the proposed question at issue, that balance was bound to be overturned. This was reflected in the way in which Yeltsin's proposed formula for the April 1993 referendum was repudiated by one observer as a pseudo-choice: no more than a plebiscite for himself and for autocracy. It was tantamount, therefore, to the 'destruction of one branch of the state' by another. [152]

We know from the literature on post-authoritarian transitions that a consensus among the political elite and popular legitimacy of the new institutions can facilitate successful transition to representative democracy. It is clear that neither Khasbulatov nor Yeltsin was prepared to forge such a consensus. Indeed, on this occasion it was to be Khasbulatov who upped the ante (see below). The broader political elite was divided. There were some who recognised the necessity of elite consensus if democracy was to take root in Russia. For example, Andrei Fedorov,[153] an adviser to Vice President Rutskoi, saw the proposed referendum as an opportunity to create political consensus and social stability. He called for a 'round table' as a mechanism for working out the questions to be put to the referendum, and thereby overcoming the consequences of continuing disagreement between President and Parliament on this issue. However, Gavriil Popov, as usual, was in no mood for compromise: 'Without a change of the system of power, there will be no new personnel [in power].' Political stability could only be achieved through new elections based on a new Constitution adopted by a Constituent Assembly. This would eliminate the Supreme Soviet and the Congress as political players. A Congress elected three years ago under a one-party system is not the basis for adopting a new Constitution, he argued.[154] For others, the referendum was, in a sense, too late. It was designed to publicly ratify the consolidation of a presidential

---

[151] *Ng*, 15 Dec. 1992.                              [152] *Ng*, 11 Jan. 1993.

[153] *Ng*, 19 Jan. 1993. Fedorov also saw regionalism as a threat to political stability. A number of republics and regions of the Russian Federation had indicated unwillingness to hold a referendum on their territory, threatening, according to Fedorov, the integrity of the entire political system.

[154] *Ng*, 26 Jan. 1993. Popov later argued that the October clash could have been avoided at the time of the referendum had there been a clear vote for the President as well as the Parliament to go to early elections. Yeltsin himself was willing to do so, but representatives from DemRossiia, knowing that a new election was 'tantamount to death' rejected the 'Yes' vote. Therefore, concluded Popov, failure to take advantage of the April referendum 'programmed the October events in advance'. *Ng*, 10 Dec. 1992.

republic that was already underway. Yeltsin was charged with having established three unconditionally loyal inner 'circles' which were ready at the 'necessary moment' to block the so-called conservatives.[155] The 'first circle' was composed of long-standing allies such as Viktor Iliushin; the second was that group of advisers until recent times headed by Burbulis;[156] and the third those institutions formally independent of the President but created on his initiative and financed from the presidential budget. These institutions and their finances were independent of any legislative control. The main purpose of the 'third circle' was to influence government ministries, control their activities and, 'in an extraordinary situation, possibly substitute for them'.[157] In other words, these three circles created a de facto presidential republic in advance of the referendum.

Having ' "bound" Chernomyrdin hand and foot' with Gaidar's old cabinet,[158] Yeltsin was preoccupied with his continuing joust with Khasbulatov over the forthcoming referendum. For Yeltsin the immediate public priority was stability. To that end he proposed a reconciliation pact with the Parliament, but this appeared to be just a holding operation while laying the grounds for a referendum which would tip the constitutional balance once and for all in the President's favour. However, during January there was a widespread feeling among the political elite, including many republican leaders, that holding a referendum in the current climate could lead to violence and the disintegration of the country.[159] But Yeltsin was adamant: any new constitution would not be adopted by the current corps of People's Deputies. However the strength of elite opinion prompted him to begin searching for a compromise, bringing him in early 1993 to favour election for the Parliament in 1994, a year in advance of a presidential election.[160]

---

[155] *Ng*, 26 Jan. 1993.

[156] In preparation for the impending clash with the Supreme Soviet, within presidential and government ranks a regrouping of forces took place. A 'general staff', led by Burbulis, was formed to promote the referendum. The think-tank 'RF- politika', strengthened by the presence of Poltoranin and Shakhrai, would provide the 'agitprop' for this staff. A demonstration in support of the presidential version of the referendum would be organized through DemRossiia. Meanwhile, preparation of a Constituent Assembly was underway. It was intended to play a dual role: if Yeltsin wins the referendum it would adopt the new 'presidential constitution'; in the event of defeat, it could present itself as a visible alternative to the 'red-brown congress'—ready to take power: *Ng*, 12 Jan. 1993.

[157] *Ng*, 26 Jan. 1993.                    [158] *Ng*, 10 Feb. 1993.

[159] Sakwa, *Russian Politics*, 125.

[160] Speech of Yeltsin on Russian Television, 18 Feb. 1993. Within the President's advisory team Shumeiko was most intent on going to referendum; Shakhrai proposed a temporary accord with the Supreme Soviet; while Filatov proposed pursuing both approaches. See the reports in *Rossiiskie vesti*, 20 Feb. 1993 (Yeltsin's address) and *Megapolis-Express*, 24 Feb. 1993, *CDPSP*, XLV, 7 (1993), 4.

Khasbulatov saw it otherwise. He believed that the road to political stability lay through the existing Congress of People's Deputies, not a referendum. To that end he favoured the convening of an extraordinary Congress. Indeed, in December the Supreme Soviet had begun preparing its 'secret weapon': bringing forward the Eighth Congress to March in order to anticipate the April referendum. The Congress would then at least be able to impose its version of the referendum rather than Yeltsin's, which was to propose the dispersal of the Congress.[161] Doubting the wisdom of any referendum at all (he believed that there had been sufficient amendments to the Constitution already by the Congress to make it democratic), with the support of Rutskoi, he repudiated the December agreement on the grounds that it was unconstitutional and made under duress.[162] Arguing that the constitutional crisis was artificially manufactured by the democrats who were intent on installing a 'neototalitarian' dictatorship, he argued for *simultaneous* elections of President and legislature.[163]

In February 1993 Yeltsin acquiesced in the convening of an extraordinary Congress, but merely as a prelude to a referendum. Khasbulatov, however, was intent on resolving the impasse through the Congress. Among his concerns was to eliminate what he called the 'dualism of executive power' by transferring control over the government from President to Parliament.[164] For Khasbulatov, the soviets were the bulwark against dictatorship. Speaking to regional soviet leaders in February, he urged that local soviets should have the final say over appointments of local security and interior officials, and should subordinate all executive officials to the soviet's authority. The soviets in turn should be subordinate to the Presidium of the Supreme Soviet, a proposal which, if implemented, would have completely sidelined the President and re-instituted parliamentary rule.

The extraordinary Eighth Congress, which met on 10–13 March 1993, brought the spectre of dual power into sharp focus. On 12 March the Congress abrogated the December compromise with Yeltsin, rebuffing his proposals for a referendum,[165] and depriving him of his previously virtually unrestricted right to issue decrees (which could now be overturned by a simple parliamentary majority), to appoint regional heads of administration or presidential

---

[161] *Ng*, 24 Dec. 1992.

[162] Brudny, 'Ruslan Khasbulatov', 9.

[163] *Izvestiia*, 20 Feb. 1993; 23 Feb. 1993.

[164] *Izvestiia*, 26 Feb. 1993.

[165] The Seventh Congress of People's Deputies on 12 December 1992 had adopted a nine-point resolution brokered by Zorkin: 'On the Stabilisation of the Constitutional System.' Under this resolution, a referendum on the adoption of a new constitution was to be held in April 1993. Meanwhile, the existing balance between executive and legislature would remain in place, that is, the President would retain his right to rule by decree: see Sakwa, *Russian Politics*, 124; *Ng*, 16 Mar. 1993.

representatives, and to appoint ministers without parliamentary approval.[166] The Supreme Soviet sought to shift the axis of executive power away from the presidency to the government and make the latter responsible to the Parliament. The right of the Council of Ministers to initiate legislation, by-passing the presidency, was affirmed,[167] as the Parliament sought to split the government from Yeltsin. In addition, in a defensive move, a constitutional amendment was adopted providing for the automatic impeachment of the President should he seek to dissolve the Parliament. Emboldened, and acting like a head of government, Khasbulatov made overtures to his CIS counter-parts for support, an initiative that Yeltsin evidently found threatening.[168] Parliamentarism was on the counter-offensive against presidentialism.

The Congress had been a stinging defeat for the President, but now there was fear that he might settle accounts with the Parliament by force. According to Zorkin, 'the tank variant hung in the air.'[169] The leadership of the Federation of Independent Trade Unions of Russia prepared for the declaration of a state of emergency. But it was evident that Yeltsin lacked the power to do this: not only were the deputies against him, but also Zorkin and Rutskoi. It was unclear too how the power ministries would act. The provincial heads of administration too came out against repressive measures. Neither was there certainty about the allegiances of republican and regional leaders nor about the possible repercussions for the federation.[170] In sum, Yeltsin felt unable to act decisively because there was no elite consensus to do so.

Yeltsin needed to build such a consensus, to rally public and elite support to cut the ground from under the feet of the Congress. He found support to act decisively against the Parliament both within and without his apparatus. Both his Security Council and Presidential Council urged him to act.[171] There were those who proposed he declare a state of emergency. But in the main, he was

---

[166] Sakwa, *Russian Politics*, 125.

[167] In fact the Congress of People's Deputies reactivated three previously 'frozen' articles of the constitution which facilitated 'legislative initiative' on the part of the government and allowed the Supreme Soviet to suspend presidential decrees or terminate them. *Rossiiskie vesti*, 16 Mar. 1993, *CDPSP*, XLV, 10 (1993), 11.

[168] *Ng*, 20 Mar. 1993.     [169] *Ng*, 17 Mar. 1993.

[170] Appeals to republican and regional leaders by both sides in this contest were seen as strengthening separatist tendencies at the expense of the centre. Concern was expressed too at the Congress that a referendum threatened national unity: *Ng*, 16 Mar. 1993. In February the heads of Russia's republics had expressed the fear that the April referendum could tear the Federation asunder: see Sakwa, *Russian Politics*, 125.

[171] Member of the Presidential Council Migranian argued that Yeltsin was the only person who could do this and that he should take the initiative while he had no obvious competitors and the public standing of the Congress was so low, and immediately propose pre-term elections and a referendum: *Ng*, 17 Mar. 1993.

urged to resort to a referendum.[172] Support for the President was sought too among his peers in the CIS. He found strong support for his position among rather more powerful international players: the leaders of the USA and Western Europe.[173]

Encouraged, Yeltsin moved quickly to resolve the impasse. In a television address on 20 March he declared 'special rule' for five weeks. All parliamentary vetoes of presidential authority were null and void and there would now be a referendum on 25 April. His declared intention was to resolve a 'crisis of power' brought on by the Eighth Congress which he condemned as a 'dress rehearsal for revenge by members of the former Party nomenklatura.'[174] But evidently Yeltsin was still not sufficiently confident to act decisively against his opponents. Constitutional Court chief Zorkin declared the assertion of 'special rule' unconstitutional, and other members of the broad political elite made their unease known. When Yeltsin's decree was published, on 24 March, it did not mention special rule, dissolution of the Congress, or suspension of the Supreme Soviet.[175]

The contest between President and legislature now intensified. An 'extraordinary' Ninth Congress convened on 26–29 March. An attempt at compromise by Khasbulatov, who at a meeting with Yeltsin on 27 March agreed to early elections for both Parliament and President, was rebuffed by the Congress. The angry deputies now held votes to remove Khasbulatov and impeach Yeltsin, but both failed narrowly. Although the Congress proceeded to strip Yeltsin of even more powers, it did not overturn the announced referendum. But when the questions for the referendum were announced, it was clear that they had been designed within the Parliament in an attempt to undercut Yeltsin's credibility. By asking whether voters had confidence in the President and supported his policies, the parliamentary leadership hoped to strip the vestiges of legitimacy away from both the President and the policies associated with his unpopular government.

Yeltsin's referendum went ahead as scheduled, with more than 50 per cent of eligible voters required to vote in order to make questions 3 and 4 (which were

---

[172] *Ng*, 20 Mar. 1993. Support apparently was not forthcoming from a coercive institution: internal security. Viktor Barannikov, a staunch Yeltsin loyalist, was unwilling to embroil the security service in political chicanery. Reluctant to act against the National Salvation Front without legal grounds, his failure to support unequivocally Yeltsin's 20 March declaration, and apparent reluctance to use force against the populace should the President consider it necessary, led to his dismissal for alleged corruption: *Ng*, 31 July 1993.

[173] *Izvestiia*, 18 Mar. 1993.

[174] *Rossiiskie vesti*, 23 Mar. 1993, *CDPSP*, XLV, 12 (1993), 1–2.

[175] Sakwa, *Russian Politics*, 126.

1

seen to involve constitutional issues) legally valid.[176] Yeltsin received unexpected support in the referendum, in which 64.5 per cent of eligible voters participated.[177] The results were as shown in Table 4.1.[178] The unexpectedly high votes of confidence in the President and approval of his policies was a shock for his parliamentary foes, and although the votes on the latter two 'constitutional' questions were not binding, the relative votes in favour of early elections constituted a moral victory for the President. However, this generally positive outcome for Yeltsin was tempered by the regional breakdown. Of the 89 administrative regions of Russia, in 20 a majority of voters expressed no confidence in Yeltsin, in 31 a majority opposed his socio-economic policies, and 43 favoured early presidential elections; but in 75 regions a majority favoured early parliamentary elections. Thus although the referendum strengthened Yeltsin by showing that he could generate greater popular support than the parliament throughout Russia (and especially in the large cities), the outcome remained indecisive.

TABLE 4.1. *Results of Yeltsin's referendum*

| Question | Yes | | No | | Spoiled ballots |
|---|---|---|---|---|---|
| | % of vote | % of electorate | % of vote | % of electorate | |
| 1. Do you have confidence in the President of the Russian Federation, Boris Yeltsin? | 58.7 | 37.3 | 39.2 | 25.2 | 2.1 |
| 2. Do you approve of the socio-economic policies carried out by the President of the RF and the government of the RF since 1992? | 53.0 | 34.0 | 44.6 | 28.6 | 2.4 |
| 3. Do you consider it necessary to hold early elections to the presidency of the RF? | 49.5 | 31.7 | 47.1 | 30.2 | 3.4 |
| 4. Do you consider it necessary to hold early elections of the people's deputies of the RF? | 67.2 | 43.1 | 30.1 | 19.3 | 2.7 |

[176] Alexander Rahr, 'The Roots of the Power Struggle', *RFE/RL Research Report*, 2: 20 (14 May 1993), 12–13.

[177] Vladimir Mau, 'Politicheskaia ekonomiia Rossiiskikh reform: opyt 1993 goda', Sm 1 (1994), 37.

[178] Results as reported in Sakwa, *Russian Politics*, 391.

Plebiscitary politics favoured the incumbent President, but the referendum did not resolve the basic crisis of institutional legitimacy that the stand-off between President and Parliament entailed. Their continual attempts to discredit each other undermined the capacity of the government to take decisive action on the economy. Above all, they discredited the institutions of state as a whole. The stalemate threatened to drag down the entire edifice of constitutional rule, including the Constitutional Court, which was increasingly drawn into the fray on the side of the parliament. Further, as each side sought to win allies among provincial elites, central government was weakened. While not immediately threatening the integrity of the Russian state, as nationalist separatism had fatally done in the Soviet Union, it eroded central authority, exacerbating the tensions between the centre and the regions, impeding the implementation of economic policy at the level of the Russian state as a whole.[179] In this respect, the question of who was winning and who was losing in this tournament made little sense. What was increasingly at stake was the legitimacy of the new political regime, which was charged with bringing about the capitalist transformation of Russia. Failure to resolve this impasse threatened not only to bog down this transformation but (once again) raised the spectre of 'civil confrontation.'[180]

Such a confrontation was not long in coming. May Day saw a bloody clash with oppositionists in Moscow, which left 579 of them injured and one police officer dead. Khasbulatov interpreted this clash in terms of Yeltsin's desire to create the conditions under which he could act decisively against the Parliament and thereby take advantage of the two-thirds vote in favour of early elections. The referendum, he argued, had weakened the state. The clash was merely a provocation by Yeltsin and his allies among the Moscow city authorities to set the scene for removing the Parliament.[181]

Having won a popular vote of confidence in himself and his policies, Yeltsin went on the political offensive. He moved to have a new Constitution adopted by a Constitutional Assembly.[182] The draft anticipated the Constitution that would finally be adopted in December. While provision was made for enhanced human rights and civil liberties, the commitment to social rights (right to work, free housing and education, etc.) that had been a feature of the previous constitution were omitted. This would be a Constitution for a capitalist state. Most striking about the new Constitution was the proposed strengthening of presidential authority. It would become, in the words of one

---

[179] Mau, 'Politicheskaia', 35. On concessions by the centre to regional authorities in return for their 'nominal support', see Alpatov, 'Vozmozhen', 71.
[180] *Moskovskie novosti*, 4 Apr. 1993, *CDPSP*, XLV, 13 (1993), 10–11.
[181] *Rossiiskaia gazeta*, 5 May 1993.                    [182] Mau, 'Politicheskaia', 40.

analyst, a 'regime of personal power', Tsarism in all but name.[183] While the President's nomination to the post of Prime Minister required parliamentary approval, he could make other ministerial appointments 'in consultation' with the upper house , or Federation Council, of the new bicameral legislature. The government would be directly subordinated to him. He could also appoint the top officials in the executive, and present candidates for Prosecutor General and judges in all Federal Courts. The Central Bank would also be subordinate to the President. In short, the President would have a decisive grip on the sinews of state power: personnel and money. Further, there would be few checks on this power. The President was able to dissolve the bicameral legislature and call new elections, while impeachment of the President was a difficult process and could be carried out only by the Federation Council (which was to consist of the elected heads of Russia's republics and the heads of administrations—i.e., Yeltsin's counterparts in the regions). The draft Constitution was in every sense a product of the proposal for an authoritarian presidential republic which Shakhrai and Burbulis had been putting forward since early 1992. But there were still several obstacles on the path to its realization, notably the Constitutional Court and the Congress of People's Deputies. Indeed, a new constitution could only be introduced through the existing parliament.

In June a Constitutional Assembly was convened by Yeltsin in an attempt to circumvent this opposition. But the impasse remained. Despite the adoption of a draft Basic Law by the Constitutional Assembly, which Yeltsin viewed as *the* draft, the Supreme Soviet continued to consider it as only an alternative to the draft of its own Constitutional Commission. The Assembly came up with a new draft in July, representing a synthesis of many elements of the opposing presidential and parliamentary drafts, but there could be no agreement on the basic question of power: parliamentary or presidential supremacy. It was apparent that the attempt by the presidency to achieve 'shock' constitutional reform had bogged down. But it was equally apparent that Yeltsin was intent on securing his version of the Constitution. In the eyes of one observer,[184] if this could not be secured through the Congress of People's Deputies, then the issue of who would decide—Parliament in its current make-up, a new Parliament, or a special Constitutional Assembly—would be put to referendum. In the end the matter was to be put to a popular vote without reference either to the Soviet-era Parliament or any other institution (see below).

After the April referendum, the struggle over economic policy took a virulent political form. A 'war of programmes' broke out between President and Parliament, as the Supreme Soviet countered the government's acceleration of

---

[183] *Megapolis-Express*, 5 May 1993, *CDPSP*, XLV, 18 (1993), 7. The draft was published in *Izvestiia*, 30 Apr. 1993.
[184] *Segodnia*, 23 July 1993, *CDPSP*, XLIV, 28 (Aug. 1993), 5–6.

privatization and tight credit and monetary policies.[185] It passed a series of anti-privatization resolutions and on 20 July suspended a presidential decree accelerating privatization, referring it to the Constitutional Court. That month Parliament proposed a US$23 billion deficit budget to subsidise industry, which would have increased the public sector deficit to about 25 per cent of GDP. Yeltsin, under pressure from the IMF, twice vetoed the Parliament's inflationary budget.[186]

The struggle between President and Parliament was compounded by a split within the government itself over economic policy. In April Lobov was appointed First Deputy Prime Minister and Minister of Economics. Renowned for his pro-inflationary views, he was immediately at loggerheads with the deflationary views of his formal subordinates, Anatoly Chubais and Boris Fedorov, heads of the State Committee on Property and the Ministry of Finance respectively. The appointment of Lobov reflected the inconsistent stance of the President, who vacillated between inflationary and extreme-deflationary policies. The leadership of the Supreme Soviet tried to exploit the vacillations of the President and the division within the government. It hoped to split the government in order to isolate the extreme neo-liberals, and with them the President.[187]

By the beginning of September it was clear that the Supreme Soviet and the President were on a collision course. Both sides had been courting regional authorities, and the Supreme Soviet had been pressing on with its own plans for constitutional reform. This constituted a major danger for Yeltsin, because the Parliament had the power to adopt constitutional amendments regardless of the views of the President. Amid allegations and counter-allegations of corruption, Rutskoi was dismissed as Vice President while Gaidar returned to the government as First Deputy Prime Minister. The Supreme Soviet was threatening to adopt normative acts that would give them control over the government and reduce the President to a 'decorative figure'. Equally, Yeltsin was determined to resolve once and for all what he and his supporters regarded as untenable: 'dual power'. The Parliament was threatened with dissolution.[188]

According to one observer, a presidential *coup d'état* was in the making.[189] But there were clearly risks involved. There was the danger of detonating a

---

[185] In May the government signed a three-month agreement with the Central Bank tightening credit. Meanwhile the Parliament abolished the Supreme Soviet Committee for Economic Reform which, chaired by S. N. Krasavchenko, was considered pro-government. Mau, 'Politicheskaia', 39–40.

[186] At the beginning of September, the IMF informed the Russian government that no IMF money would be available until the budget was settled: Jonathan W. Moses, 'The *Eighteenth Brumaire* of Boris Yeltsin', *Security Dialogue*, 25: 3 (1994), 339.

[187] Mau, 'Politicheskaia', 38, 42. See also *Rossiiskaia gazeta*, 11 Sept. 1993.

[188] *Izvestiia*, 10 Sept. 1993.     [189] *Rossiiskaia gazeta*, 11 Sept. 1993.

social explosion. There was also the uncertainty of which coercive apparatuses Yeltsin had at his disposal. Steps towards a resolution of what Yeltsin called the 'question of power' were already being undertaken within the presidential apparatus. The most notable signs of this were the reshuffling of personnel within the crucial power ministries and apparatuses. In July Barannikov had been dismissed as security minister, to be replaced by a former KGB officer, Nikolai Golushko. An army general was appointed head of the border forces, which were now incorporated into the structures of the Ministry of Internal Affairs. The Secretary of the Security Council, Marshal Shaposhnikov, not two months in the job, had resigned.[190] Yeltsin now moved to seek support from the Ministry of Internal Affairs, under General Viktor Yerin, the Security Ministry under Golushko, and from the army, headed by Grachev.[191] He could rely on the forces of internal order, but at best the military was an uncertain ally. Yeltsin tried to shore up his military support by visiting bases in the vicinity of Moscow. At the height of the confrontation, however, Defence Minister Grachev declared the military to be '100%' behind Yeltsin.[192] But later analysis indicates it was a reluctant military that answered Yeltsin's appeal for support. It was the Ministry of Internal Affairs that was the vital player.[193] Nevertheless, the military advantage lay with the President; the Parliament had virtually no armed forces at its disposal.[194] Even so, on the eve of his strike against the Parliament, the forces at the President's disposal were less than resolute.

The Bonapartist coup[195] came on 21 September 1993 when, in a televised address, Yeltsin terminated the activities of the Supreme Soviet and the

[190] An interesting insight into the function of the Security Council and its relations with the President is provided by Shaposhnikov's departure. His predecessor, Skokov, had fallen foul of competition with the power ministries. Shaposhnikov soon discovered that all that was required of him was 'political loyalty to the President and a minimum of activity'. As for the Security Council 'it was no more than a part of the presidential administration, intended to organise deliberations of Boris Yeltsin with "specific" departments, but not at all for the elaboration—at long last—of a unified conception of national security and coordination of its implementation' *Ng*, 12 Aug. 1993.

[191] He could rely upon three Moscow-based forces—the Main Administration of the Defence of the Russian Federation, the Kremlin Presidential Regiment, and the Moscow OMON—and possibly MVD units. But these could only control the capital. Only the army could act nationally. However, its young officers were mindful of the consequences of acting illegally. Further, the commanders of units located in the regions were under the sway of the local leaders to whom they were indebted for their living conditions. The bulk of regional leaders had more than once come out against unconstitutional acts: *Izvestiia*, 10 Sept. 1993.

[192] *Segodniia*, 30 Sept. 1993, *CDPSP*, XLV, 39 (1993), 6.

[193] *Ng*, 9 Oct. 1993. For support for this view, see Yeltsin's own account in Boris Yeltsin, *The View from the Kremlin*, trans. Catherine A. Fitzpatrick (New York, HarperCollins, 1994).

[194] *Rossiiskaia gazeta*, 11 Sept. 1993.

[195] The analogy is with Louis Bonaparte's coup of December 1851 against the French legislative assembly. This was the culmination of a campaign by a populist, elected

Congress of People's Deputies. The notorious Decree No. 1400 suspended the existing political arrangements. Henceforth, legislative functions would be exercised by a new bicameral Federal Assembly. Elections for that assembly would be held on 11–12 December. Until then, Russia would be ruled by presidential decrees and government resolutions. The decree also suspended the Constitutional Court (it was to remain suspended for two years) and brought the Central Bank and the Prosecutor-General under the authority of the President pending the election.[196] The next twenty-four hours saw a flurry of counter-decrees from the Supreme Soviet and the Tenth Congress of People's Deputies meeting in an emergency session: Yeltsin was dismissed as President; Rutskoi installed as acting-President; and Yeltsin's decree sent to the Constitutional Court, which found against him.[197]

The course of the confrontation between the President and the Parliament is well known.[198] An armed stand-off between the Parliament and the President escalated into a violent confrontation on 3 October. A histrionic appeal by Rutskoi, standing on the balcony of the White House, to attack the office of Moscow's mayor and Ostankino television station provided the perfect pretext for Yeltsin to declare a state of emergency. On 4 October front-line tanks shelled the Parliament into submission, at the cost of an estimated 146 lives. Rutskoi, Khasbulatov, Barannikov and twenty-seven other leading oppositionists were gaoled. Several opposition publications, notably *Pravda*, *Sovetskaia Rossiia* and *Den'*, were suspended, as were several opposition organizations. Among them were the National Salvation Front, the Russian Communist Workers' Party, and the Officers' Union. Seizing the moment, Yeltsin dissolved local and regional soviets, decreed a plebiscite be held on 12 December on a draft Constitution (to be agreed between the Constitutional Assembly and the parliamentary Constitutional Commission which Yeltsin now headed), and banned a number of parties and movements from participating in the December elections.[199]

President against a conservative legislature, which he swept away in the name of democracy, ratifying his actions with a plebiscite. For an interesting contemporary discussion, see 'Lui bonapart ili general peron?', *Ng*, 8 Oct. 1993.

[196]  *Ng*, 22 Sept. 1993.

[197]  For the text of these decrees see *CDPSP*, XLV, 38 (1993), 6.

[198]  See Vladimir Berezovsky and Vladimir Cherviakov, 'Osennii politicheskii krizis. Sentiabr'skaia i oktiabr'skaia fazy', *Svobodnaia mysl'*, 15 (Oct. 1993), 12–42; Archie Brown, 'The October Crisis of 1993: Context and Implications', *Post-Soviet Affairs* 9: 3 (1993), 183–95; Alexander Buzgalin and Andrei Kolganov, *Bloody October in Moscow: Political Repression in the Name of Reform*, trans. Renfrey Clarke (New York: Monthly Review Press, 1994).

[199]  For a list of these, see *Ng*, 11 Nov. 1993. Some were later permitted to participate in the election.

Throughout the entire confrontation the people of Russia were mute spectators of violent theatre. This was an intra-elite struggle, fought without popular participation. The parliamentary forces, including Rutskoi in particular, overestimated popular sympathy for the defence of the separation of powers and the rule of law. They erroneously thought this was a re-run of August 1991. Furthermore, the Parliament was geographically isolated from the elite interests it represented, the traditional industrial directorate which was largely regionally based. Yeltsin had the advantage here. Moscow was the principal base for the emergent financial-commercial elite that sympathised with him. He also was able to appeal to an etatist political tradition of the good Tsar defending the interests of the populace. In doing so he was tapping into the political torpor of a populace traumatized by shock therapy and years of incessant change and fruitless promises. In contrast to the period 1989–91, which had seen considerable tension between political authority and politically mobilized sections of the populace, 1992–93 had witnessed a significant downturn of social and political activism. Participation in political meetings and industrial action, particularly political strikes, was minimal.[200] In short, civil society was inert in the face of a major crisis in state authority (see Chapter 6). The victory of the executive branch of state over the legislative and judicial branches enabled the President to codify his supremacy by the imposition of a new Constitution, and with it the marginalization of civil society in matters of state.

In the void created by the absence of stable party institutions, the presidency had come to the fore. In this regard the adoption on 12 December 1993 of the new Constitution, though there were suspicions the figures had been falsified,[201] was a defining moment. It made constitutional what the events of 3 October had established as fact: the supremacy of the presidency. October–December 1993 was a watershed in the consolidation of Yeltsin's power. It was to lay the basis for a period of relative quiescence in Russian politics. It allowed the newly emerging political and economic elites to draw breath while they stabilised, if not consolidated, their rule. A vital component of this was to legitimize the new elite and the new regime in their own eyes, as well as that of public opinion. Through the new Constitution they sought to

---

[200] Mau, 'Politicheskaia', 37.

[201] Official figures declared that on a turn out of 54.8% , 58.4% of voters approved of the Constitution, well in excess of the 50% of voters required to participate to validate the document: Sakwa, *Russian Politics*, 391. However it was later suggested that only 46.1% of the electorate had actually participated, thereby, if true, invalidating adoption of the Constitution. To be adopted, the Constitution required the participation of at least 50% of the electorate and the support of 50% of those who voted: see *Izvestiia*, 4 May 1994; *Ng*, 28 June 1994; *Ng*, 19 July 1994.

give legal sanction to the informal power structures that shaped the Yeltsin regime.[202] But the Constitution was also designed to minimize the vagaries of the electoral process that could threaten the still fragile regime and the interests of the new oligarchy that it had spawned through privatization (see Chapter 6).

[202] Tomas Grekhem, 'Novyi rossiiskii rezhim', *Ng*, 23 Nov. 1995.

# 5

# A Debilitated President

The forced dissolution of the Parliament seemed unambiguously to resolve the running sore that had poisoned Russian politics since 1991 by giving Yeltsin the victory over his opponents that he had long sought. The terms of this victory were consolidated in the new Constitution adopted in December. This Constitution decisively shifted power into the President's hands. The President was the Head of State. He alone had the power to appoint and remove deputy prime ministers and ministers, and with the consent of the lower house (the State Duma) he appointed the Prime Minister. Under certain circumstances, the President could dissolve the State Duma. The President could recommend to the State Duma the candidate for directorship of the Central Bank, and to the Federation Council (the upper house), candidates for judicial offices. He was to form and head the Security Council. He was also commander-in-chief of the military, determined the basic guidelines of domestic and foreign policy, possessed the right of legislative initiative, could issue decrees having the force of law, and could introduce a state of emergency (with confirmation by the Federation Council) in the country as a whole or in specific regions. He was also given specific responsibility for ensuring 'the coordinated functioning and collaboration of bodies of state power'.

The impressive panoply of presidential powers reflected a constitutional order constructed in such a way as to avoid any repetition of a serious challenge to executive authority by the legislature, and in so doing minimize for the President the uncertainty of the electoral process. With the government created not by the legislature but by the President and deriving its authority from him, the Duma had little capacity to oversee the executive. It did have the responsibility for passing (and thereby also holding up) laws, including the budget introduced by the goverment, but every law it passed required presidential assent. If the President vetoed legislation adopted by the Parliament, this veto could only be overridden by a two-thirds vote of both chambers of the Federal Assembly. The Duma could vote no confidence in the government, but if repeated within three months, the President could dissolve the Duma and call for parliamentary elections, an unpalatable prospect for deputies anxious to retain their positions and the privileges that go with them. On several occasions since 1993 threatened votes of no confidence failed to materialize for precisely this reason. Similarly, the Parliament could reject the President's nominee for Prime Minister, but should it do so three times, the President was required to send it to elections, a threat that Yeltsin was to use successfully in mid-1998 to secure the installation of the unpopular Sergei Kirienko as prime minister. A major reduction in the power of the new legislature compared to its predecessor was its inability to amend the Constitution independently. Chapters 1, 2, and 9 of the Constitution could be amended only by a specially convened Constitutional Assembly following a favourable vote by three-fifths of the members of both houses. Chapters 3–8 could be amended by a two-thirds vote of the members of the legislative organs of the administrative regions of the federation. Impeachment of the President was also difficult, requiring a two-thirds vote of the members of both houses plus confirmation of the correctness of the charges and the validity of the procedure followed by respectively the Supreme and Constitutional Courts.

It is clear that the division of powers was decisively weighted in favour of the President and against the legislature. From Yeltsin's perspective it was probably just as well that this was the case given the results of the December election to the State Duma. Despite the fact that opposition forces were severely restricted in their capacity to compete effectively during the campaign (the prevention of some opposition organizations from participating, the closure of some press outlets, restrictions on criticism of the President or the draft Constitution), pro-Yeltsin parties did not do as well as expected. The electoral system was a mixed proportional and majoritarian system. People voted in individual constituencies for local members to fill half the seats in the State Duma,[1] while the other half were filled on a proportional basis from national lists presented by each party. In the proportional vote, a 5 per cent threshold was instituted to filter out very small parties. The results for those parties exceeding the 5 per cent threshold were as shown in Table 5.1.[2] The two explicitly pro-government parties, Russia's Choice (headed by Gaidar) and PRES (headed by Shakhrai) polled only 22.2 per cent of the vote, while the vote for the avowedly oppositionist parties (LDPR, KPRF and the Agrarian Party) totalled 43.2 per cent. The total 'democrat' vote (Russia's Choice, Yabloko, PRES and Sobchak's

---

[1] The Federation Council was to consist of two representative from each of the administrative regions of the country, one from the executive and one from the legislature. In this first instance, such people were elected, but such elections tended to be held on a local, non-party basis.

[2] This and the following election data may be found in Richard Sakwa, *Russian Politics and Society*, 2nd edn. (London and New York, Routledge, 1996) 107, 391–2.

TABLE 5.1. *Parliamentary election results, 1993*

| Party/bloc | Party list | | Single member | Total seats | |
|---|---|---|---|---|---|
| | % | Seats | Seats | Number | % |
| Russia's Choice | 15.51 | 40 | 30 | 70 | 15.6 |
| Liberal Democrats | 22.92 | 59 | 5 | 64 | 14.2 |
| KPRF | 12.40 | 32 | 16 | 48 | 10.7 |
| Agrarian Party | 7.99 | 21 | 12 | 33 | 7.3 |
| Yabloko | 7.86 | 20 | 3 | 23 | 5.1 |
| Women of Russia | 8.13 | 21 | 2 | 23 | 5.1 |
| PRES | 6.76 | 18 | 1 | 19 | 4.0 |
| DPR | 5.52 | 14 | 1 | 15 | 3.3 |

group) was just less than a third, at 33.2 per cent. Clearly, the election had been a rebuff to the President and his government.

The unexpectedly strong showing of parties opposed to radical marketization, notably Zhirinovsky's LDPR and the KPRF, were grounds for concern in relation to the long-term stability of the regime and Yeltsin in particular. Failure to achieve any discernible improvement in the economy was eroding support for market reforms and for the President personally. In the two and a half years between Yeltsin's election as President and the adoption of his new Constitution (12 June 1991–12 December 1993), support for the President had declined by some 18 million votes. In the eight months since the April 1993 referendum, support for the President had dropped by about 4.5 million votes. On a monthly basis since the summer of 1991, Yeltsin's popularity had been declining on average at a rate of 0.6 million voters per month.[3] Participation by voters had also steadily fallen, from a high of 74.7 per cent in mid-1991 to, officially, 54.8 per cent in December 1993, confirming growing disenchantment with the political process on the part of the citizenry.[4] The narrowing of political support for the 'above-party Head of State', in the context of a growing socio-economic crisis, put Yeltsin in a precarious position. Concern within Yeltsin's circle saw an attempt at the end of March–beginning of April 1994 to establish Gaidar's Russia's Choice as a presidential party, which could lay the groundwork for presidential elections. Several leading figures joined the party, among them Minister of Foreign Affairs Kozyrev, Deputy Prime Minister Chubais and head of the Presidential Administration Filatov. The hope was

[3] Vladimir Berezovsky, 'Vladimir Zhirinovsky kak phenomenon Rossiisskoi politiki', *Svobodnaia mysl'* (henceforth *Sm*), 4 (1994), 107. These estimates are apparently based on unofficial estimates for the numbers who voted for the December 1993 Constitution.

[4] See Sakwa, *Russian Politics*, 390–1.

that Yeltsin would assume the role of leader of the radical monetarists, abandoning his self-styled role as a 'social and political arbiter'.[5] Yeltsin, however, continued to distance himself from all such projects. Instead he turned to strengthening his grip on the instruments of state.

In this he was aided by the fact that the new Constitution not only ensured that the President had enormous authority to make and enforce the law, but also the 'quasi-judicial' authority to interpret it. The President virtually appropriated the right of the Constitutional Court to review legislation. He alone appointed its members. These functions were reinforced by the fact that in the course of re-establishing a Constitutional Court, the President set about restricting its authority. It would not be able to judge the constitutionality of the activities of government officials if they were not incorporated into written legislation. It could not rule on the constitutionality of political parties. Nor could its Chairman do more than preside over its meetings. The last restriction was designed to prevent a repetition of the high-profile political role that its last chairman, Zorkin, had played. In general, Yeltsin clearly set about structuring the court to ensure not only that it would not impede his authority as its predecessor had done, but that it would be little more than an appendage of his apparatus.[6]

Yeltsin had learned the lessons of 1992–93 well. Russia would be a presidential system of government. In this respect the new order was redolent of the 1958 Constitution adopted by the Fifth French Republic under Charles de Gaulle. But at least the French National Assembly had the right to elect a Prime Minister and could monitor the government. The Russian Duma had no such rights, and any attempt to assert control over the executive opened the way to its own dissolution. Accordingly, Yeltsin could ignore the significant vote in December 1993 against the harsh economic policies pursued to date and appoint a government that reflected his priorities rather than those of the electorate.

Following the late 1993 dissolution of the old Parliament and the virtual imposition of a new Constitution, the axis of intra-elite struggle shifted. Previously it had been a life and death struggle between the executive and the legislature, but now, although there were at times tensions and disagreements, they were not allowed to reach the degree of intensity that had characterized the earlier period. There were a number of reasons for this. One is that the constitutional ambiguity which had been evident earlier was now removed as the Constitution established new rules of the political game. In addition, members

[5] Vladimir Berezovsky, 'Dva politicheskikh lageria federal'noi elity Rossii', *Sm*, 9 (June 1994), 69.

[6] See Vera Tolz, 'Problems in Building Democratic Institutions in Russia', *RFE/RL Research Report*, 3: 9 (4 Mar. 1994), 1–7.

of the elite realized both how damaging the former conflict had been to the longer term aspirations for the development of a stable Russian political system and how dangerous it had been for the members of the elite. They now acknowledged the need for compromise in their actions. They also realized that further elections were due in a few short years, and therefore for the oppositionists, the potential opportunity to grasp for themselves the reins of presidential power. But also important was the changed composition of the government. The new Chernomyrdin government was dominated by centrists, as leading democrats like Gaidar and Fedorov departed. The new government followed a more moderate course, including bigger budget deficits, fewer cuts to military spending and a stronger stance toward the West. As a result there was much less ideological dissonance between the government and the legislature than there had been previously. But this changed nature of the government had implications for relations within the executive branch.

If the contest before had been between executive and legislature, now it became a contest within the branches of the executive, that is, within and between the presidential and governmental apparatuses, though it was much more muted than that between President and legislature had been.[7] Although there were rivalries within the presidential and governmental camps, broadly the former was inclined to a harsh monetarist course and voucher privatization while the latter wanted a less harsh monetary regime, greater support for domestic industry and its reorganisation on the basis of financial-industrial groups. In effect Chernomyrdin was picking up where the Supreme Soviet had left off, though not in such a confrontational fashion.

But the President and his circle were resolved to dominate affairs of state and would brook no rival, even one who at the critical juncture of October 1993 had demonstrated total loyalty, as Chernomyrdin had done. According to one observer,[8] the presidential camp was a 'coalition' of forces, among them: an 'inner circle', led by Yeltsin's personal assistant Viktor Iliushin, leaders of the bloc Russia's Choice, such as Gaidar, the so-called 'nomenklatura-politicians' of the Presidential Administration headed by Filatov, the Security Council headed by the 'personal friend' of the President Oleg Lobov, the General Procurator Aleksei Iliushenko, and the Speaker of the Federation Council Vladimir Shumeiko. Among the pro-government forces centred around Chernomyrdin were the technocrats overseeing the economy, 'social liberals' drawn from the Moscow academic elite, members of the 'industrial

[7] Tomas Grekhem, 'Novyi rossiiskii rezhim', *Nezavisimaia gazeta* (henceforth *Ng*) 23 Nov. 1995. Even in the earlier period there had been tension between the presidential apparatus and the government, especially between Petrov and the Gaidar government. For discussion of this, see *Ng*, 24 Jan., 14 Feb. 1992; *Izvestiia*, 19 Feb. 1992.

[8] Berezovsky, 'Dva politicheskikh lageria', 68–76.

directorate' who favoured state intervention (the fuel and energy, the agricultural and the export-oriented military industries), a segment of 'new business', and some regional leaders. Among Chernomyrdin's key supporters were First Deputy Prime Minister Oleg Soskovets, linked with the 'industrial directorate' and the trade unions, Central Bank Chairman Viktor Gerashchenko, and the Deputy Prime Minister responsible for agriculture, Aleksandr Zaveriukha, a prominent member of the Agrarian Party. Chernomyrdin also had tentative support from leaders of the Party of Russian Unity and Accord (PRES), notably Deputy Prime Ministers Aleksandr Shokhin and Sergei Shakhrai. The period October 1993–February 1994 saw a determined attempt by pro-Chernomyrdin forces to strengthen his independent role and re-orient government policy in the interests of domestic, export-oriented industry.

This challenge did not go unanswered by those who advocated integrating Russia into the world market and stringent budgetary constraints. A counter programme to accelerate economic policy in accordance with IMF guidelines and strengthen the weight of the monetarists in government was launched by Russia's Choice chief, First Deputy Prime Minister Gaidar, immediately after the December elections. Then, in the new year a campaign was initiated from within Yeltsin's camp to discredit Chernomyrdin as a possible presidential contender. These initiatives to counter Chernomyrdin's growing stature were reinforced by a determined drive in late 1993–early 1994 to limit the prime minister's influence on strategic policy matters and to legalise presidential supervision over him. A subdivision of the Presidential Administration was formed to oversee government economic policy and to ensure that it vetted financial documents submitted for the President's signature.[9]

More ominously, by a decree issued on 21 December that disbanded the Ministry of Security, the coercive apparatuses of the state became the exclusive province of the President.[10] He alone controlled the power ministries of defence and internal affairs, and the security and intelligence agencies: the Federal Counter-intelligence Service (FSK, the successor to the Ministry of Security), the Foreign Intelligence Service (SVR), the Federal Border Service (FPS). The bringing of the Federal Agency for Government Communications and Information (FAPSI) under the President meant that he gained direct oversight of the mass media. In February 1994 the President established a system of direct communications with the commanders of all the army formations.[11] These structures represented a formidable presidential coercive apparatus. In the guise of the 76,000 strong FSK, the former KGB had risen

---

[9] Berezovsky, 'Dva politicheskikh lageria', 81.

[10] See Viktor Yasman, 'Security Services Reorganized: All Power to the Russian President?', *RFE/RL Research Report*, 6 (11 Feb. 1994), 7–14.

[11] *Ng*, 23 Dec. 1995; Berezovsky, 'Dva politicheskikh lageria', 81, 83.

'from the ashes', in the words of Sergei Stepashin, FSK head from 1994 to mid-1995. In April 1995, the FSK was re-named the Federal Security Service (FSB) and accorded vastly expanded surveillance powers. Former Kremlin commandant Barsukov, himself a graduate of the KGB Ninth Directorate, took over the FSB from July 1995 to June 1996.[12]

The MVD in particular developed as a powerful military apparatus in its own right, separate from the army. The MVD, rather than the army, was the spearhead of the Kremlin's war against Chechnya that was unleashed in December 1994. As an issue of internal security, the war was prosecuted under the command of MVD General Anatoly Kulikov.[13] Under Kulikov, who replaced Yerin as interior minister after the Budennovsk hostage debacle, the MVD enhanced its military capacity and its responsibilities. According to one report, it had at its disposal some 300,000 interior forces and had acquired an array of artillery, light tanks and helicopters, suitable for maintaining domestic order.[14] In early 1997 MVD forces were assigned to collect taxes, even though there already existed tax police. Until his dismissal as interior minister on 22 March 1998, Kulikov was widely regarded as the most influential minister in the government.[15]

In addition to MVD and FSB forces, it was at this time that Yeltsin consolidated his own armed forces. After the violent confrontation in October 1993, which saw hesitant army support for Yeltsin, an 'essential step'[16] in guaranteeing the capacity of the President to fend off any threat from civil or military authorities was the strengthening of military formations at the personal disposal of the President. Barsukov's 40,000 strong Main Security Directorate (GUO) undertook an unprecedented concentration of special forces, including the Alpha and Vympel squads, together with a special tank regiment. In March 1994, Barsukov was appointed to the cabinet. Meanwhile, the Presidential Security Service (PSB), under the command of Yeltsin's friend and chief bodyguard, Aleksandr Korzhakov, had been carved out of the GUO. Korzhakov could, if necessary, exercise authority over the highest state officials. Both these praetorians were notorious for their interference in matters of state.[17]

---

[12] David Mandel, 'The Russian Working Class and the Labour Movement in Year Four of "Shock Therapy" ', in David Mandel (ed.), *The Former 'State Socialist' World: Views from the Left* (Montreal/New York/London, Black Rose,1996), 26; Sakwa, *Russian Politics*, 73.

[13] Sakwa, *Russian Politics*, 73, 311.

[14] Boris Kagarlitsky, 'Russia's "Big Cop" ', *Green Left Weekly*, 12 Feb. 1997, 12. Sakwa, *Russian Politics*, 73, gives a much more modest figure of 70,000 Interior Troops (VV), half of whom were members of a mobile strike force, opnaz.

[15] *Kommersant Vlast'*, 2 (27 Jan. 1998), 13–15.

[16] Berezovsky, 'Dva politicheskikh lageria', 81–2.

[17] Ibid., 81–2. After the February 1994 amnesty of the parliamentary insurgents, Korzhakov personally interrogated the General Procurator, A. Kazannik. On 30 November

The war in Chechnya seems to have reflected the considerable, if not pre-ponderant, influence of the organs of security on state policy. Korzhakov, FSK chief Stepashin and MVD head Yerin, together with nationalities minister Nikolai Yegorov and Security Council Secretary Lobov, were members of what has been called the 'party of war': those who favoured a military solution in Chechnya.[18] Whether it is possible to attribute the war to the machinations of the power ministries alone rather than the President and his government as a whole is open to debate. But it does point to praetorian tendencies in politics, particularly when Korzhakov was pre-eminent, as a feature of the Yeltsin regime. The ministries of internal order occupied a privileged position in influencing presidential decision-making, with little or no parliamentary over-sight.

The contrast here is with the role of the military, particularly the army. Despite persistent speculation that military rule has been in the offing in Russia, it has not eventuated. Although the military has played a critical role on a couple of occasions since 1991, the military has not been a major player in Russian politics, let alone a serious threat to civilian authority. The unwill-ingness of the Soviet military to flout legal civilian authority and comply with the directives of the emergency committee in August 1991 contributed to the failure of the putsch.[19] After some hesitation, the military, under General Pavel Grachev, finally threw its weight behind the President in October 1993, shelling the Parliament into submission. The subsequent announcement of a new military doctrine seemed to suggest that the military would be rewarded for its loyalty to Yeltsin by an enhanced influence on policy. It was not to be. Despite initial enthusiasm on the part of Defence Minister Grachev, the army more generally was a reluctant participant in the Chechen war. Indeed there was considerable resentment by the military at being dragged into the conflict, only to find the politicians blaming the army for military failures.[20] The mil-itary has certainly not been a beneficiary of the Russian transformation. On the contrary, it has been one of the most serious casualties of neo-liberal eco-nomics. Promises of reform, to create a more modern, smaller, better equipped, professional army in place of the huge conscript army bequeathed by the Soviet Union, have come to nought. Declining budgetary allocations

1994, two days before his infamous raid on the Mostbank, Korzhakov took it upon himself to suggest policy and appointments to the Prime Minister. Querying decisions of former economics minister Shokhin in regard to fuel and energy policy, he suggested Chernomyrdin appoint First Deputy Prime Minister Soskovets to a commission to oversee policy in this area: *Izvestiia*, 22 Dec. 1994.

[18] Sakwa, *Russian Politics*, 74.
[19] Vladimir Serebrianikkov, 'Armiia i politika', *Sm*, 2 (Jan. 1992), 72.
[20] Sakwa, *Russian Politics*, 311.

have created a demoralized, corrupt, under-equipped military, whose ill-fed conscripts are far from battle ready, as the debacle in Chechnya graphically illustrated. In Yeltsin's Russia, with the rise of the internal security forces, the old military–industrial complex has been eclipsed by what one observer has called a 'military–police complex'.[21] In these circumstances, the Bonapartism of the Yeltsin regime rests not on the armed forces, of which he is commander in chief, but on the agencies of internal order in association with the presidential apparatus.

These developments were coupled with the resurgence of the Security Council as a major instrument of presidential power. Under Lobov, it supervised the functioning of the remnants of the military–industrial complex. It also built up an apparatus that effectively duplicated those of the government, enabling it to circumscribe the powers of the Prime Minister and interfere in the workings of his government. If need be, 'in the interests of national security', the Security Council could be elevated to a 'coordinating' body of government. Its authority was ensured by several presidential decrees, including that on 'Responsibility for Attempts to Violate Social Harmony'. In the guise of defending Russia's economic security from crime and corruption, the Security Council also gained oversight of the development of government economic policy. In addition, in concert with the intelligence services, the Council gained considerable control over senior government appointments.[22]

As an instrument to extend presidential authority *vis-à-vis* that of the government, the State-Legal Administration (GPU) now came into its own.[23] Already the GPU's position in relation to the Ministry of Justice had been strengthened by an April 1993 presidential decision to establish a Centre for Legal Information rivalling that of the ministry. A massive data base gave the Centre a monopoly on legal and administrative data. Suspected of having been initiated by Shakhrai, this trespass on the authority of the government has been interpreted as a conspiracy to 'concentrate the executive's information resources in the presidency'. By 1994 the government's own Legal Department was required to seek GPU final certification of the legality of government laws. During 1994 Yeltsin increasingly relied on rule by decree, a tendency that placed the GPU at the centre of this struggle. However, Yeltsin rarely initiated decrees himself. Rather, in the eyes of one observer, 'like a monarch in the era between absolutism and constitutionalism, he respond[ed] to proposals submitted by officials who want[ed] the President's imprimatur on their project.'[24]

---

[21] Kagarlitsky, 'Russia's "Big Cop" '.

[22] Berezovsky, 'Dva politicheskikh lageria', 84.

[23] Eugene Huskey, 'The State-Legal Administration and the Politics of Redundancy', *Post-Soviet Affairs*, 11: 2 (1995), 126, n. 30.

[24] Ibid. 118, 130.

Yeltsin's counter-measures against Chernomyrdin's government also included the establishment within the presidential apparatus of a *de facto* department of agitation and propaganda called the Administration for Information Security, which directly competed with the government's own press service. Control over economic policy was secured by the President's Expert group headed by Aleksandr Livshits, and the financial and budgetary administration of the Presidential Administration. Yeltsin's seizure of the initiative against Chernomyrdin was codified in six decrees on the economy,[25] capped off with his criticism of the work of the cabinet in May 1994. All told, Yeltsin's initiatives to secure the whip hand in relation to government policy formation and implementation were designed to limit Chernomyrdin's capacity to act as an independent political player, and therefore a possible rival. Yeltsin's personal control over the coercive apparatuses ensured not only his unchallenged supremacy within the state. It also provided an armed bulwark for his regime, in the context of increasing social tension and diminishing social support for the extreme neo-liberals within Chernomyrdin's government.[26]

By 1994 the new presidential state was a bureaucratic leviathan in the making. Ironically, the Russian revolution against the Soviet administrative–command state had spawned a presidential apparatus far larger than its Central Committee predecessor, dwarfing similar bureaucracies in the West and that of the Russian legislature. By 1994 it was estimated that the presidential staff numbered from 5,000 to 27,000, depending on the number of institutions included.[27] The permanent professional staff of the Presidential Administration alone numbered 2,180. The total 500 billion rouble budgetary allocation for the President's Administration of Affairs and that of his Administration for Planning and Special Programmes was more than 2.7 times that allocated to the State Duma (180 billion roubles) and 6.5 times (76 billion) that allocated to the Federation Council.[28] These figures by themselves are good indicators that in the new Russian state the presidential apparatus controlled the lion's share of resources—and therefore power.

The formation of an apparatus immediately subordinate to the President himself, the 'party of power' as it has sometimes been called,[29] was pivotal to

---

[25] For discussion of these, see *Izvestiia*, 24 May 1994 and *Segodnia*, 24, 28 May 1994.
[26] Berezovsky, 'Dva politicheskikh lageria', 82–3.
[27] Huskey, 'The State-Legal Administration', 116 and n. 5.          [28] Ibid., 116 and n. 5.
[29] This concept has been used in a variety of ways. In the press it is often a synonym for those who formally occupy positions of power. At other times the 'party of power' is equated with those elite groupings who pursue policies at odds with those of the President and the government. Others have virtually equated it with the apex of the Russian state as such: 'the conglomerate of forces which constitute the axis of executive power', from the President himself to the administrative apparatus as a whole: Sergei Khenkin, ' "Partiia vlasti": rossiiskii variant', *Pro et Contra*, 1: 1 (Autumn 1996), 32–3.

attempts to put the new Russian administration on a stable footing and to consolidate decision-making in the President's hands. This was the fulcrum of relations between the President and other elites: in the government, in the legislature and, especially, the emerging Russian bourgeoisie. In the years since Yeltsin became President of Russia, an array of institutions have waxed and waned under a variety of names. But it is not so much the institutional matrix that has shaped the new state, but Yeltsin's entourage—the network of informal, personal relations with the President himself. Accordingly, Yeltsin's regnum has been marked by the rise and fall of personal careers.

By 1994 the contours of this entourage and its modus operandi were well established. Access to the President, rather than formal status, tended to define where a particular official stood in the hierarchy of power. Accordingly those in the President's inner circle were usually regarded as the most powerful. But this hierarchy of power was constantly in flux. Nobody, not even those closest to the President, had security of tenure. After his victory over the Soviet centre, Yeltsin never tired of claiming that the new Russian state was strong because, unlike Gorbachev's Union presidency, the Russian President was surrounded by completely loyal personnel. Nevertheless, in the course of the next few years there were those whose independent political ambitions would be their undoing. Throughout these shifts of personnel, the President's inner circle included many people lacking definite political views but with good informal relations with him.[30]

At the heart of Yeltsin's entourage, as late as 1996, was one of these, Viktor Iliushin, his old Sverdlovsk comrade-in-arms since 1977. A 'prudent, reserved, experienced apparatchik', Iliushin was accused by disgruntled democrats of acting as a 'filter' to block information to the President (an accusation reminiscent of the kind 'the good Tsar surrounded by bad advisers'!). When it suited him, Iliushin disregarded the opinions of others, whatever his formal obligations. Iliushin blithely ignored, for instance, the fact that on more than one occasion decrees prepared by him were incompatible with other legal acts, which vexed the President's own GPU which had a responsibility to ensure that presidential decrees were legally consistent. Such was Iliushin's influence that he eclipsed even the heads of the Presidential Administration. At the end of 1992 he had been instrumental in removing Yury Petrov, the first chief of Yeltsin's administration. A measure of Iliushin's personal influence is the fact that he was Yeltsin's closest confidant at the time of the September–October 1993 confrontation with the Supreme Soviet, when the President's authority was on the line. It was Iliushin who was entrusted with preparing in secret the

---

[30] *Izvestiia*, 2 July 1994. For a diagrammatic representation of the presidential apparatus as it stood at the end of 1992 see *Kto est' chto: politicheskaiia Moskva* (Moscow: Satallakhu, 1993), 99.

notorious decree No. 1400, the presidential declaration of war on the Parliament.[31] Not even the GPU was consulted about this decree.[32]

Throughout his presidency, right up until just before the second round of the 1996 presidential elections, one of the individuals closest to the President was the head of his personal bodyguard, Aleksandr Korzhakov. A former major in the KGB Ninth Directorate, which had once been responsible for the security of the highest ranking Soviet politicians, Korzhakov attached himself to Yeltsin when he was first secretary of the Moscow party organization. They became, according to Korzhakov, literally 'blood brothers'.[33] Beside Yeltsin during the August putsch, on the night of 3–4 October 1993 he had played a crucial negotiating role with the Minister of Defence Pavel Grachev and the General Staff. After the White House had been shelled into submission, Korzhakov personally arrested Rutskoi and Khasbulatov. Until Korzhakov's shock dismissal before the second round of the 1996 presidential elections, he was infamous for playing a role far beyond his formal capacity. Not only a trusted confidant and adviser to Yeltsin, he directly interfered in government policy in such areas as arms exports and high technology transfers. It was Korzhakov's troops that in December 1994 clashed with security forces from Mostbank, then closely allied with Moscow mayor Yury Luzhkov.[34]

Similarly favoured relations with the President were enjoyed by General Mikhail Barsukov. In November 1991 he had become commandant of the Kremlin due to the good offices of Korzhakov. With the patronage of Petrov, Barsukov simultaneously became chief of the Main Security Directorate (GUO), which had been formed out of the old Ninth Directorate of the KGB by secret presidential decree. Both chiefs of Yeltsin's praetorian guard, Korzhakov and Barsukov, were said to be potentially 'extremely significant figures' by virtue of their direct access to the President.[35] Barsukov was rumoured to be the eyes and ears of the President in the Kremlin, eventually bringing even Burbulis to book for his tactless remarks about the President. These praetorian figures were reputedly members of the so-called 'party of war' which advocated military intervention in Chechnya and constituted what has been

---

[31] *Izvestiia*, 2 July 1994. Deputy department head of the Sverdlovsk obkom of the CPSU, Iliushin worked in the Moscow City Committee and the Central Committee of the CPSU. According to Korzhakov, the decision to decree dismissal of the Supreme Soviet was approved by Yeltsin, Kozyrev, Grachev, Yerin, Chernomyrdin, and Nikolai Golushko, acting Minister of Security: Aleksandr Korzhakov, *Boris Yeltsin: Ot rasveta do zakata* (Moscow, Interbuk, 1997), 155.

[32] Huskey, 'The State-Legal Administration', 125 n. 25.

[33] David Remnick, 'How Russia is Ruled', *New York Review of Books*, 9 Apr. 1998, p. 10.

[34] *Izvestiia*, 2 July 1994; 'Korzhakov, Aleksandr Vasilevich', *Kto est Kto v Rossii: 1997 goda* (Moscow, Olymp, 1997), 328–30; Sakwa, *Russian Politics*, 74.

[35] *Izvestiia*, 2 July 1994.

called a kind of 'new politburo'.[36] Among other prominent figures were General Procurator A. Iliushenko who headed the Control Administration of the President, N. Medvedev who (in mid-1994) headed the 'potentially very significant' Administration for Work with the Territories, and Pavel Borodin, head of the Main Socio-Productive Administration (GOPU), which was accused of exercising 'shadowy influence', through its control over financial benefits.[37]

As well as people whose relationship with Yeltsin was based on personal connections devoid of policy positions embedded in the institutional structures surrounding Yeltsin, there were some whose personal relationship with the President was underpinned by policy commitments. These were not people with long associations with the President, but a younger technocratic but highly ideological cohort that had come to his side after he had achieved power in 1991. An example of this from the earlier period was Gaidar who held leading posts in the government, but whose power and continued tenure of office depended upon the support of the President. The most important example of this sort of relationship after December 1993 was Anatoly Chubais. Chubais was a committed free marketeer, who, as we saw above, had been brought from St Petersburg to the capital by Gaidar and introduced into the Yeltsin administration under his auspices. Chubais held a series of official positions, in addition to his responsibilities for privatization, which earned him the wrath of the opposition and the disdain of the populace. In June 1992 he became a Deputy Prime Minister. Even after the departure of Gaidar in December 1992, he remained in Chernomyrdin's government. Elected a deputy as a member of Russia's Choice in December 1993, in November of the following year Yeltsin appointed him a First Deputy Prime Minister responsible for economic policy.[38] He went on in April 1995 to become Russia's representative to the World Bank and the IMF.[39] He lost these offices in January 1996 after falling out of favour with Yeltsin, who blamed him for the poor showing of Our Home is Russia (NDR) in the election.[40] But he returned to the fold two months later to head Yeltsin's re-election campaign, which opened the way for him to enter Yeltsin's inner circle. Although dependent on Yeltsin's favour, Chubais clearly had other attributes that have enabled him to survive. At this time they were

---

[36] 'Barsukov, Mikhail Ivanovich', *Kto est' Kto*, 45–6; Korzhakov, *Boris Yeltsin*, 463–4. This 'politburo' was said to include Grachev, Soskovets, and Lobov as well as Barsukov.

[37] *Izvestiia*, 2 July 1994.

[38] 'Chubais, Anatoly Borisovich', *Kto est' Kto*, 705–7.

[39] Joseph R.Blasi, Maya Kroumova, and Douglas Kruse, *Kremlin Capitalism: Privatizing the Russian Economy* (Ithaca, Cornell University Press, 1997), p. xix.

[40] *Kto est' Kto*, 705–7.

principally his achievements as the young 'father of privatization' and his standing with international financial institutions such as the IMF.[41]

The capacity of these people to wield significant influence was a result in part of the problems that existed surrounding the government. In the period before 1993, when Gaidar was prominent, Yeltsin could rely upon the support of the government much more than he felt able to do once Chernomyrdin had become Prime Minister. The stand-off that occurred between President and government discussed above meant that Yeltsin had to look more to his own apparatus for support, and this involved relying upon people with close personal relations with him. Such an outcome is natural; everyone wants to work with people they can trust, and this involves overwhelmingly an emphasis upon personal relationships. This would have been strengthened by the history of Yeltsin's personal experience of work within the Soviet apparatus, where personal relationships were of signal importance in political success. But their power was also enhanced by the personal style of the President. Yeltsin was not a leader who seemed to submerge himself in the detail of issues, preferring the grander vision, with the result that there was significant scope for his officials to exercise their own initiative. This factor was strengthened by the way in which Yeltsin would frequently disappear from the scene. Yeltsin's health was anything but robust. Rumours about a drinking problem were rife, and then he suffered heart attacks in July and October 1995, which restricted his practical involvement in day-to-day political affairs for some time. Under such circumstances, and given the desire to hide his debility from his enemies, his closest associates shouldered much of the politico-administrative load. Clearly Yeltsin's style of leadership greatly facilitated the leaching of power to members of his personal entourage. This was to become even more important following his re-election in July 1996.

Yeltsin's entourage has been described as a 'court' operating as a system of 'checks and balances'.[42] Under this system, expulsion was the punishment for those disrupting the equilibrium by pursuing their own interests too much. Meanwhile, the individual members of the entourage themselves engaged in a constant jostling not so much for positions, as for access to the 'sovereign'. This

---

[41] Elena Chinayeva, 'A Kremlin Survivor: A Profile of Deputy Prime Minister Anatolii Chubais', *Transitions* 1, 22 (1 Dec. 1995), 39.

[42] *Izvestiia*, 2 July 1994. The metaphor of Yeltsin's entourage as a court was quite common among analysts at this time. It has been described, for example, as a 'hybrid Court Apparatus', combining the 'favouritism' of court life with 'centralised autocratic power'— *Ng*, 25 Dec. 1993. While a striking metaphor, given the etatist political culture of Russia, it will require detailed empirical analysis to assess its utility. Moreover, such a metaphor may obscure as much as it reveals. Royal courts have often been highly structured by symbols and ranks, if not rules, and administrative systems are often far more personalist than they appear. Patronage and favour are by no means exclusive to 'Eastern' societies.

incessant 'apparatus struggle' took its toll on the effectiveness of the Presidential Administration. At the same time, however, it enabled the President to assume a pivotal role in the new state structure. Buttressing his enormous executive powers with the personal authority of an autocrat, Yeltsin effectively ensured that he alone had the decisive say in who or which grouping was in or out of favour. Nobody, not even his closest advisers, had permanent tenure. The democrats, expecting to come to power, had been displaced by former apparatchiki. But by early 1993 a new influx of independent figures like Yury Baturin was occurring.[43] According to one analysis, this new cohort represented a strengthening of the 'political principle' in the Presidential Administration; it was based on certain ' "progressive thinking analysts" who maintained close relations with "cultured" ' business circles. But the newcomers too were aware that their positions were no more secure than those of their predecessors on this permanent 'field of battle'.[44] In this sense, Yeltsin operated like a Stalin figure: the political elite was kept in a permanent state of insecurity, and therefore dependency on the President. Of course, should they fall out with Yeltsin, the consequences were not nearly as drastic as they were under Stalin. There were other activities, usually business, to pursue. And sometimes, as the career of Chubais testifies, favourites were even readmitted to the inner circle.

## Political Stabilization?

In the aftermath of the December election and the events that had preceded it, there was a widespread feeling that some form of reconciliation had to be brought about between the different political forces. One reflection of this was the February 1994 amnesty granted by the new legislature to the August 1991 putsch plotters and the parliamentary opponents of Yeltsin who had been arrested in October. These were both groups who had been crushed by Yeltsin, and their amnesty could have been interpreted as a slap in the face for the President, but Yeltsin did not take public issue with this. Such inaction can be interpreted as an attempt to extend an olive branch to the Parliament which,

[43] A legal expert, he was previously employed in Gorbachev's presidential apparatus, where he co-authored an alternative press law. In June 1993 he became a presidential aide responsible for appointments and was instrumental in developing the policy on military reform, in the face of opposition from Minister of Defence Igor Rodionov. In January 1994 he became Yeltsin's aide on national security and then Security Council Secretary until 1996, when he became Secretary of the Defence Council, a post he retained until 1997: 'Baturin, Yury Mikhailovich', *Kto est' Kto*, 51–2.

[44] *Izvestiia*, 2 July 1994.

contrary to expectations, was of a political hue that was unsympathetic to the President.

Another sign of this desire for reconciliation, and a major political initiative to stabilize the situation after the trauma of 1993, was Yeltsin's Civic Accord, first proposed in February 1994 and finally adopted on 28 April. It was a corporatist initiative in every sense. The Accord was intended to promote social compromise and reconciliation during the two years it was in effect, the 'most painful transition period' as the final document put it. 'Destabilising' constitutional amendments were prohibited; campaigns for pre-term presidential or parliamentary elections were banned; and the Federal Assembly was to expedite the passage of legislation. For its part, the government promised reduced inflation, financial stability and economic growth. Almost 250 public figures signed the document, as did more than 100 leading bankers and business people in May. But three major political organisations refused to sign: Yabloko, whose leader Yavlinsky dismissed it as meaningless; the Agrarian Party, which rejected bans on pre-term elections; and the KPRF, which demanded a presence in a coalition government. It was an Accord very much on the President's terms. Initiated from the top, it made no attempt at popular involvement.[45]

A particular objective of the Accord was to shore up the centre's authority, which had been eroded in the years since Gorbachev unleashed perestroika. Yeltsin was anxious to halt and reverse separatist tendencies. To this end, Moscow repudiated the previous Federal Treaty, which had accorded greater rights to republics than the regions and districts, in favour of the new Constitution that accorded equal rights to all subjects of the federation.[46] He also sought an end to the previous practice of Moscow politicians appealing to their opposite numbers in the regions for support against their opponents (as both executive and legislature had done in the heat of their struggle in 1993). The Civic Accord codified the relations between the centre and its regions. Regional leaders were promised that laws on the devolution of powers were to be enacted. They in turn committed themselves to collect taxes and transfer them to Moscow and not to violate the unity of the Federation. All but two regional leaders and all republics' leaders, except Chechnya's, signed.[47] By mid-1994 Yeltsin felt confident enough to declare that the threat of separatism had passed.[48]

[45] In fact it was designed to forestall an accord 'from below', the Accord for Russia movement, initiated by, among others, the KPRF: Vera Tolz, 'The Civic Accord: Contributing to Russia's Stability?', *RFE/RL Research Report*, 3: 19 (13 May 1994), 1–5.

[46] In February 1994 Russia concluded an agreement with Tatarstan which privileged the republic compared to other Federation subjects but which involved acceptance of its 'subject' status in the Federation.

[47] Tolz, 'The Civic Accord', 3–4; Jeremy Lester, *Modern Tsars and Princes: The Struggle for Hegemony in Russia* (London and New York, Verso, 1995), 207–8.

[48] Grekhem, 'Novyi rossiiskii'.

This proved to be rather optimistic, as Chechnya would dramatically demonstrate. Even the more modest quest for the supremacy of presidential writ at regional level remained elusive. The triumph of the executive over the legislature in 1993 did not establish a strong, unified legal-administrative regime. On the contrary, in Russia the 'system of state control practically disappeared', giving local heads of administration considerable latitude for independent decision-making. While outwardly observing presidential authority, more than a few regional leaders pursued their own policies, in the process ignoring the decrees of the President.[49]

Yeltsin thus attempted to put in place a system designed to reinforce his political supremacy by extending his authority throughout the Russian regions. He was to prove more successful in asserting his political supremacy at the centre than in extending his reach throughout Russia. Lack of cohesion, instability and constantly changing alignments of forces within the political elite weakened the Russian multinational state. The establishment of an effective central administration, a vital part of political stabilization, was hamstrung by the very nature of the new Russian state. It was, after all, the site on which the various groupings within the new oligarchy wrestled for 'political advantages'.[50]

The Civic Accord was no Moncloa Pact. It was, however, an attempt to establish elite, if not popular, consensus around political and economic life and thereby stabilise the new regime by broadening Yeltsin's support within the political elite. But events soon showed the fragility of so-called political stabilization, built as it was on uncertain economic foundations and unequal distribution of power. 'Black Tuesday', 11 October 1994, saw the rouble plummet by 22 per cent and with it Chernomyrdin's attempts to control inflation collapsed.[51] The impotence of the Parliament was demonstrated by an abortive motion of no confidence in the government initiated by the KPRF. It fell 32 votes short of the required 226, partly because of a sop to the Parliament: Yeltsin appointed Agrarian Party member Aleksandr Nazarchuk Minister of Agriculture. The Parliament was reduced to merely resolving that the government's performance was unsatisfactory.[52] Nevertheless, the illusion of stability had been punctured.[53] Yeltsin evidently felt vulnerable enough to reactivate the Security Council as a key instrument of state. It was to come to the fore in

---

[49] Khenkin, 'Partiia vlasti', 36. For a useful case study see Peter Kirkow, 'Regional Warlordism in Russia: The Case of Primorskii Krai', *Europe–Asia Studies*, 47: 6 (1995), 923–47.

[50] *Ng*, 23 Nov. 1995.

[51] Vera Tolz, 'The Shifting Sands of Stabilisation', *Transition*, 1, 2 (15 Feb. 1995), 8.

[52] Ibid. 6; Open Media Research Institute, *Annual Survey 1995* (Armonk, M. E. Sharpe Inc., 1996), 212.

[53] Tolz, 'Shifting Sands', 5.

the 29 November 1994 decision to invade Chechnya on 11 December.[54] It now included not only the President, Council Secretary Lobov and the heads of the power ministries, but Prime Minister Chernomyrdin and Foreign Minister Kozyrev.[55]

There is considerable contention over who actually decided to invade Chechnya. Political analyst Fedor Burlatsky accused Yeltsin himself.[56] Others, however, have seen the decision as an initiative by the so-called 'party of war'. According to this analysis, again of the 'good Tsar, bad advisers' type, the decision to resort to brute force rather than negotiate reflected the ascendancy of the 'party of war' over Yeltsin's loyal democrat allies, particularly Gaidar.[57] This lack of clarity about who actually decided to use armed force pointed to an absence of any clear constitutional mechanisms in Russia for taking decisions of state, as commentator Otto Latsis put it,[58] according to whom the regime was once again in 'crisis'. The informal, but relatively stable coalition of Duma deputies (especially Russia's Choice), the intelligentsia, the press and other democrat forces supporting Yeltsin and favouring continuation of the reforms had been shattered. At stake were not just the forthcoming parliamentary and presidential elections but the regime itself, which seemed in a permanent state of instability, lurching from crisis to crisis.

The war rapidly took a toll on Yeltsin's already beleaguered standing. Few Russians actively supported the war. Yeltsin blamed his advisers and the military for Russian reverses in Chechnya. The people, however, blamed the President. By January 1995, a mere month into the war, Yeltsin's popularity on a scale of 1 to 10 was a mere 2.9. It would average about that for the remainder of the year, by the end of which only 2 per cent of the population 'completely supported' the President.[59] Even those sections of the democrats which had formerly strongly supported him, including Gaidar, now turned against Yeltsin and criticized the Chechen war. Yeltsin ignored both public opinion and the Parliament. On 13 December, two days after military intervention, by an overwhelming majority the Duma passed a resolution condemning the government for not seeking a peaceful solution and calling for an end to hostilities. Yeltsin ignored this, but averted any possible parliamentary oversight of the war by not declaring a state of emergency.

---

[54]  Robert Orttung, 'Chechnya: A Painful Price', *Transition*, 1: 3 (15 Mar. 1995), 3.
[55]  Sakwa, *Russian Politics*, 146.
[56]  Fedor Burlatsky, 'Yeltsin: A Turning Point', *Transition*, 1: 3 (15 Mar. 1995), 8–9.
[57]  Orttung, 'Chechnya', 3.                               [58]  *Izvestiia*, 29 Dec. 1994.
[59]  Stephen White, Richard Rose, and Ian McAllister, *How Russia Votes* (Chatham, New Jersey, Chatham House Publishers, 1997), 170–1. Also see Fig. 8.2 on p. 169 which shows the declining popularity of Yeltsin during this period.

In these circumstances Yeltsin was forced to turn increasingly inwards to the apparatuses of state for support, particularly the Security Council. In January 1995 Finance Minister Panskov had become a non-voting member, a move that suggested increased presidential control,[60] while in February the speakers of the Federation Council and the Duma, Vladimir Shumeiko and Ivan Rybkin[61] (who already participated in a non-voting capacity) were made full voting members. The Council's limited decision-making role during the war suggests that at all times it was acting at the behest of the President, not vice versa. In the Parliament the President and his government were reliant on Zhirinovsky's support for the war, to which the democrats and the KPRF were opposed.[62]

A critical media, which defied government attempts to impose censorship and openly expressed public opposition to the war have been cited as indicators that a 'fragile' civil society existed in Russia.[63] 'Marginal' would be a more appropriate term. Constitutional arrangements enabled Yeltsin to ignore the Parliament and circumvent public and press opinion in waging war. In this, Yeltsin was aided by a compliant Constitutional Court, which was finally resurrected on 16 March 1995. In April both chambers of the Federal Assembly appealed the legality of the three presidential decrees and one government directive which were the basis of military action in Chechnya. It was argued that without formally declaring a state of emergency, which required Federation Council approval, the President did not have the authority to deploy military forces in Russia. Initial rejection of the case by the Court, purely on the basis of technical irregularities in the documents submitted by the Council, led to speculation that the Court was helping the executive buy time, thereby making the case irrelevant. When the case finally opened on 10 July, it took only six days for the Court, which did not even call Defence Minister Grachev to testify, to find Yeltsin's 9 December 1994 decree disarming illegal armed formations 'fully consistent with the constitution'.[64] This

[60] J. William Derleth, 'The Evolution of the Russian Polity: The Case of the Security Council', *Communist and Post-Communist Studies*, 29: 1 (1996), 53.

[61] This step appeared to comply with provisions in the original Law on Security that the parliamentary leadership should have permanent status on the Council. Not all agreed with this, however. Former Minister of Justice Kalmykov speculated that Yeltsin had colluded with Shumeiko and Rybkin in the Security Council to avoid having to declare a state of emergency over Chechnya, which constitutionally would have required ratification by the Federation Council: Derleth, 'Evolution', 53; Orttung, 'Chechnya', 5.

[62] Chernomyrdin met with Zhirinovsky to defeat a legislative initiative by Russia's Choice on 11 January 1995 to restrict the President's war-making capacities. See Orttung, 'Chechnya', 5 and Burlatsky, 'Yeltsin', 9: 'Chechnya turned the Russian political spectrum upside down.'

[63] Tolz, 'Shifting Sands', 5.

[64] Laura Belin and Robert W. Orttung, 'On the Political Front, Slow Progress Towards Democracy', *Annual Survey 1995*, 218.

decision was clearly a victory for Yeltsin. There were now no legal obstacles to prosecution of the war. Once again the Constitutional Court was playing an important political role, but unlike in 1993, this time it was firmly on the side of the executive. In fact now, under the new constitutional arrangements, it was little more than a retainer for the President.

Several attempts during 1995 by the Duma to censure the President or his government came to nothing. The seizure of hostages in Budennovsk on 14 June 1995 by Chechen guerrillas and the subsequent loss of life when government troops stormed a hospital provoked a 21 June vote of no confidence in the government, which was adopted by 241 to 72. Under many constitutions this would have forced the government to resign; but not under Russia's Constitution. It required a second vote within three months that would have obliged the President to either dismiss the government or send the Duma to election. Chernomyrdin demanded a second vote as soon as possible and Yeltsin threatened to dismiss the Duma should it vote the wrong way; 'As I decide, so it shall be', he warned.[65]

No doubt mindful of the fate of its predecessor, on 1 July by a vote of 193 to 117, the motion of no confidence was passed, but this fell far short of the majority required to adopt it.[66] Yeltsin had actually given the deputies a way out of a vote that could have ended their careers. As a concession he had dismissed three 'power ministers' closely associated with the Chechen debacle: FSB chief Stepashin, Interior Minister Yerin and Deputy Prime Minister and Minister for Nationalities Yegorov. In substance, these dismissals changed nothing. All three were given other high-level posts. Among their replacements were some of Yeltsin's closest allies, who were equally if not more hard-line: Anatoly Kulikov, Russian commander in Chechnya who became Interior Minister, and Colonel General Barsukov, who became FSB chief.[67]

Yeltsin thus kept his hands on the levers of power, though he personally was physically weakened by the first of two heart attacks on 11 July. An attempt to impeach Yeltsin the following day initiated by the KPRF did not even get on the agenda, thanks to Zhirinovsky's LDPR which withdrew its support for the motion following Yeltsin's hospitalization. Despite his ill-health, Yeltsin was also able to fend off a challenge to his standing coming from the Prime Minister. Chernomyrdin's profile had been elevated by the formation of a new political party, Our Home is Russia (NDR), in May. But his well-publicised role in negotiating an end to the Budennovsk hostage crisis marked his emer-

---

[65] Boris Kagarlitsky, 'Chto c nami proiskhodit, ili uroki Basaeva', *Sm*, 8 (Aug. 1995), 24.

[66] The Constitution required that a majority of the total number of deputies support such a motion before it was adopted. See the discussion in White, Rose, and McAllister, *How Russia Votes*, 185.

[67] *Annual Survey 1995*, 212–13.

gence from under Yeltsin's shadow. Yeltsin's second heart attack on 26 October gave Chernomyrdin the opportunity to declare that the security ministers would answer to him and not the President while Yeltsin was incapacitated, but this attempt to assert his authority was rebuffed by Defence Minister Grachev. Although Chernomyrdin's influence was on the rise, the Prime Minister still could not overcome the power of Yeltsin's circle.[68]

Despite the powerlessness of the Parliament, Yeltsin was still concerned that it should not be a hostile forum. With one eye on the forthcoming June 1996 presidential election and the other on the December 1995 parliamentary elections, he had gone out of his way in early 1995 to try to redress his sagging popularity. A package of measures included bringing state-controlled television under his control, endorsing (at last) a political party and courting a bloc of deputies in the Duma. A key figure in these initiatives was Gorbachev's old right-hand man, Aleksandr Yakovlev. Recognising that 'whoever controls Ostankino controls Russia', as *Kommersant-Daily* so concisely put it, under his tutelage he recreated Ostankino as Russian Public Television (ORT), which became effectively 'the President's channel', despite concerted manoeuvres by the Parliament to secure control over it. Simultaneously, Yakovlev set about creating the Russian Party of Social Democracy, a party, like so many others, of no real programmatic distinction that did not even come close to crossing the 5 per cent threshold in December. This attempt to build up his electoral base was reinforced by the establishment of a 36-deputy bloc in the Duma appropriately called Stabil'nost'. This bloc identified with Yeltsin's policy and had links with bankers such as National Credit Bank's Oleg Boiko, but its participants were as much concerned with securing their parliamentary seats as supporting the President.[69] Yeltsin's attempts to improve his public standing also came to nought. Although the Parliament could not impose any effective checks upon the President, it remained an arena in which he came under continuing criticism, both before and after the parliamentary elections of December 1993. In addition the press, at least until early 1996 was very critical of him, especially following the beginning of the Chechen war; indeed, Yeltsin became a figure of ridicule in the popular television satire, 'Kukli'.

In a move which seemed to cut across the rationale underpinning the establishment of Yakovlev's party, the regime also attempted to foster a two-party system through the development of a centre-left 'loyal opposition' under Duma Speaker Ivan Rybkin and a centre-right pro-government party under Chernomyrdin. This was an attempt to construct two electoral blocs designed to sweep up the support of all but the voters at the extreme ends of the

[68] Ibid. 211.
[69] On these developments, see Robert W. Orttung, 'Yeltsin and the Spin Doctors', *Transition*, 1: 8 (26 May 1995), 11–14.

spectrum. It was thereby meant to stabilize the President's regime by ensuring a compliant majority in the Duma. In the event, Yeltsin remained aloof from the election campaign, leaving Yakovlev's, Rybkin's and Chernomyrdin's parties to make their own ways without his focused support. However this general strategy was a clear failure.

The results of the December 1995 election clearly show the failure of this strategy.[70] Only four parties crossed the 5 per cent threshold (see Table 5.2). Only one other party was able to gain the election of deputies numbering in double figures, the Agrarian Party with 20. This result was a major rebuff for the President and his supporters. The party most closely associated with the President, NDR, received less than half the votes of the President's major critics, the communists; Gaidar's party, Russia's Democratic Choice gained only 3.86 per cent of the vote and nine deputies. In contrast, the KPRF gained just less than a quarter of all votes cast, and when combined with its ally (the Agrarian Party) received 26.08 per cent. Compared with the 1993 election, it is clear that the basis of electoral support for the President and government had shrunk considerably, while the support for the communist opposition had grown significantly. Rybkin's bloc had been a victim of the narrowing of the regime's electoral base, which left no room for a 'reserve party of power'.[71] This contraction of the regime's support was in part a reaction to the stalling of the economy: a 4 per cent decline in GDP in the first eleven months of 1995, a 15 per cent fall in wages (which had temporarily stabilized in 1994) and price rises running at 220 per cent.[72] For the same reason, the KPRF was the real winner in the election. This shifted political opposition away from the chauvinist LDPR, in reality a pseudo-opposition that had paid the price for being too sup-

TABLE 5.2. *Parliamentary election results, 1995*

| Party/bloc | Party list | | Single member | Total seats | 1993 seats |
|---|---|---|---|---|---|
| | % | Number | Number | | |
| KPRF | 22.30 | 99 | 58 | 157 | 45 |
| LDPR | 11.18 | 50 | 1 | 51 | 64 |
| NDR | 10.13 | 45 | 10 | 55 | na |
| Yabloko | 6.89 | 31 | 14 | 45 | 25 |

[70] The figures are from Sakwa, *Russian Politics*, 392.

[71] Boris Kagarlitsky, 'The Russian Parliamentary Elections: Results and Prospects', *New Left Review*, 215 (Jan.–Feb. 1996), 120.

[72] Alexander Buzgalin and Andrei Kolganov, 'Russia: the Rout of the Neo-Liberals', *New Left Review*, 215, (Jan.–Feb. 1996), 131–2. Also see figures for shifts in GDP and wages in *Russian and Euro-Asian Bulletin*, 6: 8 (1997), 10, and 7: 1 (1998), 8.

portive of the government, in favour of the 'leftist' KPRF. Over all, the results were a stinging defeat for the 'party of power'. It had secured less than half of the total vote of the KPRF/Agrarian opposition.[73]

This result sent shock waves through the Yeltsin administration; within a month it had changed the composition of the government to give it a more nationalist and less reformist hue.[74] Should the results be repeated in the presidential elections, it was likely that Ziuganov and Zhirinovsky would have been contesting the second round, not Yeltsin. They demonstrated that attempts to create a Russian 'guided democracy' had failed. Despite all the financial and media resources at their disposal, the pro-government, pro-reform parties had performed badly, while predictions that a higher voter turnout would advantage the government came unstuck. The attempt to make the electoral outcome more predictable had failed.[75]

The results of the December 1995 elections, with the success of the KPRF and the humiliation of NDR, saw an enormous mobilization of resources to guarantee a victory for Yeltsin in the presidential contest. The prospects looked bleak. In January, Yeltsin's approval rating hovered around 5 per cent, with KPRF candidate Ziuganov well out in front with 17 per cent approval. Yeltsin was even lagging behind other potential candidates Grigory Yavlinsky (15 per cent), Aleksandr Lebed (14 per cent) and Vladimir Zhirinovsky (9 per cent).[76] But the prospect of a defeat for Yeltsin at the hands of the KPRF was too much for the new bourgeoisie. Their success depended on continued access to the state. Should the KPRF win office, then all the wealth they had appropriated during the past five years would be in jeopardy.[77] (See below Chapter 6).

In these circumstances, the temptation not to go to a presidential election was great indeed. Some members of the so-called 'party of war'—bodyguard Korzhakov, security chief Barsukov and First Deputy Prime Minister Soskovets, who at that time was in charge of Yeltsin's election campaign—were inclined to cancel the elections. Korzhakov reportedly felt elections were too risky; they were just a Western idea and 'democracy could be preserved without them.'[78] By

---

[73] For further analysis, see M. G. Gorkov *et al.* (eds.), *Ot Yeltsina k . . . Yeltsinu: prezidentskaiia gonka–96* (Moscow, Terra, 1997), 19.

[74] The pro-Western Foreign Minister Kozyrev was replaced by Yevgeny Primakov, who had close relations with the Arab world, Filatov was replaced as head of the presidential administration by former minister for nationalities Yegorov, and most importantly, First Deputy Prime Minister Chubais was sacked: White, Rose, and McAllister, *How Russia Votes*, 235.

[75] See Kagarlitsky, 'The Russian Parliamentary Elections', 117–28. The turnout of voters in 1995 was 64.44%, up from 54.80% in 1993. Sakwa, *Russian Politics*, 391–2.

[76] Gorkov, 'Ot Yeltsina', 83.

[77] Boris Kagarlitsky, 'Russia Before the Elections', *Green Left Weekly*, 19 June 1996, p. 21.

[78] David Remnick, 'The War for the Kremlin', *New Yorker*, 22 July 1996, pp. 47–8.

March, Yeltsin himself was seriously considering cancelling the elections. He ordered Korzhakov to investigate this as an option. As a pretext for cancellation, Korzhakov seized on a Duma resolution adopted on 15 March denouncing the Belovezha Accords ending the USSR. Next day the necessary presidential decrees were drafted: for the dissolution of the Parliament, banning of the Communist Party and cancellation of the election. Yeltsin was brought back from the brink of a coup only by the inability of his Interior Minister Kulikov to guarantee the loyalty of his troops in such an undertaking.[79] On 6 May Korzhakov publicly declared the need to postpone the elections in the interests of stability. Yeltsin was forced to repudiate his bodyguard's declaration. Nevertheless, on the very eve of the election the President himself did not preclude the possibility of a coup: 'I will not allow the communists into power', he declared.[80] Such were the limits of the new democracy.

Meanwhile, in February, some of those who believed that the only course was to go to election had met at the economic summit in Davos, Switzerland. One of the wealthiest of the new bourgeoisie, Boris Berezovsky, head of a vast conglomerate of car dealerships (Logovaz), media outlets (Russian Public Television, the journal *Ogonek* and the newspaper *Nezavisimaia gazeta*) and banks, teamed up with an arch rival Vladimir Gusinsky, head of Mostbank and owner of NTV public television. These 'politicized capitalists' were the core of a group of businessmen who threw their vast financial and media resources behind Yeltsin.[81] Chubais, who had fallen from grace in January 1996, in March returned to the fold to head Yeltsin's new election team.

Chubais's return was not welcomed by his rivals in the presidential and government administrations.[82] Throughout the campaign there was bitter rivalry between the Chubais and Soskovets teams. An attempt to establish a joint 14-member election council proved untenable. But it was the Chubais media-led approach that won the day. Yeltsin began to turn the electoral tide in a campaign that 'gave new meaning to the phrase "the advantages of incumbency." '[83] Yeltsin was on the hustings, making thirty-three trips in four

[79] Remnick, 'War for the Kremlin', pp. 47–8. See also B. Yeltsin, 'Duma stavit pod somnenie vozmozhnosti provedeniia prezidentskikh vyborov' and S. Kurginian, 'U propasti. Politicheskii krizis 15–18 marta 1996 goda', Gorkov, 'Ot Yeltsina', 169–70, 184–5.

[80] A. Korzhakov, 'Esli vybory sostoiatsiia, izbezhat' borby ne udastsiia . . .', Gorkov, 'Ot Yeltsina', 279–80; Remnick, 'War for the Kremlin', 50.

[81] Both Berezovsky and Gusinsky recognised the importance of investing in the media, not so much for profit as for the shaping of public opinion and exercising political influence: Ivan Zasursky, 'Politika, dengi i pressa v sovremennoi Rossii', *Sm*, 10 (1996), 14–16.

[82] David Hoffman, 'Only Elite Benefit in People's Capitalism', *Guardian Weekly*, 25 Jan. 1998, 15.

[83] Remnick, 'War for the Kremlin', 49.

months that culminated in a rock concert in Red Square in June. Previously debilitated by his heart disorder, he now projected an image of youthful vigour, but at considerable cost to his health: he suffered a heart attack between the election rounds, though this was concealed from the voters at the time. Drawing illegally on state funds, he distributed electoral largesse estimated at US$11billion, which left Russia's commitments to IMF budgetary requirements in tatters.[84] As the elections grew closer, an anti-communist media campaign of McCarthyite intensity depicted Yeltsin as a bulwark against a return to Stalinism, making the election a stark choice: 'back to revolutions and shocks or forward to stability and welfare'. It was a pseudo-choice, framed as a referendum.[85] The election was not a choice between systems: a capitalist or a communist Russia. The KPRF projected a mixed message. On the one hand it had advanced a vaguely Keynesian economic policy, but on the other it had advocated some renationalization of industry and increased state intervention. There was considerable uncertainty about what the communists actually stood for. Nevertheless to many, they appeared to offer a programme for national capitalist development, tailored to the chauvinist conceptions of the 'popular patriotic bloc' which supported Ziuganov's candidacy.[86]

A critical part of Yeltsin's strategy was to promote a third candidate who would draw away part of the nationalist vote that would otherwise have gone to Ziuganov. As it later emerged, a deal was struck with Lebed who campaigned on a strongly nationalist platform, with the promise of a high-level appointment.[87] From March onwards, money and campaign advice flowed his way from the Yeltsin camp so that in the first round of the voting on 16 June, he secured a surprise 14.52 per cent of the vote, almost twice as much as Yavlinsky with 7.34 per cent. Yeltsin himself came in first with 35.28 per cent of the vote, ahead of Ziuganov on 32.03 per cent; Zhirinovsky had gained a paltry 5.70 per cent. This meant that in the second round some two weeks later, Yeltsin and Ziuganov would run off. Yeltsin now rewarded Lebed by appointing him Secretary of the Security Council, potentially a powerful position but, as Lebed would find to his cost, totally dependent on the President. Simultaneously he dismissed an arch rival of Lebed's, Pavel Grachev, by now a liability for Yeltsin's campaign given his close association with the Chechnya debacle and the taint of corruption. Grachev's fellow members of the 'party of

[84] David Hearst, 'Can Boris Buy the Election?', *Guardian Weekly*, 16 June 1996, p. 7.

[85] Laura Belin and Robert W. Orttung, 'Electing a Fragile Political Stability', *Transition*, 3: 2 (7 Feb. 1997), 68.

[86] Jack F. Matlock, Jr, 'The Struggle for the Kremlin', *New York Review of Books*, 8 Aug. 1996, p. 30; Renfrey Clarke, 'Russian Elections: How Yeltsin Arose from the Dead', *Green Left Weekly*, 26 June 1995, p. 15.

[87] Remnick, 'War for the Kremlin', 52. For the election statistics, see Sakwa, *Russian Politics*, 393–4.

war' soon followed suit. When two campaign aides working for Chubais were arrested by Korzhakov's guards carrying US$500,000 from a government building, Chubais with Lebed's help was able to turn the tables on his rivals. Korzhakov, Barsukov and Soskovets were dismissed on the pretext that they were interfering with the election campaign.[88] Before the second round had even occurred on 3 July, Chubais and Yeltsin's younger daughter Tatiana Diachenko, who had played a pivotal role in the campaign, had achieved unrivalled influence over the ailing President.[89]

Yeltsin's win on 3 July was decisive: 53.82 per cent to Ziuganov's 40.31 per cent; 4.83 per cent voted against both candidates. Although down from the 57.30 per cent Yeltsin had received when elected in 1991, it was a remarkable electoral turnaround for a candidate who six months earlier was polling barely 5 per cent and was incapacitated by a heart attack between rounds.[90] In part it was due to the adeptness of Yeltsin's campaign. The essential, ultimately successful, ingredients in this campaign were twofold: the widespread use of modern political technology, especially the media, and the utilisation of a team of professional political advisers and consultants. The media was crucial. Following the discussions at Davos referred to above, most of the media outlets swung in behind the President. Instead of the wholesale criticism that had been its usual fare in 1995, the media now mounted an unashamedly biased campaign, giving unstinting support to Yeltsin and heaping criticism upon his opponent. The favourable attitude the media adopted toward the President is nowhere better seen than in the way it projected him as healthy and full of vigour before the first round, and then when he had his heart attack following the first round of voting and did not play a personal part in the campaign for the second round, nothing was made of this. In organisational terms, the political decisions concerning the campaign were taken by Yeltsin's staff, but their implementation and dissemination to the electorate were undertaken by professionals. Yeltsin's campaign was quite distinct, therefore, from that conducted in December by NDR, for example, which drew its campaign organizers from government bureaucrats who thought they had no need for

---

[88] B. Yeltsin, 'Silovye struktury slishkom mnogo stali na sebia brat': Gorkov, 'Ot Yeltsina', 498–9; Matlock, 'The Struggle', 30–1. On 4 July the 20,000 strong Presidential Security Service formerly headed by Korzhakov was merged with the larger State Protection Service.

[89] According to Korzhakov, Chubais and Berezovsky were instrumental in bringing Diachenko into the campaign team. She alone had the trust of the President and was seen as the ideal intermediary. On 27 June 1997 she became Yeltsin's media adviser: Korzhakov, *Boris Yeltsin*, 355, 358, 468.

[90] For scepticism about the final results see Boris Kagarlitsky, 'Russia's Elections without Winners', *Green Left Weekly*, 17 July 1996, p. 18.

electoral advisers.[91] Yeltsin made up for his lack of a mass party by mobilizing the 'party' of the presidential apparatus.[92] It was a fiercely anti-communist campaign that successfully convinced the electorate that only Yeltsin stood between them and a return to the Gulag.[93]

Yeltsin's victory was assisted by the lack-lustre KPRF campaign. It failed to take advantage of the initial lead it had when it went into the first round of the election. Foregoing paid television advertisements, it relied on the party apparatus and an ageing membership that conducted door-to-door electioneering, distributing leaflets and stickers. In the second round, it appeared to have already admitted defeat. Instead of vigorous campaigning, it concentrated on making overtures for representation in a coalition government. These aspirations came to nought, but they were symptomatic of a demoralised organization that had basically accepted the rules of the new political game. For the KPRF it was never a question of resuscitating a lost-Soviet past. Rather the KPRF counter-elite—an amalgam of relics of the old party-state apparatus, regional administrators and industrial managers from defence and rural-based industries—sought a legitimate place in the new capitalist Russia and a sharing of the spoils of office in the new democracy. Yeltsin's new political technology had certainly outpaced 'apparatus-command' style campaigning. But at bottom, it was the unwillingness of the KPRF to seriously attempt to mobilize popular opinion against Yeltsin's record on a number of issues—Chechnya, conscription, economic decline -that virtually handed Yeltsin the presidency.[94] Indeed, there was considerable confusion about what the KPRF stood for, with Ziuganov tailoring his message to his audience to such a focused extent that at times he seemed to be adopting two contradictory positions; both Leninist and Russian orthodox symbolism pervaded his campaign.

Yeltsin's incumbency of the presidency gave his campaign a number of advantages. Good economic news was manufactured in the lead up to the election, which the biased press did not subject to the usual scrutiny. The payment of overdue wages was promised, and in some cases, this was fulfilled. The opening of negotiations suggested that an end to the Chechen conflict was in sight. In March an accord was signed between Russia, Belarus, Kazakhstan and Kyrgyzstan foreshadowing closer integration, and in April a bilateral agreement with Belarus announced a form of 'union' between the two states, both measures which appealed to that section of the population which regretted the passing of the Soviet Union. In personnel matters, the appointment of Primakov as Foreign Minister in place of Andrei Kozyrev, who was hated by

---

[91] Khenkin, 'Partiia vlasti', 40.    [92] Gorkov, 'Ot Yeltsina', 10.

[93] B. Slavin, 'Pochemu B. Yeltsin vyigral?', Gorkov, 'Ot Yeltsina', 584–6.

[94] Clarke, 'Russian elections'; Kagarlitsky, 'Russia's Elections without Winners'; Boris Kagarlitsky, 'O prichinakh porazheniia levykh', *Sm* 9 (1996), 3–7.

those in the nationalist camp, was a concession to a significant group of critics of Yeltsin. The President also used the considerable resources at his disposal for dispensing largesse as he travelled around the regions campaigning. He was also able to win over many regional elites by suggesting that he would be a President who would be much less intrusive in local affairs than his opponent. And finally, Yeltsin played upon the image he had sought to project since 1991 of being the populist President who ruled for all rather than being tied to any specific sectional group or party.

The presidential campaign was sharply polarized—an 'either–or' campaign. The nearer the elections got, and the more intense the contest, the more Yeltsin was portrayed as the 'symbol of a legitimate state and as a figure binding together a split, atomised Russian society.' Furthermore, Yeltsin, as the incumbent, was able to take advantage of the traditional Russian attitude to the Head of State: 'the Tsar cannot cease to be the Tsar.' In this sense, the elections showed not only the efficacy of the mass media in the campaign, but also the resilience of the traditional 'state principle' in Russian political culture.[95]

## A Political Vacuum

Yeltsin's emphatic victory in the presidential election should have been the beginning of a period when the President dominated the Russian political scene even more than he had before. His victory seemed to legitimate the consolidation of presidential power that had been brought about on the basis of the 1993 Constitution. His performance placed the results of the parliamentary election in the shade, while his achievement in coming from so far behind at the start of the year seemed to suggest that Russian political life was his personally to mould as he wished. But this was more appearance than substance. The role played in his victory by high-level business supporters and their media outlets was suggestive of the way in which much of Russian politics was now bound up with the views and outlooks of economic elites. Their links with the President's campaign machine, embedded in part in the presidential apparatus, was consistent with the large role being played in Russian public life by the entourage around Yeltsin. And given Yeltsin's ill health, and the consequent relative passivity of the person of the President throughout much of 1996 and extending into 1997, those personal advisers and functionaries found the scope for them to play an independent role in political life greatly enhanced.

---

[95] Khenkin, 'Partiia vlasti', 40.

During the pre-election campaign the 'party of power' probably achieved its apogee of strength. It saw an unprecedented rallying of forces both inside and outside the political elite, a 'merger of the party of power and the media', to prevent a KPRF victory.[96] This disparate coalition soon broke up once victory was secured. Tensions broke out with the appointment in mid-July of Chubais as Yeltsin's chief of staff,[97] despite Yeltsin's declaration just before the second round of the elections that Chubais would not be holding high office. Chubais's elevation to the second most powerful position in the country was cemented by a decree in mid-August requiring all draft presidential decrees to go through the chief of staff alone.[98] Chubais was now in the position to vet all presidential decisions. Chubais' strategic location became apparent when on 5 September it was finally announced that Yeltsin was unwell and would be undergoing major heart surgery, which was to take Yeltsin out of regular public life until early 1997. During his operation, formal authority temporarily passed to Prime Minister Chernomyrdin, as required by the Constitution. But real authority lay with the President's regent: his chief of staff.

From the outset Chubais had in his sights the new Security Council Secretary, Aleksandr Lebed, against whom he now instigated a media campaign. With Yeltsin's re-election as President in mid-1996 and Lebed's appointment as Security Council Secretary, the Council looked set to assume a central role again. A presidential decree of 10 July made the Council responsible for defending Russia's vital social, economic, defence, environmental, and information interests.[99] At the end of August, Lebed negotiated a Chechen settlement, which earned him the enmity of Interior Minister Kulikov, whom Lebed blamed for the debacle in Chechnya when Grozny was seized by the separatists. On 16 October Kulikov accused Lebed of plotting a military coup. The next day Lebed was unceremoniously dismissed on national television by the President, who accused Lebed of using his position to promote his own presidential ambitions.[100] Once more Yeltsin had demonstrated his willingness to use allies, then dispense with them when it suited him. He had also demonstrated again that real power resided in his apparat. It would not be the last time.

As reward for support in the election campaign, Yeltsin appointed two prominent businessmen to his administration. The banker Vladimir Potanin

[96] The role of the mass media during the presidential elections was 'not a step towards democracy', according to the European Press Institute (EMI), which monitored the media during the election. EMI found that in violation of the March 1996 electoral law, the media had overwhelmingly supported Yeltsin's campaign. Yeltsin had occupied 53% of the transmission time received by the candidates. Both state-owned television (ORT and RTR) and the privately owned (by Gusinsky) NTV had thrown themselves behind Yeltsin: Zasursky, 'Politika', 17–18.

[97] *Ng*, 16 July 1996.  [98] *Izvestiia*, 23 Aug. 1996.
[99] Sakwa, *Russian Politics*, 146.  [100] Gorkov, 'Ot Yeltsina', 620.

became a Deputy Prime Minister responsible for economic policy and privatization, while Boris Berezovsky became Deputy Secretary of the Security Council responsible for Chechnya. This constituted the entry into formal political office of representatives of leading financial-business interests, colloquially called 'the oligarchs',[101] who had supported Yeltsin's re-election bid and were intent on using their political connections to further their economic ambitions. Allegations about corruption and Berezovsky's Israeli citizenship led to calls from Duma Speaker and Communist Party member Gennady Seleznev for Berezovsky to resign. Yeltsin ignored this call, as he did similar accusations against Chubais. Chubais was accused of direct involvement in illegal campaign financing and of falsely claiming that his two aides arrested by Korzhakov had the US$500,000 planted on them. Chubais not only remained at his post, but on 7 March 1997 Yeltsin once more made Chubais a First Deputy Prime Minister. The Duma, despite its incremental increase in organization and influence since 1995, was powerless to restrict the newly re-elected President.[102]

In addition to Chubais, Yeltsin also brought Boris Nemtsov, who had made his reputation as a reformer in the city of Nizhnii Novgorod, into the cabinet as the other First Deputy Prime Minister. These so-called 'young wolves' were determined to carry the privatisation process a step further by breaking up the 'natural monopolies', such as Gazprom, state-owned oil companies, and even the railways. This set the stage for a clash of interests over lucrative government assets. An auction for communications giant Sviazinvest and for Norilsk Nickel set for July 1997 generated intense rivalry between potential bidders. Despite the hopes of Mostbank chief Gusinsky, controlling interests in both Sviazinvest and Norilsk Nickel were secured by arch rival Oneksimbank magnate Potanin, who resigned as Deputy Prime Minister in order to bid. Such public squabbling between the major bankers saw the President call them in for a public dressing-down. Such behaviour, he suggested, detracted from the over-all standing of the bankers and the political process as a whole. The Sviazinvest and Norilsk Nickel affairs eventually cost Berezovsky his position as Deputy Secretary of the Security Council. He was dismissed in November

---

[101] This originally comprised the seven who came together to support Yeltsin in 1996: Vladimir Potanin of Oneksimbank, Mikhail Khodorkovsky of Bank Menatep, Vladimir Gusinsky of Most Group, Mikhail Fridman of Alfa Group, Vagit Alikperov of Lukoil, Aleksandr Smolensky of Stolichnyi Bank, and Berezovsky. Two others later became associated with this group: Vladimir Vinogradov of Inkombank and Rem Viakhirev of Gazprom.

[102] Belin and Orttung, 'Electing a Fragile Political Stability', 69–70. For a claim that the Duma has been getting gradually stronger, see Robert W. Orttung and Scott Parrish, 'From Confrontation to Cooperation in Russia', *Transition*, 2: 25 (13 Dec. 1996), 20.

amid bitter recriminations against Chubais for allegedly favouring Potanin.[103] Once again, Yeltsin was acting as the supreme arbiter, this time among the elite beneficiaries of the privatization policies introduced by his favourite—Chubais.

But even Yeltsin could not protect Chubais forever. Scandals and constant accusations of corrupt behaviour, including promises of a lucrative advance on an unpublished book on privatization which came to light in November 1997, brought him into disrepute. As a result he was removed as Finance Minister but retained his post as First Deputy Prime Minister. No doubt this was some satisfaction for two of Chubais's main rivals, Berezovsky and Chernomyrdin. Berezovsky felt his bank had been excluded from its fair share of the latest cycle of privatization. The Prime Minister saw Chubais and Nemtsov as threats to his position and that of the fuel and energy sector with which he identified. Outwardly, Yeltsin, stood behind his government. In early 1998 he hailed the achievements of the Chernomyrdin government while promising Chubais and Nemtsov would remain in office until the year 2000. But it was not to be. Falling oil prices, rising state debt, the odour of corruption and the politically destabilizing infighting between Chernomyrdin and Chubais forced an ailing Yeltsin to act. On 23 March 1998 Yeltsin dismissed the Prime Minister and his cabinet, including Interior Minister General Anatoly Kulikov who apparently had gathered too much power in his hands. In doing so, in the words of one observer, Yeltsin 'acted like the ancient Persian ruler who, on learning of the enmity between two of his courtiers, had both of them executed.'[104] Yeltsin now chose a former junior minister, Sergei Kirienko, as Prime Minister. This choice was widely opposed in the Duma, which on two occasions voted not to ratify Yeltsin's choice. However, in the context of growing economic crisis brought on by the Asian financial crisis, the moderate stance and image projected by Kirienko, and threats by the President to dissolve the Duma, Yeltsin's choice was finally accepted on 24 April 1998. His dominance over the Parliament was once again apparent for all to see. But perhaps even more reflective of his dominance was the fact that, in mid-1998, Yeltsin brought Chubais back once again, this time as presidential envoy to international financial institutions with the rank of Deputy Prime Minister[105] to conduct negotiations with the IMF for assistance to deal with the economic crisis.[106] Despite

---

[103] See e.g. the article by Ulyan Kerzonov in *Nezavisimaia gazeta*, 13 Sept. 1997. *Ng* is widely seen as the mouthpiece of Berezovsky.

[104] Boris Kagarlitsky, 'Russia: New Government No Threat to Neo-Liberalism', *Green Left Weekly*, 312 (1 Apr. 1998).

[105] *Segodnia*, 18 June 1998.

[106] For an interesting discussion of this, see Konstantin Smirnov, 'Rossiia poluchit po polnoi programme', *Kommersant Vlast'*, 27 (21 July 1998).

ınpopularity, Chubais had been brought back into the centre
President. Of course he had never been too far from it; in April
en appointed chairman of the electricity giant United Energy

, of Chernomyrdin, the ramming of the Kirienko appointment
throug.. /uma, and the re-appointment of Chubais seemed to suggest that
Yeltsin was a powerful and vigorous figure. But this appearance was deceptive.
Yeltsin never fully recovered from his heart operation at the end of 1996.
During the subsequent years he was physically unable to bear the full workload
demanded by his office. His involvement in affairs of state was increasingly
punctuated by withdrawals from public activity, returning only to intervene at
critical junctures. The effect of what in practice was a part-time President was
the leaching of power away from the President personally, despite the continued power of the presidency. This leaching of power favoured two political
actors: successive Prime Ministers, and an informal group of advisers and confidants around Yeltsin usually referred to as 'the family'. The precise identity of
this latter group has been a matter of some debate, but it included Yeltsin's
daughter Tatiana Diachenko, Berezovsky (reputed to be the personal financial
adviser to Yeltsin's family), Chubais, head of the Presidential Administration
Aleksandr Voloshin and his predecessor Valentin Yumashev, and head of
Sibneft oil company Roman Abramovich. Although the interests of these
people did not always coincide, they were united in their desire to sustain their
own positions of power, influence and wealth, even after Yeltsin's departure
from the scene. With Yeltsin's ill health, their influence expanded greatly, chiefly
because of their personal conduit to the President through his daughter.

The political stabilization at the upper level of the Russian state that the
replacement of Chernomyrdin by Kirienko was meant to bring about was
destroyed by the economic crisis of August 1998. Russia had accumulated
debts of US$140 billion, and by mid-1998 these consumed 30 per cent of the
federal budget.[107] Government attempts to raise revenues through the sale of
short-term government bonds (GKUs), privatization of the state-owned oil
producer Rosneft, and increased income tax collections (the Kirienko government particularly sought to target business and the 'oligarchs') failed. Despite
a massive US$22.6 billion rescue package for Russia put together by the IMF
and World Bank, investor confidence, already shaken by the Asian crisis, fell.
Finally on 17 August Russia effectively devalued its currency, something Yeltsin
had vowed he would never allow,[108] and defaulted on some of its debts. The

[107] Boris Kagarlitsky, 'Testimony Before the Banking and Financial Services United
States House of Representatives Hearing To Examine the Russian Economic Crisis and the
International Monetary Fund', 10 Sept. 1998. Johnson's Russia List 2384, 13 Oct. 1998.
[108] *Ng*, 15 Aug. 1998.

Russian state was bankrupt. On 23 August, the Kirienko government was dismissed, less than six months after it was appointed.

The attempt to form a new government exposed how Yeltsin's authority had been weakened by the financial crisis. Twice he had his initial nominee for Prime Minister, Viktor Chernomyrdin, rejected by the Duma; one further rejection would have given Yeltsin the power to dismiss the Parliament and send it to new elections. The KPRF, which when previously faced with the prospect of the dissolution of the Duma had buckled, this time refused to accept Chernomyrdin's nomination despite its previous good relations with him. In part this rejection was on the grounds that, as Prime Minister between December 1992 and March 1998, Chernomyrdin had presided over Russia's precipitous decline and was therefore discredited in the public eye.[109] But the kiss of death came when Yeltsin announced that he regarded Chernomyrdin as his successor.[110] When Yeltsin's willingness to concede the Prime Minister's right to form the government in consultation with the Duma did not sway the Parliament,[111] Yeltsin was forced to compromise.

On 11 September an alternative, acceptable, nominee for Prime Minister was announced: former Gorbachev politburo member, head of foreign intelligence and foreign minister Yevgeny Primakov. Although Primakov's nomination was overwhelmingly endorsed by the Duma and welcomed by the KPRF, it is a measure of the impasse that Russia found itself in that it took another three weeks for Primakov to finalize his cabinet. Some politicians refused to serve in the new government and another resigned after being appointed. Finally Primakov settled on a cabinet that would maximize his political support. He appointed the KPRF's Yury Masliukov as Deputy Prime Minister for the economy, a prominent monetarist Mikhail Zadornov as Finance Minister, and the LDPR's Sergei Kalashnikov as Minister for Labour.

Despite Primakov's proclaimed intention of re-establishing some controls over the economy, something depicted in some quarters as a threatened reversion to Soviet era command economics, the new Prime Minister evidently opted to observe 'the imperatives of the global market place', as US President Bill Clinton had insisted bluntly on 1 September when he dropped in to Moscow to shore up the tottering Yeltsin regime.[112] Among Primakov's first acts in mid-September was to arrange a debt swap for Russia's ailing banks. This entailed borrowing from the reserves that they were required to deposit with the Central Bank, and then repaying them using the worthless government bonds that the Kirienko administration had previously defaulted on.

---

[109] *Izvestiia*, 10 Sept. 1998.  [110] *Obshchaia gazeta*, 3–9 Sept. 1998.
[111] *Ng*, 8 Sept. 1998.
[112] S. Holland, 'Clinton Bluntly Tells Russia to Keep Reforms', *Reuters*, 1 Sept. 1998.

This was a gift to the bankers.[113] Meanwhile Primakov promised to pay billions of roubles in wage and pension arrears.

Rather than a radical change of course, stabilisation proved to be the hallmark of Primakov's short-lived government as it tried to ride out the financial crisis and a threatening social storm. Fears of a social upheaval were real. In a country dependent on imports for 50 per cent of foodstuffs and suffering a 60 per cent fall of the rouble in the space of three weeks, social tensions were high. With several of the major banks insolvent, many of the 'new middle class' in Moscow and St Petersburg, hitherto an electoral bulwark of the Yeltsin regime, were impoverished overnight or thrown out of work. Although a nationwide protest of 7 October failed to mobilize the millions promised by the Federation of Independent Trade Unions,[114] there were worrying signs of discontent in many of the regions where new forms of militant protest, such as the blockading of railways, erupted.[115] Centrifugal tendencies, already evident earlier in the Yeltsin period, were stimulated by the crisis, as regional elites reacted by sequestering local and financial material resources, including food, and denying them to the Moscow centre.[116] The authorities in Yakutia asserted control over its gold production and limited sales to Moscow and the banks.[117] Fear that Russia would disintegrate into warring fiefs raised its head again.

Believing itself faced with an insoluble dilemma—if the government did not print roubles, wages would continue to go unpaid with the fear of social unrest, but if they did print money inflation would rapidly erode its value— Primakov steered a middle course: a modest increase in the money supply.[118] The new government was under intense pressure from the IMF, which was insistent that deflationary policies were essential for the continuation of the reforms and a necessary condition for the provision of further financial assistance. The IMF was disconcerted by Primakov's reappointment of Viktor Gerashchenko as head of the Central Bank, associating him with what they regarded as profligate fiscal policies during his previous tenure in 1992–94. The Fund rejected out of hand the proposal in the government's draft plan, announced on 2 November, to print roubles in order to plug a 70 billion rouble (approximately US$4.4 billion) budget deficit. To deliver on the next US$4.3 billion loan instalment, the IMF urged Primakov to adopt a 'realistic'

[113] Renfrey Clarke, 'Russian Government Blows Wage Arrears to Save Oligarchs', *Green Left Weekly*, 30 Sept. 1998, p. 21.

[114] *Ng*, 8 Oct. 1998.

[115] Also see R. Clarke, 'On Strike at the Volkov Mine', Johnson's Russia List 2427, 13 Oct. 1998.

[116] *Ng*, 8 Sept. 1998.

[117] P. Reeves, 'Russia's Regions Start to Rebel as Kremlin's Grip Weakens', *Independent* (UK), 7 Sept. 1998.

[118] See the interview with Finance Minister Mikhail Zadornov, *Izvestiia*, 14 Oct. 1998.

budget.[119] Primakov duly did, although it took Masliukov's threat to resign to force the Duma to accept it at the second reading.[120]

Overall, Primakov marked time in the face of Russia's impasse, although he mooted policies that on occasion seemed to hark back to Soviet times. In response to the regionalist tendencies he suggested that regional governors should be appointed rather than elected. Reflecting his disenchantment with the market (which he had been among the first to embrace at the time of perestroika's demise), he spoke about creating a huge, new state-owned oil company, ridiculed by *Izvestiia* as a 'collective oil farm'.[121] In an attempt to appease militant miners, there were promises to double state subsidies for the coal industry.[122] There was also a significant slowing of privatisation; Sviazinvest and Rosneft were retained in state hands 'because they were going to be sold for a song'.[123] But there was no overall anti-crisis programme; Primakov maintained a holding operation. There was no restructuring of the banking system and the rouble continued to fall in value against the dollar. Above all, Primakov resiled from any attempt to renationalize industry, the worst fear of his opponents at home and abroad. Instead he focused on winning the support of domestic interests by modest financial inducements while observing sufficient budgetary stringency to procure enough Western financial aid to roll over the US\$4.5 billion due to be repaid to the IMF in 1999 for earlier loans. It was not until the NATO offensive in Yugoslavia in March 1999, when the Western powers wanted Russia on side, that an in principle agreement with the IMF was forthcoming.

Despite the enormity of the problems facing Russia, Primakov's ability seemingly to at least hold the line saw his popularity rise. An upturn in industrial output and food production (fostered by the weak rouble which increased domestic demand and exports and make imports more expensive), strong support in the Duma with whom he was able to work cooperatively, and his high public profile as de facto Vice President as he filled the vacuum created by the ailing President throughout much of this period, all worked in his favour, temporarily at least. Primakov began increasingly to look like a presidential contender in 2000. This was not an attractive proposition in the eyes of 'the family'. Primakov was not one of them, his instincts seemed to be more state regulatory than free market in essence, he was believed to have retained much of his communist past in both style and substance, and it was by no means clear that he would safeguard their interests either, in the run-up to the election or, if he was elected, after it. Furthermore their position seemed in danger of eroding. Several of the bankers who had thrown their weight behind Yeltsin in 1996 had

[119] S. Rao, 'Cabinet Approves Plan for Economy', *Moscow Times*, 3 Nov. 1998.
[120] *Izvestiia*, 21 Jan. 1999; *Ng*, 21 Jan. 1999.     [121] *Izvestiia*, 27 Jan. 1999.
[122] *Kommersant*, 2 Feb. 1999.     [123] *Izvestiia*, 15 Oct. 1998.

been badly burned by the August financial crisis, particularly Smolensky, Potanin and Khodorkovsky. Vinogradov's Inkombank, reportedly Russia's second largest, had ceased to exist.[124] Furthermore in early 1999 Berezovsky became a particular target of the Prosecutor-General Yury Skuratov in relation to bribery and spying charges, which were part of a wider investigation into high-level corruption in the Kremlin, Government, and Central Bank. Skuratov was widely seen as having been encouraged in this by Primakov. Berezovsky's dismissal as CIS Executive Secretary in March was an attempt by Yeltsin to distance himself from the odour arising from Berezovsky's activities.

The danger to 'the family' and to Yeltsin seemed stark by March 1999. The KPRF had initiated a campaign to impeach Yeltsin on five grounds[125] and there was a widespread consensus that such a vote could succeed on at least one of the charges. Furthermore, Yeltsin's attempts to fend off Skuratov's investigation were weakened when the Federation Council refused to assent to the removal of the Prosecutor-General. It soon became apparent, however, that Yeltsin and those around him were determined to claw back his authority. The first sign of this came with a reshuffling of the cabinet on 28 April, which saw Interior Minister Sergei Stapashin promoted to First Deputy Prime Minister, equal in standing to Masliukov. Hints that Primakov might soon be removed came from head of the Presidential Administration Aleksandr Voloshin, who accused the Prime Minister of failing to deter a vote against Skuratov in the upper house and against Yeltsin in the lower house. Primakov was also accused of failing to strike a credit deal with the IMF, and was publicly disparaged by Yeltsin. The coup de grace came on 12 May when Yeltsin sacked Primakov, appointing Stepashin in his stead. Although Primakov's failure to reinvigorate the economy was given as the principal reason for his dismissal, more immediate factors included Yeltsin's determination that the President rather than the Prime Minister should occupy centre stage in Russian politics (especially in the context of the crisis surrounding events in Kosovo), and the concern to defend the position and prerogatives enjoyed by 'the family'. Primakov's sacking at this time once again demonstrated that for the clique surrounding the President, personal interests prevailed over those of Russia as a state.

The sacking seemed to presage yet another political crisis, coming as it did on the eve of the 15 May Duma impeachment vote. The failure by the Duma to ratify the President's nominee for Prime Minister on three occasions opened the way for its dismissal, but once impeachment proceedings were underway,

---

[124] *Ng*, 28 Oct. 1998.

[125] The five 'criminal' charges which were the basis for impeachment under the Constitution were the launching of the war against Chechnya, dissolution of the USSR in 1991, dispersal of the Parliament by force in 1993, the collapse of the Russian military, and pursuit of economic 'genocidal' policies against the population.

the Duma could not legally be dismissed. A constitutional stand-off threatened. But it was not to be. Despite a year's preparation, the KPRF failed to muster the necessary two-thirds vote required for impeachment on any of the five charges. Within days of the vote, on 18 May the Duma meekly confirmed Stepashin as Prime Minister. The appointment of the Colonel-General in charge of interior ministry forces was an unambiguous warning to the Duma of the President's resolve. In an election year, the deputies had no stomach for a fight; dismissal would mean the loss of vital resources for campaigning, such as offices, communications, travel, and photocopying.

Stepashin was a long-standing Yeltsin loyalist. In October 1993 the former head of the Supreme Soviet's security committee had gone over to the President. In 1994 he was an active contributor to the intervention in Chechnya, including the Budennovsk hostage debacle, after which he had lost his position. Now he was back, this time as Prime Minister and, it seemed, determined to demonstrate that he was no mere minion of the Kremlin. However, he was unable to have his way in the selection of his ministers. Some of his recommendations were rejected by Yeltsin, who also forced upon him former railways minister Nikolai Aksenenko as First Deputy Prime Minister. This appointment, and Aksenenko's expansion of his brief to include economic affairs, prompted the resignation of Mikhail Zadornov. The appointment of Aksenenko, and of Sibneft head Roman Abramovich, to the government was widely seen as reflecting 'family' and 'oligarch' influence.[126] So too was Stepashin's sudden, unexplained dismissal on 9 August. His replacement, Security Council Secretary and FSB head Vladimir Putin, had even closer connections with Yeltsin's circle. With fighting once again in the northern Caucasus region, financial scandals implicating both Yeltsin personally and his daughter Tatiana Diachenko, parliamentary elections scheduled for December 1999, and rumours circulating about the possible imposition of emergency rule, Putin's links with the security apparatuses seemed to have their advantages. This was enough for Yeltsin also to anoint Putin as his preferred candidate for the presidential election scheduled for the middle of 2000.

The events of spring 1999 underlined the central role in the Russian system occupied by the presidency. But it also showed in sharp outline the paradox at the heart of the Russian system. A constitutionally powerful presidency was occupied by someone whose physical capacities prevented him from adequately playing out that role, with the result that power was effectively devolved into the hands of a shadowy camarilla surrounding the President. The squabbles, differences, and disagreements within this group was a crucial element structuring Russian politics. So much depended upon who had the

[126] *Kommersant Den'gi*, 21 (2 June 1999), 7–9; *Kommersant*, 27 May 1999.

ear of the President and whether he was capable of making decisions rather than the institutional imperatives flowing from the Constitution. The lack of adequate institutional checks on the President and the absence of a firm institutional structure within which the presidency was embedded, meant that whenever the President was sick or otherwise indisposed, power rested in the hands of unelected assistants and advisers, including his immediate family. Against them it was difficult for other institutions to prevail. Particularly important in this regard is the fact that such elite politics was largely removed from popular political input, which was impeded by a dearth of effective vehicles for mass democratic politics. This was a reflection of the weakness of civil society.

# 6

# A Stunted Civil Society

---

The course of independent Russian politics has been shaped overwhelmingly by the dynamics of elite interaction and conflict focused principally upon the presidency. Civil society forces have played little part in this. Certainly the populace was called upon to play a part through the 1993 referendum and successive elections, changing opinion polls have registered popular preferences and at times have influenced the course of elite politics, and the parties have sometimes been influential through the legislature. But these have essentially been marginal roles. The basic contours of the political system and the thrust of Russian politics have been determined by elite action and elite preferences largely untrammelled by actors outside that elite. This raises the question why civil society forces have not been sufficiently developed to be able to exercise greater influence on the shape of events. Under Gorbachev there had been clear evidence of the growth of civil society forces and the concentration of their activity at the republican level. The new Russian regime came to power professing democratic principles, which should have been conducive to the growth and development of such forces. But a robust and vigorous civil society has not emerged. Why is this so? Why have the major groups in Russian society been unable to throw up the sorts of organizational vehicles which would enable them to play an active, continuing part in political life?

## The Rise of a New Bourgeoisie[1]

The newly emerging Russian bourgeoisie, although new, did not spring fully-fledged from the fall of Soviet communism. It was gestating within the Soviet

[1] Social science is not value free, nor is the terminology it employs. An array of terms has emerged to describe, if not define, those who dominate the post-Soviet Russian economy: 'elite', 'entrepreneurs', 'business class', 'oligarchy', 'ruling class', 'capitalists', 'nomenklatura-bourgeoisie'. All of them carry implications about the way these groups function. Often, too, their use implies approval or otherwise. 'Elite', for example, usually refers to

command economy. Without property rights, however, the Soviet bureaucracy could not emulate the merchant capital that grew within the incubus of Western feudalism, eventually seeking political power commensurate with its economic power. Rather it was an 'aspirant' bourgeoisie, an 'acquisition class' in waiting, that could only begin really to take shape with the political defeat of the CPSU.[2] It was not, therefore, a new Russian bourgeoisie that gave rise to the ideologues of the market, rather it was neo-liberal ideologues and politicians who set about creating a capitalist class.[3] For this reason the Russian transformation has been first and foremost politically driven from above.

Three sources of the Russian bourgeoisie can be identified: the previous Soviet elite, independent entrepreneurs, and the criminal world, although the boundaries between them are not nearly as clear as these categories imply.[4] The Soviet elite, especially those drawn from the administrative–economic hierarchy, has been an important source giving rise to the popular term 'nomenklatura-bourgeoisie'. In effect this involved elite transformation, the 'metamorphosis of power' into property,[5] by which elements of a bureaucratic elite have transformed themselves into an embryonic capitalist class. The other two sources were less reliant on access to state property gained through official

stratification of power, wealth or status, but without necessarily implying conflict or exploitation. 'Class', used in the Marxist sense, is related to ownership of property or lack of it. It implies conflict and exploitation. 'Nomenklatura' and 'oligarch' are both employed in Russia and Western political science to refer to the Soviet and post-Soviet elites, usually with a strong whiff of disapproval. 'Entrepreneurs' or 'business class' clearly carries a more positive connotation. From time to time we employ some of those terms, but in the main we refer to the 'bourgeoisie', by which is meant those who are the owners and controllers of large capital, principally in the financial, commercial, and industrial sectors of the economy. The term 'bourgeoisie' is not necessarily synonymous with contemporary capitalist classes outside Russia nor with their forerunners in Western Europe, although we think there are useful historical parallels to be drawn. It should be clear from our discussion what we mean by 'bourgeoisie' in the current Russian context. For a consideration of this question see Anna Ostapchuk, 'Alkhimiia elity', *Pro et Contra*, 1: 1 (Autumn 1996), 104–11. For criticism of the term 'oligarchy', which suggests it is a media-created 'illusion', see Anders Aslund, 'The Myth of the Oligarchy', *Moscow Times*, Jan. 1998, p. 8.

[2] David Lane, *The Rise and Fall of State Socialism: Industrial Society and the Socialist State* (Oxford, Polity, 1996), 164–71. For an argument regarding the development of a pro-capitalist coalition that coalesced around Yeltsin in opposition to Gorbachev's Soviet Union, see David M. Kotz with Fred Weir, *Revolution from Above: The Demise of the Soviet System* (London and New York, Routledge, 1997).

[3] Roi Medvedev, 'Novyi klass Rossiiskogo obshchestva', *Svobodnaia mysl'*, (henceforth *Sm*), 8 (1997), 58.

[4] Graeme Gill, 'Democratization, the Bourgeoisie and Russia', *Government and Opposition*, 33: 3 (Summer 1998), 311.

[5] Bill Lomax, 'From Death to Resurrection: The Metamorphosis of Power in Eastern Europe', *Critique*, 25 (1993), 47–84.

position, but were able to exploit the changed economic conditions to accumulate significant economic wealth.

The new resource and financial sector which, after its long gestation during the late Soviet period as what one observer has called an 'invisible' bureaucratic, 'merchant' class,[6] had welcomed Gorbachev's perestroika as a chance to transform itself openly into a commercial class capable of asserting its own interests.[7] As indicated earlier, during the Brezhnev period in particular, many leading figures in the economic-administrative apparatus had been able to take advantage of their positions both to appropriate state resources and to position themselves in such a way as effectively to create a platform from which a future post-Soviet bourgeoisie could emerge. This is certainly the way some contemporary observers have interpreted this. For example, this process has been described as the transformation of the 'soldiers of the party' into the 'merchants of the party' during the late Soviet period. The crucial turning point was seen to be the 1974 oil crisis, from which the USSR as an energy supplier benefited significantly, until about 1982. The resultant 'super profits' from oil underpinned the expansion of the military–industrial complex and accelerated their 'shadow' appropriation by the monopolies of the 'bureaucratic market'. Perestroika relaxed the coercive administrative constraints on these nouveau riche administrators of the resource sector.[8] The collapse of the old Union and the unambiguous adoption of marketization by the Yeltsin administration gave this embryonic new class an unprecedented opportunity to develop itself. The particular approach that Gaidar pursued in relation to marketisation was a crucial factor here. 'Gaidarnomiks' was not just the abstract application of free market principles in Russia. It voiced and met the interests of the resource and financial sector. The adoption of price liberalization as a precursor to privatization and the floating of the rouble particularly benefited the new commercial class. It saw the unprecedented concentration of money in the hands of the new speculative-commercial class, at the expense of the productive sectors and the populace as a whole. Simultaneously, the abolition of the state monopoly of foreign trade and of the Central Bank's control over exchange rates saw a radical reorienting of the economy to the external market. Under Gaidar, raw materials exports and capital outflow became the predominant mode of the integration of Russia into the world capitalist economy. The energy sector was one of the chief beneficiaries of this process and by mid-1992 one of its executives was in the government: Viktor Chernomyrdin.

---

[6] *Nezavisimaia gazeta* (henceforth *Ng*), 11 Jan. 1993.   [7] Ibid.

[8] Ibid. But on the timing, see the argument in Graeme Gill and Roderic Pitty, *Power in the Party: The Organization of Power and Central–Republican Relations in the CPSU* (London, Macmillan, 1997).

Private appropriation of state property has been a key mechanism for the formation of the new bourgeoisie. Before official privatization began in Russia, 'prikhvatizatsiia' (a play on the Russian verb khvatat', to grab or snatch) was under way in the last years of the Soviet era. As early as 1987 the Komsomol, ironically overseen by the relatively conservative Yegor Ligachev, provided a rich pool of new entrepreneurs. Taking advantage of the 1988 Soviet law on cooperative enterprises, a quiet 'political embourgeoisment' took place among the young Komsomol leadership. From 1989 onwards they were joined by their 'elder brothers' in the party.[9]

The second stage of the crystallisation of the new entrepreneurs occurred in 1990–91, with the weakening of legal restraints on commercial activity. This period saw the emergence of small entrepreneurs, joint-stock societies and private firms. But it also saw increasing financial obstacles to business development for those who were not in the position to have access to cheap credit. As a consequence this period saw a rash of middleman activities and the eruption of large-scale stock-broking and commercial institutions. Trade, commerce, middleman activities and financial consultancies flourished.[10]

Privileged access to the outside world saw joint ventures established under the immediate tutelage of the party.[11] The first commercial banks, supported by the state, exploited black market currency exchange rates to enrich themselves. Property dealing was a vital factor in the formation of the new entrepreneurs. Nomenklatura firms, semi-commercial structures set up by officials to exploit the new opportunities, alone could engage in property transactions. And the best state property was sold to nomenklatura firms. In fact the nomenklatura 'sold itself its own property'. On this basis, for example, the powerful Most Group of banks bought buildings in Moscow for less than half their market value.[12]

In effect, what took place from 1991 onwards, was a process that has been described as 'privatisation of the state by the state'.[13] Ministries were turned into businesses with former officials at the helm. Senior officials now became shareholders; deputy ministers became bank presidents; and ministers became consultants. During 1988–89 banks had proliferated as they were broken up into commercial banks or created by the Ministry of Finance. But management, steadfastly nomenklatura in origin, remained the same. A 1992–93 sur-

[9] V. V. Radaev (ed.), *Stanovlenie novogo Rossiiskogo predprinimatel'stva (Sotsiologicheskii aspekt)* (Moscow, Institute of Economics, Russian Academy of Sciences, 1993), 57.

[10] Ibid.

[11] Olga Kryshtanovskaia and Stephen White, 'From Soviet *Nomenklatura* to Russian Elite', *Europe–Asia Studies*, 48: 5 (1996), 719.

[12] Kryshtanovskaia and White. See also A. Kol'ev, *Miatezh nomenklatury: Moskva 1990–93* (Moscow, Intellekt, 1995, second corrected edn.), 46–84.

[13] *Izvestiia*, 10 Jan. 1996.

vey of Russia's top 100 businessmen found that fourteen came from USSR state banks, 51 per cent of which took up private business in 1990.[14] Approximately 50 per cent of the major Russian banks were established by managers of Soviet era enterprises and ministries. A striking example of this is the head of what was once the largest state bank in the USSR, Promstroibank. Its former president, Yakov Dubenetsky, turned it into a joint stock company with himself at the helm. Former officials of the Ministry of Foreign Affairs, once the official interface between the capitalist world and the Soviet Union, have also figured prominently among the new bourgeoisie. A former Foreign Ministry press officer, Vadim Biriukov, went into partnership with the publisher of the French magazine *Figaro*. Biriukov went on to become editor in chief of *Delovie Liudi*, part of the seed money for which came from Progress Publishers.[15]

Komsomol centres had been particularly well placed to convert assets into cash. Of the 100 businessmen surveyed above, seventeen were former Komsomol apparatchiks. More than 50 per cent of these started their businesses out of the offices of the Komsomol Centres for the Scientific and Technical Creativity of Youth (NTTM), which acted as intermediaries on 'scientific-technical matters' between Soviet and foreign enterprises.[16] Some of the leading bankers in Yeltsin's Russia cut their teeth in the Komsomol. Prominent among them have been former NTTM director Mikhail Khodorkovsky, the founder of Menatep which was in 1996 ranked the ninth most influential enterprise in the country, and the head of Inkombank, Vladimir Vinogradov, ranked sixteenth. Aleksandr Shcherbakov, the chairman of the board of Finist Bank, which was founded with 700 million roubles from the Komsomol, was previously a Komsomol Central Committee member.[17]

[14] Kotz and Weir, *Revolution*, 119 citing Olga Kryshtanovskaia, 'Transformatsiia staroi nomenklatury v novuiu Rossiiskuiu elitu: Tezisy doklada', unpublished paper, Moscow, May 1994.

[15] Kotz and Weir, *Revolution*, 123.

[16] According to the founding director of NTTM, Mikhail Khodorkovsky, 'We gave people the chance to pursue scientific research for pay, not simply for the publication of articles and academic titles'—'Mikail Borisovich, Khodorkovsky', in *Kto est' kto v Rossii 1997 god* (Moscow, Olymp, 1997), 683. For a description of the scepticism of former Komsomol First Secretary Viktor I. Mironenko towards socialism and enthusiasm for Thatcherism, see Kotz and Weir, *Revolution*, 119.

[17] N. Lapina, *Rossiiskie ekonomicheskie elity i modeli natsional'nogo razvitiia* (Moscow, Russian Academy of Sciences, 1997), pp. 10–11. The rise of Khodorkovsky and Menatep is instructive. Khodorkovsky had no personal capital. This came from party and state funds: the NTTM Centre, the central planning State Committee for Science and Technology and the state Zhilsotsbank. Initially official property of a Moscow municipal district, with profits going to its labour collective, Menatep bought out its three founding agencies. In 1990 it became a joint-stock company: Kotz and Weir, *Revolution*, 120–1.

This process of so-called 'spontaneous privatisation' soon involved enterprise managers and political officials as well. Both were able to take advantage
of their strategic location to transfer property into their own hands, usually in
the guise of joint stock companies, while many political officials moved into
the financial sector.[18] Managers tended to take over industrial enterprises. Of
the 100 businessmen surveyed above, 23 per cent were previously 'industrialists'. Of these, just over a half came from the industrial ministries and state
committees of the USSR or the RSFSR. Approximately a quarter (26 per cent)
were directors of large state industrial enterprises. Generally, the 'industrialists' took to private business in 1989–91, particularly in 1990. In other words,
this sector of the bourgeoisie was moving to establish itself before the Soviet
Union disappeared. But this did not necessarily mean the end of careers for the
old Soviet elite. Many of those in the previous central planning apparatus
became consultants to the new businesses. The former head of Gosplan from
1965 to 1985, Nikolai Baibakov, went on to became a consultant to Gazprom.[19]

The offspring of elite families have been another source of the new bourgeoisie. In the survey cited above, they constituted 8 per cent of the new entrepreneurs. Once again, social influence came into play. Often, they were the
children of the party-state elite who had international connections, particularly Ministry of Foreign Affairs officials. Their offspring were very well educated and were able to take advantage of their links with the outside world. As
among the komsomoltsy, many were quick to take up the chance of private
business, especially in 1987. Likewise, many of the scions of former
Communist Party politicians seem to have taken to capitalism with relish.
Striking in this regard is Vladimir Sterligov, the grandson of the former, noto-
riously hard-line, ideology chief Mikhail Suslov. In mid-1991, Sterligov made
the move from *Pravda* to commercial banking.[20]

Overall, the transformation of the Soviet bureaucratic elite to nascent bourgeoisie has been dominated by economic apparatchiks rather than by former
Communist Party politicians. The latter have been eclipsed by younger leaders
drawn from the Komsomol. A 1995 survey[21] found that while 61 per cent of
the new business elite had nomenklatura origins, only 13.1 per cent had a party
background. Former managers of the economy and the Komsomol were
equally well-represented: 37.7 per cent in both cases.

Conspicuous by their absence from the new bourgeoisie has been the former
Soviet military elite. Lacking access to resources capable of being converted
into commodities on a large scale, its members have not been in the position

---

[18] Gill, 'Democratization', 313–14.                [19] Kotz and Weir, *Revolution*, 122.
[20] Ibid. 119–20, 124.
[21] *Izvestiia*, 10 Jan. 1996; Kryshtanovskaia and White, 'From Soviet *Nomenklatura*',
Table 8, p. 729.

to convert themselves into private capitalists. This has not, however, prevented the emergence of a military mafia engaging in corrupt commercial activity such as weapons sales.[22]

The second source of the new bourgeoisie were so-called 'samorodki', persons of exceptional talents who became independent entrepreneurs.[23] Some of these came from the so-called coloured markets which in the 1960s and 1970s filled the gaps in the Soviet economy, particularly in the repair and service sectors. An important element of the move to the market in the late Soviet era was the legalization of much coloured market activity. Other independent entrepreneurs arose from a variety of sectors of Soviet society, including well-connected 'technical specialists': scientists, engineers, technicians, inventors and so on.[24] Relying on their personal contacts rather than their technical know-how, they took advantage of controlled prices and shortages for trade and financial speculation. Often they bought up goods from state enterprises and resold them on the domestic market at much higher prices. An even more lucrative avenue was to procure cheap Soviet raw materials and then export them illegally at world market prices. Speculators invested in gold, molybdenum or foreign currencies, the value of which rose as the Soviet economy declined.[25]

The samorodki have concentrated their activity in a different sector of the economy from that of the ex-nomenklatura, which tends to be concentrated in banking, resources and industry. The samorodki have carved out a niche in export/import, trade and middleman activities, as well as banking.[26] The opening up of the market in Russia, particularly the price liberalization of January 1992, favoured trade and financial speculation where a lower level of starting capital was required and which could take advantage of the price differentials between the domestic and the world market.[27] This was an environment that suited the outsiders. Professionals, often those with a technical background such as scientists and engineers, have figured prominently in Russian small to medium business, such as it is. A 1993 survey found they made up 25.8 per cent of Moscow entrepreneurs, though they were still

---

[22] For an argument suggesting the importance of the military's 'socialist' socialization as a factor here, see Kotz and Weir, *Revolution*, 261, n. 43.

[23] See Kryshtanovskaia in ibid. 118. It should be noted that samorodki made up only 5% of Kryshtanovskaia's sample.

[24] A good example of someone who used his personal talents plus contacts to enrich himself is Boris Berezovsky. Head of Logovaz, he was a mathematician who used his contacts with the head of the giant Soviet automobile concern, Avtovaz, to build up a very profitable car dealership in 1989: 'Berezovsky, Boris Abramovich', Kto est' Kto, 62–4.

[25] Kotz and Weir, *Revolution*, 116–17.

[26] Lapina, *Rossiiskie*, 29.

[27] Medvedev, 'Novyi klass', 60.

overshadowed by former enterprise managers who made up 68.1 per cent.[28] Even so, about half the banks were established by independent entrepreneurs.[29]

Another group of outsiders, the criminal world, has provided the third source of the new Russian bourgeoisie. This is the most difficult group to define. In the Soviet era virtually any kind of private commercial activity was regarded as criminal, both officially and in popular consciousness; witness the negative reaction of Soviet citizens to the first co-operative activity. In Russia the term 'mafia' has taken on a variety of meanings, from everday crime to corruption at the highest levels of authority.[30] This points, however, to the fact that much spontaneous privatization was not sanctioned by law. This blurring of criminal and legitimate business activity makes it difficult to establish precise boundaries between this and the other sectors identified above. Despite suggestions that the criminal world erupted from the underground once the restraining hand of the Communist Party state was lifted, it seems that a criminal bourgeoisie emerged with the monetarization of the Russian economy.[31] This would fit with the image of organised crime operating, initially at least, on the margins of the economy, in its non-productive areas. The parasitic nature of criminal activity is suggested by the fact that it has tended to be concentrated in the areas where quick returns can be made for little investment: retail and wholesale trade, advertising, show business, prostitution, money laundering, trade (smuggling) and banking.[32] By 1993 criminal activity was making inroads into the bastions of the new economy. The then president of the Association of Russian Banks, Sergei Yegorov, wrote to president Yeltsin complaining that 'all of society and new financial and entrepreneurial institutions have become the target of well-organised, well-equipped bandits.'[33] In the absence of a strong independent state, protectionism, extortion and murder have become a mafia hallmark.[34]

---

[28]  V. Radaev in Kotz and Weir, *Revolution*, 117.

[29]  Gill, 'Democratization', 315; Lapina Rossiiskie, 11.

[30]  Lapina, *Rossiiskie*, 20. For one discussion of crime, see Stephen Handelman, *Comrade Criminal: Russia's New Mafiya* (New Haven, Yale University Press, 1985).

[31]  Medvedev, 'Novyi klass', 58 argues that few from the Soviet 'shadow economy' of the 1970s became 'new Russians' in the 1990s. Finding it difficult to adapt to the legalization of business, they gravitated towards organized crime.

[32]  Lapina, *Rossiiskie*, 20.

[33]  Cited in Kotz and Weir, *Revolution*, 184. They also cite a 1994 report prepared for the president which found that 70% to 80% of private banks and businesses in the major cities were forced to make payments of between 10% and 20% of their revenues to organized crime.

[34]  Federico Varese, 'Is Sicily the Future of Russia? Private Protection and the Rise of the Russian Mafia', *Archives europeenes de sociologie*, 35 (1994), 224–58.

The criminal world might also overlap with the entrepreneurial sector mentioned above in the form of speculative (vremenshchiki) capitalists. Generally drawn from the banking, financial and stock-market groupings, the vremenshchiki sought immediate commercial gain by dubious means, exploiting the market upsurge that accompanied the emergence of an independent Russia. They have often fallen as fast as they have risen. A prime example was Sergei Mavrodi, head of the failed MMM financial pyramid who went on to be elected a Duma deputy in 1995 in order to gain immunity from prosecution for his economic activities. But the mafia has not remained entirely on the margins of the economy. With the onset of the monetary stage of privatization, organized crime, with plenty of liquid assets and a willingness to resort to armed force, moved in to corner shares of major Russian industrial enterprises.[35] On this basis, according to former dissident Roy Medvedev, the 'criminalisation of Russian society has outstripped the development of private business.'[36]

The appellation 'new bourgeoisie' is appropriate for the nascent Russian capitalist class, even though it is far from homogeneous in its origins and make up. Few of the democrats who paved the way for Yeltsin's meteoric rise joined the upper echelons of the new bourgeoisie, even though they had helped to create the conditions for its emergence.[37] Much of the industrial sector of the Russian economy is in the hands of those who were formerly lords of Soviet industry. In effecting this transition, it is not just a certain continuity of personnel that has been maintained, but also the traditional social-bonding between members of the old nomenklatura preserving what has been called its 'unique estate-class consciousness.'[38] In contrast, the commercial–financial sectors seem to be the province of those without high office in the Soviet period but who were in a position to take advantage of the changing conditions. One-time Security Council deputy secretary Berezovsky is a classic case of this.

In this regard, *blat*, personal contacts, particularly for the first wave of young entrepreneurs, was vital for the formation of the new bourgeoisie, lacking as it did the necessary personal wealth. Connections meant access to public resources on a favourable basis and helped to overcome bureaucratic obstacles to going into private business. Friends, acquaintances, relations and administrative contacts smoothed the way. The registration of firms, accommodation, opening of

---

[35] Lapina, *Rossiiskie*, 18, 20: 'Privatisation, taken together with other components of shock therapy, has been the major cause of the rapid expansion of organised crime and corruption.'

[36] Medvedev, 'Novyi klass', 71.          [37] Ibid. 64; *Izvestiia* 10 Jan. 1996.

[38] Tatiana Zaslavskaia, *Rossiiskoe obshchestvo na sotsial'nom izlome: vzgliad iznutri* (Moscow, VTsIOM/MVSSEN, 1997), 228.

bank accounts, information about tax arrangements, market possibilities, and illicitly procuring public resources on a favourable basis, were all facilitated by personal connections and bribery rather than formal channels. In these circumstances, it is hardly surprising that the old guard (party apparatchiks, enterprise managers, and heads of administration) were particularly well placed to become prominent members of the new bourgeoisie.[39] This strategic location also enabled them to profit from the policy of privatization pursued by the government[40] that was a principal means of the acquisition of property by this new bourgeoisie. Indeed, the privatization of state assets was probably the most important form of capital accumulation for the new bourgeoisie.

When we look at the structure of the nascent Russian bourgeoisie as a whole, what we see is a class whose wealth is concentrated overwhelmingly in the financial and resource sectors at the expense of the industrial sectors. It is not a class involved in productive investment, technological innovation or employment creation. On the contrary, capital flight has been one of the growth areas for the new bourgeoisie.[41] This is a class that has accumulated extraordinary wealth at a time when the Russian economy as a whole has suffered a catastrophic decline. It is in many respects at best a rentier class and at worst a criminal class, deriving much of its wealth as it has from the plundering of state resources accumulated in the Soviet era or the evasion of state obligations, such as taxes. In this respect there may be historical analogies with European merchant capital that 'preserves and deepens underdevelopment'[42]

[39] Alena Ledeneva, 'Neformal'naia sfera i blat: grazhdanskoe obshchestvo ili (post)sovetskaiia korporativnost'?', *Pro et Contra*, 2: 4 (Autumn 1997), 113–24. She makes the important point that the onset of a money economy at the same time has disrupted and diminished the importance of personal connections, though it has far from eliminated them. Blat, she suggests, has taken on a different form: 'corporatism' meaning mutual support among those whom one identifies as one's own. This has become particularly important in a situation of a criminal environment characterised by weakly defined legal and economic regulations.

[40] There is a large Western literature on this. For example, Stephen Fortescue, 'Privatisation of Russian Industry', *Australian Journal of Political Science*, 29: 1 (March 1994); Simon Clarke, 'Privatization and the Development of Capitalism in Russia', *New Left Review*, 196 (1992); Simon Johnson and Heidi Kroll, 'Managerial Strategies for Spontaneous Privatisation', *Soviet Economy*, 7: 4 (1991); Peter Rutland, 'Privatisation in Russia: One Step Forward: Two Steps Back?', *Europe–Asia Studies*, 46: 7 (1994); Michael McFaul, 'State Power, Institutional Change, and the Politics of Privatization in Russia', *World Politics*, 47: 2 (Jan. 1995). See also Roi Medvedev, *Chubais i vaucher: Iz istorii rossiiskoi privatizatsii* (Moscow, Impeto, 1997), and Aleksandr Bim, 'Privatizatsiia v Rossii: problemy blizhaishei perspektivy', *Sm*, 4 (1993).

[41] Vladimir Tikhomirov, 'Capital Flight from Post-Soviet Russia', *Europe–Asia Studies*, 49: 4 (1997), 591–615.

[42] Michael Burawoy and Pavel Krotov, 'The Soviet Transition from Socialism to Capitalism: Worker Control and Economic Bargaining in the Wood Industry', *American Sociological Review*, 75 (1992), 16–38.

or perhaps US robber barons of the late nineteenth century, although ultimately at least the latter's activities contributed to overall economic development. In the modern era a closer analogy may be the capitalist elites of the underdeveloped world, such as Latin America, concentrated as they are in commerce and trade, or even African states, such as Zaire where a kleptocracy drained the treasury while the infrastructure collapsed around them. In both cases, and Russia is no exception here, a weak domestic bourgeoisie exhibits a high degree of economic and political dependence internally on its domestic state and externally on the capitalist metropoles.[43] The principal question for our purposes is the implications the particular structure of the bourgeoisie has for the Russian political system.

The distinctive feature of the modern Russian bourgeoisie is its relationship with the state. The state has been both its progenitor and midwife. Much of the economic elite issued from the old state apparatus, particularly from those who oversaw the economy. The government's privatization programme legitimised private appropriation of property and simultaneously provided the state resources which have nurtured the fledgling bourgeoisie. Further, the government has provided a fertile political environment to foster the growth of its most dynamic sector, the resource–financial sector. With the October 1993 defeat of the old Supreme Soviet the presidential and, to a lesser extent, the governmental apparatuses of the state have been unrivalled as loci of political power, creating a heavy material and political dependence by the new bourgeoisie on the executive apparatus of government. The new legislature, the Duma, has had little political clout and therefore little attraction as a channel for new economic elites to advance their interests. In contrast to the long-established, socially confident, and relatively independent capitalist entrepreneurs in the West, who exercise powerful influence over the state, the nascent Russian bourgeoisie is dependent to a much greater degree on the patronage of the Russian state. However, there is considerable co-dependence here too, as demonstrated by the way the bankers and the media closed ranks around Yeltsin in the lead up to the 1996 presidential elections.

The economic dependence of the new bourgeoisie on the state is well documented. The way in which businesses utilise the largesse of the state to escape market competition, accumulate resources and ensconce themselves as monopolies (Gazprom and United Energy System are good examples of corporations which have achieved such positions because of state assistance) has

---

[43] See Hamza Alavi, 'State and Class under Peripheral Capitalism', Hamza Alavi and Teodor Shanin (eds.), *Introduction to the Sociology of 'Developing Societies'* (London, Macmillan, 1982), 289–307.

led some observers to categorise the Russian bourgeoisie as 'rent-seeking'.[44] Rather than look outwards towards the developing market, or to actively promoting a market themselves, they have looked to state resources to advantage themselves commercially. The banks have been particularly busy in this regard. The strongest of them were those which, in the absence of a federal treasury, acted as bankers to the Russian government. While holding government funds, they were able to reap massive returns for loans they made, even using government moneys to procure state assets. The system of private banks acting as state banker remained in place until 1997.[45] It was through this that the notorious 'loans for shares' deal emerged. Desperate to increase revenues from privatization, and perhaps also concerned to compensate the banks for the blow to their profits that the introduction of the rouble corridor constituted,[46] on 31 August 1995 Yeltsin authorized the auctioning of twenty-nine state-owned enterprises to a small group of banks. The bank that offered the highest loan to the government would win a block of shares, which they could sell after September 1996. It was nothing less than a way for the banks to procure some of Russia's most valuable state companies at extremely low prices. Government initiatives providing for the establishment of Financial Industrial Groups (FIGs) were also particularly beneficial to seven major banking groups, the so-called 'seven boyars'.[47] They were able to use these measures to expand their control in the industrial and resource areas and thereby build up more broadly-based economic empires.

An honest, if less than eloquent, comment by Berezovsky sums up the motivation of the nascent Russian bourgeoisie: 'Profits! It's too early for that—we're still dividing up the property.'[48] Such a statement is indicative of the fact that this is a bourgeoisie in the making, still bearing the birthmarks of its Soviet origins, where political influence was paramount for economic performance. This approach has been categorised by Gaidar as 'bureaucratic markets' as

---

[44] Joel Hellman, 'Bureaucrats vs Markets? Rethinking the Bureaucratic Response to Market Reform in Centrally Planned Economies', in Susan Gross Solomon (ed.), *Beyond Sovietology: Essays in Politics and History* (Armonk, M. E. Sharpe Inc., 1993), 54.

[45] Gill, 'Democratization', 320; David Hoffman, 'Only Elite Benefit in People's Capitalism', *Guardian Weekly*, 25 Jan. 1998, 15. See also Joseph R. Blasi, Maya Kroumova, and Douglas Kruse, *Kremlin Capitalism: Privatizing the Russian Economy* (Ithaca, Cornell University Press, 1997), 74.

[46] In July 1995 the government announced that the rouble would not be allowed to fluctuate in value beyond the range 4,300–4,900 roubles to the US dollar. This rouble corridor limited the wild fluctuations in value which the banks had used to generate large speculative profits.

[47] Promstroibank, Vneshtorgbank, Menatep, Oneksimbank, Rossiiskii Kredit, Inkombank and Mostbank: *Izvestiia*, 10 Jan. 1996.

[48] Cited in Hoffman, 'Only Elite Benefit'.

opposed to so-called 'free markets'.[49] With limited initial resources available to the aspirant bourgeoisie, access to state resources has been a vital source of starting capital and profits. But state resources are finite and access to them crucial. In reality currying political influence tends to be the primary objective of the new bourgeoisie rather than the pursuit of profit through commercial endeavour. Hence from time to time fierce struggles have broken out within the economic elite around market competition, access to state resources and government economic policy which would favour them. Such struggles are compounded by the dualism of Russian executive power: some financial groups have more influence in the government, others with the presidency.[50]

The first open instance of this was in the lead-up to the dispersal of Parliament in 1993, which saw a political victory that favoured the finance–resources sector over the industrial sector which had in the main supported the Parliament. A new phase of intra-economic elite struggle broke out after so-called 'Black Tuesday', 11 October 1994. That day the exchange rate for the rouble plummeted by 22 per cent. It was a clear signal that the fragile Russian financial system was in danger of collapse. On a rapidly contracting economic foundation, there was little room for all the new bourgeoisie which had come to the fore since 1992. From late 1994 onwards clashes broke out between the leading players, especially the energy producers and the banks, which disputed who would be the beneficiaries of privatization. Symptomatic of these tensions within the business elite and their political allies was the December 1994 armed raid by presidential security forces on the offices of Mostbank, then firmly allied with Moscow Mayor Yury Luzhkov. The renewed slowing down of the economy in autumn 1994 brought a further decline in average living standards and reduced the flow of resources to the state to stabilize the economy. Additional resources had to be found within the economic elite. The upshot was that this burden was borne by the banks rather than the energy sector. From July 1995, the banks were forced to bear the cost of a fixed exchange rate. The rouble corridor was sustained by forcing a sharp increase in Central Bank reserve requirements of between 5–20 per cent, at a cost to the banks of US$2 billion, putting further strain on an already shaky sector. The energy sector emerged, temporarily at least, as the beneficiaries of this intra-elite struggle. Under their immediate champion, Prime Minister Chernomyrdin, the fuel and energy complex reached new heights of power. The launching of a new party Our Home is Russia (NDR), in the lead-up to the

---

[49] Gill, 'Democratisation', 321. Whether there has ever been such a phenomenon as the 'free market' is open to question. Given Gaidar's status as the ideologue of the market in Russia, such a conception is hardly surprising.

[50] Aleksei Zudin, 'Biznes i politika v prezidentskoi kampanii 1996 goda', *Pro et Contra* 1: 1 (Autumn 1996), 49–50.

December 1995 elections was an attempt, it has been argued, 'to reorganise politically the entire new capitalist class under the leadership of the energy complex.'[51]

The loans for shares scheme generated further conflict within the bourgeoisie. The banks that organised the auctions usually won them with low bids by excluding both domestic and foreign competitors. An infamous example occurred in November 1995 when Oneksimbank organized the auction for Russia's sixth largest corporation, Norilsk Nickel, and won with a bid only US$100,000 above the starting price. There was a public outcry about this practice, including from those like Inkombank, Rossiiskii Kredit and Alfa-bank who had lost out. The government conceded that, in future, auctions would be more open. In response, these disgruntled bankers sought to rebuild their bridges to the government; an aide to Chernomyrdin was appointed chairman of Alfa-bank. The auctions affair is a good illustration of the fact that, powerful as the new entrepreneurs are, the rent-seeking strategy they have adopted makes them vulnerable to state decisions against their interests.[52]

The failure of parties such as NDR and the success of the KPRF in the December 1995 elections led to a closing of ranks within the new bourgeoisie in order to secure Yeltsin's victory in the presidential elections. Thus it was almost inevitable that there would be clashes between members of the new bourgeoisie when, after the re-election of Yeltsin, a new round of privatization occurred. Already by 1996 it was estimated that an extraordinary 75 per cent of large and medium state enterprises, responsible for 70 per cent of GNP, had been privatized. All that remained were the 'natural monopolies', the jewels in the state crown, so to speak.[53]

The close structural nexus between the state and the bourgeoisie is also testified to by the fact that until recent times the government has retained significant share holdings in some of the most lucrative enterprises. For example, the national government retained 40 per cent of shares in Gazprom and 51 per cent in Russian Public Television (ORT). This pattern has been repeated at more or less all levels of government, most strikingly in Moscow and Yakutiia. Thus close commercial links persist between the state and its elite offspring.[54]

---

[51] Renfrey Clarke, 'The Economic Foundations of Russian Politics', unpublished paper, n.d., pp. 5, 8.

[52] Zudin, 'Biznes i Politika', 53.

[53] Blasi *et al.*, *Kremlin Capitalism*, 50; Stephen Fortescue, 'Privatisation, Corporate Governance and Enterprise Performance in Russia', *Russian and Euro-Asian Bulletin*, 7: 5 (May 1998), 1–2.

[54] Fortescue, 'Privatisation, Corporate Governance', 2 points out that 'the state retains shareholdings in a significant number of privatised enterprises on the basis of government decrees declaring the "strategic significance for national security" of the enterprise.'

The most striking feature of the new political system, however, is the direct representation of the emerging bourgeoisie in government. In this regard there is a contrast to be made with parliamentary politics in the West where, in general, government tends to keep private business, especially big business, at arm's length. Leaders of government tend to be drawn from educated middle layers, such as lawyers and teachers, rather than businessmen as such. There are exceptions of course, but when there are, they are usually required either to divest themselves of any business dealings that they have, or at least to suspend them. This has not been the case in Russia. A number of prominent businessmen have become senior members of government while still retaining their business interests, particularly in the wake of the 1996 presidential election; Potanin and Berezovsky are the most prominent examples. Rather than lobbying various levels of government, they became office holders in their own right, even if only temporarily. The ability to move between private business and public office has been facilitated by the common social origins of political and economic elites. It was estimated in 1996 that 75 per cent of the president's inner circle and 74.3 per cent of the government came from the nomenklatura.[55] But it is also due to the 'clan' nature of the conglomerates and their political dependency. According to Olga Kryshtanovskaia, a leading analyst of Russian elites: 'At the top of each corporate clan sits a business mogul and political ally, such as a mayor, prime minister or governor. Each clan has a bank at its core, surrounded by a commercial or industrial empire. The clan also has its defenses—media outlets, extensive private security forces, corporate intelligence and espionage.'[56] This 'tycoon model', as it has been called, clearly offers an image of the new bourgeoisie which is at odds with even a rhetorical commitment to democracy. For the new Russian bourgeoisie, government is a resource for their own political and commercial aggrandisement. It is the 'privatisation of power'.[57]

Initially it seemed as if the first cabinet under Yegor Gaidar, which lasted from late 1991 to mid-1992, was the 'first anti-lobby government' in Russia. No members of the government directly represented any particular branch of the economy. It was assumed that the Gaidar government would merely lay down the rules of the game without favouring any particular branch. Despite expectations, this situation did not last long. Within six months branch

[55] *Izvestiia*, 10 Jan. 1996.

[56] Cited in Hoffman, 'Only Elite Benefit'. The close alliance between banking capital and the power elite is also strikingly illustrated by that between Moscow mayor Luzhkov and the Most Group headed by Gusinsky. Banker to the city until 1997, Gusinsky has significant investments in the information industry, including publishing, newspapers (*Obshchaia gazeta* and *Vecherniaia gazeta*), radio (Ekho Moskvy), and television (Centre TV, TV6, NTV): Lapina, *Rossiiskie*, 12; Gill, 'Democratization', 322.

[57] Kol'ev, *Miatezh nomklatury*, 47.

interests began to emerge within the government, with the appointment of Georgy Khizha, Viktor Chernomyrdin and Vladimir Shumeiko as Deputy Prime Ministers at the end of May–beginning of June 1992. At this stage, however, it was not the fuel and energy complex (TEK) or Gazprom that were the real beneficiaries. It was the military–industrial complex (VPK). It was well represented. Khizha, appointed to a specially created position of Deputy Prime Minister with responsibility for the military industrial complex and industry as a whole, was supported by five other high-ranking representatives of the defence industries. Thus in the second half of 1992 the VPK was represented in government by a singularly powerful sextet. Despite this, the VPK proved incapable of securing sustained government support for its conversion to high-tech civilian industry or to become a highly competitive arms exporter. With the demise of the Soviet Union, and the subsequent reduction of government orders, the influence of the VPK quickly dissipated.[58]

But as the fortunes of the heavy industry and arms producers waned, those of the fuel and energy complex waxed. In mid-1992 it appeared as if the TEK would amount to nothing more than a 'milch cow of market reform'.[59] The turning point was the appointment of Chernomyrdin as Prime Minister in December 1992. The appointment of Chernomyrdin effectively cemented an alliance between the executive apparatus and the fuel and energy elite. In addition to Chernomyrdin, Yury Shafrannik, an oil industry executive from the Tiumen region, was appointed Minister for Fuel and Energy, while the head of the ministry, Vladimir Kvasov, came straight from the management of Gazprom.

The TEK's unique status as an internationally competitive earner of export revenue gave it a strategic role in the Russian economy, to its decided advantage in relations with the government. Among the benefits were low export duties, unrestricted control over hard currency earnings and tax-exempt funds, such as the Gazprom Stabilisation Fund. At the same time the government turned a blind eye to irregularities in bookkeeping and the failure of the sector to meet its tax obligations. It was not all one way, however. In return the oil and energy complex was expected to provide resources to consumers, including agricultural producers who were unable to pay. And from time to time the TEK met the revenue obligations of regional governments to the

---

[58]  In addition, in February 1992 The League for Assistance to the Defence Industries was established by some of the principal figures in the industry. The League actively lobbied for defence industry interests throughout 1992 and into 1993: Yakov Pappe, 'Otraslevye lobbi v pravitel'stve Rossii (1992–1996)', *Pro et Contra*, 1: 1 (Autumn 1996), 63–4. On Gaidar's 'anti-lobby government', see also Sergei Peregudov and Irina Semenenko, 'Lobbying Business Interests in Russia', *Democratization*, 3: 2 (1996), 119.

[59]  Pappe, 'Otraslevye', 64.

Federal budget. It was deemed to be the 'second budget' of the country.[60] Such has been the weight of the oil-energy sector in the executive that it has virtually ignored the legislature.[61] Of course, this also says a great deal about the insignificance of the Russian legislature as an arm of government.

The direct involvement of the new bourgeoisie in government is clearly embodied in the continued role of Chernomyrdin from mid-1992 until March 1998. A former Soviet minister of the gas industry and managing director of Gazprom, Chernomyrdin was elevated to Prime Minister at the end of 1992, a post he retained until his dismissal in March 1998. An apparent source of political and economic stability amidst turbulent politics, Chernomyrdin had seemed unassailable.[62] Gazprom has been well represented at the highest echelons. P. Rodionov, a member of the Council of Directors of Gazprom, in 1996 was Minister for Oil and Energy. The chairman of the Gazprom Council of Directors, Aleksandr Kazakov, a past head of the State Committee for Property, in 1997 became deputy head of the Presidential Administration. Another Gazprom Council member, Andrei Vavilov, was first deputy minister for finance between 1992 and 1997, when he joined Interros, part of the Oneksimbank empire. Little wonder then that the chief executive of Gazprom, Rem Viakhirev, has regularly been rated the most influential entrepreneur in Russia.[63] A succession of ministers, usually no lower than deputy prime minister level,[64] have been widely seen as representing the interests of particular segments of the elite: among them, Minister for Oil and Energy Yury Shafrannik, First Deputy Prime Minister Vladimir Shumeiko (defence industries); Deputy Prime Minister Aleksandr Zaveriukha (agriculture); and First Deputy Prime Minister Oleg Soskovets (machine building and metallurgy).[65]

The presidential election campaign of 1996 well illustrates the intimate relationship between the new bourgeoisie and the executive apparatus. But it also illustrates that this is a relationship in constant flux as relations within the bourgeoisie and between it and the state wax and wane. After Ziuganov's attempt to woo business and the West at the February 1996 World Economic Forum in Davos, the spectre of a KPRF victory drove a group of bankers to call on Chubais to head up a campaign to 'stop the communists'. Chubais, at that time without any government position, soon became the direct link to business support for Yeltsin's presidential campaign.[66] According to Chubais, he

---

[60] Lapina, *Rossiiskie*, 9–10.

[61] Ibid. 7 points out that the Ministry of Oil and Energy had been unable to get one piece of legislation passed without at least significant amendment, reflecting the failure of the oil-energy producers to lobby the Duma.

[62] *Kommersant Vlast'*, 2 (27 Jan. 1998), 9–12.

[63] Lapina, *Rossiiskie*, 9; *Ng*, 20 Feb. 1997; *Kto est' Kto*, 104–5, and 278–9.

[64] Pappe, 'Otraslevye', 61.      [65] *Izvestiia*, 6 Dec. 1994; Gill, 'Democratization', 323.

[66] Zudin, 'Biznes i Politika', 50.

told the bankers he needed US$5 million to set up a campaign headquarters. Five days later it was delivered in the form of a no-interest loan.[67]

Initially, however, there was some division in the ranks of the bourgeoisie, partly as a result of the 'auctions affair', partly because of uncertainty about a Yeltsin victory and the need therefore to curry favour with other candidates. The new bourgeoisie were covering themselves in the event of a Ziuganov victory.[68] Anxious to avoid the use of force to resolve political uncertainty, on 27 April thirteen leading businessmen, mainly bankers including Berezovsky and Gusinsky who were already funding Yeltsin's campaign, publicly appealed to other candidates for 'compromise' as a 'way out of the impasse'.[69] This Appeal was seen by some analysts as a declaration by business that it was directly participating in the election campaign as a 'third force'.[70] The widely published Appeal was also seen as a lack of confidence in Yeltsin. But a tacit rebuff from Yeltsin and his endorsement by potential rivals within the elite, such as Inkombank chief Vinogradov, soon brought the recalcitrants to heel. Berezovsky, an initiator of the Appeal, sought reconciliation with the Yeltsin campaign, a further reflection of the vulnerability of the new bourgeoisie and its dependence on state patronage. The Association of Russian Banks and the Round Table of Business of Russia then threw themselves wholeheartedly behind the Yeltsin campaign.[71] So too did the media they controlled. To the fore in the media campaign were the two largest and most influential television networks, Independent Television (NTV) and Russian Public Television (ORT). Mostbank head Gusinsky and Gazprom, both financial backers of Yeltsin's campaign, are major NTV shareholders. Another major contributor to the Yeltsin campaign, Boris Berezovsky, head of Logovaz and owner of the major daily newspaper *Nezavisimaia gazeta*, has a major stake in ORT.[72]

Success brought its rewards. Several of those previously shut out of the inner circle were brought back. NTV's role cemented an alliance between Mostgroup and Gazprom. Vinogradov became a confidant of Moscow mayor Luzhkov, who actively campaigned for Yeltsin (and for his own election).[73] Berezovsky's appointment as Deputy Secretary of the Security Council and Potanin's as First

---

[67] Hoffman, 'Only Elite Benefit'.

[68] Apart from support from entrepreneurs linked with traditional Soviet industry, Mosbiznesbank and (perhaps) Promstroibank were rumoured to have contributed to the KPRF campaign: Zudin, 'Biznes i Politika', 58–9, n. 10.

[69] 'Vyiti iz tupika!', M. G. Gorkov *et al.* (eds.), *Ot Yeltsina k . . . Yeltsinu: prezidentskaia gonka–96* (Moscow, Terra, 1997), 261–4.

[70] Zudin, 'Biznes i Politika', 52.          [71] Ibid. 54–5.

[72] David Hoffman, 'Powerful Few Rule Russian Mass Media', *The Washington Post*, 31 Mar. 1997.

[73] Zudin, 'Biznes i Politika', 56, n. 9.

Deputy Prime Minister are further instances of this. Thus, for a time at least, the banks gained direct representation in strategic sections of the state.[74]

The meshing of private business and public administration is not restricted to the apex of the elite. Many of the privatised industries drew their middle-level staff from the ministries from which they had emerged. Such people retained their personal linkages and contacts with the government apparatus. Gazprom, once again, provides a striking instance of this process, initially even continuing to operate from the old ministry premises. This continuity of personnel at management level of the new enterprises has important implications for political decision-making and for the democratic process as a whole. It suggests that in Russia today, as in the Soviet era, personal connections and networking are at least as important, if not more so, than formal institutional channels in influencing and determining decision-making.[75]

Social clubs and thinktanks, a cluster of which sprang up in 1993–94, have become important venues for networking among the political, intellectual and business elite.[76] Among the most influential have been Club 93, established in May 1993 by the Politika Fund thinktank, the Realists Club, the Moscow International Oil Club (MMNK), and especially the club On Big Nikitskoi Street (NBN). Club 93 included among its members Bank Menatep head Khodorkovsky, Mostbank head Gusinsky and political scientist Andrannik Migranian. Each month they meet for analytical discussions 'at the highest level'. The Realists, also established in 1993, was described as 'left-centrist' by one of its founders Yury Petrov, former head of the presidential administration. It numbered among its members the Vice President of the Russian Union of Industrialists and Entrepreneurs (RSPP) Aleksandr Vladislav, the leader of the (Federation of Independent Trade Unions) (FNPR), Mikhail Shmakov, members of the Federal Council and provincial governors. MMNK, founded by its patron Chernomyrdin in 1994, had as its honourary chairman Boris Nemtsov. It included some forty Russian and international oil and gas corporations among its members, although later it opened its doors to the bankers, as they began buying into the fuel and energy sector. NBN, one of the most influential clubs, left no doubt about its politics: 'No radicals—communists or leftists!', declared its founders in 1993, among them Yegor Gaidar. Oleg Boiko, head of National Credit bank and chair of the party Russia's Democratic Choice, as the first NBN president was described as the 'embodiment of the internal alliance of power and business'. This proposition was borne out by

[74] Lapina, *Rossiiskie*, 12. The other key point of contact for the banks with the government is the Central Bank. Unlike the oil-energy sector, the banks gave considerable attention to the legislature. In 1993 and 1995 they financed the campaigns of many Duma deputies, across a fairly broad political spectrum, from Russia's Choice to the LDPR.

[75] Gill, 'Democratization', 324.          [76] Zudin, 'Biznes i Politika', 48.

NBN's forty corporate members, among them, Oneksimbank and Bank Menatep, and its politician members, notably Anatoly Chubais. Elite clubs like these are discreet meeting places for key corporate and political players, both domestic and international. If investors wanted to discuss taxes, then they could dine with the head of the tax service. If they wanted to establish good relations with the Duma, then they could meet with a faction leader, a Zhirinovsky or a Yavlinsky.[77] This club culture was part of the broader culture underpinning the relationship between state and new bourgeoisie, a culture of personal networks, cronyism and covert deals.

Formal lobby groups, associations of business people formed to promote their collective interests, have also been active.[78] But notions of lobbying and even influence are feeble conceptions for understanding politics in a context where those who are enriching themselves at the expense of the state are themselves exercising state power.[79] Similarly, a focus on political parties needs to take account both of the fact that the bourgeoisie is deeply embedded in the state and the weakness of political parties allied with that bourgeoisie. The failure of business-backed parties to establish any significant electoral base (a question we address below), in stark contrast to the KPRF, has encouraged Russian business to focus its attention on the executive rather more than the legislative branch of government. Undoubtedly too, the obvious weakness of the legislature compared to the executive has encouraged this focus. This clearly has implications for the attitude of the bourgeoisie towards representative democracy. A direct presence in the machinery of government short-circuits the need for active participation in politics at a more popular level. Above all, the monopolization of power by an executive presidency has fostered a destabilizing, permanent struggle for political influence and economic advantage among the elite focused on the president and his bureaucratic apparatus. In a more parliamentary system such rivalry would be more likely to be shared around the other branches of government, taking considerable heat out of the struggle. But the struggle for influence over the presidency has intensified the 'clanisation' of Russian politics, characterised by corruption, feuding, and palace conspiracies.[80]

---

[77] *Kommersant Vlast'*, 2 (27 Jan. 1998), 33–6. See also *Ng*, 20 July 1994.

[78] Peregudov and Semenenko, 'Lobbying'.

[79] Similar reservations are expressed by Pappe, 'Otraslevye', 61. He utilises the concept of 'branch representation' rather than 'lobbying', a term that is poorly defined and has never been widespread in Russia. By branch representation he means a highly placed politician, at least a Deputy Prime Minister, often drawn from a particular 'branch', for example, oil or diamonds (as distinct from a sector or complex, i.e., a group of industries [otrasly] that are similar, technologically or economically, for example, the military-industrial complex).

[80] Vladimir Berezovsky, 'Dva politicheskikh lagereia federal'noi elity Rossii', *Sm*, 9 (June 1994), 86.

The absence of a developed market, the weakness of formal rules and laws governing conflicts of interest, and, conversely, a propensity for informal, personalized connections manifested in the club and lobbying culture in Russia undoubtedly militate against the establishment of the sorts of procedural norms usually associated with democratic government in the West. But this begs the question of why the Russian bourgeoisie has not to date shown particularly strong inclinations in favour of such norms. The answer to this seems to lie in the nature of the Russian bourgeoisie and the state. Both are in process of formation and both depend on each other for support, as well as externally on the support of foreign capitalist states (especially the USA and Germany) and international capitalist institutions such as the IMF. The fact that the Russian bourgeoisie is immature, concentrated in the commercial–financial sector and lacks any strong domestic social support other than the state gives it a particular predilection for authoritarian rather than democratic rule. In this respect it is more akin to the bourgeoisie of Latin America than that of Western Europe or North America.[81] It has never been enamoured of the notion of democracy except as rhetoric. Pinochet's Chile or South Korea have often been the preferred models for 'democracy'. Stolichnyi Bank head Aleksandr Smolensky has stated that he prefers executive rule, openly acknowledging that the unpredictablity of elections to the Duma 'terrified' him.[82] Similarly, one of Russia's leading investors, L. Skoptsov, in the lead-up to the 1995 Duma elections, declared himself 'passionately negative about elections. If I see free elections will bring to power people who will totally destroy the country, what am I supposed to say? Let my country be destroyed but at least Western democracy will prevail? No. Instead, I say let Western democracy die; I value my country more.'[83] Rather than work openly through the political process, and thereby encourage the development of civil society organizations, the bourgeoisie prefers to work through its informal channels to the political elite.

It is self-evident that elite representation and the implementation of policies that advantage that elite generally, if at times disadvantaging individual elements of it, are close correlates. On the whole, in the years since Yeltsin came to power, there has been a close correlation between those social layers that have been winners socially and economically, and those that have had a presence in the apparatus of government. It is noticeable that this does not include

---

[81] See V. G. Khoros (ed.), *Avtoritarizm i demokratiia v razvivaiushchikhsia stranakh* (Moscow, Nauka, 1996).

[82] 'Smolensky, Aleksandr Pavlovich', *Kto est' Kto*, 596–7.

[83] Cited in David Mandel, 'The Russian Working Class and the Labour Movement in Year Four of "Shock Therapy" ', in David Mandel (ed.), *The Former 'State Socialist' World: Views from the Left* (Montreal, New York and London, Black Rose, 1996), 27.

all of the economic elite. It is clear that a tiny segment of the bourgeoisie has been advantaged at the expense of the traditional industrial elite. Yet despite the enormous influence that the ascendant Russian new bourgeoisie exercises over the Russian state, it would be wrong to merely see the latter as simply a creature of that class. On the contrary, to date the state has acted more or less as an independent third power balancing the interests of the declining industrial, military, and agricultural complexes against those of the rising energy, financial, and commercial sectors. Paradoxically, this precarious equilibrium has provided relative social and economic stability and has compensated for the weakness of the state.[84] It also helps to explain the Bonapartist tendencies of Yeltsin in arbitrating between the interests of economic elites while being beholden to none.

## The Working Class

By its nature and intent, shock therapy was directed against the industrial sector of the Soviet economy. If a market system was to be established, the large industrial conglomerates with huge, under-utilised workforces had to be broken up. But this meant not only the destruction of places of work of millions of people and the associated work patterns that went with them, but the whole Soviet socio-economic infrastructure which had both sustained and shaped the Soviet working class. In this sense, shock therapy has struck at the immediate interests of the working class.[85] The social pact that existed in Soviet society almost until its demise ensured basic social guarantees (right of employment, housing, health care and basic education) provided by the 'workers' state' in return for political passivity.[86] The free market aspirations of the Yeltsin administration have seen a radical withdrawal of state responsibility for social welfare and the exposure of enterprises, which once provided many of these services, to the market. Such a programme has necessarily entailed both social dislocation and a radical reduction in workers' incomes. Accordingly, its successful implementation has required a compliant labour movement. This has been a risky strategy, with the danger of provoking a social

---

[84] Peregudov and Semenenko, 'Lobbying', 136.

[85] As Gowan puts it 'There is . . . a central dimension to the liberalisation shock: a sudden, dramatic weakening of the social power of the industrial working class' Peter Gowan, 'Neo-Liberal Theory and Practice for Eastern Europe', *New Left Review*, 213 (Sept.–Oct. 1995), 14.

[86] For discussions of this, see the sources cited in Chapter 2, n. 42.

backlash from the working class.[87] Nevertheless, shock therapy has been surprisingly successful at slashing living standards with a minimum of social resistance.

The relative passivity of the working class has been caused in part by the collapse of the Russian economy.[88] This has severely constrained the bargaining power of organized labour. Crucial to this has been the reduction of many workers to a virtual subsistence standard of living. Workers in state industries, such as health, education, and defence, have found themselves below the poverty line.[89] Even those industrial workers with the highest cash incomes, such as those in the oil and gas industry, have found their incomes squeezed by the fact that they live in high-cost areas.[90] Furthermore, workers now increasingly pay for services, such as childcare, healthcare and housing that were previously part of their social wage. Women in particular have suffered as a result of these developments.

The delay or non-payment of wages has compounded the problem of reduced incomes and services. In June 1997 wage arrears totalled an astronomical 54 trillion roubles (US$10 billion). An additional nine trillion roubles was owed to the army. According to one study, across the economy, an average five weeks' wages was owed to workers, double what had been in 1992. However this average masks real discrepancies. The average delay for enterprises and organisations which actually reported payment arrears in January 1997 was nearly three months. Furthermore, 5 per cent of workers had not been paid for more than six months. While unpaid wages per worker in Moscow stood at 166,000 roubles, in the Arctic Circle it reached three million roubles. Among those most in arrears were teachers and coal miners, ironical given the support the latter had given Yeltsin in his quest for the presidency. Eighty per cent of the unpaid wages were owed by enterprises. Five per cent was the direct responsibility of the central government.[91] Meanwhile it is

[87] Tatiana Zaslavskaia, 'Sotsial'naia struktura sovremennogo Rossiiskogo obshchestva' in Zaslavskaia, *Rossiiskoe obshchestvo*, 238–9.

[88] There are numerous analyses of this. See e.g. Vadim Medvedev, 'Otvedena li ugroza katastrofi', *Sm*, 7 (1996); A. Chebanova, 'Rossiia v 1996 godu: ekonomicheskii pod'em eshche daleko', *Sm*, 11 (1996).

[89] 'Public employee wages remain the lowest in the economy, ranging from 58 per cent of the national average in culture and arts, to 70 per cent in health and 74 per cent in science': Mandel, 'The Russian Working Class', 9.

[90] Penny Morvant and Peter Rutland, 'Russian Workers Face the Market', *Transition*, 2, 13 (28 June 1996), 7.

[91] 'ICFTU Campaign on the Non-Payment of Wages in Russia', Campaign Newsletter, 1 (July/Aug. 1997). In the lead-up to the presidential elections the government had actually received money from the IMF to pay off arrears. In more recent times, it has resorted to selling off assets to meet arrears. Many enterprises claim that their inability to pay wages on time has been a result of the government's (and other customers') failure to pay their bills.

estimated that 12 per cent of employees are paid in kind, in anything from tampons to wheelbarrows. When wage arrears are met, more often in the case of public than private employees, there is no compensation for inflation, a practice that has been labelled 'state robbery'. Anxious to head off any wide-scale protest against arrears, the government has selectively paid off debts to different sectors of the workforce located in different regions.[92] Indeed, this was a significant feature of Yeltsin's 1996 re-election campaign. In such dire circumstances, a struggle for survival defines Russian working class life today. Of those without a job, a mere 10 per cent survive on unemployment benefits of US $20 per month. For those with a job, a second job or longer hours is quite common. It has also been reported that 72 per cent of wage earners were growing vegetables on garden plots,[93] with the summer months generally seeing a lull in industrial and political activity as workers are busy tending these plots.[94]

Unemployment in Russia has remained relatively low, despite a collapse of production of the order of 50 per cent since 1990.[95] At the end of 1995 some 6 million workers were officially unemployed, a mere 8.2 per cent of the workforce.[96] As befits an economy that is rapidly being incorporated into the international capitalist economy, unemployment is highest in the traditional industrial sectors of the economy. Growth in employment has occurred only in trade, finance, and services, especially in Moscow where such businesses are concentrated. In other words, employment growth has occurred only in those sectors meeting the needs of the new commercial capitalism, such as the private security business. However, official unemployment figures masked considerable *de facto* unemployment. At the end 1995 real unemployment was estimated to be 13.7 per cent. Unemployment has also been disguised, in the guise of reduced hours and 'administrative leave', that is, forced leave. The latter has become commonplace since 1993, despite the fact that it is illegal. According to law, extra leave beyond what is normal can only be voluntary. In February 1995 some five million workers, out of a total workforce of 74.1 million, were on reduced hours or administrative leave. In the latter case, this meant that they were receiving less than half their normal take-home pay. In fact though, 1.5 million were not being paid at all. Should those on forced leave and reduced work be added to those actually out of work, the real unemployment rate may be as high as 20 per cent.[97]

Notwithstanding shock therapy, the government has been reluctant to see mass unemployment. Not only might forcing the pace provoke mass opposi-

[92]  Mandel, 'The Russian Working Class', 7.
[93]  Morvant and Rutland, 'Russian Workers', 7.
[94]  Mandel, 'The Russian Working Class', 67.
[95]  'Sotsial'naia tsena ekonomicheskogo krizisa', *Sm*, 4 (1995), 3, Table 1.
[96]  Medvedev, 'Otvedena', 78.        [97]  Mandel, 'The Russian Working Class', 2–3.

tion, putting in place an adequate social security system to cope with mass unemployment would impose extraordinary demands on the exchequer. Despite the rhetoric of the market, there have been few factory closures due to bankruptcies, which would throw masses of unemployed onto the streets, threatening social and political instability.[98] Nevertheless, the very phenomenon of unemployment has caught the Russian working class off guard, accustomed as it has been for three generations to guaranteed full employment.[99]

A significant factor in the demobilization of the working class has been the strengthening of managerial power under the new regime. Under the Soviet system the authoritarian paternalism of management was tempered by a kind of enterprise corporatism. Under perestroika, there was some shifting of the balance between management and workers in favour of the latter. This was facilitated by self-management legislation, which allowed for the election of work collective councils and administrators, and reinforced by the emergence of the working class as an independent social force, at least in some areas. But under the impact of privatization 'the independent power of enterprise directors is greater than at any time under Soviet rule'.[100] It has been politically expedient for the government to enhance the formal rights of workers as shareholders, while in reality excluding them from participating in the running of the enterprise as producers.[101] Freed from the constraints of party and central planning oversight, with little or no shareholder rights, and negligible worker influence, management has become a law unto itself. Monopolising information about the enterprise's economic situation, managers have increased their arbitrary authority over wages, the designation of the skill categories of workers and over lay-offs. Privatization also provided a pretext for management to marginalize or even eliminate union influence, if need be, by harassment or even violence against unionists.[102] Workers' fears of unemployment, especially in the wake of the August 1998 financial crisis, also strengthened managerial control. The resulting enhancement of managerial prerogatives has been registered by pronounced and growing differentials between managers' and

[98] Peregudov and Semenenko, 'Lobbying Business', 134.

[99] Article 37 of the previous Soviet constitution guaranteed the right to a job. Indeed, until April 1991 it remained a crime in Russia not to work. But Article 37 of the new Russian Constitution merely states 'Labour is free'.

[100] Mandel, 'The Russian Working Class', 35. See also Blasi *et al.*, *Kremlin Capitalism*, 82: 'Managers took advantage of the process [of privatization] to build up their own power. Top managers captured control of the firms far in excess of the share ownership they gained.'

[101] Mandel, 'The Russian Working Class', 36.

[102] Paul T. Christensen, 'Why Russia Lacks a Labor Movement', *Transition*, 4: 7 (Dec. 1997), 46–7. For example, special police were called into a strike at the VAZ automobile plant in September 1994, the management of which has close links with government politicians: Mandel, 'The Russian Working Class', 43–5.

workers' incomes. Yet the strengthening of managerial authority has been an uneven and contradictory process. Its development varies from sector to sector and the Soviet tradition of managerial paternalism remains an important factor in the unwillingness of factories to shed labour for economic reasons.

The extraordinarily difficult economic situation confronted by workers and the resulting struggle for subsistence goes a long way towards explaining the relatively low level of organized resistance to these processes and the political apathy that has characterized Russian society in the Yeltsin era. Important here too has been government policy, which has directly hindered the development of labour solidarity: the selective payment of back wages and the linkage of wages to enterprise performance have been significant barriers to the development of a broad sense of working-class solidarity.[103] The relative quiescence of the working class has also had significant consequences for the development of a union movement.

The inertia of the working class is in part a reflection of the weakness of the trade union movement, which one would expect in such circumstances to be a significant champion of working-class interests. This weakness is the product not only of parlous economic circumstances but also of the policies pursued by the trade union leadership. Judged by membership, the Russian trade union movement is, potentially at least, extremely powerful. The Federation of Independent Trade Unions of Russia (FNPR), the successor to the Soviet era Russian trade unions, has 60 million members out of a workforce 72.5 million strong. In addition to the FNPR, which covers 90 per cent of union membership, there are the so-called 'free' trade unions. These were originally formed in opposition to the existing Soviet trade unions.[104] The prime example is the Independent Miners' Union, which grew out of the struggles that erupted in 1989. Though small and fragmented, until recent times it was more likely to confront management who, unlike the situation in the FNPR, are not members. In recent times though, with a downturn in the mining industry, there have been tensions between regional and national leaders. Such has been the depth of the crisis in the mining industry, that there has even been some cooperation with FNPR. Nevertheless, the independent trade unions tend to be craft unions, based on skilled workers—engine drivers, pilots, dockers, min-

[103] Mandel, 'The Russian Working Class'.

[104] Not without a little help from the US government. It has channelled millions of dollars through the AFL-CIO in an attempt to fashion a labour movement more to its own liking. After 1989 links were established with the miners' unions. In 1992 the Free Trade Union Institute opened in Moscow. Hostile to the FNPR, it supported the 'independent' unions, funding a newspaper, an education programme, finances, and equipment. See Renfrey Clarke, 'Cold War and Workers' Solidarity: US Trade Unions in Russia', *Green Left Weekly*, (20 Aug. 1997).

ers—who are geographically concentrated and with little identification with wage-earners as a whole.[105]

Rather than opposing the drive to the market, the FNPR embraced it. They did so under a barrage of ideological pressure from the political elite and the media, which discredited Soviet socialism or any alternative to the market. Instead the FNPR tried to ameliorate the excesses of capitalism by such measures as wage indexation, an endeavour in which it clearly failed.[106] Some union leaders actually argued that withdrawal of state support and privatization would at least force enterprises to pursue private investment. Others even maintained that Russian unions would only become 'real' unions when they faced 'real' private owners.[107] Unfortunately the contrary proved to be the case: after privatization workers and their unions had less power than ever.[108]

The FNPR tried to find a place for itself in the new capitalist order by embracing the corporatist doctrine of 'social partnership' officially advocated by the Russian state. Effectively an arm of the state in the Soviet era, in a labour shortage economy it could still have significant influence on management policies. In the post-Soviet era the FNPR sought to collaborate with both management and state, but the blows against wage-earners resulting from shock therapy ultimately were to push the unions to confront the state. In January 1992 a Tripartite Commission of government, trade unions and management was established to deal with wages and disputes. It proved, however, to be a two-part arrangement: with the government seeking to ignore both trade unions and management, the FNPR tended to ally itself with management against the government. This was not mere collusion. Nor was it compromise. The FNPR actually covered managers as well as workers. This reflected the fact that in the Soviet era, managers were not the representatives of private capital and had a common interest with their workforce in dealing with the central planners and other enterprises. Now they again found themselves with a common interest in confronting the consequences of the economic policies of the central government. The very existence of the enterprise, in which both management and labour had a mutually vested interest, was at stake. But such an

---

[105] Christensen, 'Why Russia', 49.

[106] In 1990–1 a significant worker self-management movement arose, based on the work-collective councils initiated under the 1987 Law on the State Enterprise. But it never became an independent mass movement. Instead it hitched itself to Yeltsin's campaign for Russian sovereignty. Once Yeltsin was in power he turned his back on the movement (just as he did with DemRossiia). The self-management movement then disintegrated, restricting itself to maximizing workers' share-holdings under the privatisation programme. Mandel, 'The Russian Working Class', 31–2.

[107] Ibid. 33.

[108] Blasi *et al.*, *Kremlin Capitalism*, 114.

alliance, and the continued presence of management within the membership, is a serious obstacle to the FNPR representing workers as a social class.[109]

Given this sort of membership and its concentration in the industrial sector, the FNPR had supported the parliamentary side in the dispute with Yeltsin. After the FNPR executive denounced Yeltsin's September 1993 dismissal of the Supreme Soviet and called for a strike in defence of the Constitution, the government retaliated. It took control of the Social Insurance Fund[110] and dismantled the state-funded but trade union-run occupational health and safety inspectorate. Thus the FNPR was deprived of two key functions it had previously administered. In these circumstances, shortly after the October 1993 confrontation, an extraordinary congress elected a new FNPR leadership committed to a conciliatory approach towards Yeltsin. In part this moderation was the direct result of the intimidating violence of October coupled with government threats to dissolve the union federation, expropriate its property and end the automatic collection of union dues.[111]

The new leadership went on to sign Yeltsin's 1994 Civic Accord, committing itself to cooperation with the government. The FNPR has been as good as its word, adopting an extraordinarily restrained response to the economic crisis. In general it refrained from shutting down production, calling mass protests or raising political demands. Rather, in line with the general acceptance by the union movement of the government's overall course to capitalism, if not necessarily its method of implementation, national union leaders advocated active participation by their local affiliates in privatisation to secure worker representation on newly elected boards of directors. This was a vain hope. Even where workers were the largest shareholders, it proved difficult to have their representatives elected. There are even reports that where workers tried to exercise their rights as shareholders, violence was used to stop them.[112]

Despite widespread fears and rumours of a labour movement backlash, organized resistance to the assault on living standards has been relatively restrained. There have been thousands of strikes involving millions of workers across a wide range of occupations, a good indicator that Russian workers are neither passive by nature nor happy with the reforms. But in times of economic depression strikes are at best a defensive weapon, and in Russia they have been of limited duration and breadth. Almost 2 million worker days were lost in 1992, as female health workers led the initial industrial reaction to shock

---

[109] Christensen, 'Why Russia', 48.

[110] These were funds managed by the unions and enterprises to provide social welfare provisions for their members/workers.

[111] Mandel, 'The Russian Working Class', 25.

[112] Fortescue, 'Privatisation, Corporate Governance', 3: 'Coercion and manipulation have been much in evidence.'

therapy. But in 1993 this fell sharply to a mere 236,800 worker days lost affecting only 264 organizations. In 1994 worker days lost increased to 755,000, affecting 514 organizations. But 1995 saw a big jump in these figures, to 1.36 million worker days lost affecting 8,856 organisations. The number of strikers also rose dramatically over this period, from 155,000 to 489,000 particularly among education, health, transport, and communications workers. The first half of 1997 saw five times as many strikes as the first half of 1996. Workers in the nuclear industry marched to Moscow and submarine repairers blocked the Trans-Siberian railway. Adopting a more political stance, aviation workers called for the impeachment of Yeltsin. Increasingly, the initiative has passed from miners to teachers, health, and energy workers. Slowly, the FNPR has adopted a more militant stance. On 27 March 1997 it proclaimed a 'Day of Action'. Estimates of participation ranged from a low of 1.2 million by the government to a high of 5.1 million by the FNPR. Either way this means at most 7 per cent of the work force participated, a tiny fraction of the FNPR membership.[113] Despite increases in strike action, in terms of the overall workforce, the figures remained low.[114]

Furthermore strikes have generally been of limited duration and had limited objectives. Mainly warning strikes, few have gone beyond a few days or even hours. The majority of strikes have been directed at securing the back-payment of wages. There have, however, been protest strikes against deteriorating working conditions in dangerous industries, such as mining.[115] Workers have been fearful of losing the employment they have or of providing an excuse for the closure of their enterprise or plant, many of which are already technically bankrupt. This could mean the loss of ancillary social benefits provided by the enterprise.[116] Moreover, most union leaders and workers think that the government is primarily responsible for the current crisis and that in these circumstances there is little that can be done at enterprise level to rectify the situation.[117] For this reason, the majority of strikes appear to be directed against the Federal government or regional authorities, rather than enterprise managers. At the same time, the decentralisation of the economy has seen the regionalization of industrial action by workers, often in concert with local

[113] Christensen, 'Why Russia', 44.

[114] Figures drawn from Morvant and Rutland, 'Russian Workers', 10, Table 2.

[115] The increase in industrial accidents reflects not only lack of investment in new equipment and poor labour discipline, but also the failure of the government to adequately compensate for union overseeing of safety standards, which the government took over in 1993. Spending on labour safety by enterprises has dropped by two-thirds. Whereas one worker in 14,000 is killed on the job in the USA, in Russia one in 9,000 dies on the job. Blasi *et al.*, *Kremlin Capitalism*, 114.

[116] Christensen, 'Why Russia', 45–6.

[117] Mandel, 'The Russian Working Class', 46.

management or political leaders, directed at the central government. Often the shared objective is to obtain extra central funding for a particular industry. The net effect has been to create a kind of 'local and regional corporatism' which impedes coordinated nation-wide action.[118]

In addition, the government, rather than courting the labour movement, has set out to limit its capacity to act. A 1991 law prohibited strikes that threaten the lives or health of other citizens. On the defensive in these circumstances, workers have resorted to blockades and even hunger strikes. In December 1995, adults and children in the oil town of Usinsk in the far northern Komi Republic went on a hunger strike for better conditions. April 1996 saw firefighters in Norilsk on a hunger strike for six days to protest against wage arrears. In one of the most sustained actions, in mid-1998 miners blockaded the Trans-Siberian railway, demanding the back payment of wages. But such actions have been a sign of desperation on the part of the Russian working class rather than of militancy.

So worker frustration has not been directed into a sustained and coordinated campaign by the union movement. Important here has also been the attitude of many workers toward unions and their role in the industrial sphere. Many workers, and the leadership of the majority union, still see their organization as responsible for the 'social sphere' of the enterprise and therefore on common ground with management. Nor have rank-and-file workers indicated they have much confidence in their industrial organisations. A survey conducted in April 1994 found that nearly three-quarters of the workers interviewed said that unions played either no role or a negative role in Russia. A poll conducted the following September found that a mere 11.5 per cent of those interviewed would turn to their unions to defend their interests in the workplace.[119] As a consequence there has been relatively little attempt to build a union movement that relies on its own independent strength. The Russian labour movement has exhibited nothing like the militancy that erupted among Soviet miners in 1989. Then the miners promised to be a critical element, if not the core, of an emerging civil society. If the labour movement was to play such a role, it would have to engage actively in politics. But trade union involvement in politics has been limited.

The national union leadership has generally shied clear of politicising industrial action, demonstrating a pronounced 'allergy to politics'.[120] The FNPR specifically declared its second national protest called in October 1994 (the first was in April) purely economic. It demanded payment of arrears and a programme to stop mass unemployment. The same two demands were put for-

---

[118] Christensen, 'Why Russia', 48.
[119] Cited in Morvant and Rutland, 'Russian Workers', 11.
[120] Christensen, 'Why Russia', 50.

ward at another national protest called in April 1995. Despite its apparent determination to limit the political implications of its campaigns, the very fact that the FNPR leadership focused its call for overcoming arrears on the government rather than enterprise management had a certain political logic to it. This was given expression at local and regional demonstrations held in October 1994. Nearly half of these called for the government's resignation and early presidential and parliamentary elections. This sentiment was evidently growing. By April 1995 a clear majority of these demonstrations were advancing such demands. In response to such sentiment, and having called out hundreds of thousands of workers to little effect, the FNPR national leadership evidently chose to channel this growing political sentiment into the electoral arena. It declared that the next stage of its campaign would be participation in the December 1995 Duma elections.[121]

The trade unions did not participate in the December 1993 legislative elections, although in the previous two years there had been some discussion within the FNPR about establishing a labour party. Similar discussions preceded the December 1995 Duma election.[122] But in general, the trade unions have eschewed promoting an independent political course for the labour movement as a whole. Rather, their guiding principle has been one of lobbying, the 'politics of intercession' as it has been called: linking up with non-labour centrist and liberal political forces with the intention of getting them to intercede with the ministry responsible for the particular economic sector which they cover.[123] The fuel and energy sector unions, having failed to establish an electoral bloc with management, turned to collaborating with NDR. In the lead-up to the December 1995 elections, the Confederation of Free Transport Unions established an electoral alliance with DemRossiia.[124] The Metal Foundry and Mine Workers' Union, which split from the FNPR at a national level and has links with AFL-CIO representatives in Russia, aligned itself with Yavlinsky's Yabloko. The Union of Trade Workers and the Union of Educational Workers linked up with the centrist Women of Russia, while one of the strongest groups of the alternative trade unions, Sotsprof, gave its support to Vladimir Polevanov's bloc 'For the Homeland'. Various regional union organizations allied themselves with the Congress of Russian Communities[125] or the KPRF, although no national union has sought to ally itself with the communists. Local trade union organizations covering agriculture have been the basis of the Agrarian Party.

[121] Ibid. 47–8.
[122] Boris Kagarlitsky, 'Russian Trade Unions and the 1995 Elections', *Green Left Weekly*, 1 Nov. 1995, 19.
[123] Mandel, 'The Russian Working Class', 64.                    [124] Ibid. 61
[125] Ibid. 64–5; Kagarlitsky, 'Russian Trade Unions'.

At national level, the FNPR has been as cautious in the electoral arena as it has been conciliatory in the industrial arena. In both cases it has sought to avoid confrontation. In the political arena it has concentrated on lobbying the government rather than mobilizing its membership in public actions. Initially the FNPR entertained the notion of supporting State Duma Speaker Ivan Rybkin's pro-Yeltsin left-centrist bloc, an initiative that was apparently foisted on the union by the government. However, this manoeuvre was rejected at the August 1995 session of the conference of the 'Trade Unions of Russia—to the Elections' movement. When the FNPR finally did decide to enter the electoral arena, it chose to ally itself with those it saw as its natural allies in the industrial arena: the managers, particularly those from the military–industrial complex. In September 1995 the FNPR announced a bloc with the Russian Union of Industrialists and Entrepreneurs (RSPP) and an electoral alliance with the Russian United Industrial Party led by Arkady Volsky and Vladimir Shcherbakov (who was close to then First Deputy Prime Minister Oleg Soskovets). A joint statement called for a redirection of economic policy in the 'interests of the entire society', for 'social partnership rather than confrontation' and a 'responsible' legislature.[126]

In entering into such an alliance, the FNPR demonstrated its anxiety to avoid confrontation, its reluctance to mobilize its membership and its illusions about the legislature as a vehicle for defending the interests of its members from the ravages of government economic policy. At the same time the FNPR leadership demonstrated common ground with that wing of the enterprise managers which, while willingly embracing the market, sought increased state intervention, a strong state sector, protection of the domestic market and a 'socially oriented' market. Contesting the election as the Trade Unions and Industrialists of Russia–Union of Labour, this alliance won only 1.6 per cent of the list vote, and returned only one representative from a constituency.[127] In this sense, the FNPR was pursuing the same electoral orientation as the alternative unions. Almost all of these alliances were directed at weak centrist parties, which had little electoral appeal but which hoped that the unions would deliver them thousands if not millions of votes. It proved a vain hope. In the December 1995 elections, none of them crossed the 5 per cent threshold.

A strong, active labour movement is a key component of a vigorous civil society. A weak labour movement has almost invariably betokened a weak civil society. But the conciliatory policies towards the government pursued by the trade unions and their failure to participate actively in the political arena has impeded the development of labour as a kernel of an active civil society. In

---

[126] Cited in Mandel, 'The Russian Working Class', 62.

[127] Stephen White, Richard Rose, and Ian McAllister, *How Russia Votes* (Chatham, New Jersey, Chatham House, 1997), 208, 224.

1989–91 organized labour had seemed set to play such a role as part of a general upsurge of civic activism. Militant, highly organized Siberian miners had played an important part in weakening Gorbachev. Yeltsin successfully harnessed this labor militancy to his quest for power in 1991, only to cast it aside once he had succeeded in doing so. The inertia of the Russian labour movement, particularly its inability and apparent unwillingness to coordinate sustained and effective industrial and political activity on a Russia-wide scale, has sapped the morale of its membership. Widespread political apathy derives not only from the necessity to survive, but the sense that given the relentless decline in living standards, industrial and political action is futile. As a result, the political initiative has been left in the hands of the state, which has been emboldened by the apparent passivity of the organized working class. The imposition of the market and electoral democracy has 'disempowered' workers, leaving them as little more than bystanders in the privatization process and the Russian transformation as a whole.[128]

## An Impoverished Peasantry

Aside from a stable, cooperative labour movement, a prosperous farming class, together with a prosperous urban middle class, has been the backbone of stable democracies in developed capitalist countries. Gaullism and its successors in France, the Liberal Democratic Party in Japan, Christian Democracy in Germany, and the Democrat-Republican party system in the USA, have all derived a considerable part of their political strength from a conservative, prosperous farming class. Russia has had no family farm tradition, and it was not until the dissolution of the parliament in autumn 1993 that measures were taken to make this possible.[129]

However, far from prospering in the new market, Russian agriculture went into precipitous decline, a victim of the free market policies pursued from 1992 onwards. With price liberalization, a scissors crisis gripped agriculture as a gap opened up between industrial and agricultural prices, to the decided disadvantage of the countryside.[130] Monopoly conditions in industry saw sharp increases in the price of machinery, fuel and livestock, while agricultural

[128] Morvant and Rutland, 'Russian Workers', 6.

[129] A Yeltsin decree of October 1993 created a free market in land and abolished the compulsory state purchase of agricultural produce, while Article 9 of the new Constitution allowed for private ownership of land.

[130] Richard Sakwa, *Russian Politics and Society*, 2nd edn. (London and New York, Routledge, 1996), 248.

prices, output and productivity fell, victims of a lack of demand, seed, credit, and equipment. Between 1991 and 1994, prices for industrial inputs rose 5.7 times faster than prices for agricultural output.[131] Agricultural production plummeted. According to a 1995 World Bank estimate, agricultural output since 1990 fell by 45–50 per cent compared to the 1986–90 average. This was approximately double the decline experienced by agriculture as a consequence of Stalin's forced collectivization.[132] Agricultural production was also hit by the introduction of the rouble corridor in 1995. The strong rouble enabled increased food imports, thereby stifling the demand for domestic produce. An estimated 70 per cent of the meat in Moscow was imported,[133] leading to fears that if Russia were to stop food imports, large cities would be on rations. However, the August 1998 crisis, with its devaluation of the rouble, stimulated food production within Russia.

Private farming has proved a dismal failure. Initially the number of farms rose from a mere 31,000 in October 1991 to 258,000 in July 1993.[134] But the numbers soon shrank after September 1993 because of the abolition of cheap state credit. Private bank interest, however, remained prohibitively high. By late 1994 more farms were being disbanded than were being created. 'Grossly undercapitalised' subsistence farming has proved unviable. In 1995, one-third of farms lacked even a tractor. Fixated with the myth of the family farm, reform of Russian agriculture has concentrated on privatization, to the detriment of an efficient market in agricultural inputs and outputs.[135] The net result has been not reform of the agricultural system but precipitously near complete collapse.[136]

Despite the views of some observers,[137] there is little evidence to support the claim that privatization of agriculture has been bedevilled by nomenklatura privatization, as in industry. So-called 'red landlords' have been intent on keeping their farms intact and ensuring the survival of their desperate, often aged, workforce. 'People have to live' is a common refrain. This paternalism means farm managers, have been reluctant to dispense with the social support

---

[131] Stephen K. Wegren and Frank A. Durgin, 'Why Agrarian Reform is Failing', *Transition,* 1: 19 (20 Oct. 1995), 50.

[132] Ibid. 50–1.

[133] Renfrey Clarke, 'Mexico City in Moscow', *Links,* 6, (Jan.–Apr. 1996), 65–77.

[134] Sakwa, '*Russian Politics,* 248.

[135] Wegren and Durgin, 'Why Agrarian Reform', 53.

[136] As 'a rural economy which had been an essentially credit-run "cash minimal" economy, became almost overnight, a totally cash-based "nil-credit" economy' collapse was averted only by partial reversion to the old state credit system and the emergence of barter.' Gavin Kitching, 'The Development of Agrarian Capitalism in Russia 1991–97: A Theoretical Outline', unpublished paper, Sydney, Dec. 1997, p. 3.

[137] See, e.g. Sakwa, *Russian Politics,* 248 who claims farm managers have sold land to local elites rather than to their own collective farmers.

provided by the collective farm, such as clinics, a cultural centre, nurseries, and primary schools.[138] Privatization of collective agriculture has been seen as a threat to village society and economy.[139] The result has been a political back-lash rather than support for the government. In 1993 the Agrarian Party and in 1995 and 1996 the KPRF were the principal beneficiaries of rural disen-chantment. This was a response both to the effects of government policies and to the way in which these policies were foisted on the countryside from above, with little popular input. Rural Russia's 'fear in the face of changes' foisted on them by alien urban authorities, who took little or no account of the peas-antry's opinions and preferences, galvanized rural support for communist and nationalist parties.[140]

There were attempts to organise popular support for private farming, but they were feeble and effectively undermined by government policy. As early as January 1990 an Association of Peasant Farms and Agricultural Co-operatives of Russia (AKKOR) was established with government support. But its attempt to represent farming interests was undercut by the government's credit restric-tions of September 1993, despite the fact that AKKOR had supported the President in his confrontation with the Parliament. Concern that disaffection with agricultural policies was driving private farmers into the arms of the Agrarian Party saw the setting up of a more political organization to promote farmers' interests. In December 1994 the president of AKKOR, Vladimir Bashmachnikov, established the Union of Landowners. Initially distancing itself from the government, in the lead-up to the December 1995 Duma elec-tions Bashmachnikov took his organization into an electoral bloc with NDR. Thus the interests of rural Russia were effectively subordinated to those of urban Russia.[141]

The net effect politically has been the failure of the new regime to build a rural constituency and the inability of rural inhabitants to organise success-fully to defend their interests. This situation has been compounded by the fail-ure to construct another social pillar of stable political democracies, a strong urban middle class.

---

[138] Kitching, 'The Development', 12, n. 2, 13–14.

[139] 'Opinion polls consistently showed that rural residents opposed decollectivisation': Wegren and Durgin, 'Why Agrarian', 53.

[140] German Diligensky, 'Chto my zhnaem o demokratii i grazhdanskoi obshchestve?', *Pro et Contra*, 2: 4 (Autumn 1997), 13. He also makes the point that the regions of European Russia to the south of Moscow, tend to be more conservative than those to the north and north-west.

[141] Wegren and Durgin, 'Why Agrarian', 54.

## A Weak Urban Middle Class

It is the urban middle class spawned by modern capitalism that provides the solid centre that sustains modern liberal democracy. Conversely its absence, as in developing countries, is often seen as an impediment to democratization. Moreover, its social degradation, as in Weimar Germany, may see the emergence of fascism. In Russia such a middle class, as it is understood in post-industrial Western capitalism, is weakly developed. At best it is a 'proto-layer', as Zaslavskaia has put it, a potential middle class: small proprietors, semi-proprietors, middle-level officials, the most qualified specialists and employees. The middle class, such as it is, consists of professionals, managers or supervisors in banks or foreign firms or those providing skilled services such as language interpreting and computer consulting.[142] According to Zaslavskaia's calculations, the so-called middle class in Russia today is usually younger, male, well educated and urban. A quarter of this new layer lives in Moscow and St Petersburg. They make up approximately a quarter of the economically active population, a much lower percentage and with lower social status than their Western counterparts who act as a 'social stabiliser'.[143]

A potential source of a modern middle class in Russia is the intelligentsia, with their high levels of education and professional skills. The intelligentsia had expected to reap the benefits of the move towards democratic capitalism. But the outcome has been otherwise. The political exclusion of the 'democratic' intelligentsia has been reflected in the social and economic demise of the intelligentsia as a whole. They have experienced not only a pronounced deterioration in their living conditions but also significant income differentiation. The weakness of the Russian middle class is a reflection of the polarisation of wealth in Russian society. A 1995 comparison of household money income in the USA and Russia indicated this. It showed not only that the top and bottom 20 per cent of Russian households had a larger share of income than in the USA, but that the three middle quintiles in Russia had a smaller share of income than their US counterparts.[144]

Many of those Russians who have made it into the private sector, such as managers, economists and legal specialists, are well qualified and well paid. Commerce is a sector that actually experienced a doubling of income relative

---

[142] Kotz and Weir, *Revolution*, 181. Professionals as normally understood in the West—i.e. doctors, lawyers, teachers—have largely been marginalised in economic terms in post-Soviet Russia.

[143] Zaslavskaia ' Sotsial'naia struktura', 233, 238–9.

[144] Kotz and Weir, *Revolution*, 182.

to the average over 1989–94.[145] Beneath them, however, is a large layer of scientific and technical specialists working in the VPK and other export industries. At the bottom, are those employed in the social sciences and humanities in the state sector.[146] The scientific intelligentsia, once the pride of the industrially based Soviet economy, have suffered an extraordinary reversal of fortunes. Whereas in 1989 their wages were 20 per cent above the average, by 1994 they had suffered a decline of about one-third. A brain drain has been one result, scientists departing for overseas, working for foreign firms in Russia, or abandoning science for more lucrative employment in commerce, even of the most rudimentary kind. A survey conducted in 1992–93 of almost one thousand Moscow street traders found that 36.8 per cent were students, researchers, engineers, teachers, or doctors.[147] Moreover, such small-scale trading has not fostered a middle class based on small business. Despite the rhetorical commitment of the Russian government to 'peoples' capitalism', and even legal and financial support for small business, voucher privatization, price liberalization, and a harsh tax regime, coupled with racketeering, have been major obstacles to the emergence of a middle class based on small business, with the partial exception of Moscow city.[148]

While the new middle class has been the principal social support for economic transformation, it is as yet 'too small to serve as a guarantor of social stability'.[149] The exceptions to this are in the metropoles of St Petersburg and particularly Moscow. The concentration of wealth in the Russian capital created a social layer that, at least until the August 1998 financial crisis, was the principal beneficiary of capitalism in terms of income and access to consumer goods and services. The success of Mayor Luzhkov's populist politics in part seems to have rested on this relatively prosperous middle layer. It is hardly surprising either that Russia's two major cities have consistently voted for pro-capitalist parties and against the KPRF. But Moscow is not Russia. The middle class remains small, weak and vulnerable; the crisis of August 1998 caused the impoverishment of a significant section of this group virtually overnight. This weakness has significant implications for the development of a party system

---

[145] Ibid. 183–4. The collapse of research funding and wages in the scientific sector has been a serious obstacle to the young entering science careers, a trend which has serious implications for the long-term maintenance of scientific and technical development in Russia. Research and development expenditures fell from 3.1% of GDP in 1990 to 1.2% in 1992: Jody Overland and Michael Spagat, 'Human Capital and Russia's Economic Transformation', *Transition*, 2, 13 (28 June 1996), 13.

[146] Zaslavskaia, 'Sotsial'naia struktura', 231.

[147] Cited in Overland and Spagat, 'Human Capital', 14.

[148] Elena Bragina, 'Malyi biznes: sostoianie i problemy', *Sm*, 11 (1995), 86–94.

[149] Zaslavskaia, 'Sotsial'naia struktura', 233, 238–9.

since, historically, such a class has been crucial for the growth of mass-based democratic parties.

## Political Parties

In established representative democracies, the existence of well-defined social interests articulated through a party system has usually been regarded as essential for a viable political system. Certainly, the establishment of a party system has been seen as a *sine qua non* for a successful post-authoritarian transition. A party system, operating through elections, is a key linkage between civil society and the state: it is a means of articulating the varied interests of civil society (such as capital and labour) and keeping political elites accountable while providing a basis of legitimation for political activity. Social interests utilize parties to mobilise electoral constituencies and channel their support into governmental institutions. The electoral system, marginalising political extremes, encourages centrist parties, which provide much of the ballast for political stability.

In the case of Russia, the dearth of well-delineated social interests, particularly at a popular level, self-consciously seeking to advance their political interests through institutionalized means, has taken its toll on the development of a meaningful party system. Economic and political upheaval has resulted in social disorientation and political inertia. As a consequence, political parties have developed in a social vacuum, weakly rooted in an inchoate society and lacking sustained links with the state.[150] This situation has been a major impediment to the establishment of a stable polity.

The problem for Russia has been a structural one. There has been no social basis to establish a stable party system, such as exists in the West, that could ensure political stability. There has been no social basis to create either mass-based conservative parties of the Christian Democratic and Gaullist type, or social democratic parties, which have been the bulwarks of West European democracy. As we have seen, Russia lacks the prosperous rural community that has been the backbone of conservative parties in the West. On the contrary, shock therapy has been to the detriment of the countryside, slashing both output and incomes. As a consequence the countryside has voted against Yeltsin and his programme, throwing their support behind the KPRF and their Agrarian Party allies instead. Moreover, the depth of Russia's economic crisis has meant that the state has been unable to put in place the dense network of

---

[150] Marcia A. Weigle, 'Political Participation and Party Formation in Russia, 1985–1992: Institutionalizing Democracy?', *Russian Review*, 53 (Apr. 1994), 240–1.

welfare-state social services which in the West underpin the support of urban workers for social democratic parties. Indeed, a central feature of the Russian transition has been the radical destruction of the soviet-era welfare state. In these circumstances, the urban working classes (with the signal exception of Moscow and St Petersburg) have tended to look towards the successors to the old communist party or to nationalist parties.

The loss of the CPSU's monopoly of the political process formally in March 1990, the introduction of parliamentary political institutions such as the Congress of People's Deputies, and the subsequent banning of party political activity within social institutions such as factories or the military, brought about a significant shift in the conception of politics in Russia, even before it became a separate state. The displacement of the Soviet territorial-production basis of politics by a territorial-electoral system brought about the separation of politics from social institutions. This separation of electoral politics into a discrete realm, in effect a narrowing of the potential arena of politics, reached its logical conclusion with the final abolition of the soviet system. The replacement of class by citizenship as the (formal) basis of the political system, signalled by the elimination of labour collectives as electoral institutions, was accompanied by the formation of parties as vote-gathering machines but not as vehicles for political participation.

Paradoxically, this reduction of politics to party-electoral activity coincided with a surge in political activity, as we saw above. The flourishing of the informal civil associations fostered a plethora of amorphous 'parties'. In 1991 there were some 457 associations of which perhaps 100 resembled parties. Eighteen social movements and nine political parties came together to officially establish DemRossiia in October 1990, a movement of 200,000–300,000 that Yeltsin successfully rode to power in June the following year.[151] Soon after the defeat of the August 1991 putsch, however, DemRossiia began to fragment, having lost its *raison d'être* as an anti-communist coalition supporting Yeltsin's struggle with the centre. Conflict broke out over the construction of the new Russian state, over Russian nationalism and economic policy, as well as who controlled the organization. The fragmentation of DemRossiia in late 1991–early 1992 immobilised what had been a highly organized movement and gave rise to a plethora of new pseudo-parties and political blocs.[152] By mid-1992 there were some 1,200 parties operating in Russia.[153] But they were

[151] Weigle, 'Political Participation', 259–61; *Kto est' chto: politicheskaiia Moskva* (Moscow, Satallakhu, 1993), 197. For a four-phase periodisation of the emergence of parties in Russia, see Sakwa, *Russian Politics*, 77–91.

[152] Weigle, 'Political Participation', 262–4.

[153] Ian McAllister and Stephen White, 'Democracy, Political Parties and Party Formation in Postcommunist Russia', *Party Politics*, 1: 1 (1995), 52.

hamstrung by their organisational weakness and by their failure to put down any social roots.

The one exception seemed to be the political bloc Civic Union, formally established on 21 June 1992. It was an amalgam principally of Aleksandr Rutskoi's People's Party of Free Russia (PPSR), Nikolai Travkin's Democratic Party of Russia (DPR) and Arkady Volsky's All-Russian Union Renewal, an off-shoot of his Russian Union of Industrialists and Entrepreneurs (RSPP).[154] Civic Union represented the directors of large former-state enterprises who were anxious to head off bankruptcy under the impact of shock therapy. Largely through Volsky, Civic Union successfully pressured Yeltsin to admit representatives of the industrial directorate into the cabinet and to guarantee continued state subsidies. After the December 1992 Seventh CPD and Gaidar's departure from government, Yeltsin courted Civic Union, mindful of its relatively strong social base and as a counter-weight to mounting opposition in the parliament.[155] In the December 1993 Duma elections, of the parties representing business interests only Civic Union gained the required 100,000 signatures for registration on the party list. However it failed to secure the necessary 5 per cent of the vote to achieve party list representation in the Duma, although it did win twenty seats in the single seat competition. But Civic Union's moment of glory was fleeting. It soon began to wither away, as did its constituent parties. Volsky failed to establish an industrial party on the basis of RSPP as a conservative party along Western lines by broadening out its social support to include a rural constituency. The industrialists gathered around Civic Union made overtures to the Agrarian Party to form a bloc, but they were pre-empted by the KPRF.[156]

The fate of Civic Union was common to all attempts to create a 'party of capital'. Not one party representing the bourgeoisie contested the December 1993 elections on a separate list.[157] The Party of Economic Freedom, founded by the entrepreneurial surgeon Sviatoslav Fedorov and Konstantin Borovoi in May 1992, could not muster enough signatures to participate in the 1993 elections, even though its founders boasted it had more than 200,000 supporters by its first congress in December 1992.[158] In the December 1995 legislative elections business parties were even less successful. The Trade Unions and Industrialists of Russia–Union of Labour, a new party of industrialists and trade unionists founded by Civic Union leader Volsky and leading trade union officials, secured only one seat with 1.6 per cent of the vote.[159]

[154] Sakwa, *Russian Politics*, 82. For details of the parties and blocs see *Kto est' chto*, 170 ff.
[155] Weigle, 'Political Participation', 265, 267.                     [156] *Ng*, 1 Dec. 1993.
[157] Valery Krasnov, 'Ot vyborov–93 k vyboram–95', *Sm*, 10 (1995), 22.
[158] Jeremy Lester, *Modern Tsars and Princes: The Struggle for Hegemony in Russia* (London and New York, Verso, 1995), 107–8; *Kto est' chto*, 324–34.
[159] White, Rose and McAllister, *How Russia Votes*, 224. See also Peregudov and Semenenko, 'Lobby Business', 123–4.

By May 1993 there were an extraordinary 1,800 pseudo-parties in existence. Russia, it has been correctly observed, had 'moved from being a one-party state to a non-party state'.[160] These new pseudo-parties ranged right across the political spectrum from extreme left to extreme right. In the main these parties were more like movements than electoral parties as such. Those that had representation in the Supreme Soviet exhibited no firm factional discipline. The fact that parties did not form the government left them with little reason for existence. Anticipating parliamentary elections, in the context of the Parliament's stand off with the President, there were two initiatives in September 1993 to create political support for Yeltsin, both coming out of DemRossiia: Gaidar's Russia's Choice, later Russia's Democratic Choice (DVR), and Sergei Shakhrai's Party of Russian Unity and Accord (PRES). Russia's Choice was intended to be the 'party of power', while PRES kept a slight distance from Yeltsin, possibly because it was covertly supported by Chernomyrdin. Neither flourished in the 1993 elections: Russia's Choice won 15.5 per cent and PRES 6.8 per cent of the vote.[161]

For all their democratic shortcomings, the December 1993 elections were the first genuine multi-party elections in post-Soviet Russia and they signalled the emergence of political forces capable of acting independently of the executive. Yet the successful organisations scarcely qualified as parties, lacking as they did clear programmatic distinctions and binding discipline on their deputies. Fluid in their composition, with deputies forming alliances as it suited them, they were often little more than creatures of dominant personalities, such as Zhirinovsky's LDPR, a situation encouraged by the fact that half the seats were based on individual candidature rather than party lists. The development of party politics was also hindered by the preoccupation of the Duma deputies not so much with politics as with lobbying on behalf of commercial interests, which had actively promoted candidates during the campaign. The formation of serious electoral parties was also impeded by the fact that as in Soviet times, there was no obligation to form a government based on party representation in the legislature. Nevertheless, the Parliament was more than a democratic screen for Yeltsin. Given the narrowness of his own base of support and the enormity of the tasks of transformation, the president would be forced more than once to seek the cooperation of the Duma in implementing government policies, if only to share around the political responsibility for decision-making. [162]

---

[160] Sakwa, *Russian Politics*, 80.

[161] Sergei Khenkin, ' "Partiia vlasti": rossiiskii variant', *Pro et Contra*, 1: 1 (Autumn 1996), 37–8; White, Rose, and McAllister, *How Russia Votes*, 112; Sakwa, *Russian Politics*, 81.

[162] Krasnov, 'Ot vyborov-93', 13–14.

Amidst the plethora of 'would be' parties that have waxed and waned since 1991, the KPRF stands out as the only one approximating a stable party formation with a real electoral constituency. With half a million members and 20,000 local organizations, it is unrivalled as a nationally organized party with real grass roots support. Its success in the December 1995 elections, where it secured 22.3 per cent of the vote and 157 seats, was testimony not only to voter disenchantment with the direction of government policy, but also to the ability of the KPRF to organize its members and its adaptation to electoral competition.[163] Yet this adaptation has been accompanied by a failure to seriously embed itself in any social soil, most obviously amongst the organized working class which it might be assumed, given its Leninist lineage, would be its natural constituency. Instead the KPRF has pitched its programme in the broadest, non-class, nationalist terms,[164] seeking thereby the widest electoral appeal. This was much clearer during the presidential election than during the parliamentary poll, when its message was much less mixed.[165] But it has made this electoral appeal without seriously anchoring itself in any social constituency in particular, with the possible exceptions of elderly rural dwellers, managers of former collective farms, and members of the nomenklatura who have not benefited from neo-liberalism.

The KPRF has eschewed active engagement with civil society forces. It distanced itself from the October 1993 conflict. Likewise, it has shown at best lukewarm support for industrial or other mass action against Russia's neo-liberal course. Instead, in pursuit of its 'strategic compromise', it has focused on winning elections and lobbying the government, since 1995 in particular with one eye on the possibility of entering a coalition. From mid-1994 on, and again after the 1996 presidential election, a close working relationship developed between the KPRF and Chernomyrdin. Acting like a loyal opposition, the KPRF voted in favour of Chernomyrdin's successive budgets, fearful that their rejection might strengthen the hand of the champion of neo-liberalism, Chubais. The net result has been that the one major Russia-wide political party has channelled its energies into the narrowest of electoral strategies. Fearing that social protest might erupt into social upheaval, it has effectively turned its

---

[163] Kagarlitsky, 'The Russian Parliamentary Elections', 118. Following the April 1993 referendum, the KPRF resolved at its May 1993 Central Committee plenum to seek a peaceful, electoral road to power: Dzhoan Urban and Valerii Solovei, 'Kommunisticheskoe dvizhenie v postsovetskoi Rossii', *Sm*, 3 (Mar. 1997), 20.

[164] See Jeremy Lester, 'Overdosing on Nationalism: Gennadii Zyuganov and the Communist Party of the Russian Federation', *New Left Review*, 221, (Jan.–Feb. 1997), 34–53.

[165] For the fullest study of the party, see Joan Barth Urban and Valerii D. Solovei, *Russia's Communists at the Crossroads* (Boulder, Westview, 1997).

back on an unorganised, directionless civil society. In this sense, it has become a 'major factor in the stability' of the Yeltsin regime.[166]

The failure of Russia to generate a party system truly embedded in civil society is exemplified by the abortive attempts to found a viable 'party of power'. In contrast to the situation in liberal democracies where parties generally form governments, in Russia there have actually been attempts by the government to form parties. In early 1995 conditions seemed propitious for the establishment of a 'party of power'. By then, after the political upheavals of 1993 and the struggles over the redistribution of property had subsided, 'stability' became the order of the day. This was a notion that evidently tapped the mood of the populace at large, exhausted by continual instability and political infighting.[167] In these circumstances, the political elite around the executive moved to establish a two-party system, along US lines. This was interpreted by one commentator as an attempt to create a right-centrist bloc that would be the basis of government while a left-centrist social democratic type of bloc would win the State Duma speakership.[168] Such a plan did not come to pass. There was no discernible difference between these blocs. The speaker of the Duma, Rybkin, previously closely aligned with the agrarians and the communists, was now seen as aligning himself with the president.

Chernomyrdin's attempt in May 1995 to form a right-centrist bloc based on NDR was no more successful. Intended to consolidate relations between the central and regional elites in order to head off a communist party and/or nationalist challenge in the December 1995 elections, it was primarily an elite formation with little or no mass base. The platform of NDR was based on three fundamental principles: a 'strong state', a 'liberal economy', and 'real social change'. In reality, however, the binding principle of NDR was one of elite orientation towards the executive power. This was exactly how NDR was seen by the electorate—the 'party of the bosses'[169] responsible for the social costs of the transformation. Accordingly, in December 1995 it garnered a mere 10.13 per cent of the votes, despite the considerable financial and media resources it had at its disposal. Though this was enough to make it the second largest faction in the Duma, NDR's ostensibly centrist platform had little appeal for the electorate. Neither was whole-hearted support forthcoming from either the regional elite or the President, who had originally endorsed it.[170]

NDR proved singularly unsuccessful in addressing a particular priority of the political elite: the need to establish a viable, national party to ensure

[166] Urban and Solovei, 'Kommunisticheskoe dvizhenie', 21, 27; Boris Kagarlitsky, 'Five Years of the Communist Party of the Russian Federation', *Green Left Weekly*, 6 Apr. 1998, p. 22.
[167] Khenkin, ' "Partiia vlasti" ', 37–8.     [168] Ibid. 38.     [169] Ibid. 39.
[170] Ibid.

political succession in the event of Yeltsin's death or inability to carry out his duties. The pivotal role of Yeltsin as the guarantor of state stability had injected a certain urgency into the situation, given his poor state of health and uncertainty about the mechanisms for political succession. Moreover, NDR failed not simply because it was formed by the government, rather than vice versa, but also because it excluded other members of the political class. For this reason, for example, Aleksandr Lebed built his own independent political bloc 'For Truth and Order!' It was no accident that soon after NDR entered the Duma, it ceased to exist in all but name, abandoned by many of its leading cadre.[171]

While there was a higher turnout for the December 1995 elections than for those two years previously (64.44 per cent as opposed to the official figure of 54.8 per cent), and there was an increase in grass roots activism, these did nothing to dispel a chronic feature of Russian political life to date: a low level of party participation and identification, and pronounced popular scepticism towards parties and their activities.[172] The December 1995 elections did, however, have the virtue of sorting out the so-called 'divan parties' from the real parties. Some 300 parties had pursued 200,000 signatures each to be on the ballot. Forty-three party lists finally contested the election, but, as shown above, only four crossed the 5 per cent threshold. Though indicative of the apparent emergence of an embryonic party system, the election displayed all the weaknesses of the system. A plethora of organizations with barely distinguishable programmes, they were often not much more than mechanisms for satisfying the electoral ambitions of particular individuals, who fought for a place at the head of a party list to win a single member seat, even if the party did not cross the 5 per cent threshold. As in its predecessor, many of the deputies and parties in the new Duma were direct representatives of commercial and industrial lobbies. This situation impeded party development. The various elite business interests acted as partial substitutes for political parties, directly participating in the political system and 'turning the parliament into an institution where interest representation has developed on an unprecedented scale.'[173]

A combination of factors has impeded the emergence of a viable party system in Russia. Difficulties of organisation stemming from the size of the country, the difficulties of cheap, regular communication, and the limited resources available to many people have been important here. But undoubtedly an entrenched political culture shaped by an overweening state has stifled the emergence of autonomous political activity, an étatist tradition that has been continued under the Russian presidency. The refusal of Yeltsin to seriously

---

[171] Khenkin, ' "Partiia vlasti" ', 42.
[172] McAllister and White, 'Democracy', 56–7.
[173] Peregudov and Semenenko, 'Lobbying Business', 130.

embrace party politics, preferring instead to project himself as the representative of popular interests, coupled with the fact that the presidential apparatus has been the axis of politics, has marginalised the legislature, in parliamentary democracies the arena of party politics. The political impediments to formation of a party system have been compounded by the inhospitable social environment of post-Soviet Russia. The failure to sustain mass movements that could generate active parties, combined with the crystallisation of elite business interests that have relied not only on direct connections with the apparatus of state but a presence in it, have been major barriers to the emergence of a party system. Likewise, the development of a stable ruling party has been impeded by the failure of the regime to realize the expectations raised by the 'heroic days' of August 1991. There have been no tangible benefits that could provide a basis for the political and economic elites to build a mass political party, particularly given the weakness of a middle class that could provide the basis of centrist politics.[174] The very same social and economic factors, however, have also impeded the emergence of mass-based opposition parties and a vital civil society that could sustain them.

## A Languishing Civil Society

A flourishing civil society was a goal of the new Russia. It has plainly not come to pass. Rather than an active citizenry participating in the political life of the country, generating new and vibrant institutions and reinvigorating old ones, the opposite has been the case. Social interests have not crystallised. There has been a withdrawal from public life. Cynicism about politics and politicians pervades popular consciousness. With the exception of the KPRF, parties have little independent life and a scant mass base. Trade unions have a large membership but active participation and sustained, concerted industrial action has yet to appear. There has been no flowering of civil society.[175]

---

[174] Krasnov, 'Ot vyborov-93', 20.

[175] A similar argument is advanced by Diligensky, 'Chto My', 5–22. Diligensky, along with several other contributors to the discussion in this issue of the journal, argues that the very notion of civil society, derived as it is from the Western, especially the Anglo-American, tradition is problematic for Russia. A survey conducted in June 1993 found that half those surveyed had little or no idea of the meaning of democracy, while only 5% identified democracy with 'popularly elected government'. 'As a whole', writes Diligensky (p. 17), 'the concept of "democracy" is for Russian society an abstraction, borrowed from an alien (Western) experience.' For an attempt to resurrect obshchestvennost' (roughly, 'community') as an indigenous feature of Russian civic life, see Vadim Volkov, 'Obshchestvennost': zabytaia praktika grazhdanskogo obshchestva', *Pro et Contra*, 2: 4 (Autumn 1997), 77–91.

In good part the withering of civil society so soon after the formation of the Russian Federation is the obverse of the monopolization of political decision-making by the executive branch of the state. Whatever its rhetoric, by concentrating power in the executive at the expense of the legislative organs, the capacity of the citizenry to actively participate in political life has been undermined. But the torpor of political life is also a by-product of dashed expectations. Instead of the cornucopia of the market trumpeted by the mass media and the democrat politicians came a harsh economic regime, a brutal war in Chechnya, crime and corruption, and uncertainty about the political direction of the country. The consequence has been that the mass of the populace has retreated into a sullen preoccupation with the need to survive in a harsh market. The majority yearns for 'order' rather than democracy, which they equate with 'disorder'.[176] Furthermore, those sections of society which elsewhere have often been important forces pressing for an opening of the political system, have been conspicuous by their failure to do so in Russia. The new bourgeoisie has for the most part been content to function on the basis of personal contacts and connections rather than through civil society organs. The labour movement, despite some bouts of militancy, has proved incapable of sustained mobilization, while the middle class has remained weak and politically inert. In these circumstances civil society in Russia has languished with the result that society generally has lacked the means to shape the course of Russian political life. Politics has become the exclusive domain of a warring elite, which, in the absence of mass involvement or support, clings to an authoritarian style of presidency in the person of Boris Yeltsin as a substitute for democracy.

---

[176] Diligensky, 'Chtmo My', 11–12, 18. He makes much of the fact that no mass movement developed in opposition to the Chechen war, unlike that in the West against the war in Vietnam. Human rights advocates and mothers of soldiers organizations remained isolated. The government and military ignored public opinion in relation to the war.

# 7

# Conclusion

A crucial factor shaping the course of political developments in the Soviet Union and then Russia from 1985 has been the weakness of civil society forces and the inability of a vibrant and robust civil society to establish itself. As argued in Chapter 1, the operation of civil society forces is central to the achievement of a democratic outcome in cases of regime crisis. Civil society forces put pressure on political elites, forcing them to make decisions on the basis of considerations wider than their own narrow self-interest. They act as negotiating partners with regime elites, their links into an active citizen community acting as an important anchor holding the reform process on a democratic course. Through their continuing involvement in the process, they are the best guarantors of a democratic outcome. Where such forces are unable to insert themselves into the process, where they cannot become powerful interlocutors with regime elites and force a broader perspective on them, regime elites are better able to structure the process to achieve an outcome which better suits their needs but falls short of democracy. Such an outcome may fulfil the formal, institutional requirements of democracy, but it will lack its substantive essence. It has been the weakness of such civil society forces in the Soviet Union and Russia which has left excessive power in the hands of political elites and undercut the emergence of a stable and robust democracy.

When elements within the Soviet political elite became convinced that the economic difficulties confronting the Soviet Union required a reformist response, they did not envisage this as necessitating any widespread support from within the populace. It was assumed that the changes to the economic structure that were required could be implemented from above, as had been the case in the past, and that therefore the principal political imperative would be the maintenance of support for reform within the state, most importantly at the apex. In other words, for many in the elite this was seen as simply a technocratic type of Soviet reform, like that sponsored by Kosygin in the mid-60s. However, it soon became clear that the economic difficulties were but the most obvious signs of a deeper malaise within the Soviet polity more broadly, and that any attempt to combat this was going to have to go much further than

Soviet reform efforts had gone in the past. Acknowledgement of the greater
seriousness of the problem, added to the emerging opposition to some elements of the proposed solution among lower-level officials, encouraged those
in the reformist coalition around Gorbachev to seek to mobilise popular support for their efforts. From late 1986, Gorbachev and his immediate supporters tried to enlist popular support in their struggle with those more
conservative elements within the political structure who sought to weaken the
course of change. As economic (and general social) conditions deteriorated,
and as the solutions considered became increasingly radical (with the assump-
tion that these would cause further economic pain to the populace) and therefore generated even stronger opposition, the need for popular support
mounted.

However, this search for popular support faced major problems. Soviet society constituted an unpromising base for the quick generation of those sorts of
civil society organizations which could have organized and focused popular
feeling. The Soviet political system proved incapable, if it ever had been, of acting as a conduit for autonomous popular interests. The official monism had
been antithetical to the development of independent organisation and to the
emergence of a public arena for the contestation of ideas, either within or outside its structure. As a result, when Gorbachev and his supporters looked for
support from within the populace, there were no established structures for the
carriage of such support. If support was to be regularized and strong, it needed
to be organized and focused, and this could only come about through the creation of an effective civil society. The reformist wing of the Soviet elite did
make some progress here, but it was overwhelmingly too late to have much
effect. Freedom of the press was initially tolerated and then legalized, thereby
providing a voice predominantly for the intelligentsia, who had been encouraged to become involved by the freeing of Sakharov; but the intelligentsia ultimately used this freedom to express its disillusionment with perestroika and to
repudiate the entire Soviet experience. Provision was made for competitive
elections, but only belatedly for competitive parties. A parliamentary arena for
the discussion of issues was created, but its functioning was hindered by the
absence of stable parties within it and by the distrust which many of the politically active had for it because of the way it was set up. Increasingly too it
became a forum for the disenchanted intelligentsia. Furthermore the reformist
section of the elite did not push firmly for the growth of independent organizations within society, such as stable political parties or an organized labour
movement that might have been used as a counter-weight against the conservatives. When such organizations did emerge, like the miners' movement, little or no attempt was made to win them over or to support their development.
Instead they were left to be mobilized by others, like Yeltsin. The only organi-

zations that did emerge and gain support within reformist elite circles were some of the national fronts, but through their actions, these effectively further undercut the emergence of a Soviet civil society.

Not only was the stimulus for civil society development from the top half-hearted, but the force for it coming from below was also muted. Conscious political activity supporting reform did emerge within society, principally among the intelligentsia of the major cities. This tended to take two forms. First, the emergence of the national fronts, which initially began as pro-perestroika forces but, harnessed by nationalist elites, soon developed into organizations pressing for changes in the federal structure, to which chief elements in the reformist section of the Soviet elite were resistant. Their priorities lay in restructuring the federation rather than the sorts of political and economic changes which Gorbachev sought to bring about in Soviet society as a whole; nationalist concerns displaced those more associated with civil society. Ultimately, these developed into centrifugal forces that rent the USSR asunder. Second, the democrats, who were actually more important in the Russian Federation than popularly based nationalist forces. While the democrats initially emerged as supporters of perestroika, as the reform process bogged down they became disillusioned by what they saw as the vacillations of the Gorbachev leadership. Increasingly they saw the wholesale introduction of the market as the way forward and cast in their lot with the new leader of Russian nationalism, Boris Yeltsin. In this way, they put the nascent organizations of civil society at the service of the second level of the political elite and in the service of Russian national interests in preference to those of the USSR. Under the banner of Russian sovereignty the beginnings of civil society became suborned to a convergence of the economic interests of the embryonic Russian bourgeoisie, the political interests of Boris Yeltsin and his circle, and the national interests of sections of the Russian political elite.

The weakness of civil society, and the fact that from 1989 onwards those proponents of change who were politically active focused on supporting Yeltsin, meant that the main course of the struggle for change during the Soviet period was, as in the traditional Soviet pattern, confined largely to the summit of the political structure. The struggle for Soviet reform was fought at elite levels, with the reformers frequently out-manoeuvring their opponents without ever finally killing them off, while a war of attrition against the changes was waged by many officials at lower levels. Clearly the mobilization of the rank-and-file through the existing structures was having some effect, not least in terms of rendering the traditional structure incoherent and of fundamentally weakening the conservative opposition, but it could not so strengthen the reformists that they could be encouraged to mount a decisive action to get rid of their opponents with the secure hope of success. The result was that the conflict remained defined principally in terms of Soviet norms, and although some of those norms may have been shaken, this did not open the way for the mobilization of popular forces to the degree necessary to vanquish the opponents of perestroika.

In this conflict at the top of the Soviet structure, there was no agreement between the two sides over the retirement of one from the field. Although the conservatives were on the defensive throughout most of this period, they remained firmly in place at many levels of the structure. The resultant stalemate took its toll on the reformers too. As perestroika stalled and the economy foundered, reform of Soviet state socialism was abandoned. Gorbachev and his associates cast desperately about for an alternative political and economic system. They found it in an executive presidency and the market, a rapid change of heart that was symptomatic of a loss of commitment to the traditional structures of the Soviet system at the highest echelons of the political elite. It took the abortive putsch of August 1991 and the seizure of the opportunity this presented by Yeltsin to remove the conservative wing of the Soviet elite to break this stalemate. But Yeltsin also removed the reformist wing. Unlike Gorbachev and his allies, Yeltsin and his circle effectively mobilized support to the degree necessary to undercut the Soviet centre. Power then slipped into the hands of the Russian wing of the political elite that emerged in 1990.

The final rupturing of power at the centre and the opportunity this presented for the Russian republican elite to seize power and displace its formal superiors was a result of the fundamental tensions at the heart of the process of change, represented in the shift from reform to transformation. The nature of the change sought by Gorbachev, involving both economic and political liberalisation, generated a dynamic which the central leadership could not control. As reform became increasingly radical, it transcended the existing institutions, seeking their effective replacement rather than their alteration. This was reflected in the official programme sponsored by Gorbachev; the shift from single communist party monopoly to a multi-party presidential republic with the CPSU becoming a social democratic party, and the shift from an economy in which state regulation played the predominant part to one in which market forces were primary, are the two main facets of this. But this change in the official programme was difficult to achieve, characterized by reverses and setbacks, and opposed at each step of the way by elements in both the leadership and at lower levels of the political structure. This change was also propelled by the redrawing of the public agenda, something which after 1989 was outside the control of the central elite. As actors from lower levels of society, including some republican elites, nationalist movements and civic opposition forces, pressed for more and more change, the shift to transformation was achieved. The result was the cracking open of the old system and the collapse of the Union, a development which created new opportunities for those possessing the resources to take advantage of them. For political elites and those active in the political arena, the prospect was access to political power. For those who had already begun to take advantage of the opportunities created in the economic sphere, including those who were to be the basis of the new bourgeoisie, those opportunities expanded considerably.

Given the uncertain rules of the political game in the newly independent Russia, and the stand-off that was to develop between President and legislature, the situation seemed ripe for decisive intervention by forces from outside the political elite. However, here the legacy of the Gorbachev period was crucial. The weakness of civil society forces at the time of the disintegration of the Union meant that those loosely labelled 'democrats' who had supported Yeltsin in his moves against the Soviet centre had no solid, independent social basis from which to project their influence into the realms of elite politics. Consequently when Yeltsin failed to include the democrats in his plans for the construction of a new political structure, and with the legislative side to the dispute tainted by the prominence of communists, the democrats were left on the sidelines. They could not play a powerful independent role; instead, the polarization of politics meant that, if they were to play a part at all, they appeared to have little alternative but to act merely as vocal supporters (or critics) of the path pursued by the President and his government. As a personalist president, eschewing any form of presidential party, Yeltsin turned his back on the democrat movement that he had ridden to power, thereby denying it a role as a vehicle of popular involvement with close links to the summit of power. The former politburo member closed ranks with former members of the nomenklatura,while other sections of the nomenklatura busily reconfigured themselves as a new Russian bourgeoisie.

While the collapse of the Soviet system seemed to open the way to the development of those institutions which are seen as vital to the linking of civil society to the political process, political parties, the results were mixed. A large number of parties burst onto the Russian scene, but few have been both long-lasting and important. Hampered by difficulties of organization and resources, a culture of division and dissent, and the prominence of individual personalities, most parties were unable to extend an organisational presence across the country. Furthermore, their development was not greatly promoted by that which is generally seen as encouraging party development, elections. The 1993 election was called suddenly, giving parties little warning, with the result that they had only some ten weeks between announcement of the election and actual balloting. This was clearly insufficient time to enable regular and stable parties to emerge. Following that election and the introduction of the new

Constitution, the clearly subordinate status of the Duma and the avowedly non-party status of the Federation Council provided little incentive for potential activists to invest much in party creation. The presidency was clearly the locus of power rather than the legislature, and Yeltsin's hegemonic non-party model provided little incentive for parties to be developed in the lead-up to this election. So this combination of Yeltsin's style and the implications of the electoral process as it was worked out in Russia stood in the way of effective party development.

The capacity of civil society to emerge strongly during the post-1991 period was also impeded by what has been called a ' social adaptation crisis'[1] engendered by the abrupt embrace of capitalism, which cut a swathe through the fabric of established social, political and economic relations. The popular response to the trauma associated with shock therapy and its aftermath, has been apathy and disillusionment rather than political mobilization. As people have struggled to make ends meet, their efforts have turned much more to coping with the rigours of daily living rather than trying to participate in the political system. The widespread distrust of politicians and the political system has led to an opting out; levels of electoral participation are at the low end of the OECD countries. This means that there has been little stimulus from the populace for the generation of civil society organizations, as people have turned away even from those levels of involvement attained under Gorbachev. Popular commitment to sustained involvement in politics has therefore been absent.

The effect of the weakness of civil society during the Yeltsin period has been that politics has remained overwhelmingly the preserve of the elite. Certainly the populace has been given a say on certain occasions: the April 1993 referendum, the December 1993 legislative election and constitutional plebiscite, the December 1995 legislative election and the June/July 1996 presidential election. But the tendency has been towards plebiscitary elections: 'for' or 'against' the 'reforms'; 'for' or 'against' the President, a style of politics that hinges on competing personalities rather than political programmes. There has been no sustained involvement in political affairs by civil society forces, with the possible exception of discussion in the media. While much of the media remains free of government control and discussion in it is vigorous and wide-ranging, the small circulation of much of the print media and its lack of connection with the lives of many of the populace, at least when it discusses political issues, not to mention its role as the mouthpiece of a few wealthy magnates who have used it to advance their own interests (most dramatically during the 1996 presidential elections), means that it cannot stimulate a mature civil society.

[1] *Crisis in Mortality, Health and Nutrition*, Florence, UNICEF, Economies in Transition Studies, Regional Monitoring Report, 2 (August 1994), p. vi.

A stunted civil society cannot exercise significant influence in the structuring of Russian politics. It cannot provide a powerful partner with which regime elites can negotiate and cooperate to create a stable democratic structure. In this context, it might appear that the prospects for democracy rest overwhelmingly upon the political elites. But this would be a shaky basis for democratic development. There can be no reliance on the existing elites to create democratic structures and to ensure their observance. In post-authoritarian transitions, ruling elites are often reluctant democratizers, particularly given the considerable uncertainty that is introduced into the political system once restrictions are lifted on political activity and competitive politics is put in place, which may threaten the social prerogatives of the elite. In moving to democracy, elites are usually anxious to write predictability into the new rules of the game. In the Russian case, the September–October 1993 dissolution of the Congress of People's Deputies and Supreme Soviet stands as a striking instance of one political actor forcefully breaking the rules as they were understood, thereby throwing those rules into a contingent light. Despite the concerted attempt through the December 1993 Constitution to structure politics in such a way as to eliminate any contingency, principally by ensuring the overweening authority of the President, and a considerable degree of observance of the rules of the game as laid down in the Constitution, it is by no means certain that those rules have become embedded in the system. The serious discussion in the Russian media in 1998–99 about the prospect that Yeltsin might seek a third presidential term reflects doubts about the capacity of the formal rules of the system to gain normative authority, itself a reflection of the problematic commitment on the part of the political elite to the rules that they themselves put in place in the name of democracy.

Furthermore the absence of effective civil society oversight has left the way clear for the entry into political life of powerful business elites formally located outside the bounds of the political system. The emergence of a fledgling bourgeoisie in Russia, which lacks any solid mass social support and with a tenuous hold on economic life that makes it dependent on state support, has been a serious obstacle to the establishment of a democratic polity. Its determination that there should be no popular or legal constraints on its appropriation and use of wealth accumulated in the Soviet era, coupled with continuous infighting over scarce resources, has facilitated the emergence of a kind of 'soft Bonapartism'[2] in Yeltsin's Russia: a personalist, populist, plebiscitary regime,

---

[2] Aleksandr Tarasov, *Provokatsiia: versiia sobytii 3–4 oktiabriia 1993 g. v Moskve. Postskriptum iz 1994-go* (Moscow, 'Feniks', 1994), 53. For a discussion of the concept of Bonapartism see Ralph Miliband, *Marxism and Politics* (Oxford, Oxford University Press, 1977). For an analysis of the Yeltsin regime in terms of an allied concept ' Caesarism', see Jeremy Lester, *Modern Tsars and Princes: The Struggle for Hegemony in Russia* (London/New

that rests on the administrative and coercive apparatuses of the state and that by seemingly elevating itself above society, acts as an arbitrator and preserver of the new bourgeoisie's interests as a whole. If the grip of the new bourgeoisie on political life is strengthened, and they continue to see their interests as being served by operating through private channels behind a democratic facade, in the absence of a vibrant civil society and democratically committed elite, there is little in the way of their consolidation of power. Historically, the surest barrier against this has been a strong civil society, including an assertive labour movement allied with other popular social forces. In the continuing absence of this, it would be a brave person who was convinced of the triumph of democracy in Russia in the new millennium.

Ultimately this question will have to await the departure of Yeltsin from the political scene. If he is replaced by someone who is committed to the position (adopted by many after the 1993 adoption of the Constitution) that what was needed was a weakening of the institution of President and a strengthening of Parliament, then the strength of the personalist presidential system may be tempered. A better balance between presidency and parliament would go some way to strengthening democracy in Russia. But fundamental to achievement of this remains the development of a mature civil society, something which in turn depends in part upon the ending of the economic crisis conditions which have been afflicting Russian society. Also central to this is the curbing of the new bourgeoisie and the reining in of the power at least elements of this have been able to achieve. This involves both political will and state capacity, and up until now, both have been lacking. The setting in place of the conditions which would facilitate the consolidation of Russian democracy is a large task, but unless it is done the likelihood of the emergence of a democratic polity from the process of Soviet/Russian transformation is unlikely.

York, Verso, 1995). For an interpretation of the Yeltsin regime drawing on these and related concepts, see Roger D. Markwick, 'What Kind of a State is the Russian State—If There Is One?', *The Journal of Communist Studies and Transition Politics*, 15: 4 (Dec. 1999), 111–30.

# BIBLIOGRAPHY

## Newspapers

*Argumenty i fakty*
*Current Digest of the Soviet Press*
*Current Digest of the Post-Soviet Press*
*The Financial Times*
*Foreign Broadcast Information Service*
*Green Left Weekly*
*The Guardian Weekly*
*The Independent* (UK)
*Izvestiia*
*Izvestiia Ts.K. KPSS*
*Kommersant*
*Kommersant Den'gi*
*Kommersant Vlast'*
*Komsomol'skaia Pravda*
*Moskovskie novosti*
*The Moscow Times*
*Nezavisimaia gazeta*
*Obshchaia gazeta*
*Partiinaia zhizn'*
*Pravda*
*Reuters*
*Rossiiskaia gazeta*
*Russian and Euro-Asian Bulletin*
*Segodnia*
*Sovetskaia Kul'tura*
*Sovetskaia Rossiia*
*Vedomosti Verkhovnogo Soveta Soiuza Sovetskikh Sotsialisticheskikh Respublik*

## Books and Articles

ALAVI, HAMZA, 'State and Class Under Peripheral Capitalism', in Hamza Alavi and
  Teodor Shanin (eds.) *Introduction to the Sociology of 'Developing Societies'* (London,
  Macmillan, 1982), 289–307.

ALMOND, GABRIEL A. and COLEMAN, JAMES S., *The Politics of the Developing Areas* (Princeton, Princeton University Press, 1960).

ALPATOV, VLADIMIR, 'Vozmozhen li Rossiiskii "Pakt Monkloa" ', *Svobodnaia mysl'* 13, (Sept. 1993), 67–76.

APTER, DAVID E., *The Politics of Modernization* (Chicago, University of Chicago Press, 1965).

ASLUND, ANDERS, 'Gorbachev's Economic Advisors', *Soviet Economy* 3: 3 (1987), 246–69.

—— *Gorbachev's Struggle for Economic Reform* (Ithaca, Cornell University Press, 1987).

BATTLE, JOHN M., 'Uskorenie, Glasnost and Perestroika: The Pattern of Reform under Gorbachev', *Soviet Studies*, 40: 3 (July 1988), 367–84.

BELIN LAURA, and ORTTUNG, ROBERT W., 'Electing a Fragile Political Stability', *Transition*, 3: 2 (7 Feb. 1997), 67–70.

BEREZOVSKY, VLADIMIR, 'Vladimir Zhirinovsky kak phenomenon Rossiisskoi politiki', *Svobodnaia mysl'*, 4 (Mar. 1994), 96–109.

—— 'Dva politicheskikh lagereia federal'noi elity Rossii', *Svobodnaia mysl'*, 9 (June 1994), 67–86.

—— and CHERVIAKOV, VLADIMIR, 'Osennii politicheskii krizis. Sentiabr'skaia i oktiabr'skaia fazy', *Svobodnaia mysl'*, 15 (Oct. 1993), 12–42.

BIALER, SEWERYN, *The Soviet Paradox: External Expansion, Internal Decline* (New York, Alfred A. Knopf, 1987).

BIM, ALEKSANDR, 'Privatizatsiia v Rossii: problemy blizhaishei perspektivy', *Svobodnaia mysl'*, 4 (Mar. 1993), 70–81.

BLASI, JOSEPH R., KROUMOVA, MAYA and KRUSE, DOUGLAS, *Kremlin Capitalism: Privatizing the Russian Economy* (Ithaca, Cornell University Press, 1997).

BRAGINA, ELENA, 'Malyi biznes: sostoianie i problemy', *Svobodnaia mysl'*, 11 (1995), 86–94.

BROVKIN, VLADIMIR, 'Revolution from Below: Informal Political Associations in Russia 1988–1989', *Soviet Studies*, 42: 2 (Apr. 1990), 233–57.

BROWN, ARCHIE, 'Andropov: Discipline and Reform?', *Problems of Communism*, 32: 1 (Jan.–Feb. 1983), 18–24.

—— 'The October Crisis of 1993: Context and Implications', *Post-Soviet Affairs*, 9: 3 (1993), 183–95.

—— *The Gorbachev Factor* (Oxford, Oxford University Press, 1996).

BRUDNY, YITZHAK M., 'Ruslan Khasbulatov, Aleksandr Rutskoi, and Intraelite Conflict in Postcommunist Russia, 1991–1994', in Timothy J. Colton and Robert C. Tucker (eds.), *Patterns in Post-Soviet Leadership* (Boulder, Westview, 1995), 75–101.

BUNCE, VALERIE, 'The Political Economy of the Brezhnev Era: The Rise and Fall of Corporatism', *British Journal of Political Science*, 13: 2 (1983), 129–58.

—— 'Should Transitologists be Grounded?', *Slavic Review*, 54: 1 (Spring 1995), 111–27.

—— 'Paper Curtains and Paper Tigers', *Slavic Review*, 54: 4 (Winter 1995), 979–87.

BURAWOY, MICHAEL and KROTOV, PAVEL, 'The Soviet Transition from Socialism to Capitalism: Worker Control and Economic Bargaining in the Wood Industry', *American Sociological Review*, 75 (1992), 16–38.

BURLATSKY, FEDOR, 'Yeltsin: A Turning Point', *Transition*, 1: 3 (15 Mar. 1995), 8–9.

BUSYGINA, IRINA, 'Predstaviteli prezidenta', *Svobodnaia mysl'*, 4 (1996), 52–61.

BUZGALIN, ALEXANDER and KOLGANOV, ANDREI, *Bloody October in Moscow: Political Repression in the Name of Reform*, trans. Renfrey Clarke, (New York, Monthly Review Press, 1994).

—— 'Russia: The Rout of the Neo-Liberals', *New Left Review*, 215 (Jan.–Feb. 1996), 129–36.

CHEBANOVA, A., 'Rossiia v 1996 godu: ekonomicheskii pod'em eshche daleko', *Svobodnaia mysl'*, 11 (1996), 59–74.

CHIESA, GIULETTO, 'The 28th Congress of the CPSU', *Problems of Communism*, 39: 4 (July–Aug. 1990), 24–38.

—— with NORTHROP, DOUGLAS TAYLOR, *Transition to Democracy: Political Change in the Soviet Union, 1987–1991* (Hanover, University Press of New England, 1993).

CHINAYEVA, ELENA, 'A Kremlin Survivor: A Profile of Deputy Prime Minister Anatolii Chubais', *Transitions*, 1: 22 (1 Dec. 1995), 38, 39, 69.

CHRISTENSEN, PAUL T., 'Why Russia Lacks a Labor Movement', *Transition*, 4: 7 (Dec. 1997), 44–51.

CLARK, WILLIAM A., *Crime and Punishment in Soviet Officialdom: Combating Corruption in the Political Elite, 1965–1990* (Armonk, M. E. Sharpe Inc., 1993).

—— 'Presidential Prefects in the Russian Provinces: Yeltsin's Regional Cadres Policy', in Graeme Gill (ed.), *Elites and Leadership in Russian Politics* (London, Macmillan, 1998), 24–51.

CLARKE, RENFREY, 'The Economic Foundations of Russian Politics', unpublished paper, n.d., 1–15.

—— 'Mexico City in Moscow', *Links*, 6 (Jan.–Apr. 1996), 65–77.

CLARKE, SIMON, 'Privatization and the Development of Capitalism in Russia', *New Left Review*, 196: 11–12 (1992), 3–27.

COHEN, STEPHEN F., 'The Friends and Foes of Change: Reformism and Conservatism in the Soviet Union', *Slavic Review*, 38: 2 (June 1979), 187–202.

COLTON, TIMOTHY, *The Dilemma of Reform in the Soviet Union* (Washington, Council on Foreign Relations, 1986).

CONQUEST, ROBERT, *The Nation Killers* (London, Macmillan, 1970).

COOK, LINDA J., 'Brezhnev's "Social Contract" and Gorbachev's Reforms', *Soviet Studies*, 44: 1 (1992), 37–56.

*Crisis in Mortality, Health and Nutrition*, Florence, UNICEF, Economies in Transition Studies. Regional Monitoring Report No. 2 (1994).

CRITCHLOW, JAMES, ' "Corruption", Nationalism and the Native Elites in Soviet Central Asia', *The Journal of Communist Studies*, 4: 2 (June 1988), 142–61.

DANIELS, ROBERT V., 'Stalin's Rise to Dictatorship, 1922–29', in Alexander Dallin and Alan F. Weston (eds.), *Politics in the Soviet Union: 7 Cases* (New York, Harcourt, Brace and World Inc., 1966), 1–38.

DAVIES, R. W., *Soviet History in the Gorbachev Revolution* (Bloomington, Indiana University Press, 1989).

—— *Soviet History in the Yeltsin Era* (London, Macmillan, 1997).

DERLETH, J. WILLIAM, 'The Evolution of the Russian Polity: The Case of the Security Council', *Communist and Post-Communist Studies*, 29: 1 (1996), 43–58.

DEUDNEY, DANIEL and IKENBERRY, G. JOHN, 'Soviet Reform and the End of the Cold War: Explaining Large-scale Historical Change', *Review of International Studies*, 17 (1991), 225–50.

—— 'The International Sources of Soviet Change', *International Security*, 16: 3 (Winter 1991/2), 74–118.

DEVLIN, JUDITH, *The Rise of the Russian Democrats: The Causes and Consequences of the Elite Revolution* (Aldershot, Edward Elgar, 1995).

DIAMOND, LARRY, 'Economic Development and Democracy Reconsidered', *American Behavioral Scientist*, 35: 4/5 (Mar./June 1992), 450–99.

DILIGENSKY, GERMAN, 'Chto my zhnaem o demokratii i grazhdanskoi obshchestve?', *Pro et Contra*, 2: 4 (Autumn 1997), 5–22.

DING, X. L., 'Institutional Amphibiousness and the Transition from Communism: The Case of China', *British Journal of Political Science*, 24: 3 (1994), 293–318.

DUNLOP, JOHN B., *The Rise of Russia and the Fall of the Soviet Empire* (Princeton, Princeton University Press, 1993).

FILTZER, DONALD, *Soviet Workers and the Collapse of Perestroika: The Soviet Labour Process and Gorbachev's Reforms 1985–1991* (Cambridge, Cambridge University Press, 1994).

FISH, M. STEVEN, *Democracy from Scratch: Opposition and Regime in the New Russian Revolution* (Princeton, Princeton University Press, 1995).

FORTESCUE, STEPHEN, 'Privatisation of Russian Industry', *Australian Journal of Political Science*, 29: 1 (Mar. 1994), 135–53.

—— 'Privatisation, Corporate Governance and Enterprise Performance in Russia', *Russian and Euro-Asian Bulletin*, 7: 5 (May 1998), 1–10.

FRIEDGUT, THEODORE and SIEGELBAUM, LEWIS, 'Perestroika from Below: The Soviet Miners' Strike and its Aftermath', *New Left Review*, 181 (1990), 5–32.

FRYE, TIMOTHY, 'A Politics of Institutional Choice: Post-Communist Presidencies', *Comparative Political Studies*, 30: 5 (Oct. 1997), 523–52.

GAIDAR, YEGOR, *Gosudarstvo i evoliutsiia* (Moscow, Evraziia, 1995).

GILL, GRAEME, 'Institutionalisation and Revolution: Rules and the Soviet Political System', *Soviet Studies*, 37: 2 (Apr. 1985), 212–26.

—— 'Khrushchev and Systemic Development', in Martin McCauley (ed.), *Khrushchev and Khrushchevism* (London, Macmillan, 1987).

—— *The Origins of the Stalinist Political System* (Cambridge, Cambridge University Press, 1990).

—— *The Collapse of a Single-Party System: The Disintegration of the Communist Party of the Soviet Union* (Cambridge, Cambridge University Press, 1994).

—— 'Liberalization and Democratization in the Soviet Union and Russia', *Democratization*, 2: 3 (Autumn 1995), 313–36.

—— 'Russian State-Building and the Problems of Geopolitics', *Archives europeennes de sociologie*, 37: 1 (1996), 77–103.

—— 'Democratization, the Bourgeoisie and Russia', *Government and Opposition*, 33: 3 (Summer 1998), 307–29.

—— *The Dynamics of Democratization: Elites, Civil Society and the Transition Process* (London, Macmillan, 2000).

—— and PITTY, RODERIC, *Power in the Party: The Organization of Power and Central–Republican Relations in the CPSU* (London, Macmillan, 1997).

GLEISNER, JEFF, 'The Lessons of March: The Apparatus Fights Back', *Détente*, 15 (1989), 19–24.

GOODING, JOHN, 'Gorbachev and Democracy', *Soviet Studies*, 42: 2 (Apr. 1990), 195–231.

—— 'The XXVIII Congress of the CPSU in Perspective', *Soviet Studies*, 43: 2 (1991), 237–54.

GORBACHEV, MIKHAIL S., *Izbrannye rechi i stat'i*, II (Moscow, Politizdat, 1987).

—— *Perestroika i novoe myshlenie dlia nashei strany i vsego mira* (Moscow, Politizdat, 1987).

—— *Avgustovskii putch. Prichiny i sledstviia* (Moscow, Novosti, 1991).

—— *Memoirs* (London, Doubleday, 1996).

'Gorbachev and the Coup: An Exchange', *New York Review of Books*, 26 June 1997, 67–8.

GORKOV, M. G., *et al.* (eds.), *Ot Yeltsina k . . . Yeltsinu: prezidentskaiia gonka–96* (Moscow, Terra, 1997).

GOWAN, PETER, 'Neo-Liberal Theory and Practice for Eastern Europe', *New Left Review*, 213 (Sept.–Oct. 1995), 3–60.

GRACHEV, ANDREI S., *Final Days: The Inside Story of the Collapse of the Soviet Union* (Boulder, Harper-Collins, 1995).

GURKOV, IGOR, *Popular Response to Russian Privatization: Surveys in Enterprises*, Centre for the Study of Public Policy, University of Strathclyde, Studies in Public Policy Number 245 (1995).

HAHN, GORDON M., 'The First Reorganisation of the CPSU Central Committee *Apparat* under *Perestroika*', *Europe–Asia Studies*, 49: 2 (Mar. 1997), 281–302.

HAHN, JEFFREY, 'An Experiment in Competition: The 1987 Elections to the Local Soviets', *Slavic Review*, 47: 2 (Fall 1988), 434–47.

HANDELMAN, STEPHEN, *Comrade Criminal: Russia's New Mafiya* (New Haven, Yale University Press, 1985).

HAUSLOHNER, PETER, 'Gorbachev's Social Contract', *Soviet Economy*, 3: 1 (1987), 54–89.

HAUSNER, JERZY, JESSOP, BOB, and NIELSEN, KLAUS (eds.), *Strategic Choice and Path-Dependency in Post-Socialism. Institutional Dynamics in the Transformation Process* (Aldershot, Edward Elgar, 1995).

HELLMAN, JOEL S., 'Bureaucrats vs Markets? Rethinking the Bureaucratic Response to Market Reform in Centrally Planned Economies', in Susan Gross Solomon (ed.), *Beyond Sovietology: Essays in Politics and History* (Armonk, M. E. Sharpe Inc., 1993), 53–93.

HILL, RONALD J., 'The Twenty-eighth CPSU Congress', *The Journal of Communist Studies*, 7: 1 (Mar. 1991), 95–105.

HOLMES, LESLIE, *The End of Communist Power: Anti-Corruption Campaigns and Legitimation Crisis* (Melbourne, Melbourne University Press, 1993).

HOSKING, GEOFFREY, *The Awakening of the Soviet Union* (London, Heinemann, 1990).

—— AVES, JONATHAN and DUNCAN, PETER J. S., *The Road to Post-Communism. Independent Political Movements in the Soviet Union 1985–1991* (London, Pinter, 1992).

HOUGH, JERRY F., *Russia and the West: Gorbachev and the Politics of Reform* (New York, Simon and Schuster, 1988).

—— *Democratization and Revolution in the USSR 1985–1991* (Washington, Brookings, 1997).

HUNTINGTON, SAMUEL P., *The Third Wave: Democratization in the Late Twentieth Century* (Norman, University of Oklahoma Press, 1991).

—— 'Will More Countries Become Democratic?', *Political Science Quarterly*, 99: 2 (1984), 193–218.

HUSKEY, EUGENE, 'The State-Legal Administration and the Politics of Redundancy', *Post-Soviet Affairs*, 11: 2 (1995), 115–43.

'ICFTU Campaign on the Non-Payment of Wages in Russia', Campaign Newsletter, 1 (July/Aug. 1997).

INOZEMSTEV, VLADIMIR, 'Na pereput'e', *Svobodnaia mysl'*, 13 (Sept. 1992), 20–6.

JOHNSON, SIMON and KROLL, HEIDI, 'Managerial Strategies for Spontaneous Privatisation', *Soviet Economy*, 7: 4 (1991), 281–316.

KAGARLITSKY, BORIS, 'Chto c nami proiskhodit, ili uroki Basaeva', *Svobodnaia mysl'*, 8 (Aug. 1995), 18–25.

—— 'The Russian Parliamentary Elections: Results and Prospects', *New Left Review*, 215 (Jan.–Feb. 1996), 117–28.

—— 'O prichinakh porazheniia levykh', *Svobodnaia mysl'*, 9 (1996), 3–7.

KARL, TERRY LYNN, 'Dilemmas of Democratization in Latin America', *Comparative Politics*, 23: 1 (Oct. 1990), 1–21.

—— and SCHMITTER, PHILIPPE C., 'From an Iron Curtain to a Paper Curtain: Grounding Transitologists or Students of Postcommunism?', *Slavic Review*, 54: 4 (Winter 1995), 965–78.

KEANE, JOHN, *Democracy and Civil Society* (New York, Verso, 1988).

KELLEY, DONALD R., 'Gorbachev's Democratic Revolution: Coping with Pluralism in Soviet and Post-Soviet Politics', in Gary D. Wekkin, Donald E. Whistler, Michael A. Kelley, and Michael A. Maggiotto (eds.), *Building Democracy in One-Party Systems. Theoretical Problems and Cross-Nation Experiences* (Westport, Praeger, 1993), 169–89.

KENNEDY, PAUL, 'What Gorbachev Is Up Against', *The Atlantic Monthly* (June 1987), 29–43.

KHENKIN, SERGEI, ' "Partiia vlasti": rossiiskii variant', *Pro et Contra*, 1: 1 (Autumn 1996), 32–45.

KHOROS, V. G. (ed.), *Avtoritarizm i demokratiia v razvivaiushchikhsia stranakh* (Moscow, Nauka, 1996).

KIRKOW, PETER, 'Regional Warlordism in Russia: The Case of Primorskii Krai', *Europe–Asia Studies*, 47: 6 (1995), 923–47.

KITCHING, GAVIN, 'The Development of Agrarian Capitalism in Russia 1991–97: A Theoretical Outline', unpublished paper, Sydney, Dec. 1997, pp. 1–16.

KLOPYZHNIKOVA, NATALIIA, 'Nastroeniia krest'ianstva i agrarnoe reformirovanie', *Svobodnaia mysl'*, 5 (1995), 15–26.

KOL'EV, A., *Miatezh nomenklatury: Moskva 1990–93* (Moscow, Intellekt, 1995), 2nd corrected edn.

KORZHAKOV, ALEKSANDR, *Boris Yeltsin: Ot rassveta do zakata* (Moscow, Interbuk, 1997).

KOTZ, DAVID M. with WEIR, FRED, *Revolution from Above: The Demise of the Soviet System* (London and New York, Routledge, 1997).

KRASNOV, VALERII, 'Ot vyborov–93 k vyboram–95', *Svobodnaia mysl'*, 10 (1995), 12–40.

KRYSHTANOVSKAIA, OLGA and WHITE, STEPHEN, 'From Soviet *Nomenklatura* to Russian Elite', *Europe–Asia Studies*, 48: 5 (July 1996), 711–33.

*Kto est' chto. Politicheskaia Moskva 1993* (Moscow, Satallakhu, 1993).

*Kto est Kto v Rossii: 1997 goda* (Moscow, Olymp, 1997).

KULLBERG, JUDITH S., 'The Ideological Roots of Elite Political Conflict in Post-Soviet Russia', *Europe–Asia Studies*, 46: 6 (Sept. 1994), 929–53.

LANE, DAVID, *The Rise and Fall of State Socialism: Industrial Society and the Socialist State* (Oxford, Polity, 1996).

LAPINA, N., *Rossiiskie ekonomicheskie elity i modeli natsional'nogo razvitiia* (Moscow, Russian Academy of Sciences, 1997).

LEDENEVA, ALENA, 'Neformal'naia sfera i blat: grazhdanskoe obshchestvo ili (post)sovetskaiia korporativnost'?', *Pro et Contra*, 2: 4 (Autumn 1997), 113–24.

LENTINI, PETER, 'Reforming the Electoral System: The 1989 Elections to the USSR Congress of People's Deputies', *The Journal of Communist Studies*, 7: 1 (Mar. 1991), 69–94.

LESTER, JEREMY, *Modern Tsars and Princes: The Struggle for Hegemony in Russia* (London, New York, Verso, 1995).

—— 'Overdosing on Nationalism: Gennadii Zyuganov and the Communist Party of the Russian Federation', *New Left Review*, 221 (Jan.–Feb. 1997), 34–53.

LEWIN, MOSHE, *Political Undercurrents in Soviet Economic Debates: From Bukharin to the Modern Reformers* (London, Pluto Press, 1975).

—— *The Gorbachev Phenomenon: A Historical Interpretation* (Berkeley, University of California Press, 1989).

LIGACHEV, E. K., *Izbrannye rechi i stat'i* (Moscow, Politizdat, 1989).

LIGACHEV, YEGOR, *Inside Gorbachev's Kremlin: The Memoirs of Yegor Ligachev* (Boulder, Westview Press, 1996).

LINZ, JUAN J. and VALENZUELA, ARTURO, *The Failure of Presidential Democracy* (Baltimore, Johns Hopkins University Press, 1994).

LIPSET, SEYMOUR MARTIN, 'Some Social Requisites of Democracy: Economic Development and Political Legitimacy', *American Political Science Review*, 53: 1 (Mar. 1959), 69–105.

LIPSET, SEYMOUR MARTIN, SOONG, KYOUNG-RYUNG, and TORRES, JOHN CHARLES, 'A Comparative Analysis of the Social Requisites of Democracy', *International Social Science Journal*, 136 (May 1993), 155–75.

LOMAX, BILL, 'From Death to Resurrection: The Metamorphosis of Power in Eastern Europe', *Critique*, 25 (1993), 47–84.

LOWENTHAL, RICHARD, 'Development vs Utopia in Communist Policy', in Chalmers Johnson (ed.), *Change in Communist Systems* (Stanford, Stanford University Press, 1970), 35–116.

LUDLAM, JANINE, 'Reform and the Redefinition of the Social Contract Under Gorbachev', *World Politics*, 43: 2 (Jan. 1991), 284–312.

LUKACS, GEORG, 'Reflections on the Cult of Stalin', *Survey*, 47 (Apr. 1963), 105–11.

McALLISTER, IAN and WHITE, STEPHEN, 'Democracy, Political Parties and Party Formation in Postcommunist Russia', *Party Politics*, 1: 1 (1995), 49–72.

McFAUL, MICHAEL and MARKOV, SERGEI, *The Troubled Birth of Russian Democracy: Parties, Personalities and Programs* (Stanford, Hoover Institution Press, 1993).

—— 'State Power, Institutional Change, and the Politics of Privatization in Russia', *World Politics* 47: 2 (Jan. 1995), 210–43.

MALIUTIN, M. V., 'Neformaly v perestroike: opyt i perspektivy', Yu. Afanas'ev (ed.), *Inogo ne dano* (Progress, Moscow, 1988).

MANDEL, DAVID, 'The Russian Working Class and the Labour Movement in Year Four of "Shock Therapy" ', in David Mandel (ed.), *The Former 'State Socialist' World: Views from the Left* (Montreal/New York/London: Black Rose,1996), 1–74.

MANN, MICHAEL, 'The Autonomous Power of the State: Its Origins, Mechanisms and Results', in John A. Hall (ed.), *States in History* (Oxford, Blackwell, 1986), 109–36.

MARKWICK, ROGER D., 'A Discipline in Transition?: From Sovietology to "Transitology" ', *The Journal of Communist Studies and Transition Politics*, 12: 3 (Sept. 1996), 255–76.

—— 'An Uncivil Society: Moscow in Political Change', in Vladimir Tikhomirov (ed.), *In Search of Identity: Five Years Since the Fall of the Soviet Union* (Melbourne, University of Melbourne, Centre for Russian and Euro-Asian Studies, 1996), 40–9.

—— 'What Kind of a State Is the Russian State—If There Is One?', *The Journal of Communist Studies and Transition Politics*, 15: 4 (Dec. 1999), 111–30.

MARSH, ROBERT M., 'Authoritarian and Democratic Transitions in National Political Systems', *International Journal of Comparative Sociology*, 32: 3–4 (1991), 219–32.

MATLOCK Jr, JACK, 'The Struggle for the Kremlin', *New York Review of Books*, 8 Aug. 1996, 28–34.

—— 'Gorbachev: Lingering Mysteries', *New York Review of Books*, 19 Dec. 1996, 34–9.

—— 'Success Story', *New York Review of Books*, 25 Sept. 1997, pp. 67–74.

MAU, VLADIMIR, 'Politicheskaia ekonomicheskaia Rossiiskikh reform: opyt 1993 goda', *Svobodnaia mysl'*, 1 (Jan 1994), 34–46.

MEDVEDEV, ROI, *Chubais i vaucher: Iz istorii rossiiskoi privatizatsii* (Moscow, Impeto, 1997).

—— 'Novyi klass Rossiiskogo obshchestva', *Svobodnaia mysl'*, 8 (Aug. 1998), 58–71.

MEDVEDEV, VADIM, 'Otvedena li ygroza katastrofi', *Svobodnaia mysl'*, 7 (1996), 74–85.

MEDVEDEV, ZHORES, *Andropov: His Life and Death* (Oxford, Blackwell, 1983).

MICKIEWICZ, ELLEN, 'Mobilization and Reform: Political Communication Policy Under Gorbachev', *PS: Political Science and Politics*, 19: 2 (June 1989), 199–207.

MILIBAND, RALPH, *Marxism and Politics* (Oxford, Oxford University Press, 1977).

MILLER, JOHN, *Mikhail Gorbachev and the End of Soviet Power* (London, Macmillan, 1993).

MOLTZ, JAMES CLAY, 'Divergent Learning and the Failed Politics of Soviet Economic Reform', *World Politics*, 45: 2 (Jan. 1993), 301–25.

MONTGOMERY, KATHLEEN and REMINGTON, THOMAS F., 'Regime Transition and the 1990 Soviet Republican Elections', *Journal of Communist Studies and Transition Politics*, 10: 1 (Mar. 1994), 55–79.

MOORE, MICK, 'Democracy and Development in Cross-National Perspective: A New Look at the Statistics', *Democratization*, 2: 2 (Summer 1995), 1–19.

MORVANT, PENNY, and RUTLAND, PETER, 'Russian Workers Face the Market', *Transition* 2: 13 (28 June 1996), 6–11.

MOSES, JOEL C., 'Democratic Reform in the Gorbachev Era: Dimensions of Reform in the Soviet Union, 1986–1989', *Russian Review*, 48: 3 (July 1989), 235–69.

MOSES, JONATHAN W., 'The *Eighteenth Brumaire* of Boris Yeltsin', *Security Dialogue*, 25: 3 (1994), 335–47.

MUIZNIEKS, NILS R., 'The Influence of the Baltic Popular Movements on the Process of Soviet Disintegration', *Europe–Asia Studies*, 47: 1 (1995), 3–25.

NEKRICH, ALEXANDER M., *The Punished Peoples* (New York, Norton, 1978).

NOVE, ALEC, *The Soviet Economic System* (London, Allen & Unwin, 1980).

—— *Glasnost in Action. Cultural Renaissance in Russia* (Boston, Unwin Hyman, 1989).

'Novosibirsk Report, The', *Survey*, 28: 1 (Spring 1984), 88–108.

O'DONNELL, GUILLERMO, SCHMITTER, PHILIPPE C., and WHITEHEAD, LAURENCE (eds.), *Transitions from Authoritarian Rule: Prospects for Democracy* (Baltimore, Johns Hopkins University Press, 1986).

*O merakh po ozdorovleniiu ekonomiki, etapakh ekonomicheskoi reformy i printsipal'nykh podkhodakh k razrabotke trinadtsatogo piatiletnogo plana* (Moscow, 1990).

Open Media Research Institute, *Annual Survey 1995* (Armonk, M. E. Sharpe Inc., 1996).

ORTTUNG, ROBERT W., 'The Russian Right and the Dilemmas of Party Organisation', *Soviet Studies*, 44: 3 (1992), 445–78.

—— 'Chechnya: A Painful Price', *Transition*, 1: 3 (15 Mar. 1995), 3–7.

—— 'Yeltsin and the Spin Doctors', *Transition*, 1: 8 (26 May 1995), 11–14.

—— and PARRISH, SCOTT, 'From Confrontation to Cooperation in Russia', *Transition* 2: 25 (13 Dec. 1996), 16–20.

OSTAPCHUK, ANNA, 'Alkhimiia elity', *Pro et Contra*, 1: 1 (Autumn 1996), 104–11.

OVERLAND, JODY and SPAGAT, MICHAEL, 'Human Capital and Russia's Economic Transformation', *Transition*, 2: 13 (28 June 1996), 12–15.

PAPPE, YAKOV, 'Otraslevye lobbi v pravitel'stve Rossii (1992–1996)', *Pro et Contra*, 1: 1 (Autumn 1996), 61–78.

PEREGUDOV, SERGEI and SEMENENKO, IRINA, 'Lobbying Business Interests in Russia', *Democratization*, 3: 2 (1996), 115–39.

*Perestroika raboty partii—vazneishaia kliuchevaia zadacha dnia* (Moscow, Politizdat, 1989).

*Pervyi s'ezd narodnykh deputatov SSSR. Stenograficheskii otchet*, (I, zd. Verkhovnogo soveta SSSR Moscow, 1989).

POPOV, GAVRIIL, 'Dangers of Democracy', *New York Review of Books*, 16 Aug. 1990, 27–8.

PRZEWORSKI, ADAM, 'Democracy as a Contingent Outcome of Conflicts', in Jon Elster and Rune Slagstad (eds.), *Constitutionalism and Democracy* (Cambridge, Cambridge University Press, 1988), 59–80.

—— *Democracy and the Market: Political and Economic Reforms in Eastern Europe and Latin America* (Cambridge, Cambridge University Press, 1991).

RADAEV, V. V., (ed.), *Stanovlenie novogo Rossiiskogo predprinimatel'stva (Sotsiologicheskii aspekt)* (Moscow, Institute of Economics, Russian Academy of Sciences, 1993).

RAHR, ALEXANDER, 'The CPSU in the 1980s: Changes in the Party Apparatus', *Journal of Communist Studies*, 7: 2 (June 1991), 161–9.

—— 'The Roots of the Power Struggle', *RFE/RL Research Report*, 2: 20 (14 May 1993), 9–15.

REDDAWAY, PETER, 'Resisting Gorbachev', *New York Review of Books*, 18 Aug. 1988, 36–41.

REES, E. A. (ed.), *The Soviet Communist Party in Disarray: The XXVIII Congress of the Communist Party of the Soviet Union* (London, Macmillan, 1992).

REMINGTON, THOMAS, 'A Socialist Pluralism of Opinions: Glasnost and Policy-Making Under Gorbachev', *The Russian Review*, 48: 3 (July 1989), 271–304.

REMNICK, DAVID, 'The War for the Kremlin', *New Yorker*, 22 July 1996, 40–57.

—— 'How Russia is Ruled', *New York Review of Books*, 9 Apr. 1998, 10–15.

RIGBY, T. H., 'Was Stalin a Disloyal Patron?', *Soviet Studies*, 38: 3 (July 1986), 311–24.

ROBINSON, NEIL, 'Parliamentary Politics under Gorbachev: Opposition and the Failure of Socialist Pluralism', *Journal of Communist Studies*, 9: 1 (Mar. 1993), 91–108.

RUTLAND, PETER, 'The Search for Stability: Ideology, Discipline, and the Cohesion of the Soviet Elite', *Studies in Comparative Communism*, 24: 1 (Mar. 1991), 25–57.

—— 'Privatisation in Russia: One Step Forward: Two Steps Back?', *Europe–Asia Studies*, 46: 7 (1994), 1109–31.

RYZHKOV, NIKOLAI, *Perestroika: istoriia predatel'stv* (Moscow, Novosti, 1992).

SAKWA, RICHARD, *Gorbachev and His Reforms 1985–1990* (London, Philip Allan, 1990).

—— 'A Cleansing Storm: The August Coup and the Triumph of Perestroika', *Journal of Communist Studies*, 9: 1 (1993), 131–49.

—— *Russian Politics and Society*, 2nd edn. (London, Routledge, 1996).

SANDLE, MARK, 'The Final Word: The Draft Party Programme of July/August 1991', *Europe–Asia Studies*, 48: 7 (Nov. 1996), 1131–50.

SCHMITTER, PHILIPPE C. with KARL, TERRY LYNN, 'The Conceptual Travels of Transitologists and Consolidologists: How Far to the East Should They Attempt to Go?', *Slavic Review*, 53: 1 (Spring 1994), 173–85.

SEDAITIS, JUDITH B. and BUTTERFIELD, JIM, (eds.), *Perestroika from Below* (Boulder, Westview, 1991).

SELIUNIN, VASILII, 'Istoki', *Novyi Mir*, 5 (1988), 162–89.

SEREBRIANIKKOV, VLADIMIR, 'Armiia i politika', *Svobodnaia mysl'*, 2 (Jan. 1992), 64–73.

SHEVARDNADZE, EDUARD, *Moi vybor. V zashchitu demokratii i svobody* (Moscow, Novosti, 1991).

SIMIS, KONSTANTIN, 'Andropov's Anticorruption Campaign', *Washington Quarterly*, 6: 3 (Summer 1983), 111–21.

SOGRIN, V., *Politicheskaia istoriia sovremennoi Rossii 1985–1994: ot Gorbacheva do Yeltsina* (Moscow, Progress-akademiia, 1994).

'Sotsial'naia tsena ekonomicheskogo krizisa', *Svobodnaia mysl'*, 4 (1995), 3–15.

STALIN, J. V., 'Address Delivered in the Kremlin Palace to the Graduates from the Red Army Academies', 4 May 1935, in J. V. Stalin, *Problems of Leninism* (Peking, Foreign Languages Press, 1976).

STEELE, JONATHAN, *Eternal Russia: Yeltsin, Gorbachev and the Mirage of Democracy* (London and Boston, Faber & Faber, 1994).

—— 'Why Gorbachev Failed', *New Left Review*, 216: 3–4 (1996), 141–52.

STEPAN, ALFRED and SKACH, CINDY, 'Constitutional Frameworks and Democratic Consolidation: Parliamentarism vs Presidentialism', *World Politics*, 46: 1 (Oct. 1993), 1–22.

SUROVELL, JEFFREY, 'Gorbachev's Last Year: Leftist or Rightist?', *Europe–Asia Studies*, 46: 3 (1994), 465–87.

—— 'Ligachev and Soviet Politics', *Soviet Studies*, 43: 2 (1991), 355–74.

TAAGEPERA, REIN, 'Baltic Elections, February–April 1990', *Electoral Studies*, 9: 4 (Dec. 1990), 303–11.

TARASOV, ALEKSANDR, *Provokatsiia: versiia sobytii 3–4 oktiabriia 1993 g. v Moskve. Postskriptum iz 1994-go* (Moscow, 'Feniks', 1994).

TARSCHYS, DANIEL, 'The Success of a Failure: Gorbachev's Alcohol Policy, 1985–88', *Europe–Asia Studies*, 45: 1 (1993), 7–25.

TEAGUE, ELIZABETH, 'Yeltsin Disbands the Soviets', *RFE/RL Research Report*, 2: 43 (29 Oct. 1993), 1–5.

' "The Gorbachev Factor" An Exchange', *New York Review of Books*, 27 Mar. 1997, 48–9.

TIKHOMIROV, VLADIMIR, 'Capital Flight from Post-Soviet Russia', *Europe–Asia Studies*, 49: 4 (1997), 591–615.

TOLZ, VERA, *The USSR's Emerging Multiparty System* (New York, Praeger, 1990).

—— 'Problems in Building Democratic Institutions in Russia', *RFE/RL Research Report*, 3: 9 (4 Mar. 1994), 1–7.

—— 'The Civic Accord: Contributing to Russia's Stability?', *RFE/RL Research Report*, 3: 19 (13 May 1994), 1–5.

TOLZ, VERA, 'The Shifting Sands of Stabilisation', *Transition*, 1: 2 (15 Feb. 1995), 5–8.

TUCKER, ROBERT C., *Stalin in Power: The Revolution from Above, 1928–1941* (New York, W. W. Norton and Co., 1990).

UNGER, ARYEH L., 'The Travails of Intra-Party Democracy in the Soviet Union: The Elections to the 19th Conference of the CPSU', *Soviet Studies*, 43: 2 (1991), 329–54.

URBAN, JOAN BARTH and SOLOVEI, VALERII D., *Russia's Communists at the Crossroads* (Boulder, Westview, 1997).

URBAN, DZHOAN and VALERII SOLOVEI, 'Kommunisticheskoe dvizhenie v postsovet-skoi Rossii', *Svobodnaia mysl'*, 3 (Mar. 1997), 14–28.

URBAN, MIKE, 'Popular Fronts and Informals', *Détente* 14 (1989), 3–8.

URBAN, MICHAEL E., *More Power to the Soviets: The Democratic Revolution in the USSR* (Aldershot, Edward Elgar, 1990).

—— 'The Soviet Multi-party System: A Moscow Roundtable', *Russia and the World*, 18 (1990), 1–6.

—— 'Boris El'tsin, Democratic Russia and the Campaign for the Russian Presidency', *Soviet Studies*, 44: 2 (1992), 187–207.

—— with VYACHESLAV IGRUNOV and SERGEI MITROKHIN, *The Rebirth of Politics in Russia* (Cambridge, Cambridge University Press, 1997).

VARESE, FEDERICO, 'Is Sicily the Future of Russia? Private Protection and the rise of the Russian Mafia', *Archives europeenes de sociologie*, 35 (1994), 224–58.

VOLKOV, VADIM, 'Obshchestvennost': zabytaia praktika grazhdanskogo obshchestva', *Pro et Contra*, 2: 4 (Autumn 1997), 77–91.

VON BEYME, KLAUS, 'Economics and Politics in a Socialist Country: Gorbachev's New Concepts', *Government and Opposition*, 23: 2 (Spring 1988), 167–85.

WALKER, RACHEL, *Six Years That Shook the World: Perestroika the Impossible Project*, (Manchester, Manchester University Press, 1993).

WEDEL, JANINE R., 'Cliques, Clans and Aid to Russia', *Transitions*, 4: 2 (July 1997), 66–71.

WEGREN, STEPHEN K. and DURGIN, FRANK A., 'Why Agrarian Reform is Failing', *Transition*, 1: 19 (20 Oct. 1995), 50–4.

WEIGLE, MARCIA A., 'Political Participation and Party Formation in Russia, 1985–1992: Institutionalizing Democracy?', *Russian Review*, 53 (Apr. 1994), 240–70.

WEISS, LINDA and HOBSON, JOHN, *States and Economic Development: A Comparative Historical Analysis* (Oxford, Polity Press, 1995).

WHEATCROFT, STEPHEN, 'Unleashing the Energy of History, Mentioning the Unmentionable and Reconstructing Soviet Historical Awareness: Moscow 1987', *Australian Slavonic and East European Studies*, 1: 1 (1987), 85–132.

—— 'Steadying the Energy of History and Probing the Limits of Glasnost: Moscow July to Dec. 1987', *Australian Slavonic and East European Studies*, 1: 2 (1987), 57–114.

WHITE, ANNE, *Democratization in Russia under Gorbachev 1985–91: The Birth of a Voluntary Sector* (London and New York, Macmillan and St Martin's Press, 1999).

WHITE, STEPHEN, 'Economic Performance and Communist Legitimacy', *World Politics*, 38: 3 (Apr. 1986), 462–82.

—— *Gorbachev and After* (Cambridge, Cambridge University Press, 1991).

—— 'The Soviet Elections of 1989: From Acclamation to Limited Choice', *Coexistence*, 28: 4 (Dec. 1991), 513–39.

—— *After Gorbachev* (Cambridge, Cambridge University Press, 1993).

—— *Russia Goes Dry* (Cambridge, Cambridge University Press, 1996).

—— 'The Failure of CPSU Democratization', *The Slavonic and East European Review*, 75: 4 (Oct. 1997), 681–97.

—— 'Russia: Presidential Leadership under Yeltsin', in Ray Taras (ed.), *Postcommunist Presidents* (Cambridge, Cambridge University Press, 1997), 38–66.

—— GILL, GRAEME, and SLIDER, DARRELL, *The Politics of Transition: Shaping a Post-Soviet Future* (Cambridge, Cambridge University Press, 1993).

—— ROSE, RICHARD, and McALLISTER, IAN, *How Russia Votes* (Chatham, NJ, Chatham House Publishers, 1997).

WILLERTON, JOHN P. 'Post-Soviet Clientelist Norms at Russian Federal Level', in Graeme Gill (ed.), *Elites and Leadership in Russian Politics* (London, Macmillan, 1998), 52–80.

—— and SHULUS, ALEKSEI A., 'Constructing a New Political Process: The Hegemonic Presidency and the Legislature', *John Marshall Law Review*, 27 (1995), 787–823.

*XXVII s'ezd kommunisticheskoi partii sovetskogo soiuza 25 fevralia–6 marta 1986 goda. Stenograficheskii otchet* (Moscow, Politizdat, 1986).

YAKOVLEV, ALEKSANDR, *Muki Prochteniia Bytiia. Perestroika: nadezhdy i real'nosti* (Moscow, Novosti, 1991).

—— *Predislovie, Obval, Posleslovie* (Moscow, Novosti, 1992).

YASMAN, VIKTOR, 'Security Services Reorganized: All Power to the Russian President?', *RFE/RL Research Report*, 6 (11 Feb. 1994), 7–14.

YEGOROV, VLADIMIR K., *Out of a Dead End into the Unknown* (Chicago, edition q, 1993).

YELTSIN, BORIS, *Ispoved' na zadannuiu temu* (Moscow, Novyi stil', 1990).

—— *The View from the Kremlin*, trans. Catherine A. Fitzpatrick (New York, Harper Collins, 1994).

YOUNG, CHRISTOPHER, 'The Strategy of Political Liberalization: A Comparative View of Gorbachev's Reforms', *World Politics*, 45: 1 (Oct. 1992), 47–65.

ZADORNOV, MIKHAIL, 'Sostoianie ekonomiki i blizhaishie perspektivy', *Svobodnaia mysl'*, 6 (Apr. 1992), 56–64.

ZASLAVSKAIA, TAT'IANA, *Rossiiskoe obshchestvo na sotsial'nom izlome: vzgliad iznutri* (Moscow, VTsIOM/MVSSEN, 1997).

ZASURSKY, IVAN, 'Politika, dengi i pressa v sovremennoi Rossii', *Svobodnaia mysl'*, 10 (1996), 3–18.

ZHANG, BAOHUI, 'Corporatism, Totalitarianism, and Transitions to Democracy', *Comparative Political Studies*, 27: 1 (Apr. 1994), 108–36.

ZUDIN, ALEKSEI, 'Biznes i politika v prezidentskoi kampanii 1996 goda', *Pro et Contra*, 1: 1 (Autumn 1996), 46–60.

# INDEX

Abramovich, Roman 198, 203
'acceleration', *see* uskorenie
Afanas'ev, Yury 68, 129
Afghanistan 46
Aganbegyan, Abel 100
Agrarian Party 172, 182, 235, 239, 242, 244
  and 1993 elections 168–9
  and 1995 elections 188–9
agriculture 17, 98, 172
  privatization 238–9
  production plummets 237–8
Aksenenko, Nikolai 203
Alksnis, Viktor 102
Alma Ata riots 39
Andreeva letter 49
Andropov, Yury 24–6
anti-alcohol campaign 32
anti-communism 191, 193, 243
anti-Semitism 45
Armenia 48, 57, 59, 73, 80, 81, 105, 106, 109
army, *see* military
authoritarianism 3, 5–6, 126–7, 250
Azerbaijan 48, 57, 80, 81, 109

Baltics 45, 64, 65, 94, 99, 103–4, 106, 108, 110
  and CPSU 86
  and popular fronts 58–9, 71–2, 114
  republican elections 81
  and sovereignty 71–2, 74–5, 77, 80–3, 109, 116
banks 97, 182, 187, 190, 195–6, 197, 199–200, 219, 222
  and August 1998 crisis 201–2
  Central Bank 161, 162 n., 164, 167, 172, 199, 200, 202, 207
  and 'loans for shares' 216, 218
  origins of 208–9, 212
Barranikov, Viktor 158 n., 163, 164
Barsukov, Mikhail 172, 178–9, 186,189, 192
Baturin, Yury 181

Belorussia 81, 109, 193
Belovezha Accords 110, 129, 190
Berezovsky, Boris 198, 202, 213, 216, 219
  and presidential elections 190, 222
  and Security Council 196–7
'Black Tuesday' 183, 217
*blat* (personal contacts) 213–14, 223–5
Boiko, Oleg 187, 223
Bonapartism 124, 137, 163–4, 175, 226, 257–8
Borodin, Pavel 179
bourgeoisie 23, 165, 166, 177, 195–6, 253, 255
  conflict within 217–18, 222, 224, 257
  and crime 212, 214
  and democracy 225, 257, 258
  and parties 244, 248–9
  and presidential election 221–2
  profile of 214–17
  rentier 214, 216
  rise of 205–26
  and social clubs 223–5
  and state 182, 189, 194, 215, 218–26, 257
Brezhnev, Leonid 15–20, 22, 24–6, 43,
Bukharin, Nikolai 48
Burbulis, Gennady 127, 128, 129, 130, 143, 145, 150, 151 n., 155, 178
Burlatsky, Fedor 184
business/businessmen, *see* bourgeoisie

Caucasus 80, 101, 106, 203
censorship 34–5
Central Asia 80, 81, 116
Chechnya 128, 142, 173, 174, 175, 178, 182–3, 191, 193, 195, 250
  Budennovsk crisis 186
  invasion of 184
Chernenko, Konstantin 25, 29
Chernobyl nuclear accident 34
Chernomyrdin, Viktor 147, 155, 178 n., 199, 220, 223, 246

Chernomyrdin, Viktor (*cont.*):
  and Chechnya 184, 185 n., 186
  dismissed 197
  and energy sector 207, 217–8
  and Gazprom 221
  his government 171–2, 179, 199
  and Our Home is Russia 186–8, 247
  rivalry with Yeltsin 175–6, 180, 186–7,
    195
Chernyaev, Anatoly 29
Chubais, Anatoly 130, 151 n., 153, 162,
    169, 181, 198, 224, 246
  career 179–80
  chief of staff 195
  envoy to IMF 197–8
  First Deputy Prime Minister 196–7
  and presidential elections 190, 192, 221
Civic Accord 182, 232
civic opposition 69, 82, 113, 114, 115, 254
Civic Union 148, 149, 150, 244
civil society 6, 21, 45, 48, 58, 62–3, 70, 86,
    97, 114–15, 119, 153, 185, 204, Ch. 6,
    7 *passim*
  forces 5–7, 20, 69, 86, 113, 120, 204, 256
'clans' 219, 224
Commonwealth of Independent States
    (CIS) 157, 158
Communist Party of the RSFSR 86, 90, 95
Communist Party of the Russian
    Federation (KPRF) 182, 183, 185,
    186, 196, 199, 202, 235, 239, 241, 242,
    244, 249
  attempts impeachment 186, 202–3
  and 1993 elections 168–9, 221
  and 1995 elections 188–9, 218
  and presidential election 191–3, 195
  profile of 246–7
Communist Party of the Soviet Union
    (CPSU):
  and August putsch 109–10
Central Committee (CC) 29–30, 40–1, 63,
    65, 67, 74–5, 77, 85, 88, 89–90, 95–6,
    99, 107
  and Constitution 70, 72, 75, 84, 85, 89
  and CPD elections 63–5
  demonstrations against 84
  downgraded 92
  democratization of 39–40, 50–2
  and Eastern Europe 75–7
  federalization of 86
  and factions 86–8, 92

marginalised 67, 78, 82
membership 88, 109
and other parties 70, 85, 113–14
party secretaries 40, 115
Politburo 65, 66, 77, 91, 92, 94
regional leaders 65, 74
republican parties 92, 94
Secretariat 25, 29–30, 33, 52, 55, 77, 92
'social democratic' 79, 87, 88, 90, 93,
    100, 107, 254
XXVII Congress 29, 31, 33, 46
XXVIII Congress 89–90, 91, 92–3, 94–5
XIX Conference 49–57, 74, 95
Congress of People's Deputies (CPD):
  Soviet 52, 59, 71, 84, 85, 91; elections to
    63–5, 81; opens 66–8; social
    composition 67
  Russian 95, 104, 122–3, 127, 135, 138,
    141, 149, 161; Sixth 142, 143, 145–7;
    Seventh 150–4, 244; Eighth 156–8;
    Ninth 158; Tenth 164
conservatism 24, 31, 45, 48, 50, 54, 62, 66,
    77, 78, 79, 93–5, 98, 105, 114–15, 254
  and Gorbachev 100–4, 106, 107–8, 112
  and Yeltsin 155
  and XIX Conference 56–7
  and XXVIII Congress 94–5
constitution:
  Constitutional Court 133, 144, 150 n.,
    151, 152, 158, 160, 161, 162, 168;
    compliant 170, 185–6
  Russian 121–2, 128, 141, 142–5, 154,
    155, 160–61; of December 1993
    167–8, 170, 182, 185, 186, 194, 195,
    257
  Soviet 67, 70, 75, 80, 81, 84, 92, 106;
    Article 6 amended 85–6, 89, 91, 92
  suspended 164
corporatism 182, 229, 231, 234
corruption 16, 20, 24–5, 28, 162, 191, 196,
    197, 202, 224, 250
coup 135, 137, 143, 149, 150, 153 n., 162,
    190, 195
  September 1993 163–4, 217, 257
crime 241, 250
and bourgeoisie 212–13
  see also mafia

democracy 2, 4–5, 121, 154, 251, 257
  as 'disorder' 250
  social basis 237, 239, 241–2

Democratic Russia (DemRossiia) 68, 84, 104, 123, 125, 129, 137, 147, 154 n., 155 n., 235, 243, 245
Democratic Party of Russia (DPR) 153, 244
democratization 2–7, 52, 65, 68, 115
of CPSU 39–40, 50–52
defined 3 n.
democrats 68, 103, 111, 117, 123, 125, 127, 142–3, 144–5, 240, 253
and Chechnya 184–5
marginalized 128–9, 148, 181, 255
destalinization 13–14, 26
Diachenko, Tatiano 192, 198, 203
'dual power' 141, 147, 156, 162
Duma 167–8, 176, 185, 196, 199, 215, 224, 245, 248, 256
attempts to censure Yeltsin 186–7, 202–3
supports Primakov 199, 201

Eastern Europe 56 n., 75–6
economy
Russian: August 1998 crisis 198–201, 229, 238, 241; collapse of 139–40; and living standards 227–8, 240–1; 'war of programmes' 161–2; and 1995 elections 188
Soviet: 8, 17–18, 23, 79; decline of 34, 98; and perestroika 37–8; and 500 Days Programme 98–100, 101, 103, 117, 119
elections 40–1, 55, 63,113
within CPSU 53–4
republican and local 80–1
Russian 155, 156, 158; December 1993 164–5, 168–9, 244, 245; December 1995 188–9, 235, 236, 239, 248; presidential 1996 189–94, 221–2, 227 n., 228
and unions 235–6
elites 2–4, 24, 74, 76, 88, 110, 114–16, 253
consensus 46, 61, 154, 157, 183
conflict 82, 91, 94, 96, 108–9, 112, 140–1, 154, 165, 224, 250, 253
and democratization 4–7, 205, 225
and intelligentsia 35
regional 10, 16, 160, 194, 200
transformation into bourgeoisie 206–7, 210
*see also* bourgeoisie; military industrial complex

Estonia, *see* Baltics
family groups 10, 12, 16, 22
Federal Assembly 164, 167, 182, 185
Federal Counter-Intelligence Service (FSK) 172–3, 174
Federal Security Service (FSB) 132, 173, 186
Federation Council 167, 171, 176, 185, 202, 223, 256
Federation of Independent Trade Unions of Russia (FNPR), *see* trade unions
Fedorov, Boris 162, 171
Filatov, Sergei 131, 136, 155n., 169, 171
Financial Industrial Groups (FIGS) 216
Foreign Intelligence Service (SVR) 172
fuel and energy complex/sector (TEK) 172, 197, 217, 220, 223, 226

Gaidar, Yegor 127, 130, 140–1, 142, 145, 146, 148, 149, 150, 152, 155, 162, 171, 216–17, 223
economic policy 172
first government 219–20
'Gaidarnomiks' 207
and Russia's Choice 168–9, 171, 245
and Russia's Democratic Choice 188, 245
and Yeltsin 179, 184
Gazprom 147, 196, 215, 218, 220, 222, 223
and Chernomyrdin 221
Geneva 36
Accords 46, 56 n.
Georgia 71, 80, 94, 105, 106, 109, 110
Gerashchenko, Viktor 147 n., 172, 200
glasnost (openness) 31–4, 39, 43, 65, 73
Glavlit (censor) 34
Golushko, Nikolai 178 n.
Gorbachev, Mikhail 22, 95, 101–4
and Afghanistan 46, 56 n.
and Andreeva letter 49
anti-alcohol campaign 32, 34
attacked by regional leaders 65–6
and August putsch 107–9
and Baltics 74–5, 77, 80
his centrism 47, 108, 112
Chairman of Supreme Soviet 67, 75, 77, 91
and Chernobyl 34
and Chernobyl 34
and Constitution 75, 85, 106
dismisses Yeltsin 46–7

Gorbachev, Mikhail (*cont.*):
  and Eastern Europe  56 n., 75–7
  and elite unity  78–9, 111–13
  and emergency powers  100
  as General Secretary  24–6, 92, 109
  and glasnost  31, 34, 39, 44
  and INF Treaty  46
  and intelligentsia  34, 38–9, 44, 57
  and market  99–100, 102, 106, 107
  and miners  237
  'new thinking'  35–6
  and perestroika  37–8, 253
  personnel policy  28–31, 43
  and popular anger  59
  and presidency  75, 83, 89, 91–3, 94, 110,
    124, 253
  and reform  26–7, 29, 38, 61–2, 93, 251,
    253
  and Reagan  36
  releases Sakharov  39
  his Security Council  102–3, 104–5
  and separatism  74–5
  and 'socialist pluralism'  43–4
  and Soviet history  43–4
  and Soviet Union  94
  strengthens position  42–3, 77
  and Thatcher  35
  'turn to the right'  79, 100
  and union treaties  83, 99–100, 102–3,
    105–7, 110–11, 117 n.
  undermines CPSU  60
  and XIX Conference  52–4, 57, 59
  and Yeltsin  100, 104–5
  government  132
  and economic policy  162
  and parties  245
  and president  167
  rivalry with president  171–2, 175, 180
Grachev, Andrei  29
Grachev, Pavel  136 n., 150, 163, 174, 178,
  185, 186, 191
Gromyko, Andrei  36, 56, 57, 111
Gusinsky, Vladimir  190, 195 n., 196, 222,
  223

Iliushenko, Aleksei  171, 179
Iliushin, Viktor  129, 155, 171, 177–8
Industrial Union  149
industry  17–18
  'industrial directorate'  171–2
  industrialists  210, 213, 226

INF Treaty  46
informals  45, 58, 69
intelligentsia  95, 96, 98, 114, 128
  disillusionment of  57, 252–3
  and glasnost  34, 44, 73
  and middle class  240–1
International Monetary Fund (IMF)  101,
  138–9, 162, 172, 179, 180, 191, 197,
  198, 200–1, 202, 225, 227 n.
Inter-Regional Group of Deputies  68, 75,
  84 n.

Kazakhstan  70, 81, 193
KGB  24–5, 100, 108, 132, 135n., 163,
  172–3
Khasbulatov, Ruslan  127, 138, 153 n., 178
  and president  141, 146, 150, 156–8, 160,
  164
Khizha, Georgy  147, 220
Khodorkovsky, Mikhail  196 n., 202, 209,
  223
Khrushchev  13–16, 19, 22, 26, 73
Kiev  81
Kirienko, Sergei  168, 199
  prime minister  197
Kirgizia  109
Komsomol  97
  source of bourgeoisie  208
Korzhakov, Aleksandr  129 n., 130, 173–4,
  178
  and presidential election  189–90, 192
Kozyrev, Andrei  129 n., 130 n., 151 n.,
  153, 169, 178 n., 184, 193
Kulikov, Anatoly  173, 186, 195, 197
Kyrgystan  80, 101, 193

labour movement, *see* working class
Landsbergis, Vytautus  81, 82, 94
'law governed state'  52
Law on Cooperatives  48, 208
Law on Secession  80, 83
Law on Security  134–5, 136, 185 n.
Law on the State Enterprise (Association)
  42, 48, 231 n.
law  53, 101, 106
Lebed, Aleksandr  195, 248
  and presidential election  189, 191–2
legislature, *see* parliament
Lenin, Vladimir  73, 88
Leningrad  81, 84, 95
  mayor  93, 107

Liberal Democratic Party of Russia (LDPR)
127, 186, 199
  and 1993 elections 168–9
  and 1995 elections 188–9
liberalization 3–5, 24, 27, 33, 40, 47–8, 63
  defined 3 n.
Ligachev, Yegor 33, 42, 111, 208
  and Andreeva letter 49
  criticised by Yeltsin 46, 56
  and glasnost 41, 43
  and Secretariat reform 55
  and XIX Conference 56
  and XXIV Congress 94–5
Lithuania, *see* Baltics
Livshits, Aleksandr 176
'loans for shares' 216, 218
Lobov, Oleg 129, 134, 162, 171, 174, 175,
  184
Lukianov, Anatoly 57
Luzhkov, Yury 178, 217, 222, 241

mafia 128, 212–3
Masliukov, Yury 199, 201, 202
mass mobilization 59, 63, 64
media 101, 115, 172, 185, 187, 256
  and glasnost 32–5, 48
  and presidential election 190–1, 192–5,
  222
middle class 19–20, 200, 240–2
Migranian, Andrannik 157 n, 223
  advocates 'strong' state 126–7
military 24, 100, 103, 104, 108, 109, 135,
  137, 150, 163, 167, 172
  and Chechnya 184
  decline 174–5
  wage arrears 227
military-industrial complex (VPK) 175,
  207, 220, 226, 236, 241
miners 70–1, 74, 101, 104, 125, 139, 201,
  227, 230–1, 233, 234, 237, 252
Ministry of Defence 135, 136 n., 152
Ministry of Foreign Affairs 135
  and bourgeoisie 209, 210
Ministry of Internal Affairs (MVD) 133,
  135, 136 n., 150, 152, 163, 173, 174,
  186, 190, 203
Ministry of Security 133, 135, 136 n., 152,
  163, 172
Moldavia 81, 101, 106, 109
Moscow 81, 84, 98, 104, 109, 160, 171
  authority fragments 80–2

mayor 93, 107, 125, 148 n., 164, 178
  and middle class 240–1

Nagorno-Karabakh, *see* Armenia
National Salvation Front 150, 164
nationalism 23, 71–2, 74, 76, 79, 80, 82,
  86, 94, 115–16
  and popular fronts 58–9, 62, 69, 253
NATO 101, 201
Nemtsov, Boris 196, 197, 223
neo-liberalism 206
'new thinking' 35
nomenklatura 50, 53, 54, 60, 82–3, 96 n.,
  129, 130, 137, 144, 171, 238
nomenklatura-bourgeoisie 206–8, 210,
  219, 255
Novo-Ogarevo agreement 105, 125

oligarchy, *see* bourgeoisie
opinion polls 88, 142 n., 149, 184
Our Home is Russia (NDR) 179, 186, 217,
  235, 248
  and 1995 elections 188–9, 192, 218, 239,
  247
  'party of the bosses' 247

parliament 122, 127, 128, 134, 147
  dismissed 163–4, 167
  impotence 183, 186–7, 196–7, 221, 224,
  250, 256
  and presidency 119–20, 125, 128,
  140–66, 168, 245, 257
  *see also* Duma; Federation Council;
  Federal Assembly
parties 6, 68, 101, 168, 242–9
  banned 164
  and civil society 242, 246–7
  first independent 58
  growth of 84–5, 243, 245, 246, 248
  weakness of 70, 85, 113–14, 165, 224,
  242–5, 248–9, 252, 255
'party of power' 176, 195, 245, 247
Party of Russian Unity and Accord (PRES)
  168–9, 172, 245
'party of war' 174, 178, 184, 189, 191–2
path dependency 7
Pavlov, Valentin 103, 105, 106, 107, 108 n.
peasantry 237–9, 242
  *see also* agriculture
perestroika (restructuring) 37, 41–2, 65, 66,
  68, 74, 79, 94, 108, 111, 133, 207, 252

perestroika (*cont.*):
  and working class 229
  front organizations for defence of 58
Petrov, Yury 129–30, 131, 177, 178, 223
Politburo 25, 29–30, 72, 75 n.
political culture 194, 248
Poltoranin, Mikhail 150–1, 155 n.
Popov, Gavriil 68, 93, 107, 128, 141, 143,
    147, 148 n., 154
populism 104
Potanin, Vladimir 196 n., 197, 202, 219,
    222–3
power ministries 134, 148, 157, 162, 163 n.,
    186
presidency:
  centrality of 149, 203–4, 224, 248, 256
  dominates Constitutional Court 170,
    185–6
  and coercion 132–4, 172–5
  and parliament 119–20, 128, 133,
    140–66, 196–7, 245, 250, 257
  powers of 122
  Presidential Administration 130, 171,
    176, 177, 181
  Presidential Council 157
  rivalry with government 132, 171–2,
    175–6
  Russian 124–5, 129, 130–3, 142–3
  and 1993 Constitution 167–8
  *see also* Gorbachev or Yeltsin
Primakov, Evgeny 77, 94
  foreign minister 193
  prime minister 199–202
prime minister:
  Soviet 103
  Russian 122, 124, 127, 146, 151, 153,
    168, 175, 198
privileges 33, 53
privatization 97, 126, 138–40, 166, 171,
    179–80, 196–7, 198, 201, 207, 218,
    241
  of agriculture 238–9
  of power 219
  of state property 208–10, 214–5
  strengthens managers 229–30
  and workers 232, 237
Pugo, Boris 103, 108 n.
Putin, Vladimir 203
putsch, August 1991 73, 93, 107–8, 112,
    115, 117 n., 126, 127, 132, 174, 178,
    181, 243, 253

referendum 105, 123, 144, 147
  of April 1993 152–6, 157 n., 158–9, 160,
    161, 246 n.
  of December 1993 164–5
reform Soviet 4, 18, 20–3, 26–7, 33, 34, 35,
    50–2, 57, 77, 93, 94–5, 99, 104, 110, 251
  dynamics of 118–19
  lack of social pact 113, 117, 120
  and perestroika 37–8, 41–2, 111–13, 116
  Russian 124, 126, 144
  and transformation 59, 61, 78–9, 96,
    113, 116, 118, 254
  unravels 60
regime 23
  change 3–7
  crisis 4, 7, 184
Rejkavik summit 36
republics 82, 98, 99, 105–6, 106, 109, 110
  of Russian Federation 149
'rouble corridor' 216–17, 238
Russia declares sovereignty 81–2, 109
Russian Communist Party, *see* Communist
    Party of the RSFSR
Russian Communist Workers' Party 164
Russian Public Television (ORT) 187, 190,
    195 n., 218, 222
Russian United Industrial Party 236
Russian Union of Industrialists and
    Entrepreneurs (RSPP) 223, 236, 244
Russian Unity 145
Russia's Choice 245
  opposes Chechan war 184–5
  and 1993 election 168–9
Russia's Democratic Choice 223, 245
  and 1995 election 188
Rutskoi, Aleksandr 125, 141 n., 154, 157,
    162, 164, 178, 244
Rybkin, Ivan 185, 187, 188, 236
Ryzhkov, Nikolai 31, 68, 94, 99–100

St Petersburg 125, 130, 240–1
Sachs, Jeffrey 138
Sakharov, Andrei 39, 64, 68, 78, 252
Scherbakov, Aleksandr 209
secession 72
  Law on 80, 83
Security Council:
  and Chechnya 183–4, 185
  under Gorbachev 102–3, 104–5
  and presidential power 174, 175, 183,
    185

under Yeltsin 122, 133–7, 149 n., 152, 157, 163, 167, 171, 191, 195, 203
Seleznev, Gennady 196
Shaffranik, Yury 220, 221
Shakhrai, Sergei 122, 129 n., 131, 132, 133, 134, 135, 136, 145, 153, 155 n., 168, 172, 175, 245
Shatalin, Stanislav (plan) 100
Shevardnadze, Eduard 31, 76, 77, 94, 103
foreign minister 36
Shmakov, Mikhail 223
shock therapy 99, 126, 138–40, 141, 142, 145, 149, 165, 242, 256
and working class 226–7
Shokhin, Aleksandr 127, 153, 172
Shumeiko, Vladimir 147, 155 n., 171, 185, 220, 221
Skokov, Yury 133, 134–5
Skuratov, Yury 202
Smolensky, Aleksandr 196 n., 202, 225
Sobchak, Anatoly 93, 107, 125, 141, 143
socialism 73
'socialist pluralism' 43–4
Soskovets, Oleg 172, 221, 236
and presidential election 189, 190, 192
soviets 40–1, 53, 82–3, 84
and 'desovietization' 141,143–4
dissolved 164
in Russia 123, 128, 148 n.
Soviet Union 23, 74, 93, 94, 105, 106, 193
collapse 1–2, 47, 73, 96, 107, 109–11, 113, 207, 253, 255
stabilization 181–3, 247
Stankevich, Sergei 124–5
Stalin 7, 10, 11–13, 16, 20, 43–4, 73, 101, 181, 191, 238
state, Soviet 6, 11, 16, 21, 52–3, 55, 115
crisis 165
bankrupt 199
'law governed' 52
political culture of 248
property 97, 98–9, 106, 109
privatization of 206–10, 214–5
Russian 119, 121, 124, 144, 154, 181
splits 79
'strong' 126–7
weakness 118–20, 121, 160, 183, 212, 226
State Legal Administration (GPU) 131–2, 135, 136–7, 175, 178
Stepashin, Sergei 173, 174, 186

prime minister 202–3
strikes 70–1, 72, 74, 75, 78, 104, 105, 106, 109, 139, 232–4
Supreme Soviet 42, 52, 67, 71–2, 75, 80, 84, 92, 105, 107
conflict with president 162, 164, 177
Russian 122, 127, 128, 141, 145, 146, 148, 149, 150, 152, 154, 155 n., 158
Sverdlovsk 'mafia' 129, 130 n., 135, 143, 177

Tajikistan 80, 109
Tatars 45
Tbilisi, *see* Georgia
Thatcher, Margaret 35
totalitarianism 20, 126
trade unions 101, 172, 230, 249
Federation of Independent Trade Unions of Russia (FNPR) 157, 200, 223, 230–6
'free' 230–1
and management 231–2, 234, 236
and politics 232, 234–6, 244
*see also* working class
transition 3, 5, 100, 103
transformation 53, 59, 61, 78, 97, 103, 106, 120, 124, 160, 237
Travkin, Nikolai 153, 244
Tretiakov, Vitaly 148 n., 150
Trotsky, Leon 43

unemployment, *see* working class
Ukraine 73, 81, 87, 109
USA 101, 199, 225, 230 n.
USSR, *see* Soviet Union
Uzbekistan 72–3, 80, 109
uskorenie (acceleration) 31–2, 37

Viakhirev, Rem 196 n., 221
Vinogradov, Vladimir 196 n., 202, 209, 222
Vladivostok initiative 36
Voloshin, Aleksandr 198, 202
Volsky, Arkady 151, 236, 244

wage arrears, *see* working class
Warsaw Treaty Organization (WTO) 76
working class 226–37, 242, 252, 257
and civil society 234, 236–7
living standards 227–8
and management 229–30, 231–2, 234

working class (*cont.*):
 passivity 227, 230, 236–7
 and privatization 232
 and shock therapy 226–7
 and strikes 232–4
 and unemployment 228–9, 234
wage arrears 227–8, 234
World Bank 179, 198, 238

Yabloko 235
Yakovlev, Alexander 42, 46, 49, 56, 77, 94, 103, 187, 188
Yavlinsky, Grigory 99, 107, 235
 and presidential election 189, 191
Yegorov, Nikolai 131, 174, 186
Yeltsin, Boris 31, 45, 61, 64, 68, 78, 94, 98, 104, 106
 against CPSU 123, 125
 appeals to XIX Conference 56
 and August putsch 109–10, 178
 his Bonapartism 124, 137, 163–4, 175, 226, 257–8
 and bourgeoisie 215, 216, 218, 221–2
 Chairman of Supreme Soviet 81, 95, 123, 124, 125, 129
 and Chechnya 184–5
 and Civic Accord 182
 and coercive apparatuses 172–6
 and constitution 128, 136, 143–4, 147, 150, 155, 160–1, 165–7
 CPD electoral victory 65
 criticises privileges 33
 and decrees 123, 151, 156, 158, 164, 167, 175, 178, 185, 190, 195
 declining support 169, 184, 187, 188–9, 242
 and democrats 123, 243
 and dictatorship 126–7
 dismisses parliament 163–4, 174, 177, 178, 232
 and Gorbachev 46–7, 100, 104–5, 117
 his health 180, 186–7, 191, 194–5, 198
 and impeachment 157, 158, 161, 168, 186, 202–3, 233
 his inner circle/entourage 129, 133, 155, 169, 171, 177–81, 187, 194–5, 198, 201, 202–4, 219, 253, 254
 and Korzhakov 173–4, 178
 and media 187
 as 'monarch' 175, 180
 and national independence 82, 116–17
 and parliament 122, 128, 133, 138, 140–66, 181–2, 196–7, 245, 249
 and political parties 187, 244, 245, 247, 248–9, 255
 praetorian politics 174, 178
 as president 106, 123–5, 127, 128, 132–3, 141, 142–6, 149, 167, 170, 180–1, 194, 197–8, 202, 203–4, 248, 250, 256
 and presidential elections 189–94
 as prime minister 127, 133, 135
 and referendum 147, 164–5
 and regions 182–3
 rivalry with Chernomyrdin 171–2, 176
 and shock therapy 138
 and soviets 123, 164
 'Stalin figure' 181
 and trade unions 232, 237
 and USA 158, 199
 weakened authority 198–9
 and XXVIII Congress 93
Yerin, Viktor 173, 174, 178 n., 186
Yumashev, Valentin 198

Zadornov, Mikhail 199, 203
Zaslavskaia, Tatiana 240
Zaveriukha, Aleksandr 172, 221
Zhirinovsky, Vladimir 127, 169, 185, 186, 245
 and presidential election 189, 191, 222
Ziuganov, Gennady:
 and presidential election 189, 191–3, 221
Zorkin, Valery 152–3, 156 n, 157, 158, 170